Popular Contention, Regime, and Transition

Popular Contention, Regime, and Transition

The Arab Revolts in Comparative Global Perspective

Edited by

EITAN Y. ALIMI

AVRAHAM SELA

MARIO SZNAJDER

OXFORD
UNIVERSITY PRESS

Oxford University Press is a department of the University of Oxford. It furthers
the University's objective of excellence in research, scholarship, and education
by publishing worldwide.Oxford is a registered trade mark of Oxford University
Press in the UK and certain other countries.

Published in the United States of America by Oxford University Press
198 Madison Avenue, New York, NY 10016, United States of America.

© Oxford University Press 2016

Library of Congress Cataloging-in-Publication Data
Names: Alimi, Eitan Y., editor. | Sela, Avraham, editor. | Sznajder, Mario, editor.
Title: Popular contention, regime, and transition : Arab revolts in comparative global perspective /
edited by Eitan Y. Alimi, Avraham Sela, and Mario Sznajder.
Description: New York : Oxford University Press, 2016. | Includes bibliographical references and index.
Identifiers: LCCN 2015038520 | ISBN 9780190203573 (hardcover : alk. paper)
Subjects: LCSH: Arab countries—Economic conditions—21st century. |
Democratization—Arab countries. | Protest movements—Arab countries. |
Arab countries—Politics and government.
Classification: LCC HC498 .P67 2016 | DDC 321.09—dc23
LC record available at http://lccn.loc.gov/2015038520

9 8 7 6 5 4 3 2 1
Printed by Sheridan Books, Inc., United States of America

For Nirit, Inger, and Laura

Contents

PART II: *Processes and Trajectories of Contention*

PART III: *Between Contention and Transition*

Acknowledgments

IT TOOK A getting together of a student of social movements and contentious politics who is fascinated with the identification of similarities and differences across cases; a specialist of Middle East and North Africa societies, states, and regimes who is respectfully skeptical about "Arab exceptionalism"; and an expert of Latin America politics and democratization who values comparative historical analysis to conceive of and commit to such a project. Our first and brief meeting led to an attempt to test the waters and to organize an early-afternoon minisymposium. The minisymposium, which took place in Jerusalem in May 2011, brought several colleagues to present their own reading and understanding of the events that were raging around us. The ideas that came up during that gathering and the intriguing, at times provocative and pressing, questions raised by panelists and other colleagues who joined us as active audience made it clear we needed to further extend our outlook on the surrounding events and weigh them in a broader theoretical and empirical context. This recognition led to a series of meetings during which we decided to expand the comparative canvas of this project. What if, we thought, we bring scholars who possess knowledge of other cases of mass-based popular contention from other parts of the globe to an intensive several-day workshop for the purpose of fleshing out cross-case similarities and differences in trajectories of contention and its outcomes under a variety of regime types? Our joint affirmative reaction led to an international workshop of three days that took place in Jerusalem, precisely one year after the 2011 minisymposium. Participants in the workshop were asked to produce original papers in a first systematic attempt to use the perspective of social movement theory, and specifically the contentious politics approach, to explain the dynamics and unfolding of the Arab revolts and to put them in comparative perspective. This, we knew, was not an easy task. Tensions stemming from different research styles and orientations, regarding, among other things, how to compare Arab and non-Arab cases, what constitutes an adequate and sound explanation, the role of theory and whether it should be developed deductively or inductively, all became a constant feature of this project. This was the case not only among us editors and between us and our collaborators, tensions which turned out to be constructive and fruitful, but also between us all and readers of various versions of the manuscript, who kept pushing us back, at times passionately on those same issues. We hope our readers, academics and nonacademics alike, will be intrigued and stimulated (even if not convinced) by our dual attempt to blur the boundaries between Arab and non-Arab waves of contention and between democracies and nondemocracies.

But regardless of the best intentions and most genuine commitments of all who participated in the actual writing of the volume, what made this project possible in the first place was the generous support of several institutions at the Hebrew University of Jerusalem. We thank the Harry S. Truman Institute for the Advancement of Peace; the Leonard Davis Institute for International Relations; the Liwerant Center for the Study of Latin America, Spain, Portugal, and their Jewish Communities; the Max Kampelman Chair for Democracy and Human Rights; the Nancy and Lawrence E. Glick Fund; the Department of Political Science at the Hebrew University; and the Hebrew University Authority for Research and Development. In addition to their financial support, for which we are grateful, we also benefited from the good intention, valuable advice, and professional help of the people behind the names of these institutions and organizations, in particular Menahem Blondheim, Judit Bokser Liwerant, Cheryl Cashriel, Avner De-Shalit, Noga Hatkevitz, Anat Illouz, Reuven Hazan, Hani Mazar, Tali Mishal, Steve Kaplan, and Naama Shpeter.

Finally, we thank those who were involved in certain earlier stages in the development of this project, contributed to its success, and helped us in shaping our ideas: Uriel Abulof, Wael Abu Uksa, Assaf David, Aziz Haidar, Mishy Harman, P. R. Kumaraswamy, Anat Lapidot-Firilla, Jacob Olupona, Eldad Pardo, Michael Shalev, Tamir Sheafer, Shaul Shenhav, and Gadi Wolfsfeld. Others who provided insightful and useful comments on specific chapters are thanked and acknowledged by our contributors in their respective chapters. Special thanks and deepest appreciation go to Marc Sherman for assisting us in preparing the index in the most professional and courteous way possible. And, last but not least, we are especially grateful for the interest shown in our project by the people at Oxford University Press, particularly James Cook, for being receptive, open-minded, and professional—an exceptional and rare combination we were fortunate to benefit from.

Eitan Y. Alimi
Avraham Sela
Mario Sznajder
Jerusalem, Israel

Contributors

Eitan Y. Alimi earned his Ph.D. in sociology from Boston College in 2004 and is now an associate professor of political science at the Hebrew University of Jerusalem. His research interests include contentious politics and social movements, radicalization and political terrorism, and conflict resolution. He has served as an editorial board member for the journal *Mobilization*. Recent publications have appeared in *Political Studies; British Journal of Political Science; Theory and Society; International Journal of Press and Politics; Comparative Politics; Mobilization; International Political Science Review*. His book *Israeli Politics and the First Palestinian Intifada* was published in 2007, and a recent book coauthored with Chares Demetriou and Lorenzo Bosi titled *The Dynamics of Radicalization: A Relational and Comparative Perspective*.

Vincent Boudreau received his Ph.D. from Cornell University in 1991 and is now dean of the Colin Powell School for Civic and Global Leadership at the City College of New York. Dr. Boudreau served as the director of the Colin L. Powell Center for Leadership and Service from 2002 through 2013. He is a professor of political science at City College and a member of the City University of New York graduate faculty. A specialist in the politics of social movements, particularly in Southeast Asia, his latest book is *Resisting Dictatorship: Repression and Protest in Southeast Asia* (2004). He also conducts research and writes on repression, government transitions to democracy, and collective violence. Dr. Boudreau's research, supported in part by a grant from the Fulbright program, has investigated the relationship between civil society, social movements, and democratization processes in Indonesia and the Philippines.

Valerie Bunce is professor of government and the Aaron Binenkorb Chair of International Studies at Cornell University. She has served as president of the Association for Slavic, Eastern European, and Eurasian Studies and vice-president of the American Political Science Association. She is a member of the American Academy of Arts and Sciences. Her most recent book (with Sharon Wolchik) is *Defeating Authoritarian Leaders in Postcommunist Countries* (2011).

Mario Diani is a professor in the Department of Sociology and social research of the University of Trento, which he joined from the University of Strathclyde in Glasgow in 2001. In 2010–2012 he was ICREA Research Professor in the Department of Political and Social Sciences of the Universitat Pompeu Fabra, Barcelona. He has worked extensively on social network approaches to social movements and collective action. His most recent books are *The Cement of Civil Society: Studying Networks in Localities* (2015) and *The Oxford Handbook of Social Movements*, coedited with Donatella della Porta (2015). His articles have appeared in *American Sociological Review, American Journal of Sociology, Environmental Politics, Theory and Society, Social Networks, Sociological Review*, and *Mobilization*, among others.

Jack A. Goldstone (Ph.D. Harvard) is the Richard Elman Family Professor and Director of the Institute for Public Policy at the Hong Kong University of Science and Technology. His classic *Revolution and Rebellion in the Early Modern World* (1991), winner of the Distinguished Scholarly Publication Award of the American Sociological Association, will be reissued in a new 25th anniversary edition this year. He has recently coedited the *Concise Encyclopaedia of Comparative Sociology* (2014) and published *Revolutions: A Very Short Introduction* (2014). Goldstone's current projects include a study of the emergence of modern economic growth and an analysis of the political impact of global population trends.

Gregory M. Maney received his Ph.D. from the University of Wisconsin–Madison. He is the Harry H. Wachtel Distinguished Professor for the Study of Nonviolent Social Change at Hofstra University. He has authored and coauthored numerous peer-reviewed academic journal articles and books focusing on peace movement discourses, the dynamics of ethnonationalist contention, and strategies for sustaining peace processes. He is the recipient or corecipient of research grants from several foundations, including the American Association of Colleges and Universities, the American Sociological Association, the National Science Foundation, the Sociological Initiatives Foundation, and the United States Institute of Peace. Dr. Maney has served in several elected professional leadership positions, including Chair of the Peace, War and Social Conflict Section of the American Sociological Association; Council Member of the Collective Behavior and Social Movements Section of the American Sociological Association; and speaker of the faculty at Hofstra University.

David S. Meyer is professor of sociology, political science, and planning, policy, and design at the University of California, Irvine. His research has focused on the impact of social movements on politics and public policy. He has published numerous articles on social movements and social change, and is author or coeditor of eight books, most recently, *The Politics of Protest: Social Movements in American* 2nd edition (2015).

Caelum Moffatt is an independent scholar who has spent almost a decade working on and in the Middle East as a research analyst for academic institutes, think-tanks, private companies, and local and international nongovernmental organizations. He studied at the University of Edinburgh and the London School of Economics before completing a Ph.D. in political science at Durham University.

Katia Pilati is assistant professor at the Department of Sociology and Social Research (DSRS) at the University of Trento, Italy. Before joining DSRS, she was a Marie Curie fellow at the Department of Political Science at the University of Geneva and a research fellow at the Université Libre de Bruxelles. Her research interests include social movements, protests in repressive contexts, political participation, and immigration. Her recent publications appeared in *European Journal of Political Science, Mobilization, Journal of Ethnic and Migration Studies, Global Networks* and include a book "Migrants' Political Participation in Exclusionary Contexts. From subcultures to radicalization." (2016).

Mario Quaranta obtained a Ph.D. in political science in 2013 from the Instituto Italiano di Scienze Umane (now Scuola Normale Superiore) in Florence, and is currently a postdoctoral fellow in the Department of Political Science at Libera Università Internazionale delle Science Sociali (LUISS) "Guido Carli" in Rome. He is also a member of the "International Center for Democracy and Democratization" at the same university. He has been a visiting scholar at the "Center for the Study of Democracy" of the University of California, Irvine. He has published articles on a variety of journals on topics concerning political participation, public opinion, and democracy.

Karen Rasler graduated with a B.A. from the University of Florida in 1974 and a Ph.D. from Florida State University in 1981. She has taught at Arizona State University, University of California–Riverside, and currently is a professor at Indiana University since 1991. Her research has focused on theories of international conflict and cooperation, the relative decline of world powers, war and state-building processes, the role of rivalries in conflict, and political violence and internal wars. Her published works can be found in journals such as the *American Political Science Review, American Journal of Political Science, American Sociological Review, World Politics, International Studies Quarterly, Journal of Conflict Resolution, Journal of Peace Research*, and *International Interactions*. She has also coauthored four books with William R. Thompson, the latest of which is *How Rivalries End* (2013).

Avraham Sela is Professor Emeritus of International Relations and a senior research fellow at the Truman Institute in the Hebrew University of Jerusalem.

He is the author of *The Decline of the Arab Israeli Conflict* (1998), coauthor of *The Palestinian Hamas* (1996, 2000), and editor of *The Political Encyclopedia of the Middle East* (2002). His current research projects include *The Public Political Thought of the Arab Spring* and *States and Transnational Volunteer Fighters in the Twentieth Century*.

Mario Sznajder is professor of political science at the Department of Political Science, the Hebrew University of Jerusalem. He has published on the ideology and practice of revolutionary syndicalism, fascism, human rights and politics, democratization, and political exile in Latin America. His latest books are *The Politics of Exile in Latin America* (2009), with Luis Roniger (updated, translated into Spanish, and published by in 2013), and *Shifting Frontiers of Citizenship: The Latin American Experience* (2012), co-edited with Luis Roniger and Carlos Forment.

Gayil Talshir has her Ph.D. from Oxford University, where she wrote a comparative analysis of the Green/New Left ideology in the UK and Germany. She is currently the head of the center for advanced public service and the head of the M.A. program for top governmental executives in public policy. Her research is on the crisis of legitimation of advanced democracies, party system change, political ideologies, and Israeli politics. Her two recent articles are on the 2013 and 2015 elections in Israel analyzing politics of identity versus ideologization processes of the Israeli party system and the influence of the social protest on institutional politics. She is currently involved in an international project on democracy and inequality and is working on a report on the state of Israeli democracy for the Shasha Center for strategic studies. She is a senior lecturer at the department of political science, the Hebrew University of Jerusalem.

Popular Contention, Regime, and Transition

Introduction—Popular Contention, Regime, and Transition

A COMPARATIVE PERSPECTIVE

Eitan Y. Alimi

ON JULY 1, 2013, following mass demonstrations in several major cities in Egypt against President Mursi's ever-greater appropriation of ruling powers, the state's military chief took a bold move and issued a 48-hour ultimatum to the president. Considering the situation unprecedented and expressing concerns over the safety and stability of the nation, Chief of Staff General 'Abd al-Fattah al-Sisi also included a stark warning with the ultimatum: "If the demands of the people are not realized within the defined period, it will be incumbent upon [the armed forces] ... to announce a road map for the future" (*Haaretz*, July 1, 2013). In a matter of hours, the army issued a second statement, clarifying that the ultimatum should in no way be seen as a military coup, but rather as an expression of genuine concern and a response to the "pulse of the Egyptian street." On July 3, after President Mursi declared his utter rejection of the ultimatum, and in the face of spreading street violent confrontations between anti-Mursi and pro-Mursi protesters, the army announced the overthrow of the elected president:

> The Egyptian Armed Forces first declared, is still declaring and will always declare that it stands distant from political forces. The Armed Forces ... have been called by the Egyptian people for help, not to hold the reins of power, yet to discharge its civil responsibility and answer demands of

responsibility.... [T]he army has called for national dialogue, yet it was rejected by the presidency.... [T]he EAF similarly on more than one occasion presented a strategic assessment domestically and internationally.... [H]opes were all pinned on national conciliation. Yet, the address of the president yesterday and before the expiry of the 48-hour ultimatum did not meet the demands of the people. As a result, it was necessary for the EAF to act on its patriotic and historic responsibility without sidelining, or marginalizing any party.... [D]uring the meeting a road map was agreed upon, which includes the following: Suspending the constitution provisionally; the chief justice of the constitutional court will declare the early presidential elections; Interim period until president elected ... securing and guaranteeing freedom of expression, freedom of media. All necessary measures will be taken to empower youth so they can take part in decision making processes. The EAF appeal to the Egyptian people with all its spectrum to steer away from violence and remain peaceful. The Armed Forces warn it will stand up firmly and strictly to any act deviating from peacefulness based on its patriotic and historic responsibility. May God save Egypt and the honorable, defiant people of Egypt.

Al-Jazeera, July 3, 2013

The Egyptian army move was, *mutatis mutandis*, a reprise of previous coups, the first of which took place in July 1952. More recently, in February 2011, the army forced President Mubarak to resign by withdrawing its support, ostensibly in response to growing claims and demands on the part of the Egyptian public as well as Western powers' pressure to heed the people's will. As in February 2011, the July 2013 coup was justified as an emergency measure meant to restructure the Egyptian political system on the basis of a revised constitution and free parliamentary and representative elections. Like the July 1952 coup, the recent ones were framed in terms of the army's "national responsibility" and impartiality, acting purely in response to the people's wishes rather than its own interests. Finally, similar to its critical move in February 2011, the July 2013 army intervention in the political process was yet another critical juncture in a long, tumultuous, and contingent path of contentious politics between forces of continuity and forces of change.

Beyond Egypt

No one would deny the historical specificities of Egypt—or of Bahrain, Libya, Jordan, and many other Middle Eastern and Northern African (MENA) countries for that matter. Each MENA country has its own particular political, cultural, demographic, geographic, social, and economic features and traits. Compared to the long-standing role of the military in Egypt as a primary institution and the ultimate political arbitrator, for example, Qadhafi's Libya kept the military forces small and away from politics, preferring to rely on tribal loyal forces that backed him against the rebel forces. Unlike the downfall of Mubarak, Qadhafi's fall was, most centrally, the result of a civil war and an international military intervention in support of the rebel forces.

More broadly, the revolts of Arab masses that began in Tunisia and soon spread to many other Arab countries took different shapes, lengths, and degrees of severity and were met by different responses of the incumbent regimes. It was mostly the autocratic "republican" states that experienced the longest and most severe types of revolts: Tunisia and Egypt have undergone intensive destabilizing mass demonstrations, political turbulence, revised constitutions, and regime changes; Yemen, Libya, and Syria experienced different levels of intrasocietal violence and, in the latter two, undecided civil war, while Algeria, Lebanon, and Sudan managed to contain the early wave of popular contention. Contrary to intuitive assumptions, the monarchies essentially escaped the social and political fate that befell the autocratic "republican" states since early 2011, though even within this authoritarian subcategory Bahrain saw large-scale and intensive popular contention, which was met with blatant repression and was the closest to a regime change; Morocco and Jordan managed their societal restiveness with minimal, mostly symbolic and preemptive economic and political gestures, and Saudi Arabia combined repression with plentiful spending.

The diversity of social and political behaviors among the Arab states in the course of the "Arab Spring" calls, once again, for reviewing the competing approaches in the study of the modern MENA states and societies, especially between students of country/area studies and of comparative politics. Whereas the former mostly engages in in-depth country cases, avoiding comparative analysis of regional states and societies (Ayeb 2011; Haddad 2012; see also, Gunning and Baron 2013), other MENA specialists are more receptive to fleshing out cross-state/society similarities and differences (Hamid 2014; Frisch 2013). These MENA comparativists have long been producing insightful works on regional distinctive commonalities of social and political history, structures and institutions, regimes and state-society relations and their significance in the context of protest politics, regimes, and reforms (Bayat 2010; Wiktorowicz 2004; Posusney and Angrist 2005; Ottaway and Choucair-Vizoso 2008; Beinin and Vairel 2011; Lynch 2014).

Although the recent Arab revolts took the community of MENA specialists by surprise and triggered self-searching debates about well-established assumptions and knowledge, such as the overemphasis on explaining authoritarian stability and resilience (Gause 2011; Toledano 2011), most have nonetheless warned against unmerited overgeneralizations and attempts to offer mono-causal explanations (Heydemann and Leenders 2013; Bellin 2012; Kurzman 2012; Yom and Gause 2012). Some of these sweeping generalizations, produced in the midst of the ongoing contention, regard, for example, the treatment of Arab regimes under the crude and unrefined category of authoritarianism and the related search for defining features (e.g., youth bulge, poverty, corruption); the argument of the revolutionizing effect of new information and communica-tion technologies (ICTs); and the often linked view of the "Arab Spring" as part of a fourth wave of democratization, a welcomed and glorious ending of "Arab Exceptionalism" (Al-Momani 2011; Filiu 2011; Grand 2011; de Vasconcelos 2011; Howard and Hussain 2013), or even a "second Arab renaissance" (Dawisha 2013).[1]

We share much of the concern over these overgeneralizations. With the added value and benefit of hindsight, it is abundantly clear that the role of ICTs was much more limited than it was sometimes argued to be and was contingent to a large degree on the authorities' response (Bishara 2012; Faris 2013; Wolfsfeld, Segev, and Sheafer 2013; Brym et al. 2014); that in many authoritarian regimes popular restiveness was translated into protest in a more limited scope and inten-sity than originally expected, with significant differences in the class/ethnic/religious/gender compositions of those mobilized (Anderson 2012; Beissinger, Jamal, and Mazur 2012; Beinin and Vairel 2013); and that, contrary to Western analysts and scholars' obsession with democratization of Middle East societies (Anderson 2006) and the consequent tendency to read the popular waves of con-tention as necessarily taking the road of democratization, in some cases the pro-cess of change ended up producing a fallback to authoritarianism (Bradley 2012; Hale 2013; Brumberg 2014). Indeed, the recent Arab revolts have witnessed only sporadic, short-term expressions of popular discontent in some, brought about certain reforms and regime change in others, and are still raging in yet other states, where revolts shook to the core the regime and political order. Variations and dissimilarities revealed themselves also in how authorities in each MENA country responded to the domestic challenges and, needless to say, in the nature and scope of the popular wave of contention and claims made in each.

Beyond the "Arab Spring"

We maintain that contention in authoritarian settings is different from liberal democratic ones, but not different in kind. Consciously avoiding a teleological-like normative approach and while respecting and being mindful of each case's particularities, we seek to broaden the comparative perspective of the recent wave of MENA revolts with non-MENA revolts. Thus far, such an undertaking has been mostly based on similarities in basic conditions and outcomes (e.g., Islamist forces' antidemocratic disposition and drive for power; Bradley 2012; Hamid 2014), with only a handful of works offering hints of similarities in dynamics of contentious politics (Beinin and Vairel 2013; Lynch 2014). Moving beyond commonalities in preconditions and outcomes to focusing systematically on *dynamics* of contentious politics—how popular discontent and restiveness is actualized and organized; how it is carried out and responded to; and the emergent paths and outcomes it takes—enables us to identify revealing *similarities in dissimilarities*, both across the MENA countries and between MENA and non-MENA countries. The similarities in dissimilarities, we argue, stem from the intricate, contingent, and indeterminate interplay among popular contention, regime, and transition, which, as the following definitions suggest, are treated in this book as processes:

- *Popular Contention*—a sustained, coordinated effort of claim-making by an informal network of individuals, groups, and/or organizations on the basis of shared interests and goals.
  The purpose of the claim-making is either for fostering or preventing political change and in interaction with elites, opponents, and allies, but most importantly with authorities, which can play the role of target or mediator (Diani 1992; Snow, Soule, and Kriesi 2004; Tilly 2004a; Tarrow 2011; Johnston 2014);[2]
- *Regime*—those arrangements, rules, practices, and styles that shape and institutionalize relations between a government and the major political and social actors within its jurisdiction, among these actors, and between both and the subject population (Hariman 1995; Tilly 2004b, 2006; Van Den Bosch 2013)[3]; and,
- *Transition*—the interval phase between one political regime (writ large) and another, entailing a full or partial shift from the existing regime, designation of another, and its operation, and involving institutional as well as noninstitutional forces (O'Donnell, Schmitter, and Whitehead 1986; Tarrow 1995; Linz and Stepan 1996; Morlino 1998; Whitehead 2002; Skaaning 2006).[4]

Positing popular contention, regime, and transition as inherently linked processes does not mean that such interconnectedness is bound to be confrontational and violent. Such interrelatedness may well unfold in a fairly routinized, stable, and regulated fashion, with the lines separating the three remaining clearer. During these "settled" times (Swidler 1986), differences in the modes of coordination (i.e., interest group vs. social movement) and dominant forms of claim-making (i.e., contained vs. transgressive), in the typical mode and style of authorities' response to and interaction with dissident groups and activists (i.e., democratic vs.

autocratic) or in the frequent scope and nature of the claims made (i.e., reformist vs. revolutionary) are more apparent and pronounced. During "unsettled" times (ibid.), however, in which political and cultural creativity become concentrated, it is not only the case that the interaction among popular contention, regime, and transition becomes intricate, contingent, and indeterminate, but also that the processual features of each take on a more rapid pace—something close to what Sidney Tarrow has called "cycles of contention" (2011), referring to the possible development of:

> [A] phase of heightened conflict across the social system, with rapid diffusion of collective action from more mobilized to less mobilized sectors, a rapid pace of innovation of the forms of contention employed, the creation of new or transformed collective action frames, a combination of organized and unorganized participation, and sequences of intensified information flow and interaction between challengers and authorities. Such widespread contention produces externalities, which give challengers at least temporary advantage and allow them to overcome the weaknesses in their resource base. It demands that states devise broad strategies of response that are repressive or facilitative, or a combination of the two. And it produces general outcomes that are more than the sum of the results of an aggregate of unconnected events. (199)

Along with many other scholars of social movements and contentious politics, Tarrow did not have in mind cycles of contention in Arab countries in particular, or in countries outside the liberal democracies of the West when he first introduced the term (1983). But he did conceptualize the idea based on the cycle of contention during the late 1960s and the 1970s in Italy, a country that had several meaningfully authoritarian, fascist-like features, which would have probably resulted in its classification as hybrid regime (Diamond 2002; Robertson 2011). Furthermore, and most notably since the mid-1990s, a growing body of work has applied social movement and contentious politics theories and models to nonliberal, nondemocratic settings, pointing to both meaningful analogies and important differences in trajectories and dynamics unfolding during cycles of contention (Goldstone 1998; Mueller 1999; Goodwin 2001; Almeida 2008). Inspired by this research direction and mode of inquiry, this book uses a contentious politics-oriented comparative perspective in order to address two complementing questions: *What can cycles of contention in other parts of the world tell us about revolts in the Arab world? And, equally important, what can the cycles of contention in the Arab world tell us about contentious politics more generally?*

From Theory to Empirics and Back: Drawing Parallels and Linking Regions

Admittedly, when popular contention crystallizes and meets the eye, widespread use of violence, whether bottom-up or top-down; capricious and arbitrary responses by authorities; and backlash of transition processes figure prominently outside the liberal democracies of the West. The still precarious transition in Tunisia; the multiparty civil wars in Syria, Iraq, and Yemen; the still raging violence along tribal and regional lines in Libya; the forceful takeover by the Egyptian Army; the turmoil in the Ukraine, Nigeria, and, from the less recent past, the Palestinian Intifada, the early troubles in Northern Ireland, the Chechen war of national liberation, or the Tiananmen Square events—are but some pointed reminders of these features' recurrence. The frequency of these features in various sorts of authoritarian regimes and the intensity with which they manifest themselves during contentious cycles have led a growing number of scholars to rethink the validity of existing theories and models of social movements and contentious politics.

Western Theories—Non-Western Cases: A Fruitful Tension

The popular revolts occurring throughout the MENA countries further validate what several scholars of social movements and contentious politics have long pointed to: Although episodes of popular contention in authoritarian-like regimes constitute the lion's share of mass political movements worldwide, theories and models of social movements in particular, and protest politics more generally, have been developed and formulated largely with liberal-democratic assumptions in mind.[5] Given that the overall character and style of a political regime strongly affects the prospects, forms, dynamics, and possibly the outcome of contention, it is no wonder that evidence of inconsistency between Western-based theories/models-driven expectations and predictions and non-Western cases have been accruing.[6] With typical foresight, McAdam, Tarrow, and Tilly (1997) have cautioned that for theories of contention to be able to cope better with extreme cases of violence, examples of Western civic contention should not be allowed to exclusively shape our models.

Importantly, this foresight has been part of a more general formulation of a research program for studying contention in a more dynamic manner—the *Dynamics of Contention* (McAdam et al. 2001), which undoubtedly has opened the way for a more nuanced, contingent, and context-sensitive analysis of contentious episodes across regime types. This has been the result, first, of treating social interaction as well as social ties, interpersonal networks, interpersonal communication, and various forms of continuous negotiation not merely as expressions of structure, rationality, consciousness, or culture, but as active sites of creation and change that figure centrally in the dynamics of contention (22). Second, it has been the result of adopting a middle-ground position between radical indeterminism (i.e., idiographic description) and one-path determinism (i.e., general laws). Our thinking about this project was largely shaped by these theoretical and comparative aspects.

Precipitating, but also responding to McAdam et al.'s work, a growing body of work has sought to remedy this deficit and identified meaningful inconsistencies. Moving beyond instances of covert, evasive-like resistance, which has long been argued to be a key characteristic of contention in highly repressive settings,[7] scholars have argued, for example, that in authoritarian-like settings, popular contention tends to focus on, and be driven by basic needs and freedoms, including securing sheer survival (Noonan 1995; Schneider 1995; Moodie 2002; Einwohner 2009; Soyer 2014). Other scholars have argued for the importance of greater attention to the less formal, illegal, personalized, and interpersonal features and practices that render certain aspects of political opportunity structures and of transition processes—such as succession, fraudulent elections, and patronage relationships—more salient when applied to authoritarian-like political settings (Brockett 1991, 2005; Bakary 1997; Bunce and Wolchik 2011; Kadivar 2013). Still others have demonstrated how central the role of political threats (not just political opportunities) is in mobilization and how omnipresent repression is, to the point of undermining the viability of everyday life as an alternative to political activism (Khawaja 1993; Boudreau 1996, 2004; Goldstone and Tilly 2001; Almeida 2008; Alimi 2009; Bayat 2010). Finally, some scholars have convincingly made the case that under authoritarian regimes, authorities and power elites are deeply and proactively involved given that popular contention tends to be perceived as an existential threat to the social sector or ethnic group they represent and typically results in harsh crackdown, a situation which often pushes activists to look outside their borders and work with other concerned and interested actors and institutions to restrain their repressors and further their cause (Brockett 1991; Keck and Sikkink 1998; Perry 2002; Bob 2005; Robertson 2011; Slater 2010; Finkel and Brudny 2012; Trejo 2012). This type of authority-centric approach—and the related view of regime as a process—is consistent with both Skocpol's (1979) and Fishman's (1990) important distinction between states and regimes and suggestion to consider the former as possessing a certain degree of autonomy from the latter. Indeed, as will be demonstrated in several contributions to this volume (and discussed further in the concluding chapter), the extent of autonomous relationship between a given state and its regime both shapes and is shaped by the course of cycles of contention. Given such an accumulation of inconsistencies between Western-based models of social movements and contentious politics and non-Western cases, doubts regarding the utility and applicability of the former have been growing, reinforcing the tendency toward particularism in the study of single cases or regions and directing attention to their unique initial conditions.

Privileging initial conditions and the often-related tendency to search for root causes of popular contention outside the liberal democracies of the West, however, can result in two closely related fallacies. The first fallacy involves the erroneous supposition that protest movements in particular, and contentious politics more generally, in authoritarian-like regimes constitute a distinct, exceptional category. While attempts at resisting dictatorship introduce certain particularities, they should not serve as a pretext for dehistoricizing these actions or assuming that similar properties or features are absent in liberal democracies. Thus, for example, direct repression certainly scores higher in authoritarian settings, and movement leaders and activists must always anticipate it and explicitly incorporate this anticipation into their plans (Boudreau 2004, 11). Yet, in most cases and even when feasible capabilities are present, authoritarians do not solely rely on repressive measures, but combine them with concessions (Rasler 1996; Maney 2007). Further, how repressive propensities and capacities ultimately play out is contingent on other factors, interactions, and events unfolding in the actual dynamics of contention (Kurzman 2004b).

The importance of moving beyond a singular view and acknowledging the meaningful differences across authoritarian-like states is underscored by the divergent forms and levels of opposition, variations in authorities' responses, and the types and degrees of transition introduced not only in the recent MENA revolts but also in other cases from different regions (Schock 2005). To better understand these differences, it is critical to avoid reifying initial conditions and root causes of contention as if they represent hard, fixed, and sharply bounded factors that *determine* outcomes (McAdam et al. 2001), and instead to explore the actual dynamics of contention as it pertains to the intricate and contingent relationships between popular contention, regimes, and transitions (be it a transition to or away from democracy, or a particular limbo configuration, inclusive of different phases, modes, and types). Evidently, despite similarities in initial conditions between Egypt and Tunisia or in root causes between Bahrain and Qatar or Saudi Arabia, large-scale popular waves of contention emerged only in some of these countries. When they did emerge, as in Egypt, Syria, Yemen, or Libya, we nevertheless observed striking dissimilarities, both in terms of trajectories and, more importantly, transitions—ranging from political reforms through coups, military takeovers, and revolutions to civil wars.

Closely related, the second fallacy involves hastily rejecting the usefulness of existing theories and models of social movements and contentious politics for making sense of non-Western contention. Present the liberal-democracy orientation of models of social movements and contentious politic, analysts should nonetheless be careful not to "throw the baby out with the bathwater," as seems to be implied in several works (see, for example, Bayat 2007; Zirakzadeh 2008, Tugal 2009; Beinin and Vairel 2011, 2013).

If we assume that episodes of contentious politics worldwide are completely different, we would have no basis for comparison, let alone for theorizing. Yet, as shown in various works on social movements and contentious politics in highly oppressive and repressive settings, even those classical analytical tools and concepts (e.g., mobilizing structures, framing or structure of political opportunities) generate important insights and advance understanding of protest movements, inclusive of religious and secularist motivated ones (Beissinger 2002; Wiktorowicz 2004; Alimi 2007; Lynch 2014). The fact that the "irregularities" identified in these and other works have been used to inform and refine the theoretical frameworks and models does not necessarily or immediately imply a "type II error," namely, sticking to one's paradigm at all cost. The point to be made based on the brutal police violence against immigrant protesters in mid-2000s France (Schneider 2005), the proactive role the federal government and security service took in order to crackdown on new left activists in the late-1960s United States (Cunningham 2003), or the retraction of civil rights and emergence of state of emergency in the post-9/11 United States (Tarrow 2015)—to give only a few examples—is that differences between cycles of contention in democracies and nondemocracies are less qualitative than first meet the eye. Although differences in certain initial conditions–related traits and features are surely present, it is how and when they gain or lose salience and consequentiality in the actual dynamics of contention that matters most; under certain contexts and over particular issues the dynamics of contention may blur the lines between "irregularities" and "regularities."

Rethinking Regional Boundaries

Consider the following events that took place decades before the "Arab Spring" and an ocean's distance from the MENA region:

On April 30, 1970, President Nixon informed the nation of US forces' incursion into Cambodia, as part of the intensifying and broadening war efforts in Vietnam. The announcement took place in the midst of an already contentious and turbulent context of a cycle of contention against the war. An antiwar coalition of movements spearheaded by Students for a Democratic Society (SDS) was among the groups that organized protest rallies, vigils, and demonstrations that began the next day across the nation. The events at Kent State University, in Ohio, were not exceptional when national guardsmen shot and killed four students, in what became known as the Kent State May 4 Massacre.[8]

Informed of several acts of vandalism and disruption, which took place at the city bar area on May 1, the city mayor declared a "state of emergency," ordered the closing of the bar area, imposed a curfew, and called in the National Guard. By the time National Guard forces arrived at Kent and immediately sealed off the city, a crowd of angered students and other individual protesters had already expressed their anger and set the on-campus Army ROTC (Reserve Officers' Training Corps) building on fire. The dynamics of action–counteraction moves between protesters and authorities and agents of social control that ensued on Sunday, May 3, resembled dynamics unfolding in other places, where each side responds to the other's move with greater severity based on a preexisting and newly developing buildup of hostility and animosity. The already escalating dynamics of harsher repressive measures and bolder and more violent protest tactics, feeding on each other, was a preview of what would come next.

Backed by Governor Rhodes's announcement from the previous day of using "every weapon possible to eradicate the problem," local and State officials decided to prevent a scheduled rally from taking place by declaring it illegal. When several hundred protesters gathered on the University Commons area, they were immediately ordered to disperse; some threw stones at the National Guardsmen in place to keep order. Equipped with rifles and tear gas canisters, the Guard managed to control the situation, with many of the protesters concentrated at several locations throughout campus. Just as the Guard forces began to withdraw and marched back to the Commons area, with only little provocation on the part of the encircled protesters, 28 Guardsmen turned around and fired indiscriminately, killing four students and wounding nine others.

Why have we chosen to focus on a specific contentious event from the larger cycle of contention in the United States? First, and more generally, because it is a useful reminder that classifications of regime types that are based on attempts to capture the internal coherence of a given regime are too broad (Tilly 2006). The United States had never given up on severe repression of stigmatized groups. Certain populations in the United States, as in other liberal democracies, have always been systematically excluded, discriminated against, oppressed, and repressed under highly authoritarian systems of rule. Indeed, the tragic events at Kent State University were not exceptional, nor isolated. On May 14, 1970, just 10 days after the Kent State shooting and regardless of the public shock, two black students were killed and 12 wounded by police forces at Jackson State University, Mississippi, under similar circumstances.

Liberal democracies, then, may well feature what Mann (1984) calls "despotic power," referring to the range of actions that the state elite is empowered to make without routine consultation with civil society groups. In like manner, it is hardly the case that the despotic power of authoritarian regimes is exercised in an indiscriminant manner vis-à-vis the entirety of the population, or that most authoritarian regimes also feature "infrastructural powers" (i.e., the capacity of the state to actually penetrate civil society and to get its actions logistically implemented throughout its territories; ibid.). These infrastructural powers inevitably rely on some degree of legitimacy and political rights, social welfare and security, and support and loyalty networks, internally as well as externally.

Needless to say, the use of despotic powers (e.g., occasional crackdowns on opposition forces, imprisonment of activists and searches legalized by emergency laws) is a far more prevalent practice in authoritarian regimes than in democracies (Linz 2000). Nonetheless, authoritarian regimes employ violent repression measuredly and some only as a last resort. More often, authoritarians exercise mixed strategies aimed at dividing and weakening their domestic opposition and, at the same time, employ political and economic forms of neopatrimonialism. This includes patronage of favorable social and political elite groups, clientelism, clannish relationships, corruption, co-optation of political rivals, and preference of customary law instead of the formal judicial system—all of which blurs the boundaries between the public and private spheres (Bach 2012).[9]

The old maxim that even the most tyrannical ruler cannot rely indefinitely on brute force—refined in a most nuanced and sophisticated manner in Mann's work—is further reinforced by considering a "deviant case"—the Israel's military government in the Occupied Territories of the West Bank and Gaza Strip. For all the draconian features of Israel's occupation of these Palestinian territories in recent decades, it is telling that during the first decade of its military rule, beginning June 1967, Israel devised a policy that aimed at preserving the social and political fabric of Palestinian society. In practice, far from being a mere acquiescence with international conventions regarding the responsibilities of occupying force, Israel continued the Jordanian policy of favoritism toward the notable leadership (mayors, parliament members, etc.) and institutions (local and municipal councils, welfare associations, economic enterprises, etc.) in return for their cooperation with the military government. In 1972, seeking to "normalize" the occupation, Israel conducted municipal elections, which left the incumbent pro-Jordanian mayors largely in place. The increased reliance on despotic powers beginning 1977, following the advent of a right-wing government led by Menachem Begin, was, more than anything else, the result of a widespread cycle of contention that took place in 1976, which was guided for the first time by local forces that were pro-Palestinian Liberation Organization (PLO).

More concretely, the second reason for our decision to use the example of the United States cycle of contention relates to the fact that even the most nuanced classification of regime types is nonetheless static. Under certain circumstances and with regard to certain issues, the struggle for reforms and claims made on authorities in liberal democracies has the potential to acquire its own dynamics and momentum and to produce features that bear meaningful similarities to contentious politics in authoritarian settings. Regarding the systematically and structurally stigmatized and oppressed Afro-American population, the Kent State event was shocking partly because of the context. Indeed, despite the painstaking achievements of civil rights activists during the 1950s and 1960s and the ongoing transition away from Jim Crow racial segregation regime, black activists and organizations' involvement in the anti–Vietnam War cycle of contention produced ample instances of brutal repression. The authorities' overreaction, it should be noted, extended to nonaggrieved/advantaged groups too. While initially enjoying civil, political, and social rights and constitutional-based citizenship protections, and being committed to nonviolence, many SDS leaders and activists gradually found themselves operating under repressive conditions, with ever-growing diminishing separation between everyday life and political activism. This not only produced intensive militancy and extreme ideologies and agendas but also, following the Kent State massacre and the round of war-like confrontations that ensued that May in universities nationwide, pushed some antiwar SDS members underground, from where they engaged in an unprecedented campaign of violence. Influencing this process, but also influenced by it, was the expansion of previous US security and intelligence agencies' programs and operations, which involved ever-growing willingness to sacrifice constitutional rights for the sake of neutralizing domestic dissent and threats (e.g., COINTELPRO and Operation CHAOS). The fact that the cycle of contention abated during the first half of the 1970s had little to do with the political program SDS sought to promote and struggle for, one of direct democracy and ending the all-powerful military-industrial complex regime that shaped Cold War politics and encouraged inhumane capitalistic imperialism. If anything, the cycle of contention prompted intense conservative reaction on the part of both institutional and noninstitutional forces (Sale 1973; Gamson 1990; Varon 2004; Jenkins 2006).

Importantly, not all instances of contention necessarily develop into a cycle, some remaining locally bounded and sporadic. Recalling Swidler's (1986) important distinction, during "settled times" and for diametrically opposing reasons, the distinction among popular contention, regime, and transition is easily conveyed, which renders the differences between authoritarian-like regimes and liberal democracies plentifully clear. Broadly speaking and in relative terms, in liberal democracies political power tends to be exercised, regulated, and constrained within a set of formal and informal rules; a shift, whether in full or in part, from one established ruling arrangement (political or economic or a combination of both) to another typically unfolds in orderly fashion; and, the separation between ordinary life spaces and routines and involvement in consequential claim-making is usually maintained. In authoritarian-like regimes, political power tends to be exercised with little if any consultation with civil society groups; transitions are rare and are usually the initiative of authoritarians meant to resolidify their positioning within the ruling elites; and, given the arbitrary and often capricious nature of the regime and the repressive and oppressive measures that come with it, there is little separation between ordinary life spaces and routines and involvement in consequential claim-making.

But some episodes of contention do develop into cycles. More than structural-like preconditions and certainly not a simple process of contagion, the generalizing of contention is more often the result of several processes at play, each producing its own influence, but always more than the aggregated sum of these influences. These processes include (1) the triggering of diffusion, extension, imitation, and reaction among groups that are usually more quiescent and have less resources, either because some are encouraged by possible receptiveness of authorities to demands of "early risers" or because their interests are threatened or undermined; (2) the innovation and creativity of new forms of contention and frames that often bring in more actors from within and outside the state; (3) the convergence and divergence of forces involving not only preexisting organizations but also the formation of new organizations as well as the appearance of more ad hoc organizing and activities; and (4) the rapidity of information flow, heightened political attention, and intensity and frequency of interactions among groups of challengers and among members of the authorities and social control/security agents, as well as between both sets of actors (Tarrow 2011, 201–6).

The intensity of contentious interactions that characterize those unsettled, agitated times, and the uncertainties, emotional and cognitive saliencies, and contingencies associated with them may take on diverse trajectories and outcomes, ranging from institutionalization, radicalization, and terrorism to counter/revolution, civil war, or de/democratization (Meyer 1993; Della Porta 1995, 2012; Koopmans 2004; Tilly 2003b; Goldstone 1998; Tarrow 2011). We are less interested in explaining one or more of these divergent outcomes, as others have done (see, for example, Lynch 2014), than in fleshing out similarities in contentious politics between MENA and non-MENA countries, as a means to a larger end: to draw parallels between democracies and nondemocracies. These similarities, we argue, stem from the processual, hyper-paced, and contentious nature

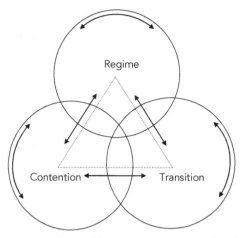

FIGURE 0.1 Interactions within and between processes in cycles of contention.

that popular contention, regime, and transition acquire and, consequently, the intricate, contingent, and indeterminate interrelation among them during cycles of contention. The analytical model (Figure 0.1) aims at capturing both the activated dynamism and accelerated pace popular contention, regime, and transition take on and the enhanced interrelatedness among them during cycles of contentious politics.

As contentious activity accelerates, interaction between challenging groups and organizations intensifies, new frames and tactics are tried, and interactions with publics, rival movements, allies, and elites, internal as well as external, take place. Regimes, too, assume more processual features, and many of those arrangements, rules, practices, and styles that shape the relations among state actors and organizations and between them and other actors, parties, and institutions (e.g., elites, the general public, and bordering and nonbordering states and institutions) are subjected to reassessment, renegotiation, or even reconfiguration by one or more actor or institution or segment of it. In like manner, cycles of contention are engines of political change; whether it is politically, economically, or culturally driven, the revolutionary situation epitomized in contentious cycles tends to speed up processes of political realignment and transformation.

Finally, the accelerated pace of popular contention, regime, and transition also generates higher interrelatedness among them, an intricate multifaceted relationship that has received fairly little scholarly attention. For various reasons, scholars of social movements, regimes, and transitions have tended to engage in a kind of a "parallel play." Scholarly divides between research traditions with their own distinct preferences, working assumptions, and research problems, have tended to discourage greater attention and attempts at theorizing these intricate linkages. Scholars of social movements, for example, have been more concerned with studying the political, cultural, and biographical consequences of contention than with exploring and specifying the reciprocal relationship between institutional and noninstitutional politics (but see, Kriesi et al. 1995; Goldstone 2003; McAdam and Tarrow 2010; Luders 2010, as notable exceptions). This kind of "movement-centric" inclination has resulted in insufficient attention not only to how authorities in particular, and regime features more generally, play a critical role in shaping the particular mode opposition groups take but also to how they seek to influence and are influenced by their own structure of political opportunities and constraints at the international level in dealing with domestic dissent.

When they do tackle the issue, social movement theorists have largely failed to engage in a more processual approach that is able to capture the various modalities of transition. From the other side of the "divide," scholars of transition treat social movements more or less as epiphenomenal to a process driven by elite realignment, defection, and contestation (Tarrow 1995; Della Porta 2014); even when transition theorists bring mass mobilization back in, they often treat it as a contributing factor to elite efforts. Yet, it is not only the case that social movements and opposition groups shape and are shaped by transitions (i.e., a shift from one phase to another, or tension and inconsistencies between one type of transition and another—as is often the case between economic and political transitions; Roberts 2014). It is also the case that in some instances, opposing movements may play an equally important role, either independently or with elite's backing, in redirecting or undermining transition or even reversing recent achievements.

Last, in their preoccupation with classifying regime types and subtypes and the search for crucial defining differences, scholars of regimes tend to settle for measures regarding the presence or absence of civil society groups and organizations or of civil liberties and freedoms (e.g., freedom of association); less frequently there is an attempt to study the influence of regime features and structures on movements (Przeworski 2008); hardly any attempt has been undertaken to explore the role played by social movements and popular contention in either safeguarding or undermining those arrangements, rules, practices, and styles that shape power relations and define regimes.

The Goal and Organization of the Book

This book's main goal is to put the recent Arab revolts in comparative perspective, as a means to a larger end: to flesh out similarities and to draw parallels between democratic and authoritarian-like regimes. Instead of treating MENA countries as monolithic and essentializing them (as the term "Arab Spring" does) or seeking to identify similar sources of discontent or "silver bullet"-like factors, we privilege a focus on the dynamics of contentious politics as they apply to the intricate, contingent, and indeterminate relationship among popular contention, regime, and transition. Privileging a focus on dynamics of contentious politics by no means implies lack of attention to and appreciation of a given case's particularities and initial conditions; nor is this book's sole task an attempt to confirm the applicability and utility of social movement theory. By asking what cycles of contention in other parts of the world can tell us about revolts in the Arab world, and what the cycles of contention in the Arab world can tell us about contentious politics more generally, we maintain a productive and useful balance between deductive and inductive modes of investigation and reasoning.

Concomitantly, and in line with the theoretical and comparative premises of the *Dynamics of Contention* research program, we do not attempt to develop a general, overarching theory of Arab and non-Arab cycles of contention; in fact we doubt such an attempt would escape oversimplification. Rather we seek (and hopefully deliver) the generation of more modest, albeit meaningful theoretical insights and statements, which is carried out by allowing both theory and empirics to bear on each other. These insights and statements are presented either in specific chapters or as threads that cut through chapters and then are addressed in the concluding chapter (e.g., the role of the military as both a central institution and a proactive actor in cycle of contention).

Inspired by the *Dynamics of Contention* research program, however, our comparative undertaking does not follow a strict analytical approach. As part of our goal to put the Arab revolts in a comparative perspective, we have allowed for a variety of comparative styles and strategies. Thus, for example, in some chapters, readers will find a broad comparative treatment of the recent Arab revolts (see the chapter by Goldstone); other chapters offer a more limited comparison of Arab and non-Arab cases (see Bunce's comparison of the 1989, color revolutions, and Arab uprisings); still other chapters build on one or more Arab cases and bring comparative evidence from non-Arab case/s (as Alimi and Meyer's chapter does) or, conversely, build on a non-Arab case/s and bring comparative evidence from one or more Arab cases (as the chapter by Pilati does). Additionally, readers will find no single or unified research strategy in the sense of relying on either variable-based or mechanism-based analysis. The diversity of comparative styles, research strategy, and the wealth of cases that comes with it are consistent with our attempt to rethink regional boundaries through unearthing theoretically insightful similarities and dissimilarities.

While contributions to this volume relate to the linkages among popular contention, regime, and transition, they nonetheless pay closer attention to one facet of this interrelatedness in particular, and are therefore organized into three distinct sections. Contributions to the first section, "Between Structure and Contention," go beyond a unidirectional line of research regarding the effects of structural factors on the willingness to rebel to probing how regime features (writ large) and authorities' responses *shape* and are *shaped by* the mode, level, and scope of popular mobilization and contention.

The section begins with Diani and Moffatt's chapter on why (and how) contentious collective action gets coordinated in different ways across different episodes or cycles of contention. The authors introduce the concept of "modes of coordination," argued to be a more nuanced, dynamic, and contingent analytical tool than the often too rigid concept of social movement, and embrace a political process–oriented framework to offer an insightful explanation to why certain modes of coordination seem to prevail over others in the MENA region. Above and beyond structural factors and root causes, the predominance of particular modes of coordination is explained by the combined influence of the capacity and propensity of repression, the presence of multiple lines of social division, and the role of local elites. Focusing more closely on varied effects of repression on protest mobilization, chapter 2, by Katia Pilati, similarly embraces an organizational perspective and argues for the explanatory payoffs found once taking into account the various ways repression shapes and is shaped by variations in organizational structure of the opposition. Based on a paired comparison of two African authoritarian regimes (Nigeria and Zimbabwe), Pilati demonstrates how the differences in levels of protest mobilization between the two cases are explained by different mechanisms of organizational structure adaptation. The generalizability of her framework and results is then discussed based on an informed analysis of several Arab uprisings as well as of migrant-based contention against exclusionary and repressive contexts in Italy and Switzerland.

The other two chapters in this section pay closer analytical attention to regime characteristics and features of the political conditions. Mario Quaranta's chapter offers a large-N comparative study of the fairly new and fragile democracies of Latin America in order to examine the influence of specific qualities of democracies on levels and forms of popular contention. The results of his analysis reveal that in regimes that are hybrid in nature, for the concept of political opportunity structure to be analytically useful it is necessary to pay close attention to those basic contextual conditions of equality, freedom, and responsiveness; to examine their interrelatedness as well as how they interact with micro-level factors at the individual level; and, equally important, to recognize that oftentimes political opportunities (or "openings") are offered by forces and institutions that are not traditionally considered political, such as the military. Whereas Quaranta discusses the generalizability of his Latin America–based results to several MENA countries, chapter 4 by Jack Goldstone takes the other direction. Based on a rich analysis of many MENA countries, Goldstone's attempt to make sense of the enormous variations in the scope and magnitude of popular contention as well as in authorities' responses (despite undeniable commonalities in root causes) generates several theoretically meaningful insights regarding often-neglected components of political opportunity structure. These components, which are particularly relevant to authoritarian regimes, and yet may well play out in democracies, are the specific character of authoritarian regimes, their resources, and their international contexts.

Essentially, the consequential claim-making entailed in popular contention embodies a threat to existing power arrangements and powerholders, which explains why the most frequent initial responses are either unresponsiveness or repression. Yet, it is possible that sustained and broadening contention, as well as specific strategy and allies, may bring about some initial signs of transition, whether declarative and symbolic or actual, albeit limited, rearrangements of power relations and practices. What is certain is that even the most symbolic gesture, say, a limited concession or reform, is likely to influence, in turn, the nature of interaction among challenging actors and groups or between them and opposing population groups that benefit from the existing power arrangements. Contributors to the second section, "Processes and Trajectories of Contention," explore these intricate and reciprocal dynamics in various ways.

Starting with processes of diffusion, Valerie Bunce's chapter examines the role of two central drivers—demonstration effects and transnational net-works—in explaining how protests against authoritarian rulers travel from one authoritarian regime to others in the same region. Comparison of three cross-national waves of popular challenges to authoritarian rule—the collapse of communism in 1989, the spread of electoral-based challenges to authoritarian rulers in post-communist Europe and Eurasia from 1998 to 2005, and the 2011 MENA uprisings—reveals meaningful cross-wave similarities without losing sight of notable dissimilarities. Moreover, the comparison also reveals the role of a third, usually overlooked driver of diffusion that was able to expand the potential for the two "primary" drivers to play a role: the early entry in each of these cross-national dynamics of a key participant (e.g., East Germany in 1989 and Egypt in the MENA events) that was ideally suited to broadcast the diffusion process to a broader swath of the region. But the expansion and evolution of cycles of contention involve additional processes and are shaped by the involvements and roles played by additional parties and actors. In chapter 6, Gregory Maney focuses on the hybrid nature of segmented composite regimes, where different groups occupy different social locations and possess unequal citizenship rights, and analyzes how this generates distinctive influences on the dynamics of contention.

Using the case of Northern Ireland ethnic democracy to develop a broader theoretical framework that applies to other "structurally similar" cases (MENA included), Maney analyzes the ways that this specific variant of segmented composite regimes influences the forms and dynamics of intergroup contention during the civil rights cycle of late 1960s and early 1970s. The chapter's main argument is that ethnic democracies, much like other regimes that are deeply divided along racial or religious lines, suffer a double legitimacy crisis, leaving authorities susceptible to challenges emanating from both minority and dominant groups. This dual crisis stems from widespread yet contradictory discourses of democracy. Both minority- and dominant-group-based ethnonationalist movements take advantage of the opportunities that discourses of democracy provide in order to challenge the legitimacy of authorities and their responses to contention. Authorities' responses to domestic challenges often backlash, and challenger groups often try to capitalize on this and mobilize external support for their cause. The ability of dissident groups to actually bring about international intervention for coping with high levels and forms of repression locally stands at the heart of chapter 7 by Eitan Alimi and David Meyer. Instrumental and normative considerations on the part of international third parties on the one hand, and the operation of transnational advocacy groups on the other, being equal, the authors make the case for the importance of examining states' nested structure of political opportunities and constraints that explains their relative power and, as a result, authoritarian rulers' space of action vis-à-vis dissident groups. Data on interstate dynamics of economic and military trades enables Alimi and Meyer to offer convincing evidence not only of the striking differences in the degree of international intervention in the cases of Egypt, Libya, and Syria but also of other cases with different regime types, such as the composite regime of Israel-Palestine and the hybrid regime of the Ukraine.

Finally, by focusing on the interconnection of several processes and their corresponding mechanisms in helping to explain the evolution as well as the outcomes of cycles of contention, chapter 8 also acts as a bridge to the theme of the next section of the volume. Based on a paired comparison between the Egyptian cycle of 2011 and the Iranian cycle of 1978–1979, Karen Rasler reminds us that in many cases the eventual trajectories and paths popular contention take are neither a mere product of macrostructural features or developments, nor action strategy and tactics of the opposition groups and organizations. Rather, in both cases highly interdependent sets of actions and reactions among multiple governmental and nongovernmental actors involved indeterminate factors and elements of spontaneity in producing the evolutionary, dynamic characteristics of both protest campaigns. Specifically, Rasler demonstrates how three crucial relational mechanisms (attribution of similarity, appropriation of mobilizing vehicles, and "carrot and stick" government strategies) were present yet operated differently in each case, contributing to the expansion of broad political processes of mobilization, coalition formation, and scale shift, which, combined, explain the outcome of each cycle.

The third, and last section of the book, "Between Contention and Transition," brings our attempt to flesh out similarities in dissimilarities between democratic and authoritarian-like regimes during cycles of contention full circle. Contributions to this section offer a sober, much needed reminder that contention does not end when transition begins, but transition processes are almost always highly contentious, hence the need to avoid treating both in linear, sequential terms. Our contributors in this section pay particular attention to the highly precarious, indeterminate, and contentious nature of the process of transition and the role played by both regime incumbents and challengers, internally as well as externally based, in driving, impeding, or reverting it altogether.

The intricate and rarely linear features of transition processes receive careful attention and treatment in Vincent Boudreau's chapter on regime transitions and popular contention in the democratizing setting of both Indonesia and the Philippines. Investigating the role of social movements in transitions and distinguishing between the activities, networks, and interests of social movement organizations, the chapter demonstrates how prodemocracy movements are not always or exclusively about democracy. Processes of antiregime mobilization, Boudreau reminds us, often draw on movement networks with a variety of interests, experiences, capacities, and orientations. Such diversity reflects movement histories—organizational and relational legacies on the one hand and emergent influences and dynamics of contention on the other. How this plays out and is carried forward to transition politics is open-ended, making the relationship between prodemocracy movements and the movement toward democracy an empirical matter. The historically informed analysis of the two similar Southeast Asian cases with different outcomes, is followed by a thought-provoking and theoretically driven discussion of parallels with the Egyptian and Tunisian contentious transitions. Processes of transition, moreover, not only are open-ended and contentious but also can involve other aspects that are not necessarily political in the strict sense of the word, which may well develop in diametrical opposition with each other. In some cases, and Chile is one in point as demonstrated in chapter 10 by Mario Sznajder, protesters seek to promote a change of fiscal regimes in the course of political transition without significantly challenging the regime. Indeed, as Sznajder demonstrates, the 2011 student-initiated cycle of protest in Chile did not challenge the democratic framework. The main demands of the reform-driven protests combine goals of deeper democratization—eliminating the last authoritarian enclaves left over from military dictatorship era—with wider upward socioeconomic mobility through better redistribution mechanisms. The main reason for that situation, the chapter demonstrates, is that societies like Chile that are characterized by deep socioeconomic gaps, have undergone processes of "economic rationalization" in which the neoliberal individualistic ethos has been imposed in parallel to the restoration of democracy. The question of how the systematic contradiction between the two dimensions of Chile's experience as a consolidating democracy that has motivated and shaped the 2011 cycle of contention may help inform our understanding of the challenges faced by some of the MENA regime transitions is addressed based on a comparison between the Chilean case and the Jordanian one in the years leading up to and during the 2011 cycle of contention. Finally, what may appear at first as an economic-driven cycle of popular contention is essentially about a crisis of political legitimacy. Closing this section, but also reconnecting more explicitly with the themes of the previous sections, chapter 11 by Gayil Talshir uses Habermas's theory of legitimation crisis to situate the Israeli protest summer of 2011 between the worldwide "Occupy" movements and the Arab revolts, and to draw insightful parallels among them in terms of how popular contention, regime, and transition interrelate. The legitimation crisis framework enables Talshir to explain, on the one hand, why movements in the recent Middle Eastern revolts seem to be slow in moving forward with democratic transition and, on the other, the quest of "Occupy" movements for a radical alternative model to representative democracy, namely, a deliberative or participatory democracy. The Israeli case, Talshir argues, can also be read and explained based on this perspective: A movement that exemplified tension between a demand for an alternative model of democracy and a demand to go back to a party-ideology-policy framework of representative democracy. Much like the Occupy movements and the MENA revolts, the Israeli summer of discontent was more than a socioeconomic-driven protest of the middle class. Essentially and substantively, the Israeli protest summer was a reaction against the democratic framework in general and, in particular, a challenge to the fragmented identity-politics that came to dominate Israeli politics over the last generation—a transition that also manifested itself in the eradication of public services and the welfare state.

Finally, tying together the various themes and insights of the book's contributions, Avraham Sela's concluding chapter critically reviews some of the main strands of research of the "Arab Spring" based on a broad historical perspective, and offers some inductive insights that inform theories of social movements and contentious politics. Some of these insights relate to the significance of regimes' political legacies and state–society relations as key factors in shaping the broadening and consolidation of cycles of contention, the impact of regionalism on cross-national diffusion of contention and political change, and the role of the military as a political player, arbitrator, or balancer in times of transition. The chapter also reflects on the recent and still ongoing contention in the region, and points out several future directions of stability and change.

Acknowledgments

Earlier versions of this introduction benefited considerably from the careful reading and useful comments of David Meyer, Avraham Sela, Mario Sznajder, and Sidney Tarrow, for which I am grateful.

Notes

1. See, Ardıç (2012) for a useful and comprehensive critical review of this literature. The Arab renaissance (*nahda*), or awakening, refers to the rise of Arab nationalism from the late 19th century to the interwar years (Antonius 1938). Dawisha (2013), however, refers to the Arab military coups of the 1950s and 1960s as the first Arab awakening.

2. Although it can be non-consequential and despite its overuse and misuse in popular discourse, we use the term protest as a synonym of contention, and interchangeably. Also, popular contention may be carried out by, and take the form of a variety of collective agents, of which a social movement is but one. In this volume, we use the term "social movement" as an analytical category, without implying a certain developmental stage and without ignoring the existence and role played by other collective agents such as interest groups, advocacy networks, or coalitions.

3. For clarity, we use the term "authoritarian" regimes as a broad category inclusive of states with totalitarian, autocratic, monarchic, or neopatrimonial features or some combination of these; "hybrid" or "mixed" regimes when referring to states with a combination of authoritarian and democratic features; and "composite" regimes when referring to states in which two different systems of rule divide different population groups along ethnic, religious, or racial lines.

4. Even though not all waves or cycles of contentious politics reach the operation or consolidation stage of transition, but all do have outcomes, we nevertheless use the former term in a nonteleological manner.

5. As will become clearer below, we use the term "assumptions" instead of "cases" because highly repressive social and political settings have never been a complete stranger to some important theorization in the field (e.g., McAdam 1999) and it is important to recognize that even in liberal democracies it is possible to have repressive settings with respect to certain populations and/or issues.

6. Inspiration for the ideas expressed here has developed jointly with Paul Almeida during a short collaboration that took the form of a panel in the American Sociological Association annual meeting in San Francisco 2009.

7. We refer to what James Scott (1985) has termed "weapons of the weak" when study-ing everyday forms of peasants' resistance in Malaysia. This type of resistance and noncompliance are excluded from the analyses throughout this volume not because we think they take place exclusively in authoritarian states, but because they tend to lack the overt, proactive, and public features of contention.

8. The information here is based on Sale's (1973) comprehensive analysis of SDS, on the President's Commission on Campus Unrest Report (a.k.a. the Scranton Report) and the May 4 Archive (http://files.eric.ed.gov/fulltext/ED083899.pdf, and http://www.may4archive.org/chronology.shtml, respectively—accessed June 1, 2014).

9. Although this type of patronage network has been conceptualized by some as the "New Authoritarianism" of MENA regimes (Jamal 2006; King 2009), several contributions to this volume demonstrate that this feature is not MENA-specific.

PART I

Between Structure and Contention

1

Modes of Coordination of Contentious Collective Action in the Middle East

Mario Diani and Caelum Moffatt

An Ongoing Conversation: Social Movement Theory and the Middle East

The momentous events of 2011 in the Middle East and North Africa (henceforth, MENA) did not develop out of the blue, but were just the most striking instance of contention among the many that had occurred across the region over the previous decades. Likewise, attempts to apply political process theory (Tarrow 2011) to Middle Eastern societies have long preceded the "Arab Spring" (see, e.g., Bennani-Chraïbi and Fillieule 2003a; Wiktorowicz 2004; Alimi 2009). Some have questioned such exercises, criticizing Western social movement theorists' tendency to focus on the role of the state and neglect changes in "behaviour, attitudes, cultural symbols and value systems" or their inability to capture the distinctiveness of movements as differentiated, dynamic, fragmented, and eclectic compositions in "constant flow and motion" (Bayat 2005, 897–98). Others have flagged the importance of engaging in a more inductive, case-specific analysis in order to capture particular contexts, networks, and practices of MENA movements (Beinin and Vairel 2011).

In this chapter we try to take such criticisms into account by treating social movements as just one of several "modes of coordination" (Diani 2012, 2013, 2015) through which collective action can be conducted. More specifically, we view social movements as the regular if informal patterns of relations between multiple actors, through which resources and symbols are circulated, solidarities and identities are reinforced, and different protest actions and organizations come to be perceived as part of the same collective project (Tarrow 2011, chap. 3). It is the combination of sustained exchanges of resources between formally independent units and longer term collective identities that sets social movements apart from short-term tactical coalitions, purposive organizations, and various types of communitarian and subcultural networks (Diani 2012, 2015, chap. 1).

At the same time, our analysis still draws heavily on the political process model of social movement research, in order to assess the reasons why certain modes of coordination seem to prevail over others in the MENA region. We focus in particular on three sets of factors: the costs of going public with expressions of dissent in largely authoritarian regimes with high levels of repression; the presence of multiple lines of social division; and the role of local elites.

We do not claim to provide a systematic, not to mention a comparative, account of the organizational forms that have developed in the MENA region in the last few years (but see Pilati's chapter in this volume on the linkage between repression, organizational forms, and mobilization). Nor do we have any aspiration to chart the highly complex processes that have followed the 2011 insurgences. More modestly, we aim to illustrate a theoretical model of the different ways in which action gets coordinated, through a number of ad hoc examples from different countries of the region (mostly Egypt and Tunisia) in the years up to 2011. We hope that our line of thinking may prompt more systematic explorations of the same events, based on our analytic framework. With these notes of caution, our argument unfolds in three steps:

- First, we recall briefly why key analytic dimensions identified by political process theory appear relevant to our understanding of collective action in the MENA region;
- Next, we illustrate how referring to "modes of coordination" might enhance our grasp of patterns of collective action in the MENA countries before the 2011 protest wave;
- Finally, we look at evidence about the 2011 events, searching for changes in modes of coordination. We wonder in particular whether social movement dynamics proper have actually developed in that phase, and under what conditions; or whether, in contrast, the "Arab Spring" has consisted mostly of the intensification of mobilization patterns already dominant in the region.

Authoritarianism, Multiple Cleavages, and Elites

Although the extent to which political process theory may be applied to MENA countries is debatable (see, e.g., Hafez 2003; Meijer 2005), it still identifies a few key mechanisms that guide our exploration of collective action even in that area. Large-scale collective action emerges through the forging of shared agendas; the development of trust bonds cutting across clans, factions, and local communities; and the creation and reinforcement of collective identities. These are hugely facilitated, and have been for a long time (Tarrow 2011, chap. 3), by the possibility of engaging in discourse and communicative action in public spaces. This is easier if (1) levels of regime authoritarianism are low, or at least perceived as diminishing; (2) the public space is structured along some major cleavage lines in reference to which actors may locate themselves, if possible from a critical angle; and (3) the elites provide allies and/or leaders to opposition movements (Kriesi 2004; Tarrow 2011).

Even allowing for significant cross-country variation, MENA polities have been largely characterized by authoritarian regimes. While these regimes have usually criminalized public displays of opposition and restricted their margins of action through violent repression (see, e.g., Singerman 2004), one should not assume that the relationship between powerholders and their opponents necessarily implies explicit violent coercion. To reduce threats from political opponents, MENA regimes have actually implemented various strategies, including various degrees of co-optation of potential challengers or toleration of moderate opponents. The complex relationship between authoritarian regimes and their domestic challengers is aptly demonstrated by the case of the Muslim Brotherhood in several countries, among them Egypt, up to the 2011 uprising, and Jordan (Robinson 2004, 119–20; Wickham 2013). Altogether, rather than the stark contrast between opponents and autocratic elites, authoritarian regimes in the Middle East seem to display complex patterns of transactions involving conflict and negotiation between rulers and challengers (Heydemann and Leenders 2013, chap. 6–7).

At the same time, one should not underestimate the fact that strong repressive apparatuses heavily discourage civic activity and in particular the forms of participation (such as large-scale coalition-building and movement activism) that most rely on public spaces and public communication. It is thus more difficult to establish networks beyond the boundaries of social and cultural milieus (religious groups, clans, urban communities) where mutual trust may be reasonably expected among members. This may have significant impacts on the prevalence of specific modes of coordination over others and on the characteristics of the actors that most successfully mobilize when regimes crumble. For example, while opposition to the Pahlevi regime in Iran was conducted significantly, if not primarily, by radical, secular activists, this group had weaker roots in communitarian and religious networks and proved less capable of mass mobilization once the regime collapsed (Robinson 2004, 118). One has to wonder how much this contributed to the move from a pluralist, polysepalous revolutionary movement to the rule of a small set of conservative Islamist organizations after the demise of the Shah.

Multiple salient cleavage lines are another relevant feature of MENA polities. Analysts have long showed that the development of sustained coalitional activity, as well as social movements, is likely to be affected by the salience of existing cleavages. When cleavages are highly salient, even other types of issue networks and coalitions tend to organize along the major identities associated with those cleavages; in contrast, cross-cutting alliances are easier when the dominant cleavages are less salient. The weakening of traditional left-right cleavages in the West since the 1980s has often been regarded as one key factor behind the spread of coalitions—and indeed social movements—mobilizing fairly heterogeneous constituencies around "new" types of issues and identities (Kriesi et al. 1995).

However, even the emergence of new cleavages and the coalitions/movements associated with them is dependent on the presence of institutional opportunities for action and on (counter)elites' capacity to articulate emerging themes into a broader political program. This is a long and contentious process (Kriesi et al. 2012). The absence of a major cleavage line or its weakening does not automatically lead to the emergence of a new cleavage, let alone a sustained one, but may simply result in the reduction of the potential for large-scale social conflicts. According to the model of pluralist politics, this may be a positive outcome as long as it reflects a pluralistic polity without major barriers to access to political influence. Where this is not the case, the most likely outcome is the fragmentation of civil society. However, MENA polities often seem to display a different pattern, characterized by the presence of multiple salient cleavages, defined along different lines. They are strong enough to increase the fragmentation of local societies, not only to prevent the emergence—and in particular the persistence—of united coalitions against autocratic rulers.

In the 2000s, the intensity of the "Islam vs. secularism" cleavage may indeed explain a lot of the difficulties encountered by the heterogeneous coalitions opposing authoritarian regimes in the area or—in Palestine—Israeli occupation, to turn into fully fledged social movements, or even to survive. The field of Islamic organizations is also highly contentious internally, marred by recurring struggles between "true" and "false" Islamists (Wiktorowicz 2004; Aburaiya 2004). And of course, social fractures are not rooted in religious conflicts only. They also draw on clan, local, and tribal solidarities, which may prove powerful obstacles to social integration in general and more specifically to the spread of inclusive types of collective action. For example, a country like Lebanon, with strong territorial enclaves defined by ethnic communities, does not provide a favorable ground for the emergence of cross-cutting alliances, if not in purely instrumental terms (Salloukh 2006; Clark and Salloukh 2013).

The above remarks point to the role that elites play in MENA polities. In general, elites in the Middle East seem to have operated to maintain and reinforce existing cleavages in order to increase their bargaining power (see, e.g., Clark 2004b; Heydemann and Leenders 2013). Genuine competition for power among elites has also been severely limited in favor of arrangements that ensured the monopoly of political influence by an inner circle of loyal elites. Polities characterized by what is sometimes referred to as a "sultanistic regime" (Goldstone 2011—see also chapter 4 in this volume) consist of an autocratic president at the apex of a Leviathan state, accompanied by a cadre of mercantile elites co-opted through a process of crony capitalism and protected by a brutally belligerent security apparatus that suppresses any appetite for protest. Collectively, the beneficiaries of this system extort public resources as an extension of their private coffers. Prior to the "Arab Spring" evidence of this system in operation was ubiquitous in the very countries that confronted popular protests, from the Ben 'Ali and Trabelsi families in Tunisia to President Mubarak's personal relationships to the military and business elites in Egypt, from Mu'ammar Qadhafi's tribal connections in Libya to President 'Ali 'Abdallah Salih's links to the Hashid Tribal Federation in Yemen, or al-Assad's ties to the Alawi community in Syria.

Even the ties between elites and oppositional actors seem to be mainly of an ascriptive nature: they are based on the solidarities originating from family and clan, and generate informal and clientelistic networks rather than associational ties (Fillieule and Bennani-Chraïbi 2003, 104). Although it can be argued that patronage politics may also contribute to mediate between different cleavages, thus playing a moderating effect on the potential for conflict (Kurtoglu Eskisar and Stroschein 2009), altogether it has further undermined the emergence of counterelites and movement entrepreneurs with the necessary leadership skills. But for social movements and coalitions to develop, political brokers are needed, capable of linking different currents and factions into a common project. For example, the long-term prospects of the Iranian opposition were kept alive by people capable of taking up precisely that role and linking Islamic and secular forces. One of them was Ali Shariati, who, particularly during his stay in France, managed successfully to combine Islam and a sense of social justice. He went beyond artificial distinctions between modernity and tradition, religious and secular, thus making of Islam a strong anticolonialist force in the 1960s Iran (Moaddel 2005, chap. 11).

The dependence of alliances across political divides on personal factors undermines their sustainability. For example, the collaboration between the Yemeni Socialist Party (YSP) and the Islamic Reform (*islah*) Party in Yemen in the early 2000s was largely a product of the personal orientations of some leaders committed to dialogue and with relatively similar positions, most prominently the

Socialist politician Jarallah Umar. His assassination in December 2002 brought the whole process virtually to an end, without ever having affected the two parties' distinctive positions and internal fragmentation (Carapico, Wedeen, and Wuerth 2002). The weakness of organizations usually prevents cooperation from developing, as organizations cannot guarantee the loyalty of their respective grassroots once specific leaders have disappeared from the scene.

The combination of high levels of repression, multiple salient cleavage lines, and patronage-oriented elites all contributed to the weakness of collective action in MENA polities and to their being portrayed, at least until 2011, as countries structurally resistant to sustained, mass forms of participation. Some analysts (e.g., Badie, cited in Bennani-Chraïbi and Fillieule 2003b, 25) even characterized Islamic societies as places where there would be no real alternative between submission and revolt. The latter (*l'émeute*) actually would characterize the political process as a whole in opposition to the concept of political demand, amenable to mediation, proper of liberal democracies. As a result, all main opposition actors from both the left and the Islamic milieus were portrayed as seriously open to the option of seizing power by force (Fillieule and Bennani-Chraïbi 2003, 89–90). And yet, the experience of 2011, as well as the years that preceded it all, suggests that the range of forms of collective action in MENA countries is more diversified than some generalizations might suggest. To illustrate this point, we need to move away from rigid dichotomies opposing the sustained and coordinated forms of collective action (Tilly's [1984] "national social movement"), typically associated with the West, to the discontinuous violent outbursts that would characterize nondemocratic societies in other parts of the world. Such a shift, one of the core themes of this volume, also requires some conceptual innovation. Let us introduce the concept of mode of coordination.

Modes of Coordination

Exploring the multiple forms of collective action is complicated by the indifference that many social movement theorists reserve to the question of the analytic peculiarity of social movements vis-à-vis other forms of collective action. For example, in her otherwise excellent analysis of Egyptian contention up to the early 2000s, Singerman (2003, 223) included within the Islamic movement all citizens trying to replace the Egyptian institutions with others closer to the principles of Islam. She also stressed the presence of organized forces acting on three levels: political; cultural—through publications, conferences, and so forth; and service delivery—addressing social needs such as education, health, and charity, mostly through the mosque and also through mutual support organizations like the Islamic banks (see also Wiktorowicz 2004, 10–12). This is a very inclusive definition; in order to capture the plurality of logics of collective action operating within each episode, and their interplay, we propose to use the concept of "mode of coordination" (Diani 2012, 2013, 2015).

By "mode of coordination"[1] we mean the relational patterns through which responses are provided to two basic collective action dilemmas, namely, the mechanisms through which *resource allocation* and *boundary definition* take place for a certain collectivity (Diani 2015, chap. 1). Decisions regarding the best use of available resources may be taken largely within the boundaries of specific organizations or groups, or they may be reached through systematic negotiations between a multiplicity of actors present in the same organizational field. Likewise, boundary definition, and the resulting collective identity, may largely focus on specific organizations, with participants in collective action addressing their loyalties and sense of belongingness to distinctive actors; or it may also imply some meaningful identification and solidarity with broader collective actors. Different combinations of responses to these basic imperatives define distinct modes of coordination.

Before proceeding to a brief illustration of such modes, we should clarify that we do not expect any model to provide a satisfactory account of any specific set of concrete experiences of mobilization. It would be pointless to ask whether Islamic activism, the complexity of which has long been pointed out (e.g., Moaddel 2002), is in itself "a social movement," an "organization," or a community-based instance of collective action; likewise, it would make little sense to classify what happened in Cairo, or in Tunis, as the outcome of a "social movement" rather than "communitarian" type of mobilization. It is far more useful to recognize that different episodes of contention may combine different logics of action at the same time. One key task for the analyst is to chart the interplay of these different logics and their evolution over time.

Social Movements

The specificity of a social movement mode of coordination is given first and foremost by the combination of dense networks of resource allocation between organizations and by processes of boundary definition between the same plural actors. In a *social movement* mode, there will be more than networks of alliances and collaborations. Of course, organizations involved in a movement dynamic will share both material and symbolic resources in order to promote more effective campaigns and will be fairly closely linked to each other. But, most important, they will also identify each other as part of a broader collective actor, whose goals and existence cannot be constrained within the boundaries of any specific protest event or campaign. The existence of collective identity linking organizations to each other will enable them to feel part of the same collective effort even when specific actions may be over and to develop more joint actions on that basis.

Until 2011, we were most likely to find evidence of social movement dynamics at work in the Palestine national mobilization and in Islamic collective action across the region and possibly in some episodes of industrial action, most notably in Egypt (e.g., Beinin 2011; see also Rasler's chapter in this volume). In both cases, however, the fit between models and reality was—and is—far from perfect. Let us look at the Palestinian case first.

A relatively close proxy of a social movement mode of coordination could have emerged from the experience of the "Ten Front," that in 1991 brought together the Islamic Resistance Movement (Hamas), the Popular Front for the Liberation of Palestine (PFLP), and other eight organizations, including the Islamic Jihad, in opposition to the peace process started with the Madrid conference the same year (Mishal and Sela 2006, 87). However, even the major organizations like Hamas or PFLP seem to have entered the coalition with the obvious goal of advancing their own organizational interest. Organizational changes, such as mergers or a commitment to full coordination with partners, were never really on the agenda. And Hamas for instance never really tried to assert its leadership on the coalition as a whole, but rather used it for its own organizational purposes (Robinson 2005, 21–22). Likewise, there were few signs of the cross-cutting memberships and interactions among associations that keep together organizational fields in Western societies and provide the basis for social movement modes of coordination (Heaney and Rojas 2008; Diani 2009). The reasons for such fragmentation are complex. Deep ideological differences, such as PFLP activists' rejection of religious fundamentalism as opposed to Hamas's view of an Islamic Palestine, prevented the elaboration of a cohesive platform and also rendered multiple individual memberships less likely (Robinson 2005, 20). As a result, the alliance seems to have been largely built on its members' rejection of negotiations with Israel and following pressure from Syria, their host country. More generally, Israel's policy of divide and rule as a foreign occupier may have similarly played some role in rendering cross-cutting alliances unlikely.[2]

It is also difficult to ascertain to what extent Islamist collective action, for which the phrase "social movement" is often used, actually displays the analytic properties of a social movement mode of coordination. While it is certainly possible to speak of Islamic collective action fields, comprising a multiplicity of Islamic organizations, and to assume that Islam represents a powerful master frame and a building block for the construction of broad identities, it seems more difficult to identify instances in which such broad feelings of identification match sustained collaborations between multiple organizations, at the same time independent and mutually committed in pursuit of shared long-term goals.

Again, a plurality of factors may account for such a state of affairs. The diffused nature of religious authority and leadership means there is no religious hierarchy favoring integration of the community of believers. In addition, fragmentation along social and geographical lines aggravates the problems deriving from personalized leadership, which further encourages competition and distances the possibility of coordination with other similar groups.

While more focused studies of relational patterns are needed before drawing firm conclusions on this issue, even the Palestinian case suggests that the focus of actors' commitment and identities be specific groups and organizations rather than broader, and vaguer, collectivities, while alliance work seems to have been driven primarily by instrumental considerations. On the other hand, sustained challenges to Israeli rule in the Occupied Territories such as the two *intifadas* of 1987–1992 and 2000–2005 (Alimi 2007) also seem to have depended heavily on the strength of the ties formed within the local community. They often provided the basis for forms of insurgency that involved actors from different persuasions. As sketchy as it may be, our reconstruction of collective action patterns in the Middle East points to the difficulties encountered by attempts to set in motion genuine social movement dynamics, implying sustained efforts conducted by heterogeneous actors sharing nonetheless a common identity. Rather than reducing all instances of collective action to a "movement," it may be useful to explore the multiplicity of ways of coordinating collective action, based on different combinations of mechanisms of resource allocation and boundary definition (Table 1.1).

Coalitional Modes

Coalitional modes of coordination are often confused with social movement dynamics, and for good reasons: in both cases, organizations get involved in dense collaborative exchanges with groups with similar concerns, addressing specific issues (van Dyke and McCammon 2010). However, in a coalitional process, interorganizational linkages will not necessarily stem from, nor will they generate, identity bonds between the organizations involved; rather, alliances and collaborations will be mostly driven by an instrumental logic. Specific events will not be linked by actors into more encompassing narratives that might assign them a broader meaning and make them part of a sustained series of actions.

When it comes to public displays of political will involving different organized actors, coalitional modes of coordination seem to be far more frequent than social movement ones in the Middle East. Alliances between political actors focusing on the opposition to local regimes rarely entail forms of

Table 1.1   A Typology of Modes of Coordination of Collective Action

	Boundary work and identity building at field level	
	Intense	Limited
Intense	**Social Movement MoC** e.g., The Ten Front (Palestine, early 1990s; very partially)	**Coalitional MoC** e.g., February 14 Movement (Bahrain, 2011) The Higher Committee for the Coordination of Nationalist Opposition Parties (Jordan)
Limited	**Subcultural/ Communitarian MoC** e.g., Neighborhood informal networks; Facebook communities	**Organizational MoC** e.g., Muslim Brotherhood

Note: None of the examples of collective action, associated with a particular mode of coordination in the table, reflect only that mode. They simply display the properties of that mode in a most pronounced way.

Source: Adapted from Diani (2012, 110; reprinted by permission © 2012 by Cambridge University Press).

collaboration that go beyond short-term, opportunistic goals to express a stronger shared identity and a common long-term political vision. This applies both to the electoral and the protest politics arena. Electoral coalitions in Lebanon, for example, suggest that rather than facilitating the creation of broader, overarching civic identities, cross-ideological alliances seem to reproduce the patronage power of ethnic leaders who allocate local spheres of influence. The net effect of this is to harden divisions nationwide (Salloukh 2006). The same difficulties apply to nonelectoral coalitions, which are often undermined by the lack of a shared vision. Coalitions involving both left-wing, secular, and Islamic actors have usually reflected, in their limited nature and scope, the difficulty of keeping together such an ideologically diverse set of allies, as partners refrain from taking up any issue that might prove controversial and on which there are well-known differences (Schwedler and Clark 2006). For example, in Jordan, the Higher Committee for the Coordination of Nationalist Opposition Parties, which includes both Communist and Ba'athist parties and the Islamic Action Front (the political branch of the Muslim Brotherhood in the country), had a self-imposed fairly narrow mandate (Clark 2006). This left little chance for cooperation on certain issues to develop and grow into joint campaigning on other issues. In such a context, the typical social movement dynamic of agenda transformation and expansion, whereby campaigns initiated on certain issues evolve into broader and/or longer-lasting alliances, was unlikely to be found.

Even where the goals pursued by coalitions seem to be very broad, they do not necessarily rest on shared principles and fundamental values. That seemed to be the case, for example, in Egypt, where before 2011 numerous extraparliamentary activities pursued high targets such as the overthrow of the regime and the challenge to imperialistic globalization, yet again without stronger bonds developing between the leftists and the Islamists involved. As the leftists said, they were working "alongside," not "with," the Islamists (Abdelrahman 2009). Changes in the approach of these actors, with radical Islamists becoming more moderate and the Muslim Brotherhood making itself closer to liberal democratic principles, did not seem to have facilitated relationships across the traditional ideological divides.

Organizational Modes

The above remarks might sound too pessimistic about the chances of developing broad and sustainable coalitions or movements in MENA countries. To put them in context, we should note that such processes do not develop easily even in democratic, affluent countries. A lot of—probably most—collective action actually takes other forms (Diani 2015, chap. 9). When it is mainly conducted within the boundaries of specific organizations (be they sects, revolutionary parties, or public and private interest groups), it is difficult to speak of social movements. If organizations broadly interested in the same themes are not involved in dense collaborations and do not share any specific identity, some of the most visible and distinctive traits of the social movement experience are missing. In such cases, *organizational* modes of coordination will prevail, as organizations focus on strengthening both their structure and their identity and try to secure control of specific issues or subsets of issues. Collaborations with other groups are relatively rare and, most importantly, scattered across a broad range of different organizations. There are no densely connected clusters of groups and associations sharing similar interests, nor do strong feelings of collective identity develop between them. While both available comparative data and experts' judgments point at the overall weakness of associational life in MENA countries (Norton 1995; Bratton 2009), religious organizations or groups directly linked to the Muslim communities (or other confessions, like the Maronites in Lebanon or the Copts in Egypt) are certainly an exception (Wiktorowicz 2000; Aburaiya 2004; Clark 2004a; Turam 2006). Even in those cases, however, and despite stereotypical views of Islamic organizations as inherently radical (see Robinson 2004, 112, for a critique), collective action has often taken a consensual—or at least, a nonovertly contentious—form rather than a conflictual form. One strength of Islamic associations has been their capacity to provide answers to prepolitical and nonpolitical needs, particularly dramatic in urban areas. In all Middle East countries, Islamic groups have addressed basic questions regarding everyday life, the managing of family relations, morality, the running of the urban economy, and so forth (Singerman 2003; Robinson 2004; Flanigan 2008; Fawaz 2014). In doing so, they have provided aggrieved communities—both of the lower and of the middle classes—with life options and with opportunities for covert resistance. For example, the fight against petty crime has proved a powerful source of influence and support for Islamic activists in local neighborhoods (Fillieule and Bennani-Chraïbi 2003, 112); so has the promotion of Islamic clinics and charitable associations (Clark 2004b).

The role of unions and industrial action should also be recognized, if with some qualification. For example, working-class organizations such as the Union Générale Tunisienne du Travail (UGTT) in Tunisia seem to have played a significant part in the opposition to the Bourguiba and later, since 1987, to the Ben 'Ali regime, maintaining some independence from the state as well as from Islamist organizations (Alexander 2000; Zemni, Smet, and Bogaert 2013). Working-class protest has also been very important in Egypt, well before the 2011 revolts, intensifying in the second half of the 2000s. As in other countries in the MENA region, Egyptian workers have mostly addressed in their protests basic "bread and butter" grievances, often the only ones that could be aired in repressive regimes (Beinin 2011). However, available accounts suggest that the Egyptian Trade Union Federation (ETUF) was far less independent from the state than UGTT in Tunisia. In the Egyptian context, most episodes of workers' contention seem to have originated at the workplace level, in a difficult relationship with the unions. While they have often prompted calls for changes in unions' leadership and approach, the coordination of strikes nationwide actually shows some elements of a movement dynamic, with informal contacts between local strikes committees (Beinin 2011, 2012).

Communitarian or Subcultural Modes

The disjunction between unions and workers' action in Egypt has often paralleled the latter's involvement in protests rooted in the local communities. For example, on April 6, 2008, in the Egyptian city of Mahallah al-Kubra, massive protests occurred against rising food prices and brutal practices of the police in preventing strikes (Beinin 2011; El Sharnoubi 2013). Much earlier than that, the so-called bread riots of 1977 expressed people's reaction to adjustment policies already advocated by the International Monetary Fund (IMF) and implemented in Egypt by Sadat (Seddon 1990; Lagi, Bertrand, and Bar-Yam 2011). Although Mahalla had seen a major instance of industrial conflict, going on in waves since 2006 at least, the 2008 events—as well as the earlier "bread riots," for that matter—were not exclusively workers' initiatives. Rather, the ties between protestors developed in several different contexts. The workplace was certainly one of them, but so were a variety of communitarian settings, youth group, and associations (Beinin 2011; El-Gobashy 2012). Altogether, one can count the 1970s protests as the first stage in the weakening of the "social contract" between the state and its citizens concerning food provision and other basic commodities.

Likewise, the reference to the role of Islamic organizations as sources of basic services for their communities provides another useful connection to what is probably the most diffuse mode of coordinating collective action in the area, namely, what we have called a "communitarian/subcultural mode of coordination" (Diani 2012; 2013). Collective action may take place in contexts in which interorganizational collaborations are rare, but actors' mutual solidarity and overall sense of identification with a given cause are relatively high. This may happen for various reasons: because the actors concerned are positively uninterested in setting up organizations and in the political work required to develop and maintain effective coalitions and because aggrieved groups are simply missing the resources and opportunities to translate their grievances into sustained collective action in the form of organizations or social movements. One should note that communitarian or subcultural modes of coordination need not be associated with a specific territory. They may also take a broader and/or virtual nature, as the spread of new forms of online activism suggests (Van de Donk et al. 2004).

In repressive contexts, community-based resistance often proved more feasible and effective than open challenges conducted through coalitions and movements. Repressive regimes have always had more difficulty eradicating organizations and networks embedded in traditional cultures and practices guarded by religious institutions or the local community—not to mention the clan or the family—than organizations and networks representing autonomous opinions and wills or performance-related (e.g., professional) activities (on this see also Wiktorowicz 2004, 22–23). For example, in Cairo, informal networks survived repression because they were by definition invisible and also because they were very much embedded in family ties; that they also operated as social capital in providing access to essential material resources further increased their efficacy as channels of covert opposition (Singerman 2003, 226–27). Likewise, informal polysepalous networks helped the *salafis* to resist repression from the Jordan state (Wiktorowicz 2000). Bayat (2005) points at the analogies between views of social movements focusing on the countercultural rather than the statist sphere (e.g., Melucci 1989) and the experience of contemporary Islamic movements. In a weak civil society with weak voluntary associations, meeting points often consist of indirectly political places like the neighborhood, the bazaar, and particularly the mosque. In authoritarian settings, where forms of resistance do not necessarily overlap with the political, a lot of attention must be given to "infrapolitical practices" (*conduites infra-politiques*; Bennani-Chraïbi and Fillieule 2003b, 31).

It is worth underlining the central role of the city as the locus where forms of resistance take place and forms of nonpolitical sociability, yet amenable to political goals, develop (Bennani-Chraïbi and Fillieule 2003b, 26). In this respect, it would be misleading to equate communitarian modes of coordination with Muslim communities, even though Islamic groups have proved particularly efficient to recruit through nonpolitical activities, such as women's Qur'anic study groups (*nadwas*) in Yemen (Clark 2004a). In his work, Bayat has emphasized the role of urban streets in providing the setting for collective action for the most deprived social groups, in a way that he explicitly labels as "non-movement," referring to its embeddedness not in specific organizations but in everyday life (Bayat 2012, 119–21). For these collectivities defined by their life in the urban streets, radical Islamism is not necessarily a major source of identification. Nor is it for small intellectual subcultures on the secular side, disenchanted even with organized political opposition yet unwilling to give up any critical perspective on current power assets, as Duboc (2011) documented in relation to Egypt.

The "Arab Spring" Changing Modes of Coordination?

On a superficial impression, the "Arab Spring" seems to have marked a turning point over the past. Certainly, and even without referring to the subsequent developments in some of the countries, the dramatic events of those months come as close as one can get to the "moments of madness" (Zolberg 1972) and the excitement of collective effervescence, long highlighted by social theory (Alberoni 1984). Accounts of the most iconic among the episodes of contention of that year, the occupation of Tahrir Square in Cairo, point to the fact that events unfolded in a manner that was neither predictable nor controllable by any of the major players involved and to the continuous flow of exchanges, communication, and negotiation among the anti-Mubarak protestors (see, e.g., El-Gobashy 2012, and other contributions to Sowers and Toensing 2012).

At the same time, those were not purely random processes resulting from the aggregation of disparate actors and the combination of divergent forces; while several different forms of coordination were at play, they combined to generate what can be legitimately regarded as a full-fledged "cycle of contention" (see the Introduction to this volume). In her analysis of the Egyptian revolt, El-Gobashy

(2012) identifies the roots of the protest in at least three different locales: the workplace, the neighborhood, and the associations (ranging from professional ones to religious ones). In our own language, the variety of modes of coordination identified in the phases preceding 2011 can also be found in the 2011 events. Coalition work was important, as it always is in phases of high political contention and regime crumbling, yet with quite different profiles, aspirations, and success across the MENA countries. In Tunisia, although the UGTT had been divided on whether to join leftist groups, such as the Tunisian Workers' Communist Party and the Democratic Patriots, in calling for an immediate end to Ben 'Ali's regime or to act as an intermediary between the community-based movement on the street and the established political order, the union decided to participate in the January 14 Front coalition. This included the Tunisian Workers Communist Party, the Democratic Patriots, and several other left-wing organizations, all opposing the Mohammed Ghannouchi transitional unity government installed on January 17, which included members of the traditional political opposition. Later, on February 11, after 28 organizations congregated in Tunis, the National Council for the Protection of the Revolution was established and supported by the January 14 Front, the UGTT, the Bar Association, the Democratic Front for Labour and Freedom, and Nahda, the Islamist party that had been a signatory of the 2005 opposition accord but publicly remained on the sidelines of the uprising.

Coalition work was similarly significant in Egypt. The January 25 coalition of mostly youth groups and organizations was supported by preexisting organizations that had been marginalized or ignored by the November elections, such as *kifaya*, the National Association for Change, the Democratic Front Party, the New Wafd Party, and the Tomorrow Party. Initially, the Muslim Brotherhood, perceived as the most structured organization operating in Egyptian civil society, did not publicly participate in the protest but permitted elements of its youth wing to join the demonstration that took place in Cairo as well as in Alexandria, Aswan, and Al-Arish (see, e.g., Ezbawy 2012). In Bahrain, the overall impact of the protest front was significantly lower, and its goals more modest. The main opposition forces since the 1990s included Shiite organizations, such as the Islamic Front for the Liberation of Bahrain and the Bahrain Islamic Freedom Movement, and leftist groups such as the Bahraini National Liberation Front and the Popular Front for the Liberation of Bahrain. By February 16, seven legal Shiite Islamist and leftist groups announced an alliance to support the "February 14 Movement," the online youth activists that initially called for the protest. The coalition demanded the release of prisoners, the resignation of the government, especially Prime Minister Khalifa bin Salman Al-Khalifa, and the abolition of the 2002 Constitution.

While attempts to establish broad coalitions are regular features of any political crisis, the role of the Internet in the promotion and coordination of the protests has attracted most attention. The Arab revolts, and in particular the events in Tunisia and Egypt, have indeed been hailed as major manifestations of a new type of "networked social movement" that would replace the coordinating efforts conducted by political organizations with coordination through the Internet (Castells 2012). While these interpretations have probably gone too far in stressing the role of new technologies, social networks such as Facebook and information and communication technology (henceforth, ICT) in general certainly helped sustain the protests. The already mentioned events in Mahallah al-Kubra in 2008 soon attracted online support in the form of a Facebook group called the April 6 Movement. Its coming to life reflected international collaborations between protesters. In 2009, Muhammad ʿAdil, a 20-year-old blogger and April 6 activist went to Belgrade to consult the Center for Applied Non-Violent Action Strategies, or CANVAS.[3] After January 25, a 26-page pamphlet widely attributed to April 6, entitled "How to Protest Intelligently," was circulated to Egyptians. It can be argued that coordinating with CANVAS enabled April 6 to articulate an agenda and mobilize people more effectively (Ezbawy 2012).

Meanwhile, online, April 6 activists used social media "to report events, alert participants about security situations, and provide legal assistance to those rounded up by state security forces" (Ishani 2011, 143–44). By the time Muhammad ʿAdil traveled to Belgrade, April 6 had 70,000 online followers (Ishani 2011, 144). Digital media experts coordinated with Italian anarchist groups on how to set up "ghost servers" in a highly censored and monitored online environment, while others attended special sessions on media training in the United States, especially "basic camera operation, steady shooting, and how to use audio recording devices" (Ishani 2011, 145). However, while April 6 activists worked to mobilize the youth for the November 2010 elections, it was a related site that attracted the most attention. Wael Ghoneim (or "Google Gandhi" as he was dubbed in the press), a Google executive based in Dubai and an April 6 activist, set up the Facebook page "We are all Khalid Saʿid" in recognition of the 28-year-old who was beaten to death by police in Alexandria on June 6, 2010. Most conspicuously, Wael Ghoneim used his social media accounts to call for a "Day of Rage" on January 25, 2011.

Overall, ICT seems to have made a substantial contribution to what appear largely as "communitarian" forms of collective action: it facilitated the creation of boundaries between people that shared a similar condition, the emergence of common grievances, and the coordination of protest activity. However, the extent to which new forms of communication actually shaped the entire "Arab Spring" is still a matter of debate (see, e.g., Lotan et al. 2011; Brym et al. 2014).

It is also disputable whether ties created on that basis are sufficient to support actions oriented not just to the fall of discredited regimes but also to securing a long-term commitment to public collective action, essential for the consolidation of democracy in the new regimes. These remarks draw our attention to the other dominant, if somehow hidden, mode of coordination at work during the "Arab Spring", namely, organizations.

In Tunisia, while members of the Progressive Democratic Party and the Tajdid Movement participated in the protests that ensued in January, it was the UGTT in particular that proved pivotal in orchestrating and organizing the aspiring social movement. In Sidi Bouzid on January 4, 2011, union teachers organized protests through a "Committee of the Marginalized" (International Crisis Group 2011, 4). As the police force became increasingly brutal in its suppression of protests, gradually giving way to the army on January 10, the movement picked up more momentum. Again, while social media websites, such as Facebook and Twitter, undoubtedly enhanced awareness and consolidated solidarity among Tunisians, they should not be solely credited with the vast physical mobilization that followed. A day after the UGTT's National Administrative Council recognized peaceful protests, the union arranged a coordinated strike on January 12 in which 30,000 took to the streets calling for an end to the regime. Two days later, on the same day as the proposed date for another general strike, Ben ʿAli fled to Saudi Arabia.

The role of Islamist organizations also deserves special attention. They certainly were not highly visible during the early phases of the 2011 campaigns, and Islamic rhetoric was largely absent from the protests. However, the instinctive assumption by commentators in the West that the "Arab Spring" represented a move away from Islam quickly turned out to be unfounded. The initial decision by Islamist organizations in Egypt not to publicly declare their support for the protests or to participate probably acted to prevent the regime from using Islamists as a scapegoat to justify its suppression of demonstrations. Nevertheless, it is clear that Islamist organizations and their social and public services contributed to mobilizing prospective activists. The same applies to other countries, such as Tunisia (Donker 2013). Moreover, it is difficult not to conclude that they were among those who profited most in the midterm from the 2011 uprisings.

Conclusions

In this chapter, we have introduced a typology of modes of coordination as an analytic tool to cope with the variety of forms of collective action that have characterized the 2011 events in the MENA countries. While the political process tradition in social movement research highlights some of the reasons why chances for large-scale social movements have been fairly limited in the MENA countries, we tried to show that a proper reading of political contention requires a richer grasp of the multiplicity of ways through which action is coordinated. There is more to contentious processes than the neat opposition between large-scale (Western) social movements and unstructured mass revolts. Accordingly, we tried to identify some concepts that might guide a deeper, systematic comparative exploration of patterns of collective action in the region. Such reconstruction is so much more urgent given the dramatic developments in Egypt, first with the seizure of power through electoral means by the Muslim Brotherhood and Mursi's attempt to Islamize Egypt, then with the military coup of July 2013, preceded by massive protests against the Islamic president.

While the political groups that profit in the midterm from a revolution are not necessarily the same that played the most central part in it (a recurrent feature of revolutions; Tilly 1993), the Egyptian case is distinctive in the level of approval that the 2013 military intervention has received, at least in its early phases, from former opponents to Mubarak. The anti-Mursi protests that preceded the coup were led by Tamarrud (Rebellion), a broad coalition backed by a range of diverse organizations such as Shayfeencom, the *kifaya* Movement, the National Salvation Front, and the April 6 Youth Movement as well as by various religious and civic leaders. In other words, power after the revolution was seized by actors, the Brotherhood, extremely distant from the publicly perceived (and Internet-propagated) ideals of democratic, liberal modernization, that public opinion associated to the 2011 uprising; later, military restoration came, again somewhat unusually, with the approval of several of the original revolutionaries and advocates of liberal modernization.

It is worth wondering whether the lack of social movement mechanisms proper might not account at least in part for the difficult transition toward a post-Mubarak regime in Egypt and the overwhelming success obtained not only by the Freedom and Justice Party, the Brotherhood political arm, but also by the al-Nour (salafi) Party and other Islamic lists. The Tunisian experience also suggests that coordination through online networks may help launch intense and—under favorable conditions—successful challenges to powerholders in the short term but may not be as effective when it comes to consolidating the relationship between activists and the larger population in a new regime. To that purpose, the sustained collaborations between multiple organizations and the deep bonds created by overlapping memberships and intense contacts between activists, typical of the social movement mode of coordination, might prove more useful. Our framework will hopefully contribute to the exploration of the complexity of the organizational dynamics that have operated in the Middle East in the first decades of the new millennium.

Acknowledgments

Earlier versions of this chapter were presented at the Rockefeller Centre, Bellagio (2005); the ASA Annual Meeting (Boston, 2008); and Durham University (2011). We are grateful to participants in those meetings and the editors of this book for their critical feedback (with special thanks to Janine Clark and Jillian Schwedler).

Notes

1. Terms like "coordination," "cooperation," or "collaboration" are often used interchangeably. In our approach, which focuses on organizational fields rather than on the behavior of discrete actors, we treat the last two as synonymous, while we use "coordination" to refer to the broader processes by which actors within a field relate—or do not relate—to each other. Some modes of coordination imply inter-organizational cooperation/collaboration, while others do not.
2. We are grateful to editors Avraham Sela and Eitan Alimi for drawing our attention to these factors.
3. CANVAS is the international advisory body emanating from *Optor!* ("Resistance!"), a grassroots youth movement in Serbia that focused on using nonviolent methods to topple Slobodan Milosevic.

Do Organizational Structures Matter for Protests in Nondemocratic African Countries?

Katia Pilati

THE CONSEQUENCES OF repression on protest in nondemocratic contexts are rather controversial. Some scholars argue that repression has a triggering effect on protest mobilization because under repressive measures, people tend to participate reactively and find alternative ways of mobilization. Others argue that repression dampens engagement in protests because of major threats related to mobilization. As Davenport suggests (2005, viii), "confronted with state repression, dissidents have been found to run away [. . .], fight harder [. . .], and alternatively run away or fight harder- [. . .]." In this framework, even less clear are the consequences of repression on organizations, the most crucial mobilizing structures in democratic contexts. Two questions are at stake in the relationships among repression, organizations, and protest mobilization, even though they may occasionally overlap. The first research question concerns how political repression—that is, any action by another group which raises the contender's cost of collective action (Tilly 1978, 100)—affects organizations. Repressive measures may dampen the overall presence of organizations and their activities. However, organizations can still operate in repressive contexts due to specific mechanisms at work, namely, "similar events that produce essentially the same immediate effects across a wide range of circumstances" (Tilly 2003a, 20). I discuss two mechanisms that may lead to enduring organizational structures in repressive contexts. First, I argue that organizations can operate thanks to apolitical agendas that are not perceived as threatening by political authorities. Second, organizations with more explicit political aims can operate thanks to mechanisms of renovation of the repertoire of actions, related to the radicalization of activities, or, on the contrary, the moderation of their repertoires of action, or the transnationalization of activities.[1]

The second research question concerns how organizations affect the likelihood of mobilizing into protests, therefore broadening the scope of the challenge. I argue that organizational structures, that is, the organizational bases and mechanisms serving to collect and use the movement's resources (Rucht 1996, 186), maintain the mobilizing capacity in repressive contexts when some of the aforementioned mechanisms are at work. Therefore, the relationship between repression and protest mobilization depends, inter-alia, on the presence of specific mechanisms enabling organizations to operate in repressive contexts. In particular, high levels of repression are likely to dampen such mechanisms, therefore leading to a weak, unstable, and fragmented organizational structure that does not act as a mobilizing structure. Conversely, under intermediate repressions, these mechanisms can work and organizations may act as mobilizing structures, although this also depends on the nature of the mechanisms at work.

This chapter addresses the two research questions in relation to the sub-Saharan African region, with a specific focus on Nigeria and Zimbabwe, two countries classified as authoritarian contexts by international indexes.[2] In the empirical analysis I discuss first the evidence on organizational structures in Nigeria and Zimbabwe. The second part of the empirical analysis, more specifically focusing on the link between organizational structures and protest mobilization, analyzes Afrobarometer public opinion survey data available for the years between 1999 and 2009. This is done by elaborating a multivariate analysis on the effect of changing organizational structures on individual protest mobilization in 16 African countries (Afrobarometer data; Bratton, Gyimah-Boadi, and Mattes 2005).[3] According to the 2006 Economist's Democracy Index (Economist 2008), most of the countries surveyed in the Afrobarometer are nondemocratic and are either considered "flawed democracies" or "hybrid regimes" with Nigeria and Zimbabwe considered, as mentioned, as "authoritarian regimes."[4]

In the conclusion, the results are discussed in relation to the implication they may have in other contexts. First, I try to draw meaningful parallels to the Middle Eastern and Northern African (MENA) region, and in particular to the Egyptian case, which, like Nigeria and Zimbabwe, was classified as an authoritarian context (Economist 2008). Second, I try to highlight how these mechanisms are not specific to authoritarian contexts, as they are also relevant to understanding dynamics of repression and mobilization in democratic contexts.

Assessing Mechanisms Linking Repression and Mobilizing Structures

Repression is one central factor that shapes many contention-related features, dynamics, and processes, such as actor constitution and the way coordination among different organizations takes shape, or the level of nonstate third party actors' intervention (see, respectively, Diani's chapter and Alimi and Meyer's chapter in this volume). There is a large scholarly debate as to whether a repressive context triggers or dampens levels of protest mobilization. Four different kinds of relationships have been postulated with regard to the relationship between repression and protests (Carey 2009, 19): a positive linear relationship, a negative linear relationship, a U-relationship, and an inverted U-relationship (see, inter alia, Gurr 1970; Tilly 1978; Lichbach and Gurr 1981; Kurzman 1996, Rasler 1996; Goldstone and Tilly 2001). However, many scholars have failed to provide details on the mechanisms affecting such relationships. As Goldstone (2003, 21) argues, "whether repression discourages or encourages protest movements depends in complex ways on the constellation of conventional party alignments [...] and the support or opposition of the public and organized counter or allied movements." Along this line of argument, the effect of repression on protest mobilization depends, inter alia, on the presence of mechanisms enabling organizations to operate in a repressive environment. Repressive contexts may have different consequences on organizations, both on the number of organizations that eventually operate under authoritarian conditions, and on the quality and forms of activities that organizations engage in. Drawing on insights by scholars investing in the political process, or political opportunity structure (POS) framework, several contextual dimensions can affect organizations and their activities. Indiscriminate repressive measures systematically targeting organizational members, their families, and organizational events and activities through harassment, arrests and detention, raids, shutdown, and seizure of offices, have deleterious effects on organizations. Scholars have also discussed the role of the army and the military (Nepstad 2011a) or elites' alignments (Brockett 1991, 264; McAdam 1996, 26). Alimi (2009) and Meyer (2003) stress the relevance of the unity of the ruling coalition, the opportunities for defection or available exit, and the international structure of political alliances in shaping protests in such countries (see Alimi and Meyer in this volume). These dimensions are all likely to have significant consequences on organizations and their activities too.

Under repression however, a few mechanisms seem to be crucial for organizations to operate. By concentrating on apolitical claims and agendas, organizations may function within the legal or legitimate framework of authoritative contexts, as they are likely to be perceived as nonthreatening by the ruling elites. For instance, organizations working in service delivery and provision, like charity organizations, sustaining the population with employment opportunities, housing, or health assistance do not represent explicit challenges for authorities. Sometimes, religious organizations can freely operate under authoritarian regimes as well (Trejo 2012). In turn, political organizations, that is, those more explicitly oriented to promote a political change or resistance to it, aiming at changing or influencing institutions and policymaking, can function in repressive contexts by means of adopting, more or less deliberately, new, renovated, and alternative forms of political actions. Under authoritative contexts political organizations need to replace their usual activities of lobbying, political networking, or linking with media in order to avoid targeted and systematic repressive measures. Three specific submechanisms related to the innovation of the repertoire of action are likely to enable organizations to operate in repressive contexts: (1) the radicalization of organizational activities, that is, the use of more confrontational activities, including engagement in violent actions; (2) the transnationalization of organizational activities, that is, their diffusion across national boundaries and states (Tarrow 1996, 52), as is the case for internationally supported nongovernmental organizations (NGOs) focusing on human rights and international law discourses; and (3) the moderation of the organizations' repertoires of action. This may occur concomitantly with the substitution of formal groups and organizations with informal political networks.

Partly, these mechanisms have been already discussed in the social movement literature although not in a unique framework, and not specifically with reference to organizational activities (e.g., Almeida 2003; Tarrow 1996; Duboc 2011; Menoret 2011; Alimi, Demetriou, and Bosi 2015). These mechanisms are not restricted to authoritarian contexts either. For instance, Tarrow has largely documented the dynamics of transnationalization of social movements' activities, models of collective actions, and organizations (Tarrow 1996, 2005). More specifically related to repressive measures, the radicalization of activities has been documented by Della Porta (1996, 69–70) when analyzing the climate of the terrorist emergency in the mid-1970s in Italy and, in particular, the reciprocal relationship between protest policing and the increasing number of violent movement groups. Della Porta concludes that "more repressive, diffuse, and hard techniques of policing tend to discourage the mass and peaceful protest while fueling the more radical fringe" (Della Porta 1996, 90). Finally, the use of moderate repertoires of action among social movement activities has been documented by scholars analyzing, for instance, women's movements. The latter have also often relied on informal and small groups at the local level, along with highly decentralized structures (Rucht 1996, 194).

The aforementioned mechanisms, enabling organizations to operate in repressive contexts, however, are likely to work differently depending on the level of repression. They may be severely weakened under high repressive measures. The latter may reduce, for instance, the presence of foreigners' investments in local organizations. Therefore, the possibility for organizations to build transnational ties thanks to foreign donors' aid or investments may be severely hindered. In other words, the relationship between repression and organizational structures is likely to follow a reversed U-shape, in line with the reversed U-shape relationship between repression and protests advanced by some scholars. Following this, engagement by organizations in apolitical activities or mechanisms of renovation of the repertoires of action should be most likely under a regime of intermediate repressiveness. In contrast, high levels of repression should most likely dampen them, leading to a weak and fragmented organizational structure. Equally, under low repression, these mechanisms are unlikely to work, as organizations may engage in their usual political activities.

Following this, considering the first research question on the link between repression and organizations, I expect that organizations may operate in repressive contexts either by engaging in apolitical issues and claims, or by renovating the repertoires of action. However, under high repressive measures these mechanisms are less likely to work (*first hypothesis*).

Before turning to the empirical analysis investigating these mechanisms in Nigeria and in Zimbabwe, in what follows, I review and discuss the literature on the mobilizing impact of organizational structures in repressive contexts. Specifically, I ask how it is possible that repressive policies reshape agendas and forms of action of organizations while preserving their mobilization capabilities.

Assessing Mechanisms Linking Organizational Structures and Protest Mobilization

Organizations have long been acknowledged as crucial for protest mobilization in democratic contexts. Involvement in all sorts of formal and informal groups contributes to gaining knowledge and skills, such as communicational and organizational abilities. The expression of shared identities developed within organizations facilitates recruitment and access in political participation and collective actions (McClurg 2003; Diani and McAdam 2003; Melucci 1989; Verba, Schlozman, and Brady 1995, 271, 304). These dynamics are also likely to occur among individuals engaged in organizations operating in repressive contexts. Evidence of the role of individual engagement in organizations for protest mobilization shows it has been crucial in sub-Saharan countries (Pilati 2011). However, when individuals resort to collective actions, the characteristics of the organizational structure are also relevant to mobilize people into protests. For instance, organizations building ties together and creating dense interorganizational networks can enable cooperation on different modes of collective actions (Diani 2015). Organizational networks help to build coalitions among organizations working on similar issues and to establish collaborations to join campaigns or to share the organization of events on common interests. Some evidence also shows that dense networks of local associational groups represented the organizational bases for powerful dissident movements in repressive contexts (Trejo 2012).

However, in repressive contexts, oppositional organizational structures may not lead to the aggregation and the mobilization of resources in the same way as it occurs in democratic contexts. Organizations may adhere to associational agendas promoted by authorities that directly serve their political mandates, consequently reinforcing clientelistic behaviors, corruption, and nepotism and promoting ideals that are not critical of the regimes (Jamal 2007). In contrast, other organizations may use alternative ways of operating, providing an organizational basis for protest mobilization. However, the impact of the organizational structure on protest mobilization also depends on the mechanisms used by organizations to operate in repressive contexts. For instance, it is uncertain whether associations active in transnational issues (i.e., human rights and humanitarian aid), such as development organizations and NGOs funded by international institutions, are "engaged in a sustained contentious interaction with powerholders" (see Tarrow 1998, 31, in Beinin and Vairel 2011, 21). Furthermore, organizations active in service delivery and provision such as educational associations, development associations, and charities may be less likely to engage in political activities than social movement organizations such as trade unions which are more likely to be involved in all forms of political mobilization. In other words, organizations born for welfare assistance, "organizations of the poor" as Piven and Cloward call them (1993, 250), are less likely to work as structures of political mobilization.

Based on the foregoing discussion, it is possible to extract a *second hypothesis* on the link between organizational structures and mobilization: I expect that individual protest mobilization can benefit from enduring organizational structures which have survived in repressive contexts thanks to alternative repertoires of actions, although the effect may also depend on mechanisms used by organizations to operate.

The following empirical investigation aims to examine the first hypothesis by analyzing the cases of Nigeria and Zimbabwe. In addition, to test the second hypothesis more specifically, I examine data on 16 sub-Saharan African countries, elaborating a multivariate analysis on the effect of durable organizational structures on individual protest mobilization.

Nigeria and Zimbabwe's Organizational Structures

Nigeria and Zimbabwe are two interesting examples of the consequences of repressive contexts on organizational structures. While Nigerian organizations are able to operate regardless of a repressive regime, very few and only weak organizations are present in Zimbabwe.

In Nigeria, the military apparatus has played a major role in the country's history, often seizing control of the country and ruling it through major periods of its history. Its last period of rule ended in 1999, following the death of the leader of the military junta Sani Abacha in 1998, president of Nigeria from 1993 to 1998, whose regime was linked to human rights violations and allegations of corruption. Since 1999, Nigeria has undertaken a progressively democratic turn. Repressive measures have not, however, stopped tout court since then. The radicalization of activities of many organizations, especially youth associations, progressively increased and was partly a response to the state of emergency in January 1999 in Bayelsa State, which had intensified repression through the military deployment of tanks and other military equipment (Ikelegbe 2001, 14–15). In addition, the Nigerian state has often lacked an adequate state police apparatus, which has been kept weak over the years, and there has been a widespread lack of collaboration among state institutions. As an illustration, the police often decline to hand over detainees to the courts because they do not trust the judges (Ikelegbe 2001). The police and the army are often perceived as a foreign occupation force, while youth militia movements, like the Bakassi Boys, are more under the control of the local population. In addition, while violent youth militia groups are often supported by the local population, they are not opposed by the police delegitimized by the population (Harnischfeger 2003). Under such circumstances, the activities by major youth groups active in the Niger Delta in the advocacy of resource control and self-determination have progressively tended to lose control. At the beginning of 1999, the Ijaw Youth Council carried out actions such as the kidnapping and/or killing of state security officials and oil company employees. Similarly, the Isoko Youth Movement carried out violent seizures of oil installations with the tacit support of some Isoko civil groups between late 1998 and early 1999 (Ikelegbe 2001, 14–15). Radicalization has not been the only way organizations in Nigeria have been operating. In the last few decades organizations have also transnationalized their actions. Transnational organizations reached their peak with the Ogoni's resistance movement in the Niger Delta during the 1990s. From the 1990s to the present, organizations like the Niger Delta Women for Justice (NDWJ) and the Environmental Rights Action/Friends of the Earth Nigeria (ERA/FoEN) have campaigned against human rights violations by the military and repeated oil spills in the Niger Delta. Together with Ken Saro-Wiwa's role in building an international network, these organizations framed the Ogoni's cause and issues in such a way as to resonate with the international community's human rights and environment discourses, and attracted the likes of transnational organizations like Greenpeace (Obi 2009, 475–76).

Organizations having no explicit political agendas have also been operating in Nigeria. Olukotun (2002) documents the deployment of traditional media—theater, oratory, folk music—in the antimilitary struggle of 1988–1999 in the Yoruba-speaking area. Business organizations have also benefited from progressively higher rates of investments in the country. Specifically, the export processing zones (EPZs) also known as the foreign-trade zone (formerly free ports), within which goods may be handled without the intervention of the customs authorities, have risen in number, especially since November 2001. While workers' rights are strictly curtailed and industrial relations are devoid of social dialogue, these areas are nonetheless supposed to be vehicles for the attraction of foreign direct investments and increases in business organizations (International Labour Office [ILO] and ITUC 2012, 1).

Finally, trade unions have survived because of a progressive freedom of workers' associations, which culminated in 2005 in the Trade Union (Amendment) Act. This allowed for the formation and affiliation of the Nigeria Labour Congress (NLC) of new trade unions (ILO and ITUC 2012, 15).

In contrast to Nigeria, Zimbabwe experienced indiscriminate repression, massive population displacement, and the suppression of opposition through harassment, intimidation, and mass urban demolitions such as those that occurred during the clean-up campaign in 2005, which led to a general demobilization and the overall destabilization of the structure of organizations (Bratton and Masunungure 2006). Zimbabwe started to formally engage in a more stable political situation only in 2008. On September 15, 2008, the Global Political Agreement (GPA) was signed by Robert Mugabe, president of the Zimbabwe African National Union—Patriotic Front (ZANU–PF), and Morgan Tsvangirai and Arthur Mutambara, the presidents of the two formations of the Movement for Democratic Change (MDC). Pursuant to the GPA, on February 5, 2009, an inclusive government was established. In this framework, there are several reasons to believe that the organizational structure in Zimbabwe had progressively weakened during the previous decade, at least until 2008 and 2009. Between 2000 and 2005 there were three national elections whose results were contested by the Movement for Democratic Change (MDC), the main opposition party formed in 1999 when the labor movement joined with opposition groups (Kamete 2009). Under these circumstances, the government coordinated well with police forces and intelligence services. Zimbabwe's military, police, security forces, and intelligence services showed consistent decisions and solid collaboration. Both the police and intelligence services were often excessively involved in every aspect of trade union life; they were present at almost all trade union events and systematically used violence, arrests, and detention as well as the harassment and torture of trade unionists as a form of intimidation. Trade unionists were often detained without eventually being charged (ILO 2009, 73–75). Workers' homes and properties in rural areas have frequently been destroyed, and workers have been forced to flee their communities with their families after becoming victims of harassment and intimidation (ILO 2009, 99). This campaign against the trade union movement amounted to a systematic violation of the freedom of association throughout the country in every sector over many years, which progressively destabilized trade unions in Zimbabwe (ILO 2009, 73).

Unlike in Nigeria, economic policies in Zimbabwe during the last decade have been largely unfavorable for the development of a strong business organizational structure because of price controls and foreign currency regulations enforced by the Zimbabwean government. In particular, the price control regulations operated regardless of the cost of production, resulting in many businesses closing down as they could not cover their costs through sales. In addition, the Reserve Bank of Zimbabwe had held a percentage of company profits for government purposes, thus depriving businesses of funds to operate. In the context of price control and foreign currency policies, prior to the establishment of the inclusive government in 2009, employers also experienced intimidation and harassment. Many employers had been "incarcerated for running their businesses," often detained in custody for up to three days, before being released without charge (ILO 2009, 121). In this context, professional organizations operating business activities have been severely undermined by the lack of economic opportunities and the presence of threats.

Overall, strong collaboration among state institutions, an unfavorable economic environment, and harsh and targeted repression, have weakened the organizational structure, and under such circumstances organizations have had very few opportunities to operate even when focusing on apolitical activities like business. In this framework, the only exception seems to be the presence of radical activities. The latter, however, rather than involving organizations, seem to be linked to individual acts or acts by small informal groups. Kamete (2010, 64) reports that young people engaged in a variety of reactive behaviors to the police cleaning up urban spaces occupied by young people. These behaviors range from complete submissiveness to violent confrontations and retaliations.

This mode of resistance, which the author calls "fighting fire with fire," includes vandalization of government and council property, especially vehicles and buildings. In some cases young people would assault officers and people they suspected of having links to security and law enforcement agencies.

The evidence reported for Nigeria and Zimbabwe suggests that the relationship between repression and organizational structures may be curvilinear, in a reversed U-shape. When repression is too harsh, as in Zimbabwe, the possibilities for organizations to operate through the mechanisms highlighted are very low, while the possibilities for mechanisms to work are higher in Nigeria, where repression was lower.

Using data from the Afrobarometer rounds, I further analyze changes in the organizational structures in Nigeria and in Zimbabwe occurred during the first decade of the millennium (*hypothesis 1*). Next, to test *hypothesis 2*, I examine which organizational structures, operating in nondemocratic contexts, are more likely to play a supportive role for individual engagement in protest actions. This is examined by elaborating on analyses of the broader sub-Saharan African region.

Methods

In the following paragraphs I discuss some characteristics of the Afrobarometer data I use in the next analyses. I also specify the dependent and the independent variables, as well as the statistical models used to elaborate the multivariate analyses.

Data Source

The data collected in the Afrobarometer surveys concerns political attitudes of citizens toward democracy, markets, and civil society as well as information on political behaviors, specifically on protest activities. The surveys employ a multistage design. Random selection procedures were used at every stage of the sampling procedure, and the sample is stratified to ensure that all major demographic segments of the population are covered. National probability samples represent a cross section of the voting age population, and the sample size in each country includes at least 1,000 individuals.

First, I use four rounds of the Afrobarometer to examine changes in the organizational structures that occurred in Nigeria and Zimbabwe between 2000 and 2008. Second, through multivariate analyses, I test how changes in the organizational structures in the broader sub-Saharan region affect individuals' probability to engage in protest.. To elaborate these analyses, I mainly employ the round 3 dataset which includes the following 16 countries: Botswana, Ghana, Lesotho,

Malawi, Mali, Namibia, Nigeria, South Africa, Tanzania, Uganda, Zambia, Zimbabwe, Cape Verde, Kenya, Mozambique, and Senegal, making up a sample of 22,849 individuals.[5]

Dependent Variable

In the multivariate analysis I examine the probability that individuals will join protests by considering one binary variable, identified by assigning a score of 1 to individuals who have attended a demonstration or protest march during the year prior to their interview in 2005–2006 (Afrobarometer Data, round 3).

Independent Variables

Among possible factors affecting the individuals' probability to join protests, the focus of my analyses lies in testing the effect of changes in the organizational structures. In addition, I employ a number of control variables to test the effects of other predictors on the individual likelihood to protest.

Changes in Organizational Structures

I consider changes in the countries' average levels of individual engagement in four types of organizations: development organizations, business organizations, trade unions, and religious organizations.[6]

Increasing average levels of engagement in organizations across years are assumed to be a proxy of enduring organizational structures (identified by positive values of the difference between years). Enduring organizational structures suggest that the types of organizations examined may have adopted, at different degrees, the above-mentioned mechanisms in order to operate in repressive contexts.

I first analyze changes in Nigeria and Zimbabwe's average levels of individual organizational engagement between 2000 and 2008 expecting that they are positive in Nigeria and negative in Zimbabwe given the high level of repression in the latter (*hypothesis 1*). Second, I test how the changes that took place in the organizational structures between 2003 (round 2 of the Afrobarometer, years 2002–2003) and 2006 (round 3 of the Afrobarometer, years 2005–2006) in 16 countries in sub-Saharan Africa affect the likelihood of individuals to participate in protests in 2006 (round 3 of the Afrobarometer, years 2005–2006).[7] Increasing average levels of engagement in the four types of organizations mentioned are expected to positively affect individual engagement in protests in 2006 although the effect may depend on the mechanisms of adaptation at work (*hypothesis 2*).

Control Variables

The multivariate analysis includes several control variables potentially affecting protest engagement—specifically, sociodemographic and socioeconomic variables (both the classical variables like gender, age, education, employment situation, and, for the specific African context, access to basic services such as housing, medical assistance, and schooling). Other variables include the level of deprivation (having gone without food, water, medical care, cooking fuel, cash income, school expenses); economic and political grievances (the perception of improved or worsened living conditions for both the individual and the country; the perception of the present vs. past political situation); network-related variables, namely religious networks and informal political networks;[8] political interest, and the perceived level of corruption. Table 2.1 shows the coding and the descriptive statistics of all variables used in the analysis by countries.

Model Specification

Given the multistage design of the Afrobarometer surveys, and given that I am interested in analyzing the effect of country-level variables, that is, the effect of changes in the organizational structures, on individual engagement in protests, I estimate multilevel models, specifically random intercept logit models. I use two levels, with individuals at level 1 and countries at level 2. I estimate the following nested models (reported in Table 2.2): Model 0 is the intercept model; model 1 includes the level-1 variables; models 2a–2d add the change in countries' mean levels of organizational engagement in the four types of organizations. For multicollinearity reasons, the level-2 variables are added one at a time in different models.

Results

Results presented below discuss, in relation to hypothesis 1, changes in the average levels of organizational engagement in Nigeria and Zimbabwe. Next, in relation to hypothesis 2, results inform on the impact of changes in the organizational structures in 16 sub-Saharan African countries on individuals' level of engagement in protest activities.

Changes in Nigeria and Zimbabwe's Organizational Structure

Figure 2.1 shows Nigeria and Zimbabwe's mean levels of organizational affiliations in the different types of organizations between the years 2000 and 2008. Apart

Table 2.1 Descriptive Statistics of All Variables Used in the Multivariate Analysis, by Country

	Protested (1 = protested at least once)	Gender (1 = male)	Age (range 18–102)	Education (0–10; 10 = holds postgraduate degree)	Has a job (0–1; 1 = has a job)	Difficulty to obtain basic services (0–4, 0 = very difficult)	Country's economic conditions 12 months ago (0–5; 5 = much better)	Individual's economic conditions 12 months ago (0–5; 5 = much better)	Level of deprivation (0–5; 5 = very high)	Perceptions of political situation (0–5; 5 = present is much better)
Botswana	0.187	0.501	37.565	3.421	0.261	2.878	2.997	2.903	1.004	3.368
Ghana	0.078	0.483	39.902	2.777	0.599	2.004	2.622	2.641	1.134	3.450
Lesotho	0.037	0.500	43.016	2.721	0.139	2.356	2.736	2.730	1.584	3.583
Malawi	0.076	0.500	34.306	2.310	0.086	2.346	2.766	2.806	1.856	3.585
Mali	0.064	0.505	42.428	1.297	0.157	2.184	2.580	2.719	1.376	3.730
Namibia	0.200	0.497	34.581	3.923	0.446	2.202	3.612	3.459	1.187	3.764
Nigeria	0.174	0.501	31.255	4.083	0.464	1.799	2.534	3.052	1.348	2.738
South Africa	0.239	0.500	39.383	4.157	0.384	2.428	3.291	3.173	0.918	3.636
Tanzania	0.172	0.498	36.715	2.762	0.315	2.475	3.013	2.911	1.410	3.457
Uganda	0.112	0.500	32.550	3.355	0.528	2.058	3.056	2.992	1.733	3.529
Zambia	0.103	0.508	33.136	4.126	0.267	2.039	2.583	2.868	1.576	3.211
Zimbabwe	0.082	0.495	37.358	3.790	0.219	2.015	1.788	1.878	2.227	2.151
Cape Verde	0.084	0.502	38.259	2.830	0.301	2.311	2.919	3.006	1.118	3.010
Kenya	0.133	0.496	35.662	3.550	0.398	2.199	2.800	2.858	1.654	3.422
Mozambique	0.249	0.499	35.272	2.249	0.224	2.063	3.317	3.032	1.645	3.212
Senegal	0.161	0.516	37.889	2.157	0.251	2.199	3.180	3.247	1.694	3.358
Total	0.141	0.500	36.450	3.207	0.338	2.205	2.881	2.927	1.440	3.331
N	22259	22849	22573	22772	22797	22849	22248	22654	22849	22849

	Informal political networks (0 = never discusses politics with friends; 1 = discusses occasionally; 2 = discusses frequently)	Religious networks (1–6; 6 = strong religious network)	Political interest (0–1; 1 = somewhat or very interested)	Level of political corruption perceived (0–3; 3 = everyone is corrupt)	Country's change in development organizational structures (2003–2006)	Country's change in business organizational structures (2003–2006)	Country's change in trade unions organizational structures (2003–2006)	Country's change in religious organizational structures (2003–2006)	N
Botswana	0.851	3.466	0.741	0.869	−0.047	−0.030	−0.032	−0.009	1,200
Ghana	1.047	4.891	0.718	0.973	0.123	0.054	0.010	0.050	1,197
Lesotho	0.927	3.812	0.827	0.609	−0.037	−0.042	−0.112	−0.184	1,161
Malawi	0.767	4.798	0.754	0.775	−0.004	0.041	0.011	−0.040	1,200
Mali	0.861	3.802	0.688	1.168	−0.019	−0.079	−0.027	−0.077	1,244
Namibia	0.902	3.494	0.776	1.090	0.049	0.004	−0.012	−0.019	1,200
Nigeria	0.979	4.814	0.597	1.657	0.103	0.047	0.030	−0.004	2,363
South Africa	0.864	3.742	0.629	1.116	0.014	0.019	0.001	−0.047	2,400
Tanzania	1.142	4.741	0.818	0.678	−0.018	−0.014	0.022	−0.176	1,304
Uganda	1.115	4.532	0.741	1.240	0.048	−0.029	−0.011	0.036	2,400
Zambia	0.862	4.859	0.564	1.246	−0.031	−0.012	−0.024	−0.015	1,200
Zimbabwe	0.924	4.115	0.568	1.293	−0.167	−0.139	−0.038	0.087	1,048
Cape Verde	0.703	3.381	0.500	0.304	0.033	−0.002	−0.014	0.099	1,256

(continued)

Table 2.1 Continued

	Informal political networks (0 = never discusses politics with friends; 1 = discusses occasionally; 2 = discusses frequently)	Religious networks (1–6; 6 = strong religious network)	Political interest (0–1; 1 = somewhat or very interested)	Level of political corruption perceived (0–3; 3 = everyone is corrupt)	Country's change in development organizational structures (2003–2006)	Country's change in business organizational structures (2003–2006)	Country's change in trade unions organizational structures (2003–2006)	Country's change in religious organizational structures (2003–2006)	N
Kenya	0.968	4.695	0.664	1.184	0.025	0.035	0.011	0.003	1,278
Mozambique	0.980	4.010	0.694	0.777	0.091	0.066	0.053	0.152	1,198
Senegal	1.131	3.103	0.719	0.747	0.035	0.040	0.025	0.110	1,200
Total	0.946	4.180	0.683	1.034	0.013	−0.010	0.014	0.052	22849
N	22570	22663	22598	22849	22849	22849	22849	22849	22849

Source: Afrobarometer surveys: round 3 (2005–2006) for the individual level variables; round 2 (2002–2003) and 3 (2005–2006) for the organizational variables.

from the religious organizational structure, Nigeria shows a constant increase in the mean participatory rate in all of the organizational types considered. This confirms that the organizational structures maintained their stability and even became stronger during the first decade of the millennium. In contrast, Zimbabwe shows negative changes, confirming that during that same decade the organizational structures progressively and widely weakened. The slight increase in the Zimbabwean development organizational structure occurred only in 2008, favored by the climate of relaxation that culminated in 2009 with the inclusive government.

Therefore, these results tend to confirm *hypothesis 1*, namely, that an enduring organizational structure in Nigeria has partly benefitted from mechanisms of redefinition of the repertoires of actions. For instance, development organizations may have benefitted from the transnationalization of activities. Likewise, business organizations may have maintained their presence thanks to apolitical agendas.

In contrast, in Zimbabwe, average levels of organizational engagement weakened throughout the first decade of the millennium. As advanced in hypothesis 1, the harsh repressive political context may have left no space for the mechanisms highlighted to take place.

Figure 2.1 also shows Nigeria and Zimbabwe's mean levels of protest engagement. The mean levels of protests in Zimbabwe were the highest in 2000 and

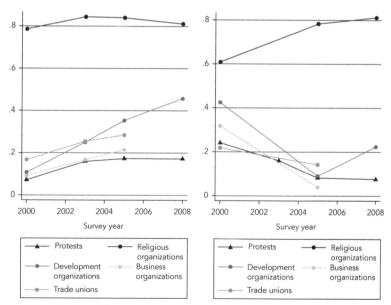

FIGURE 2.1 Levels of organizational and protest engagement in Nigeria (graph on the left) and Zimbabwe (graph on the right), 2000–2008 (countries' means).

Source: Afrobarometer surveys (rounds 1 to 4).

steadily declined over the years. In contrast to this trend, Nigerian protests were rather low in 2000, most likely due to the very recent transition to a more democratic regime, which occurred in 1999, but then protests progressively increased during the early 2000s (and especially between 2000 and 2003).

Therefore, the graph suggests that as average levels of engagement in the different types of organizations increase, the country's mean participatory rates in protests also increase, as shown by the Nigerian case. In contrast, a reversed pattern is found in Zimbabwe, where average levels of engagement in development organizations, in business organizations, and in trade unions all decrease, and the country's mean participatory rate in protests also decreases. In the next section, I test the effect of changes in the organizational structures on protest engagement in more detail through a multivariate analysis using the pooled sample of the Afrobarometer data.

The Mobilizing Role of the Organizational Structure in Sub-Saharan Countries

Table 2.2 shows the results of testing hypothesis 2, namely how changes in the average levels of organizational engagement affect protest mobilization. As I hypothesized, results show that protest engagement in 2006 is significantly affected by increasing average levels of organizational engagement across the years 2003–2006. However, not all types of organizations significantly affect protest engagement. Out of the four types of organizations observed, increasing average levels of engagement in trade unions positively affect the individual probability of engaging in protest actions in 2006. This result is consistent with studies in democratic countries, where trade unions have been long studied as classical or "old" social movement organizations (Schofer and Fourcade-Gourinchas 2001). In addition, the significant role of trade unions is consistent with studies analyzing mobilization during the 1990s in several African countries, which provide substantial evidence on trade unions' involvement in protest actions (Bratton and van de Walle 1992; Bayat 2010). An enduring business organizational structure also positively affects individual engagement in protests in 2006. Changes regarding the average level of engagement in development organizations and religious organizations are, in contrast, not significant. Both development and religious organizations are mostly involved in a-political activities such as service delivery and provision. This is especially true in sub-Saharan Africa, where these organizations are actively engaged in welfare assistance and, therefore, less likely work as structures of political mobilization. In addition, development organizations, which reflect the general increase and emergence of human rights and international law discourses, are likely to be actively engaged with transnational activities and foreign donors. The latter may orchestrate organizational agendas,

Table 2.2 Random Intercept Logit Model Estimates (standard errors in parenthesis) for Engagement in at Least One Protest Activity

	Model 0 null model		Model 1 individual level variables		Model 2a development organizations 2006–2003 structural change		Model 2b business organizations 2006–2003 structural change		Model 2c trade unions 2006–2003 structural change		Model 2d religious organizations 2006–2003 structural change	
	b	se	b	se	b	se	b	se	b	se	b	se
Gender			0.30***	(0.04)	0.30***	(0.04)	0.30***	(0.04)	0.30***	(0.04)	0.30***	(0.04)
Age			0.02*	(0.01)	0.02*	(0.01)	0.02*	(0.01)	0.02*	(0.01)	0.02*	(0.01)
Age squared			−0.00***	(0.00)	−0.00***	(0.00)	−0.00***	(0.00)	−0.00***	(0.00)	−0.00***	(0.00)
Education attained			0.06***	(0.01)	0.06***	(0.01)	0.06***	(0.01)	0.06***	(0.01)	0.06***	(0.01)
Employment status			0.16***	(0.05)	0.16***	(0.05)	0.16***	(0.05)	0.16***	(0.05)	0.16***	(0.05)
Very easy to obtain basic rights			0.08**	(0.03)	0.08**	(0.03)	0.08**	(0.03)	0.08**	(0.03)	0.08**	(0.03)
Country's economic condition 12 months ago was better			0.02	(0.03)	0.02	(0.03)	0.02	(0.03)	0.02	(0.03)	0.02	(0.03)
Respondent's living conditions 12 months ago were better			0.02	(0.03)	0.02	(0.03)	0.02	(0.03)	0.02	(0.03)	0.02	(0.03)
Very high level of deprivation			0.08***	(0.02)	0.08***	(0.02)	0.08***	(0.02)	0.08***	(0.02)	0.08***	(0.02)

(continued)

Table 2.2 Continued

	Model 0 null model		Model 1 individual level variables		Model 2a development organizations 2006–2003 structural change		Model 2b business organizations 2006–2003 structural change		Model 2c trade unions 2006–2003 structural change		Model 2d religious organizations 2006–2003 structural change	
	b	se	b	se	b	se	b	se	b	se	b	se
Present political situation better than past			-0.07**	(0.03)	-0.07**	(0.03)	-0.07**	(0.03)	-0.07**	(0.03)	-0.07**	(0.03)
Religious networks			-0.00	(0.01)	-0.00	(0.01)	-0.00	(0.01)	-0.00	(0.01)	-0.00	(0.01)
Interest in public affairs			0.34***	(0.05)	0.34***	(0.05)	0.34***	(0.05)	0.34***	(0.05)	0.34***	(0.05)
Level of corruption			0.21***	(0.03)	0.21***	(0.03)	0.21***	(0.03)	0.21***	(0.03)	0.21***	(0.03)
Informal political networks												
• Never discusses politics with friends (reference category)												
• Occasionally discusses politics with friends			0.23***	(0.06)	0.23***	(0.06)	0.23***	(0.06)	0.23***	(0.06)	0.23***	(0.06)

	(1)	(2)	(3)	(4)	(5)	(6)
• Frequently discusses politics with friends		0.78^{***} (0.07)	0.78^{***} (0.07)	0.78^{***} (0.07)	0.78^{***} (0.07)	0.78^{***} (0.07)
Changes in organizational structures (differences in country's mean level 2006–2003)						
• Development organizations			2.84 (1.95)			
• Business organizations				5.18^{*} (2.34)		
• Trade unions					10.06^{***} (2.99)	
• Religious organizations						1.74 (1.48)
Constant	-1.98^{***} (0.15)	-3.62^{***} (0.26)	-3.65^{***} (0.25)	-3.60^{***} (0.25)	-3.55^{***} (0.24)	-3.62^{***} (0.25)
country-level variance	0.33^{*} (0.12)	0.30^{**} (0.11)	0.26^{***} (0.10)	0.23^{***} (0.08)	0.17^{***} (0.06)	0.28^{***} (0.10)
LL	−8713.91	−7837.56	−7836.56	−7835.41	−7833.20	−7836.89
chi2	.	637.86	640.08	642.98	649.95	639.39
N	22,259	20,740	20,740	20,740	20,740	20,740

Source: Afrobarometer surveys: round 3 (2005–2006) for the individual level variables); round 2 (2002–2004) and 3 (2005–2006) for the organizational variables.

* $p < 0.05$,

** $p < 0.01$ and

*** $p < 0.001$.

paying particular attention to avoiding conflicts with the political élites of the countries where they are operating and therefore, not providing the organizational bases for individuals to engage in contentious politics. As to the lack of significant effect of changes in the religious organizational structures, this result is supported by the insignificant effect of religious networks. These findings are in contrast with some literature which argues that specific forms of networks among religious organizations, namely decentralized networks made up of dense local religious associations, are the basis of protest mobilization (Trejo 2012). However, these results need to be further assessed by considering, for instance, the types of networks among associations, and the professed religion, which may both have different effects on protest mobilization. Consistently with our *hypothesis 2*, the effect of the changes in the organizational structures on protest participation depend on the mechanisms used by organizations to operate in repressive contexts. In particular, results suggest that organizational structures active in transnational issues, such as development organizations, often funded by international institutions, are not likely to affect individuals' engagement in contentious actions (Tarrow 1998, 31, in Beinin and Vairel 2011, 21).

In addition to the role of formal organizational structures, the results also suggest the importance of informal networks in increasing the likelihood of protest engagement. Discussing politics with friends, either occasionally or frequently, increases the likelihood of individuals participating in protests compared with people who do not discuss politics with friends. This result partly confirms the importance of moderate repertoires of action in nondemocratic contexts which, inter alia, may benefit more from informal ties than from formal organizations (Duboc 2011; Menoret 2011).

Beyond Nigeria and Zimbabwe: Concluding Remarks

This chapter has focused on the links between repression, organizational structures, and engagement in protests. I have hypothesized that in order to understand the influence of repression on protest mobilization it is critical to look at associated changes in organizational structures. In other words, the effect of repression on protest mobilization is conditional on the presence of organizational structures as some eventually become mobilizing structures. The first hypothesis highlighted two specific mechanisms enabling organizations to operate in repressive contexts: first, the orientation of organizational activities toward apolitical issues; second the trasnationalization, the moderation, or the radicalization of political activities, which contribute to renovating the repertoire of actions. I suggested that a reversed-U relationship between repression and organizational structure may be at work, as these mechanisms are less likely to operate under high repression. The first hypothesis is confirmed. In Zimbabwe trade unions and their members have been systematically targeted, and this has hindered the development of an enduring organizational structure. The second hypothesis stressed that individual protest mobilization can benefit from stable and enduring organizational structures, although the effect may also depend on mechanisms at work allowing organizations to operate in repressive contexts. The findings indeed show that not all organizational structures affect protest mobilization. To strengthen this evidence however, more research is needed on other dimensions of the organizational structure, in particular, on the characteristics of the organizational networks which can better clarify different modalities of coordination among mobilizing actors (Diani 2015).

To what extent are the mechanisms linking repression, organizational structures, and engagement in protests discussed in the cases of Nigeria and Zimbabwe traceable, to other contexts, authoritative and democratic alike? In what follows, I first discuss similarities in other repressive contexts and then move on to discussing similarities in democratic ones.

Evidence from the Middle Eastern and Northern African Regions

Evidence from the MENA region on the mechanisms at work among organizations to operate in a repressive context are manifold. For instance, social Islam organizations active in the region partly benefit from being perceived as organizations engaged in apolitical activities (Bayat 2002). In turn, the radicalization of activities by organizations with more explicit political objectives, has occurred under the watchful eyes of the international community, given the growth of terrorist attacks in the region. Radical actions also overlapped with mechanisms of transnationalization in the region. Citizens traveling to other countries and volunteering for *Jihad* are an example (Hegghammer 2010). More specifically, concerning the transnationalization of activities, since the 1970s or 1980s the latter has been a rational strategic option of many activists in the MENA region (Vairel 2011, 28, 36). In the late 1990s, Islamic movements in Saudi Arabia turned their attention to Muslims abroad, a solution devised by the *sahwa* activists to cope with the climate of fear perpetuated by the regime and to channel students' enthusiasm in nonconfrontational directions (Menoret 2011, 48). Dynamics of moderation of the repertoires of action have also been reported. In Egypt, during the 1980s and 1990s, organizations and their members chose itineraries of deradicalization by committing themselves to social, cultural, intellectual, and artistic activities. Literary production and ongoing links with the intellectual field through acquaintances and activities such as writing for newspapers, meeting through local sections of literary groups, and writing poetry or songs in the vernacular language supported the continuation of daily resentment against the political situation (Duboc 2011, 65ff). Public gatherings organized from December 2004 to September 2005 in Egypt by *kifaya* (Enough!), an organization striving for reforms and change, were possible thanks to *Kifaya* activists' strategy to self-limit their mobilization. *Kifaya* was politically active thanks to the use of moderated repertoires of action, a result of the limits imposed on the number of people participating in the organized demonstrations and also of the choice of location of mobilization. *Kifaya* paid careful attention to the extent of mobilization, never exceeding a thousand people, and its location, mobilizing in downtown Cairo rather than in densely populated areas where too many people could gather. This enabled the organization to repeatedly denounce domestic issues related, for instance, to President Husni Mubarak's repressive regime and his attempts to enact hereditary succession (Duboc 2011, 61; Vairel 2011, 32; Beinin 2011, 185).

Several other instances provide supportive evidence of the presence of solid organizational structures for protest mobilization in the region. Considering the recent "Arab Spring" uprisings, football clubs, which likely operated thanks to their apolitical agenda, were among the most active organizations during the protests in January 2011. Evidence shows that on the January 25, 2011, the starting day of the occupation of Tahrir Square in Cairo, a march of 10,000 people was led by the leader of a football fan club league in Cairo. During the 18-day occupation of Tahrir Square, the ultras also patrolled the perimeters of the square and controlled entry (Dorsey 2012, 414). Several instances suggest that religious structures, such as those of the Muslim Brotherhood, also represented a significant mobilizing structure for protests in Egypt, especially the younger leadership (Bayat 2007). During the recent "Arab Spring" uprisings, which culminated in the occupation of Tahrir Square on January 25, 2011, the older component refrained from joining demonstrations, while the younger component promptly took part in the mobilizations (Teti and Gervasio 2011). These findings are inconsistent with my results showing a lack of significant effect of religious organizational structures in the sub-Saharan region, confirming that future research needs to assess their role in a more systematic manner.

Local and more informal networks have also been crucial mobilizing structures. Prior research reports that networks of friends and neighborhoods were imperative for protest mobilization. Beinin (2011, 183) describes the situation whereby workers' protests in Egypt between 2006 and 2009 did not rely on "movement entrepreneurs" or preexisting organizations. The Egyptian Trade Union Federation (ETUF) was an arm of the regime, and its local committees had even been an impediment to achieving workers' demands. With the exception of the support by several labor-oriented NGOs, workers' protests in Egypt mainly relied on irregular face-to-face meetings and mobile telephones, supported by family and neighborhood connections (Beinin 2011, 183). The working-class networks were thus highly localized, whereby family and neighborhood connections were of utmost importance in the daily life and in the construction of workers' neighborhoods. Similarly, in Saudi Arabia informal networks facilitated and redirected activism during the 1990s. Activists were often organized in discrete groups with no fixed boundaries (*shilla*), which tap into the state's resources, often located in areas at the periphery of the educational system and the official religious institutions (Menoret 2011, 44). Former activists of Islamic movements engaged in groups of 10 to 20 friends, who regularly met in given places like apartments, coffee shops, and private rest houses. This often led to direct involvement in political activities like engagement in the municipal elections (Menoret 2011, 57–58). Following this, further analyses on informal networks could integrate the discussion on formal organizations as mobilizing structures.

Finally, the lack of mobilizing capacity by organizations using mechanisms of transnationalization to operate in repressive contexts, is also demonstrated by some events in Morocco. In the late 1980s and 1990s "left organizations chose to internationalize their struggles but, by doing so, they also paid a heavy price in transforming their practices and programs from mobilization and street activism to participation in public policies and cooperation with authorities" (Vairel 2011, 37).

Evidence from Democratic Contexts

Although more liberal and democratic settings undoubtedly differ socially and politically, the dynamics of contention may generate meaningful similarities in terms of the mechanisms discussed throughout. The use of apolitical agendas, and the transnationalization, moderation, and radicalization of contentious repertoires can be equally useful to investigate certain dynamics pertaining to specific issues or populations that face severe contextual constraints in democracies. For instance, they are in place in the case of immigrant populations having settled in exclusionary European contexts (Cinalli and Giugni 2011). These contexts are characterized by policies and laws which grant limited individual and collective rights to migrants in order for them to integrate in the settlement countries (Pilati 2016).

Analyses in Switzerland and Italy show that migrant organizations are relatively few in number compared with other places where political contexts are more receptive and tolerant toward immigration (Eggert and Pilati 2014). In these contexts, migrant organizations mainly engage in activities implying apolitical agendas, oriented to service delivery and cultural and recreational activities. At the same time, organizations are generally isolated from the political sphere. However, while they tend to be marginalized from conventional politics, fragmented and sparsely interconnected clusters of migrant organizations are also more likely to turn to protest actions (Eggert and Pilati 2014). While evidence is scarce, some events support the argument that constraining contextual conditions linked to exclusion and racial discrimination against immigrants may be associated with forms of radicalization too. Research on some migrant youth organizations shows that radicalism is often limited to the use of symbolic violence or involves single members of organizations solving private matters through violence (Queirolo Palmas 2009; Giliberti 2014). However, a case in point regards the clashes involving immigrants in Castel Volturno, in the Province of Caserta, Southern Italy, in September 2008. Although systematic data on the role of migrant organizations during these events is not available, immigrants did organize a series of radical activities in reaction to the brutal killing of six African-origin immigrants by the organized crime groups acting in the region (*camorra*). This included protest marches, blocking of highway traffic, arson of garbage dumpsters, damage to parked cars, destruction of small business shops, and attacks on public transportation. Although differences between the Italian case and the non-democratic contexts analyzed in this chapter undoubtedly exist, the events occurred in Italy are emblematic of those exclusionary, at times severely repressive, settings that develop in democracies, and of how similar mechanisms at play help us flesh out the links between repression, organizational structures, and protest mobilization across cases and regime types.

Acknowledgments

The research leading to these results was funded by the People Programme (Marie Curie Actions) of the European Union's Seventh Framework Programme (FP7/ 2007–2013) under REA grant agreement no. PIEF-GA-2011-300444. I thank Marco Giugni, supervisor of the project at the host institution, University of Geneva. Data for this chapter was derived from the Afrobarometer, an African-led series of national public attitude surveys on democracy and governance in Africa (Afrobarometer Data; Bratton et al. 2005). I am indebted to the Afrobarometer team for their work. Finally, I am also grateful to Eitan Alimi, Avraham Sela, and Mario Sznajder for their insightful and valuable suggestions on earlier drafts, to two anonymous reviewers for their comments, and to the editors' helpful assistance.

Notes

1. Given the level of analysis, I treat them as mechanisms and not as processes. For the discussion of radicalization as a process that leads to and includes political violence see Alimi, Demetriou, and Bosi (2015).

2. According to the 2006 Economist's Democracy Index (Economist 2008), Nigeria and Zimbabwe, of which the latter has the lowest score, fall under the category of "authoritarian regimes." In turn, the Freedom House Index (Freedom House 2006) defined Nigeria as "partly free" and Zimbabwe as "not free" in 2006.

3. The Afrobarometer is a cross-sectional survey providing comparable data in different years on individual involvement in various types of organizations as well as on individual participation in protests and demonstrations.

4. Despite the usefulness of the indexes of democracy in providing a proxy for the political regimes of the countries studied, their use has raised severe criticism in relation to the complexity of the democratic phenomenon and the differences in theoretical definitions, which may not be captured by a numerical approach. Furthermore, while I address both Nigeria and Zimbabwe as authoritarian regimes, there are still innumerable differences between the two countries.

5. I use data from round 3 of the Afrobarometer survey and not the last available data, round 4, because the latter does not contain enough information on different types of organizations.

6. The use of the countries' average levels of individual organizational engagement as indicators of organizational structures has severe limitations. First, increasing average levels of countries' organizational engagement can indicate either that more individuals are affiliated to a few big organizations or that more individuals are affiliated to many small organizations. Therefore, it tells us nothing about organizational density. Second, it does not provide any information on organizational networks and the way organizations compete or collaborate with one another. Therefore, my analyses can be considered only as a very partial contribution to the analysis of the mobilizing role of organizational structures.

7. The values concerning organizational engagement in Zimbabwe in 2003 are missing. In the multivariate analysis, for the Zimbabwean case, I therefore consider changes that occurred in the mean rate of organizational engagement between 2000 and 2006. I then divide it by 2, because the time span considered is approximately double than the time covered for other countries, although this is a very rough calculation assuming that the change is steady in time.

8. To operationalize informal political networks I use a variable indicating the frequency of discussing politics with friends and neighbors. I expect that the more

people informally discuss politics, the more they are likely to join protest. I am aware that the use of this variable is highly contested because of a lack of a clear causality link and directionality of the relationship. In addition, there is redundancy to the degree that political attitudes and behaviors tend to be highly correlated, at least in democratic contexts, as it is for political interest. I nonetheless keep the variable to test the effect under repressive contextual conditions. In addition, the overall models do not change without it.

3

Qualities of Democracy, Dissatisfaction, and Contention in Latin America

THE ROLE OF EQUALITY, FREEDOM, AND RESPONSIVENESS

Mario Quaranta

POLITICAL PROTEST IS an element of democratic systems that has been seen as an indicator of both lively civil society and widespread discontent. Although noninstitutional politics in Latin American countries is no exception in terms of the influence of discontent on the willingness to protest, it is telling that widespread popular discontent is translated into actual popular contention only in some countries. In this chapter, I use the "democratic qualities" framework (Diamond and Morlino 2005; Morlino 2011) to investigate the effects of levels of political equality, freedom, and responsiveness on political protest with special attention given to the interaction between individual-level determinants, in particular dissatisfaction, and contextual ones.

The study of political protest, both legal and illegal, within a large comparative framework seems to be absent in the recent literature on Latin America. Several studies investigate the emergence of social movements in Latin American countries but tend to cover one or two cases and to focus on specific mobilization issues, such as the movements against the privatization of public services (Arce 2008), the opposition to trade negotiations (Spalding 2007), the landless movement (Ondetti 2006), the mobilization during dictatorships (Schneider 1995), and the changing authoritarian contexts

(Almeida 2008). Other studies take a comparative approach and analyze a few cases focusing on the relationship between the political structure and the social movements cycle (Brockett 2005); antineoliberal movements with a focus on urban, labor, gender, and indigenous issues (Johnston and Almeida 2006); or the politicization of ethnic cleavages and the emergence of ethnic political identities (Yashar 2005). A broader comparative framework that focuses on democratic qualities and their effect on protest cycles promises to increase understanding of differences in the levels of contention across Latin American countries. A broad comparative framework allows evaluation of the applicability of models and concepts that have been developed in Western countries, most particularly political opportunity structure (POS), in different parts of the globe. Indeed, the concept of POS has only recently begun to be applied outside the West or in less democratic settings, leading scholars to propose important adjustments and refinements to the concept based on their empirical analysis (see Moodie 2002; Alimi 2009). Given that in new or developing democracies it is usually the case that authoritarian features continue to be part of the regime and that popular contention tends to be driven by basic needs and consumption issues (Noonan 1995), it is argued that in order to use the analytical payoffs provided by the concept of POS, certain micro-macro preconditions should be taken into consideration. In addition to grievance-related factors experienced at the individual level, the "democratic qualities" framework might be useful, because it identifies constituent elements of democratic regimes that can be considered as "enablers" of popular contention. In new or consolidating democracies, elements emphasized by POS, such as the configuration of the elites or political access for social movements, may offer little analytical value for understanding the levels and forms of popular contention unless historical legacies, pathways to democratization, patterns of citizenship inclusion, and institutional configurations inform our analysis.

Latin America countries offer promising test cases. Available cross-national data—Latinobarometro (Latinobarometro Corporation 2009)—enables a systematic and rigorous comparative analysis of the separate and combined effects of macro/contextual-level and micro/individual-level measures on levels and forms of popular contention. In what follows, I review existing theories and extract hypotheses regarding the emergence of popular contention, after which I elaborate on the data and key measures used. Discussion of key findings is followed by assessing their generalizability to other structurally similar cases, particularly to several "Arab Spring" cases.

Theory

This section provides an overview of existing accounts of the determinants of political protest and formulates several hypotheses on the relationship between individual and contextual factors.

Dissatisfaction and Protest

An important body of research on why individuals engage in protest behavior deals with role of dissatisfaction. Participation in contention, it is argued, depends on the assessment of the individual personal condition against expectations or the conditions of reference groups (Buechler 2004). Gurr (1970) long ago argued that ordinary people rebel when they are in a situation of "relative deprivation," which is essentially about perceived discrepancy between capabilities and expectations. In a similar vein, Lipsky (1968) has maintained that political protest is the result of grievances growing within a society and that in these situations action becomes a "resource" for those who are marginalized and whose interests are not represented.

Studies focusing on the individual participation in protest activities have relied on the same assumption. For instance, Barnes, Farah, and Heunks (1979) argue that the "interest in the relationship between satisfaction and political behavior is at least as old as the serious study of politics [. . .] it is widely believed that happy people give rise to a tranquil polity, that those who are dissatisfied are the source of public unrest, and that the roots of political violence are often to be found in individual frustration" (1979, 381). The hypothesis that the dissatisfied would engage more in political activities has been called "disaffected radicalism" (Norris, Walgrave, and Van Aelst 2005). According to this hypothesis, citizens become involved in high-intensity forms of political action because they are not satisfied with their current situation.

This approach to the study of political protest has been extensively applied and tested, only to produce mixed results. On the one hand, personal and political dissatisfaction have not been found to be correlated with political protest (Citrin 1974; Muller and Jukam 1977; Barnes et al. 1979; Craig and Maggiotto 1981). The effects of different measures of dissatisfaction in multivariate analyses lose their significance once other variables, such as education, values, and ideology, are factored in. The lack of effect has been attributed to the fact that these analyses have been conducted in advanced industrial democracies in which political protest is more the expression of new values—postmaterialist values—produced by economic development and generational replacement (Inglehart 1990; Norris 2002; Dalton 2008; Dalton, Van Sickle, and Weldon 2010).

On the other hand, empirical research on some European cases and developing countries has yielded more confirmatory results. For example, Kriesi and Westholm (2007) show that negative evaluation of one's condition in several domains increases the probability of taking part in political action. In developing contexts, moreover, the role of grievances is more pronounced because political participation and protest are not a matter of the better educated, the upper strata, and the postmaterialists, as it happens in Western countries (Booth and Seligson 1978, Seligson and Booth 1979). Almeida (2002) argues that the grievances produced by austerity measures, in conjunction with favorable opportunity structures, namely, elections and conflict among the political elites, are factors for the mobilization of social movements. In general, in the Latin American context, the link between grievances and protest has mainly focused on the role of neoliberal economic reforms, or the deteriorating economic conditions that in general spurred dissatisfaction toward the political elites, contributed to politicizing issues, and favored mobilization (see Brockett 2005; Ondetti 2006; Arce 2008). Lastly, research on the developing countries in Latin America has indeed shown that individuals from lower socioeconomic levels join protest movements in order to formulate demands to the elected officials, while citizens with a higher socioeconomic status do not (Craig and Foweraker 1990; Escobar and Alvarez 1992; Chalmers et al. 1997).

According to this review, dissatisfaction should play a role in determining protest in developing countries (H_{1a}), and the forms of dissatisfaction (i.e., economic and political) should have a positive interaction effect (H_{1b}). That is to say, the association between economic dissatisfaction and political protest is likely to be stronger when political dissatisfaction is higher.

Qualities of Democracy and Protest

Moving beyond discontent and engagement in protest activity and seeking to account for variation in levels of protest, a second body of works focuses on the influence of political conditions and circumstances. In general, there are works on democratic regimes that suggest that freedom represents one of democracy's building blocks together with equality (Dahl 1971). These two components are interconnected in many definitions of democracy, as the first is considered a prerequisite of the second (Sartori 1987). Responsiveness, too, is often seen as an important feature of democratic regimes. Sartori (1987) argues that democracies should guarantee responsiveness (Sartori 1987), and Dahl (1970) argues that democracies are in fact characterized by the correspondence between citizens' preferences and government actions.

A more concrete literature that focuses less on democracy per se and more on how politics can either encourage or discourage protest is known as the "political process model," with its key analytical concept: the "structure of political opportunities." In brief, the characteristics of democracy "determine" the structure of political opportunities and constraints, which in turn affects the degree to which challenger groups have better bargaining position and greater political leverage (McAdam 1982; Kitschelt 1986; Kriesi et al. 1995; Tarrow 1994; Meyer 2004). Central elements of POS proposed by scholars include, for example, the configuration of political institutions, the openness of the political system, the degree of centralization versus decentralization or separation of power, the characteristics of the electoral systems, the makeup of the party system, and the presence of coalition governments.

Importantly, because these elements or facets of POS have been developed and proposed by scholars studying popular contention in advanced liberal democracies, and guided by certain material and nonmaterial assumptions, fundamental features that may have critical bearing on the emergence of popular contention outside the West have been overlooked. In this chapter, I analyze three important features of democracy—equality, freedom, and responsiveness—that are necessary (though not sufficient) for understanding the emergence of popular contention—specifically setting the conditions that facilitate engagement in contention and conducive to certain forms of contention. Nevertheless, equality, freedom, and responsiveness do not have a straightforward link to protest politics. Thus, the following overview presents various, often contradicting, hypotheses about how equality, freedom, and responsiveness are linked to political protest.

Equality is substantiated by some social rights: physical well-being, assistance and social security, work, human dignity, strike, study, healthy surroundings, and housing (see Rueschemeyer 2005; Morlino 2011). Equality facilitates political protest because it presupposes the presence of a number of social rights, which are often, but not necessarily, the product of economic development. From several sources (see Norris 2002, Dalton et al. 2010) we know that economic development improves the resources of society, which are necessary to produce citizens' mobilization. In fact, it has been argued that widespread inequality depresses political involvement, as "it increases the relative power of richer citizens" (Solt 2008, 57). According to this argument equality leads to more involvement in protest politics (H_{2a}).

Conversely, from a more rational perspective, an equal political system may be associated with less political protest. The absence of social rights can lead to protest because it indicates that the economic and social conditions are scarce and, therefore, such situations are more likely to witness political protest as a sign of deprivation (Gurr 1968). The presence of diffused dissatisfaction due to harsh living conditions and the absence of basic social rights can be seen as a determinant of political protest (Wilkes 2004). Hence, unequal societies are more likely to have political protest than equal ones. If a country provides the necessary means to reduce inequalities, citizens may have less incentive to use political protest to express their hardships (H_{2a}).

Individual *freedom* gives citizens the opportunity to express their preferences, because it substantiates political and civil rights. These two rights are basic elements of a "good democracy" (Diamond and Morlino 2005; Morlino 2011). Their presence allows citizens to choose their representatives, to compete in elections, to make claims, to criticize powerholders, to express their opinions, to move within and outside of the country, to have free information, and to assemble and associate in order to get organized (see Beetham 2005). When regimes enable and protect these rights, it is more likely that citizens and groups will engage in political protest activities because such regimes are more open and tolerant toward criticism and may also facilitate it (Dalton et al. 2010). This occurs because in such regimes citizens do not fear reprisal and the possibility of acceptance and tolerance of protest is much higher than in regimes where freedoms are present to a less extent. Therefore, freedom increases the possibilities for, and facilitates the diffusion of, political protest and, conversely, lower levels of freedom will be associated with less protest (H_{3a}). However, political protest can happen more frequently in those countries where freedoms are low, as protest actions can be the only way of expressing discontent and feeling of dissatisfaction (Davenport, Johnston, and Mueller 2005). Therefore, lack of freedom may also be associated with political protest (H_{3b}).

Responsiveness refers to "what occurs when democratic process induces the government to form and implement policies that the citizens want. When the process induces such policies consistently, we consider democracy to be of higher quality" (Powell 2005, 62). Responsiveness has often been linked to the electoral process, democratic legitimacy, and to political participation. The decreasing levels of responsiveness in Western democracies, in terms of political outputs, have been treated as a major reason for the increasing levels of political detachment and dissatisfaction, which also led to the protest waves of the 1970s (see Kaase and Newton 1995; Pharr and Putnam 2000). As governments' capacity to produce the expected policies depends on the level of government effectiveness (Morlino 2011), it is likely that countries with high levels of responsiveness will have low levels of political protest, as citizens are satisfied with the way the system addresses their issues. Following this argument, I expect that low levels of responsiveness lead to higher levels of political protest, because in such contexts citizens are less satisfied with governments' action in dealing with their needs (H_{4a}). However, a different perspective suggests that a responsive government will face more instances of demands and claim-making. This is because an effective government has more capacity to deal with new issues and to accommodate them (see Schumaker 1975), providing a positive opportunity structure for protest.[1] Accordingly, responsiveness may be associated with high levels of political protest (H_{4b}).

Dissatisfaction, Qualities of Democracy, and Protest

Individual dissatisfaction may exert a different effect on political protest depending on the specific constellation or configuration of equality, freedom, and responsiveness. In practice, the contextual characteristics may change the association between individual-level variables and the likelihood of participation in protest politics (see Anderson 2007). Furthermore, the contextual characteristics may be seen as facilitating or impeding conditions, which may affect the role of dissatisfaction in leading to political protest (see Kriesi and Westholm 2007). If a regime has a high level of income inequality it is likely that the role of dissatisfaction in predicting political protest will be higher. I therefore expect inequality to have an amplifying effect on dissatisfaction in predicting political protest (H_5). Additionally, I argue that dissatisfaction will have less effect in countries where citizens have more possibilities to express their needs. As such, in countries where political and civil rights are safeguarded, it is possible to expect dissatisfaction to be less relevant in predicting political protest (H_6). The effect of responsiveness is similar to freedom and equality. If a given regime were able to respond effectively to citizens' demands, citizens would be more satisfied, both politically and personally. Moreover, in responsive systems the levels of political efficacy are higher, because citizens perceive that the elected officials care about them. Following this argument, I expect that in more responsive political systems the effect of dissatisfaction on levels and forms of protest will be less pronounced than in unresponsive political systems (H_7).

Data and Method

Individual-level data come from the Latinobarometro series (Latinobarometro Corporation 2009) between 1996 and 2008. The countries included in this study are Argentina, Bolivia, Brazil, Chile, Colombia, Costa Rica, Ecuador, El Salvador, Guatemala, Honduras, Mexico, Nicaragua, Panama, Paraguay, Peru, República Dominicana, Uruguay, and Venezuela.[2] To provide a more general assessment of political protest, I use two items that ask whether or not the respondent has taken part in "authorized demonstrations" and whether or not the respondent has "occupied land, buildings or factories."[3] I follow Marsh and Kaase's (1979) approach to distinguish between conventional and nonconventional/disruptive

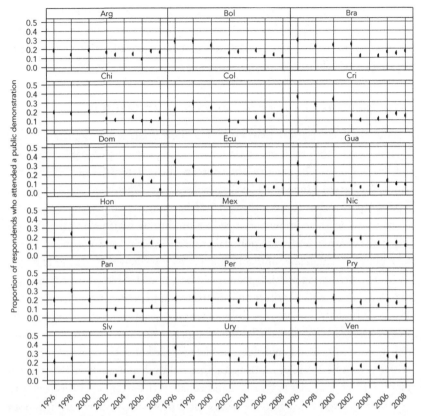

FIGURE 3.1 Proportions of respondents who declared to have attended a public demonstration in Latin American countries between 1996 and 2008, with 95% confidence intervals.

forms of political participation, a distinction consistent with works by other scholars (Tilly 1978; Tarrow 1994). The two forms of actions can be considered noninstitutional forms of participation, as the first challenges the authorities yet remains within the bounds of legal norms and the second are illegal but peaceful forms of protest (Dalton 1988).

Figures 3.1 and 3.2 show the proportion of respondents who attended authorized demonstrations and who occupied land, buildings, or factories in the Latin American countries included in this study for the years in which the indicators are available. As can be seen, in most of the countries, the proportion of citizens attending demonstrations has decreased over time. For example, in Costa Rica, Bolivia, Ecuador, El Salvador, and Nicaragua the decrease has been quite substantial. In other countries, such as Venezuela, there was an increase around 2006 accompanied by a decrease in the following years. As far as occupying land, buildings, or factories is concerned, we see that this mode of political protest is

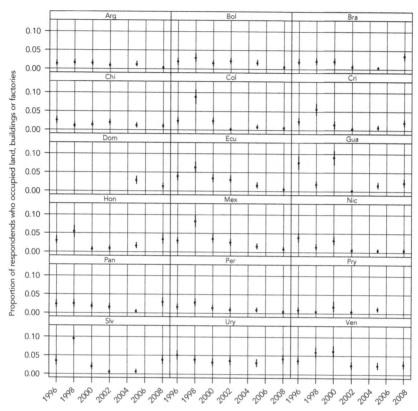

FIGURE 3.2 Proportions of respondents who declared to have occupied land, buildings, or factories in Latin American countries between 1996 and 2008, with 95% confidence intervals.

not a "popular" form of action. It appears also that the proportion of respondents who engaged in this form of protest decreased over time. In fact, in some countries, such as Colombia, Ecuador, Guatemala, Honduras, Mexico, and El Salvador, the proportion of those who occupied land, buildings, or factories was around 0.10 between 1996 and 1998, while afterward the proportion drops substantively. All in all, there is a substantial amount of variation across countries and over time. Protest politics appears to be mutable in Latin American countries, but in general it seems that these two forms of political protest are less and less present in these Latin American countries.

Several independent variables were used in order to make sense of variation in the two forms of political protest. The independent variables belong to two groups: individual and contextual. The individual variables are selected to test the hypothesis that dissatisfaction is associated with the propensity to engage in political protest activities. Our variables of interest are two. The first is an indicator measuring the dissatisfaction with the current state of the national economy, which ranges from −2 (low dissatisfaction) to 2 (high dissatisfaction). The second is a scale measuring distrust in political institutions, which is constructed using two indicators: distrust in parliament and distrust in political parties. The scale ranges from −2 (low distrust) to 2 (high distrust). I also use some control variables in order to account for other relevant hypotheses outlined in the literature (Barnes and Kaase 1979, Parry, Moyser, and Day 1992, Norris 2002, Dalton 2008).[4]

In order to test hypotheses 2–4 (i.e., that equality may or may not lead to higher protest, that the presence or absence of freedom may or may not widen (instead of enlarging) the possibilities for political protest, and that low or high levels of responsiveness may or may not lead to higher levels of political protest) I have used contextual data coming from three sources. Inequality is measured using the Gini Index, which measures how unequal the income distribution in a country is (World Bank 2011);[5] freedom is measured using the Freedom House composite index (Freedom House 2012), which measures the extent to which civil liberties and political rights are present in a regime, and it ranges from 1 (high freedom) to 7 (low freedom). To measure responsiveness,[6] I have used a composite index, inclusive of the "Government Effectiveness" Index, which "captures perceptions of the quality of public services, the quality of the civil service and the degree of its independence from political pressures, the quality of policy formulation and implementation, and the credibility of the government's commitment to such policies" (Kaufmann, Kraay, and Mastruzzi 2009). The index ranges from −2.5 to 2.5, where the first figure gauges low government effectiveness, and the second high government effectiveness. I have also controlled for the level of economic development, as it has been argued that it is a powerful predictor of political protest (Dalton et al. 2010). I use the natural logarithm of the gross domestic product (GDP) per capita (World Bank 2011).

Given that the overall analytical framework focuses on individuals nested in countries and over time, I have used multilevel modeling to test the hypotheses (see Gelman and Hill 2006). This type of statistical model allows taking into account several levels of analysis at the same time, estimating the effects of variables working at different levels on the individual behavior. Using these models, it is possible to understand whether the individual variables as well as the contextual variables predict individual political protest. In particular, for this study I use cross-classified multilevel models, as the respondents are nested both in countries and years (see Western 1998; Rasbash and Browne 2008). I use binomial logistic models, as the dependent variables are dichotomous.

Finally, it is important to note that five models for each dependent variable are estimated: a model with only the individual-level variables, a model adding the interaction between distrust in political institutions and dissatisfaction with the national economy, a model adding the contextual variables, a model adding the interaction terms between the contextual variables and dissatisfaction with the national economy, and a model adding the interaction terms between the contextual variables and distrust in political institutions.

Results

Table 3.1 reports the estimates of the multilevel models predicting the probability of attending public demonstrations. Included in the first model are individual-level factors only. At first sight, it seems that almost all the individual factors are statistically significant. It appears also that there is a clear gender gap, a finding consistent with a well-known argument regarding gender being a source of political inequality in terms of women's status (Desposato and Norrander 2009). Age has a nonlinear association with the dependent variable. Education shows the expected association with the probability of attending a demonstration. We see that as the level of education increases, the probability of attending a demonstration increases as well. This result is in line with the current literature, which mainly focuses on Western countries (Inglehart 1979; Dalton 2008). Income has also an expected association with the probability of attending a demonstration. Having a low income, or at least a perception of it, decreases the probability of attending a demonstration. These findings basically confirm that the socioeconomic status model (Brady, Verba, and Schlozman 1995; Verba, Schlozman, and Brady 1995) is valid also for Latin American countries.

Regarding the first hypothesis, we see that dissatisfaction with the national economy has a positive association with the probability of attending a demonstration. This means that the perception that the national economy is running badly translates into a high probability of attending demonstrations. In fact, a respondent who is satisfied with the national economic situation has probability of attending a demonstration of 0.14, while a respondent who is dissatisfied with national economic situation has a probability of 0.16. However, the role of this variable does not appear to be decisive. This has, of course, a positive and statistically significant association with the dependent variable, but it is not very strong. The other variable of interest, distrust in political institutions, has a negative association with the dependent variable. A respondent with a low level of distrust has a probability of attending a demonstration of 0.20, while a respondent

Table 3.1 Multilevel Models Predicting the Probability of Attending Public Demonstrations

	(1)	(2)	(3)	(4)	(5)
Intercept	−2.528	−2.520	9.804	10.565	10.386
	(0.000)	(0.000)	(0.000)	(0.000)	(0.000)
Woman	−0.282	−0.282	−0.282	−0.283	−0.282
	(0.000)	(0.000)	(0.000)	(0.000)	(0.000)
Age	0.036	0.036	0.036	0.036	0.036
	(0.000)	(0.000)	(0.000)	(0.000)	(0.000)
Age-squared	−0.037	−0.037	−0.037	−0.036	−0.037
	(0.000)	(0.000)	(0.000)	(0.000)	(0.000)
Low education (ref. No	0.033	0.033	0.036	0.034	0.034
education)	(0.499)	(0.500)	(0.462)	(0.487)	(0.491)
Middle education	0.142	0.141	0.138	0.137	0.137
	(0.000)	(0.000)	(0.000)	(0.000)	(0.000)
High education	0.605	0.604	0.593	0.592	0.591
	(0.000)	(0.000)	(0.000)	(0.000)	(0.000)
Still studying	0.733	0.732	0.721	0.718	0.719
	(0.000)	(0.000)	(0.000)	(0.000)	(0.000)
Income	−0.020	−0.020	−0.022	−0.021	−0.022
	(0.001)	(0.001)	(0.000)	(0.000)	(0.000)
Dissatisfaction with	0.047	0.014	0.045	−0.370	0.046
national economic	(0.000)	(0.157)	(0.000)	(0.000)	(0.000)
situation					
Distrust in political	−0.122	−0.137	−0.121	−0.119	−0.414
institutions	(0.000)	(0.000)	(0.000)	(0.000)	(0.000)
Dissatisfaction with		0.042			
national economic		(0.000)			
situation × Distrust					
in political					
institutions					
Gini Index			0.009	0.003	0.003
			(0.002)	(0.301)	(0.288)
FH Index			−0.116	−0.102	−0.113
			(0.000)	(0.000)	(0.000)
GovEff Index			0.098	0.119	0.085
			(0.100)	(0.049)	(0.165)

(continued)

Table 3.1 Continued

	(1)	(2)	(3)	(4)	(5)
log(GDP per capita)			−1.418	−1.475	−1.454
			(0.000)	(0.000)	(0.000)
Dissatisfaction with national economic situation × Gini Index				0.010 (0.000)	
Dissatisfaction with national economic situation × FH Index				−0.051 (0.000)	
Dissatisfaction with national economic situation × GovEff Index				−0.020 (0.305)	
Distrust in political institutions × Gini Index					0.006 (0.000)
Distrust in political institutions × FH Index					−0.014
					(0.188)
Distrust in political institutions × GovEff Index					0.021 (0.180)
Random effects					
Standard deviation: country	0.281	0.282	0.698	0.714	0.708
Standard deviation: year	0.253	0.255	0.224	0.227	0.225
BIC	124510	124484	124448	124443	124461
AIC	124382	124345	124280	124246	124263
N	144525	144525	144525	144525	144525

Note: entries are log-odds, *p*-values in parentheses. Number of countries: 18; number of years: 9.

with high level of distrust has a probability of 0.14. Therefore, this finding contradicts our expectations. It appears that distrust in political institutions does not encourage citizens to get involved in demonstrations. This could be due to the fact that a distrustful citizen does not believe that the political system and its institutions are attentive to his or her requests. It might be that distrust in politics reduces the sense of political efficacy and this in turn lowers the likelihood of attending demonstrations. When citizens do not trust their institutions it is because they think politics is not able to respond adequately to their problems and may deem protest a useless means of "voice."

Model 2 includes an interaction term between dissatisfaction with the national economy and distrust in political institutions, which is visually sketched in Figure 3.3 (left). The plot shows that the association between dissatisfaction with the national economy and the probability of attending a demonstration changes depending on distrust in political institutions. In fact, the probability of attending a demonstration increases as dissatisfaction with the national economy increases and if the respondent distrusts the political institutions. Conversely, when the respondent trusts the political institutions, dissatisfaction with the economy has a negative effect on the probability of attending a demonstration. This means that a combination of factors helps in understanding participation in protest actions, not just single factors (Kriesi and Westholm 2007). Dissatisfaction with the national economy works as a stronger motivational mechanism for attending a demonstration when the respondent distrusts the political institutions.

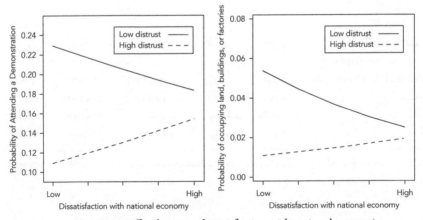

FIGURE 3.3 Interaction effect between dissatisfaction with national economic situation and distrust in political institutions on the probability of attending a public demonstration (left panel) and the probability of occupying land, buildings, or factories (right panel).

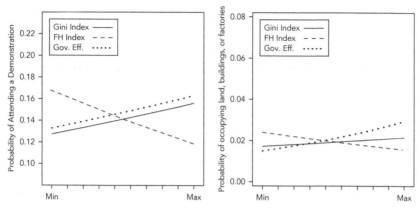

FIGURE 3.4 Association between the Gini Index, the Freedom House Index and the Government Effectiveness Index and, respectively, the probability of attending a public demonstration (left panel) and the probability of occupying land, buildings, or factories (right panel).

Model 3 includes the contextual variables measuring equality, freedom, and responsiveness. The Gini index appears to be positively associated with the dependent variable. This means (see Figure 3.4, left) that a respondent living in a society with a large level of inequality has a probability of attending a public demonstration of 0.16, while a respondent living in a country with lesser levels of inequality has a probability of 0.13. It is therefore possible to expect countries in which income is less equally distributed to produce more incentives for citizens to engage in political protest. The level of freedom, measured by the combined Freedom House score, is negatively associated with the likelihood of attending a demonstration. The coefficient suggests that the more a country denies civil and political rights the less a respondent is likely to attend a demonstration. In fact, in countries with high levels of freedoms the probability of attending a demonstration is 0.17, while in less free countries the probability drops to 0.12. In less free states, the level of repression and the absence of fundamental rights do make the practice of political protest a very risky and dangerous activity. The last variable, government effectiveness, has a positive association with the likelihood of attending a demonstration ($p = .10$). More responsive regimes may be open to activists, who, by consequence, have more incentives for protesting. In brief, a highly responsive state does not fear activists, but rather accepts protests. In practice, a responsive state provides a positive "opportunity structure" for protest (Kriesi et al. 1995). In the end, we can see that the level of economic development, measured as the logarithm of GDP per capita, is associated with the likelihood of attending demonstrations.

In models 4 and 5, I have included the interaction terms between dissatisfaction with the national economy, distrust in the political institutions, and the variables measuring inequality, freedom, and responsiveness. The estimates suggest that some democratic qualities play a role in determining the association between the probability of attending a demonstration and the measures of dissatisfaction and distrust. The interaction term between equality and dissatisfaction with the national economy is positive and statistically significant. Thus, the level of inequality mediates the association between dissatisfaction with the national economy and the likelihood of attending a demonstration. Looking at the left-hand panel of Figure 3.5, we see that the probability of attending demonstrations increases much more, in an unequal country, as dissatisfaction with national economy increases, compared with a more equal country. Therefore, it is possible to argue that the level of inequality strengthens the association between dissatisfaction with the national economy and the probability of attending demonstrations. The Freedom House Index has a negative and statistically significant effect on dissatisfaction with the national economy. In brief, in contexts where the level of freedom is low, the association between dissatisfaction with national economy and the probability of attending a demonstration is weaker than in contexts where the level of freedom is high. In contexts where citizens enjoy more freedom, low satisfaction with the national economy leads to a higher probability of attending demonstrations. In free contexts citizens are more sensitive to what they perceive about the national economy, pushing them to demonstrate and, hence, to express their voice. Conversely, in more repressive contexts the dissatisfaction with the national economy seems to have a weaker association with the likelihood of demonstrating. The last interaction term, the one concerning dissatisfaction with the national economy and the Government Effectiveness Index, suggests that the association between dissatisfaction with

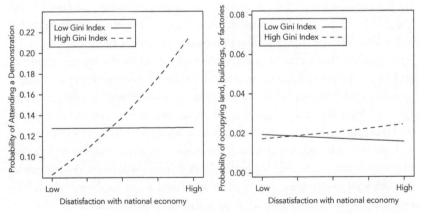

FIGURE 3.5 Interaction effect between dissatisfaction with the national economy situation and the Gini Index on the probability of attending a public demonstration (left panel) and the probability of occupying land, buildings, or factories (right panel).

the national economy and the likelihood of attending a demonstration does not change at different levels of government effectiveness. The interaction term between the Gini Index and distrust in political institutions, in model 6, is positive and statistically significant, meaning that as the level of inequality increases, the association between distrust and the probability of attending a demonstration increases as well. The other two interaction terms indicate that the association between distrust in political institutions and the probability of attending a demonstration does not change as the level of freedom and the level of responsiveness change.

Table 3.2 specifies the estimates of the models predicting the probability of occupying land, buildings, or factories. It seems that women have a lower

Table 3.2 Multilevel Models Predicting the Probability of Occupying Land, Buildings, or Factories

	(6)	(7)	(8)	(9)	(10)
Intercept	−3.873	−3.861	−0.810	−0.549	−0.804
	(0.000)	(0.000)	(0.758)	(0.823)	(0.755)
Woman	−0.332	−0.332	−0.333	−0.333	−0.333
	(0.000)	(0.000)	(0.000)	(0.000)	(0.000)
Age	0.027	0.026	0.027	0.027	0.027
	(0.001)	(0.002)	(0.001)	(0.001)	(0.001)
Age-squared	−0.037	−0.036	−0.036	−0.036	−0.036
	(0.000)	(0.000)	(0.000)	(0.000)	(0.000)
Low education (ref. No education)	−0.099	−0.099	−0.090	−0.090	−0.090
	(0.479)	(0.475)	(0.518)	(0.516)	(0.516)
Middle education	−0.204	−0.207	−0.202	−0.202	−0.202
	(0.031)	(0.029)	(0.033)	(0.033)	(0.033)
High education	−0.016	−0.021	−0.014	−0.014	−0.013
	(0.873)	(0.827)	(0.886)	(0.884)	(0.894)
Still studying	0.153	0.150	0.157	0.156	0.157
	(0.181)	(0.191)	(0.172)	(0.174)	(0.170)
Income	0.036	0.037	0.035	0.035	0.035
	(0.043)	(0.036)	(0.046)	(0.045)	(0.046)
Dissatisfaction with national economic situation	0.018	−0.027	0.020	−0.232	0.020
	(0.478)	(0.323)	(0.438)	(0.374)	(0.435)
Distrust in political institutions	−0.202	−0.237	−0.201	−0.201	−0.172
	(0.000)	(0.000)	(0.000)	(0.000)	(0.394)

(continued)

Table 3.2 Continued

	(6)	(7)	(8)	(9)	(10)
Dissatisfaction with national economic situation × Distrust in political institutions		0.086 (0.000)			
Gini Index			0.008 (0.322)	0.006 (0.537)	0.008 (0.351)
FH Index			−0.127 (0.015)	−0.124 (0.027)	−0.120 (0.029)
GovEff Index			0.282 (0.097)	0.301 (0.078)	0.278 (0.104)
log(GDP per capita)			−0.356 (0.215)	−0.369 (0.169)	−0.359 (0.202)
Dissatisfaction with national economic situation × Gini Index				0.005 (0.366)	
Dissatisfaction with national economic situation × FH Index				−0.005 (0.896)	
Dissatisfaction with national economic situation × GovEff Index				−0.015 (0.778)	
Distrust in political institutions × Gini Index					0.000 (0.971)
Distrust in political institutions × FH Index					−0.014 (0.647)
Distrust in political institutions × GovEff Index					0.011 (0.793)
Random effects					
Standard deviation: country	0.388	0.387	0.465	0.468	0.466
Standard deviation: year	0.380	0.383	0.369	0.369	0.369
BIC	20273	20264	20307	20340	20341
AIC	20150	20132	20147	20151	20152
N	93577	93577	93577	93577	93577

Note: entries are log-odds, *p*-values in parentheses. Number of countries: 18; number of years: 9.

probability of occupying land, buildings, or factories compared with men. Age has the expected curvilinear, yet weak, association with the probability of occupying property. Education has no statistically significant association with the dependent variable; therefore it does not provide useful information to predict participation in this form of action. The absence of association between education and occupying land, buildings, or factories could be due to the fact that this is a risky activity and that higher educated citizens are more able to evaluate the costs of this political action (see Barnes and Kaase 1979; Dalton 2008). As far as income is concerned, while the statistical association is not very strong, it appears that being in a situation of difficulty increases the likelihood of participating in occupying forms of protest.

Examining our central variables of interest, we see that dissatisfaction with the national economic situation is not statistically associated with the likelihood of occupying land, buildings, or factories. Distrust in political institutions is, instead, negatively associated with the dependent variable. This means that a low level of trust decreases the likelihood of occupying land, buildings, or factories. Both coefficients support the hypothesis that the higher the level of dissatisfaction the greater the probability of action. In fact, the literature on Latin America has shown that those who tend to be more involved in protest activities are also those belonging to the lower strata that may show lower levels of satisfaction (see Chalmers et al. 1997). The interaction term, in model 7, between dissatisfaction with the economy and distrust in political institutions has a positive sign, meaning that there is a more complex association between these two variables and the probability of occupation as a form of protest. This association is illustrated in the right-hand panel of Figure 3.3. The association between dissatisfaction with the economy and the probability of occupying land is positive, yet weak, when distrust in political institutions is high, while it is negative when distrust in political institutions is low. Dissatisfaction with the national economy becomes a motivating "mechanism" only when the respondent expresses distrust in political institutions.

Model 8 includes the contextual variables. The right-hand panel of Figure 3.4 shows that as the Gini Index increases the probability of doing this action does not increase very much. Indeed, it has been argued that occupying is a type of action representing a form of popular resistance to claim unproductive properties (see Ondetti 2006). However, despite its positive sign, it seems that in this case the level of inequality does not play a substantial role. The figure also shows that as the Freedom House Index increases the probability of occupying decreases: the extent to which a country is less free depresses the probability of occupying. Occupations of buildings, land, or factories occur less frequently in states in which freedoms are less guaranteed and protected. In fact, less democratic states tolerate to a lesser degree these forms of popular contention and, therefore, tend to contain or repress them (see Dalton et al. 2010). Eventually, as the Government Effectiveness Index increases the probability of occupying increases as well ($p < .10$). When the effectiveness is low the probability of occupying is about .015, when it is high the probabilities becomes .030. As for the case of demonstrations, the association between responsiveness and protest might indicate that citizens in well-functioning political systems use this form of action to make claims, as such states could be more open and able to address their claims. The GDP per capita logarithm however, is not associated with the likelihood of occupying land, buildings, or factories, which could mean that there is no difference in the levels of occupations across states with different GDP levels.

Finally, the last two models in Table 3.2 include the interaction terms between the contextual variables, dissatisfaction with the national economy and distrust in political institutions. None of the interaction terms are statistically significant. The associations between dissatisfaction with the national economy and/or distrust in political institutions and the probability of occupying land, buildings, or factories do not vary across contexts with different levels of inequality, freedom, or responsiveness.

Latin America in Comparative Perspective: Concluding Remarks

In this chapter I have explored the complex relationship between individuals and contexts in Latin America, showing that levels of protest can be explained using a large comparative framework using different levels of analysis. Indeed, contextual variables add information on the characteristics of the countries where citizens perform the protest actions. I argued that contextual factors should be taken into account in order to understand that citizens behave according to macro conditions of the political environments in which they live and that political systems define the opportunity structures for protest.

The analysis showed that in Latin America the propensity of attending a demonstration or occupying land, buildings, or factories varies quite a lot in the 18 countries considered and the period of time used. On the one hand, the relationships between equality, freedom, and responsiveness and the probability of joining the two political actions have the expected signs. On the other, the association between dissatisfaction with the national economy and attending demonstration is stronger in unequal contexts, meaning that inequalities may exacerbate discontent.

But how generalizable are these results, and can they be used to understand the patterns of political protest in other regions? The influences of two qualities of democracies—equality and responsiveness—are worth particular consideration.[7] The rising levels of inequalities and their effect on aggravating discontent as well as on the likelihood of joining protest and public demonstration and participating in occupations of public spaces have been also demonstrated in Middle Eastern and Northern African (MENA) countries before and during the recent waves dubbed the "Arab Spring" (Bayat 2002; Dalacoura 2012). For instance, some scholars have underlined the difficulties of the economies of the Arab countries and their structural problems (Noland and Pack 2007), which likely can be seen as possible causes of the popular mobilization against the regimes. A similar argument regarding the role of social grievances in explaining increasing and broadening levels of dissatisfaction and the surge of the recent revolts has been promoted by Goldstone (2011). Moreover, as shown in this chapter, citizens in Latin American countries have a higher probability to engage in demonstrations when dissatisfaction with the economic performance of their respective regimes is linked to high level of distrust in political institutions. Here, too, it is possible to point to revealing similarities with non–Latin American cases. Level of trust in political institutions has been argued to be an important explanatory intervening factor between socioeconomic-based grievances and level of mobilization for protest. This helps to explain not only variations within a given country—that is, high level of trust in the military yet low level of trust in political parties and ruling politicians, as was the case in Tunisia (Moaddel 2013)—but also cross-country/regime variations when comparing the relatively high level of trust enjoyed by the monarchies (e.g., Jordan and Morocco) with the low level of trust in those autocratic, one-party, presidential systems (e.g., Egypt and Tunisia) (Ardıç 2012).

The analysis of Latin American countries also showed that responsiveness increases the probability of joining protest. Yet, as we have also noted, responsiveness in authoritarian settings or in "new democracies" that still possess some elements from their nondemocratic past must be treated in broader terms that go beyond political institutions to include the military. Indeed, in many of the Latin American countries the military is not only the fulcrum of the regime but also often a central element of responsiveness, perceived by many as capable of coping with nationwide crises and popular discontent vis-à-vis nonresponsive political institutions. The wave of popular mobilization in Brazil is a case in point. The end of the "Brazilian miracle" and the beginning of recession of the early 1980s increased dissatisfaction with the regime, leading labor unions and other movements to mobilize in several mass demonstrations (Haggard and

Kaufman 1995). The divisions within the military between *hard-liners*, in favor of repression, and *soft-liners*, in favor of political liberalization, opened the way for opposition actors such as unions, left parties, and other organizations to gain meaningful standing and voice in the country's political arena (Berins Collier and Mahoney 1999). The inconsistency of the military, in other words, facilitated negotiations between the opposition camp and the authorities, eventually leading to acceptance of the former's demands, and in fact was also a meaningful factor in explaining the low level of violent forms of protest (see Moreira Alves 1989). In Uruguay, despite facing a deeply repressive regime, the democratic opposition surprisingly succeeded in winning the plebiscite on the new constitution drawn by the military. The defeat led to a split within the army, which in the end did not oppose the transition to democracy in a context without a violent opposition (see Linz and Stepan 1996).

Similar dynamics were observed in some Arab countries, such as Tunisia, where the military refused to fire on the demonstrators (Dalacoura 2012). The "military withdrawal" represented an opportunity for protest, as repression was no longer a perceived or actual risk. The military tolerated the mobilization, which may explain why the forms of protest were basically nonviolent actions of civil resistance (Nepstad 2011a). In Egypt, too, the widening distance between Mubarak and the armed forces ultimately played a role in decreasing repression and reinforcing the dissident forces' decision to engage in nonviolent protest (Kandil 2011). Though different in some aspects, the case of Yemen is also indicative of how the role of the military has shaped contention. In fact, the initial repression of protests led to the defection of high-ranking officials produced a fragmentation within the army, which deliberately let the opposition fight Salih's government, eventually contributing to his resignation (Knights 2013).

But if the military's role can be decisive in shaping forms of protest and, in some cases, expediting regime change and transition as a redress of popular grievances and discontent, it is possible to identify opposite scenarios that help explain escalation of protest cycles. We observed this pattern in some of the Latin America countries, such as Chile and Argentina, where the military supported and defended the authoritarian regime during the first phases of mobilization against it, leading to an escalating spiral of violence and eventual crackdown on the protesters (Garretón 1989; Navarro 1989). And we saw a similar pattern in the case of Syria, where the military, by and large, stood behind the regime's unbending and unresponsive response to the protest, leading to a ruthless, still-raging, civil war. In Bahrain too, when the measures taken to reduce discontent and protest—mainly financial concessions and promises of reforms—were revealed to be unsuccessful, the military backed up the regime and repressed the uprising with force (Barany 2011).

To conclude, this chapter argued that equality, freedom, and responsiveness, three democratic qualities, should be considered as part of the larger opportunity structure potential protesters face. These are structural conditions that may contribute to explaining level and forms of popular contention in highly repressive political settings where the conventional aspects or elements of POS are absent. The analysis of Latin America aimed at providing findings useful not only to understand political protest in this area but also to flesh out commonalities with other regions and countries, particularly the MENA countries. For all the undeniable differences in preconditions and other root causes of popular contention in countries of both regions, the point is that there may be similarities in how levels and forms of waves of popular contention emerge as a result of the open-ended and contingent interactions that are inherent to contentious episodes across time and space. This regards the importance of not only examining the interaction between individually related and contextually related factors but also recognizing that the dynamics of contention may bring about changes in those defining features and characteristics of regimes.

Acknowledgements

I thank Leonardo Morlino, the editors of this volume, and anonymous readers for Oxford University Press for comments provided on earlier versions of the chapter.

Notes

1. It might be, of course, also a matter of the state's willingness to accommodate the protesters' requests, not just the state's capacity.
2. Country labels are: Arg, Bol, Bra, Chi, Col, Cri, Dom, Ecu, Slv, Gua, Hon, Mex, Nic, Pan, Per, Pry, Ury, Ven.
3. Indicators measuring participation in other protest actions, such as participation in riots, unauthorized demonstration, or blocking the traffic are available for fewer years.
4. The control variables are gender (the reference category is woman), age and age squared to control for the curvilinear association with the dependent variable, education in categories (no education, which is the reference category, low, middle, high education, and still in education), and subjective income, which ranges from −2 (no difficulty at all) to 2 (great difficulty).

5. Given that the Gini Index has missing values, five multiple imputed datasets are produced using the other macrolevel variables.
6. For difficulties associated with measuring responsiveness, see Powell (2005).
7. For a useful discussion of the influence of freedoms, particularly the existence of civil society groups and organizations, on protest spread and participation, see Vairel (2011) and Kandil (2011).

4

Regimes, Resources, and
Regional Intervention

UNDERSTANDING THE OPENINGS AND TRAJECTORIES
FOR CONTENTION IN THE MIDDLE EAST AND
NORTH AFRICA

Jack A. Goldstone

So Much the Same, Yet So Different

The "Arab Spring" serves as an ideal natural experiment on the nature of revolutions, and in my view goes far toward favoring the state-centered theory of
revolutions as a guide to understanding such events (Skocpol 1979; Goldstone
1991; Goodwin 1997). This may seem an odd argument, inasmuch as most of the
popular and analytic focus on the Arab revolts has been on new modes of media-
driven popular mobilization and a resurgence of ideological expressions regarding everything from personal dignity, human rights, and justice to reclaiming
Islamic identities in the political sphere.

Several authors have emphasized the role of Twitter, Facebook, and satellite news media both in creating rapid flows of information among activists
and potential protestors and in unifying a broad Arab cultural space (cf. Aday
et al. 2012; Howard et al. 2011; Martin 2012; Zuckerman 2011; Lynch 2012;
although Wolfsfeld, Segev, and Sheafer 2013 argue that social media's impact
is limited by the political context, and Brym et al. 2014 claim that Twitter and
Facebook only had a major impact on the relatively few in Arab countries who
were already social-media savvy). Other authors have discussed the transformation of discourse that brought a popular emphasis on dignity and on freedom from dictatorships that ranged from Morocco to Oman (Filali-Ansary

2012). Yet threats to freedom have also been emphasized; observers have fretted that the revolutions would create ideologically rigid new centers of political Islam that would be repressive of women and minorities and be anti-Western in their outlook (Cambridge Union Society 2012; *The Australian* 2011), or that the revolutions would spawn new and even more repressive authoritarian governments (Cole 2014). In addition, scholars have examined the role of youth in these uprisings and the importance of prior labor mobilization in laying the foundation for protests (Cordesman 2011; Schwartz 2011; Lynch 2012; Gunning and Baron 2013).

Yet the thrust of this work is that everywhere across North Africa and the Middle East the conditions existed for popular protest against authoritarian regimes. Large youth cohorts faced high unemployment; families confronted rising prices for staple goods and stagnant incomes; governments were closed and egregiously corrupt; Islamist movements were gaining popular support for their social services and anticorruption stance; and knowledge that these conditions existed and were widespread was flowing through new electronic media—from cell phones and satellite television to Facebook and YouTube. Under such conditions, any number of "triggers"—from an individual setting himself on fire (as with Mohammed Bouazizi in Tunisia), to the brutal death of a young man at the hands of the police (as with Khalid Sa'id in Egypt), to a small peaceful rally on "Police Day" (January 25 in Egypt) aiming to mock and undermine police authority—had the potential to provoke substantial popular mobilization.

And indeed, that is what occurred. In swift succession, popular protests of various sizes and scopes arose everywhere across the Arab world, first in Tunisia, then in Egypt, Libya, Morocco, Algeria, Bahrain, Yemen, Oman, Kuwait, Jordan, Syria, Iraq, Saudi Arabia, and the Palestinian Territories. Yet what resulted from this common foundation of unemployment, inequality, corruption, media links, and protest differed enormously from country to country. In Tunisia, Egypt, and Yemen, cycles of protest grew into rapidly spreading waves, forcing seemingly invulnerable autocrats who had ruled for decades to surrender power, stepping down or fleeing in the face of mounting nationwide popular protests. In Libya and Syria similarly autocratic leaders instead mobilized for war and undertook an all-out military assault on their opponents; Libya's regime failed, but Syria's has so far succeeded in hanging on to power. In Algeria, Iraq, Saudi Arabia, and Bahrain, protests fizzled or were quickly snuffed out. And in Morocco, Oman, Kuwait, and Jordan, monarchs turned to varying degrees of constitutional reform and working with elected parliaments; in these cases reforms appear to have blunted popular protest by deflecting demands for revolt or revolution.

How are we to understand this enormous diversity out of what appear to be very similar fundamental conditions for mobilization? The answer lies in looking more closely at the varying character of the Arab regimes, their resources, and their international contexts. For the Arab states were hardly all similar autocracies struggling with their own people in isolation. Rather, they constituted a wide variety of states that differed in regime type, in the resources available to regimes, in the type and strength of international interventions they would incur, and in their recent experiences with popular mobilization.

Types of Authoritarian Regimes

Although we commonly divide the world into democracies and dictatorships, both of these categories are too broad, too simple, and often too static. Even putting aside the category of "anocracies" or "partial democracies" (Fearon and Latin 2003; Goldstone et al. 2010), often used for in-between type regimes, even governments that are clearly democratic, and those that are clearly autocratic, still differ among themselves *within* these categories in important respects. Democracies differ as to being parliamentary or presidential, centralized or federal, and two-party or multiparty in nature. Scholars have argued over whether these characteristics affect the stability of democracies, but so far no strong conclusions associating types of democratic institutions and stability or longevity have emerged; indeed Adserà and Boix (2007) concluded that the types of democratic institutions had only a marginal impact on regime stability compared to economic and social conditions.

The situation is different for authoritarian regimes. Barbara Geddes (1999; Geddes, Wright, and Frantz 2014) has distinguished a wide variety among them, including personalist, military, and party regimes; monarchies; and various hybrids. Moreover, there is a substantial literature in the theory of revolutions arguing that *personalist* regimes—which feature a dominant individual who came to power by military, party, or even democratic rule but who then subordinated all other political groups and individuals by making them dependent on his favor and patronage—are particularly vulnerable to revolutionary collapse in the event of widespread popular uprisings (Dix 1983; Shugart 1989; Goodwin 1994; Foran 1997; Snyder 1998; Goldstone 2001).

In addition, scholars have noted two other defining characteristics of states that bear on their political trajectories. First, as Michael Ross (2012) has argued, states that control revenues that are easily and secretly controlled, that do not require taxation, and that are large enough to give the state the ability to maintain a large cadre of elite supporters, institutions, and popular largesse, have exceptional resilience against popular demands. Profits from state-controlled fossil fuel resources, mainly oil and natural gas, provide exactly this kind of revenue. Second, as Theda Skocpol (1979) has argued, and others have confirmed (Wickham-Crowley 1992; Foran 2005), a state's position in the international states-system has major consequences for the possibilities of change (a point also affirmed by Alimi and Meyer in this volume). In smaller states, external intervention by regional powers or superpower states can shift outcomes. Strong support for the ruling regime can help it crush oppositions (as in 1848 and 1968 in Eastern Europe). Conversely, strong external support for the rebels or the loss of expected external support from allies of the regime can help a protest movement survive and succeed where it otherwise might have failed.

The conjunction of these three factors, and their variation across states in the Middle Eastern and Northern African (MENA) regions, can help us explain the varying openings and trajectories for revolts in the region. In what follows, I unpack the impacts of regime resources and alliance systems as they combined in their effects on different types of authoritarian regimes.

Explaining Divergent Openings and Trajectories

To better understand the diverse patterns among the Middle East and North African uprisings, we need to focus on the characteristics and the contexts of their regimes.

The Monarchies

Exceptionally among world regions, the MENA regions have a large number of vigorous, active hereditary monarchies that actually rule. These monarchies justify their continued rule by a combination of tradition and descent (often with links to the family of the Prophet Mohammad), and vest ultimate political authority in the head of the royal family, usually with extensive power for other family members (princes) as well (Menaldo 2012; Yom and Gause 2012; Brownlee, Masoud, and Reynolds 2013).

The monarchies of the region can be divided into those with substantial oil resources—Saudi Arabia, Kuwait, Qatar and the Emirates, and Oman—and those where oil revenues are modest or lacking—Bahrain, Morocco, and Jordan. Monarchies have certain advantages compared to personalistic, military, or party regimes when facing popular unrest. Usually, the monarch will have a reservoir of nationalist, ethnic, or religious legitimacy due to their traditional leadership role. They may be supported by a clerical elite that sanctifies their rule, and the ruler himself (or herself in regimes that allow queens to rule) may trace his or her ancestry to a highly charismatic or heroic figure. This core legitimacy may lead popular protest to focus on changing policies or personnel rather than attacking the monarchy itself. To be sure, monarchies sometimes impose themselves on diverse populations, where not all or even a majority of subjects accept the legitimacy of the ruler's position; such is the case in Bahrain (with a Sunni monarchy ruling over a majority Shi'i population), and Jordan (where conflicts in the region brought a large Palestinian population into the Bedouin kingdom). Many, if not most, monarchies also have distinct ethnic or religious minorities who are potential sources of conflict (as with Protestants in Catholic monarchies in Europe, and Shi'a within Saudi Arabia today). Monarchs cope with these issues by working to ensure that the kingdom's political and military elites are drawn from groups that *do* accept and uphold the legitimacy of the monarch and that economic elites owe their success to the monarch's continued support and favor.

In addition, monarchies have the option of sharing power with (and delegating blame to) a prime minister or elected officials, without giving up most of their privileges and power as monarchs. This power sharing can be little more than a fig leaf, as with an elected legislature that is mainly a debating forum and has no real power, or it can involve movement toward a true constitutional monarchy, in which elected officials do have real autonomy and political power and the ruler's prerogatives regarding law and policy are constrained.

Facing conditions of widespread discontent and protest, monarchies in the region took the option of sharing power or deflecting blame to elected officials, but the degree to which they did so depended on the scale of their oil revenues. The oil-poor states (Morocco and Jordan) went the furthest in their reforms; the oil-rich states (Oman, Kuwait, and Saudi Arabia) did the least. Indeed, Saudi Arabia made no significant political reforms at all and instead used its resources to shower gifts on its own population and to finance counter-revolutionary intervention in Bahrain.

Bahrain is one of two countries that demonstrate the critical role of outside intervention (Libya is the other). Bahrain faced perhaps the most massive popular protests ever seen in an authoritarian regime, in proportion to its population. Perhaps one-fifth of the entire country went into the streets to protest the ruling Sunni regime's treatment of the Shi'a majority as second-class citizens with limited rights in their own country. No regime would normally survive protests of such magnitude. Yet Bahrain's Khalifa monarchy survived thanks to massive military, logistic, and financial support from the Sunni kingdom of Saudi Arabia, which made it clear that it would not tolerate a Shi'a popular revolution on its doorstep. The variation in monarchies and their outcomes is shown in Figure 4.1.

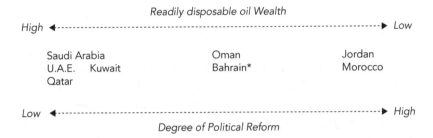

*Counter-revolution assisted by Saudi Arabia external intervention

FIGURE 4.1 Monarchies in the "Arab Spring".

The monarchies can be arrayed from left to right according to the degree to which they have oil resources that can be used to underpin their freedom of action. On the left I have placed the oil-rich regimes, on the right those without oil, and in the middle those with moderate oil resources. As can be seen, the degree of political reform arising in the wake of the Arab revolts is exactly inverse to the level of oil resources, with the exception of Bahrain, where change was arrested by intervention by Saudi Arabia in support of the status quo regime.

The Personalist Regimes

Personalist, sometimes called "sultanist," regimes are both remarkably strong yet remarkably vulnerable to collapse. In personalist regimes, a single individual— who may have begun as an elected leader or head of a military or even party regime—takes control of the national government. This leader will weaken the professional military and official bureaucracy, relying instead on a crony network of business and/or party or family associates to control the economy and government through a tight web of patronage. Because of the key role of patronage, these are sometimes referred to as "neopatrimonial" states (Eisenstadt 1978; Sharabi 1992; Goldstone 2003).

Elsewhere (Goldstone 2003, 70–71) I have described such regimes as partially modernized states in which there appears to be modern bureaucratic and party-based government, but in fact a single powerful person rules society through an extensive system of personal patronage, rather than obedience to impersonal laws. Such states may have democratic trappings, including parliaments, political parties, constitutions, and elections. However, it is recognized by all that the decisions of the chief of state are quite secure, as the patronage system, plus coercion where necessary, secures the compliance of the legislature and the political parties, the favorable interpretation of the constitution, and electoral victories.

Examples include Mexico under Porfirio Díaz, Nicaragua under the Somozas, the Philippines under Ferdinand Marcos, and Iran under the Shah.

In such states, the masses are generally depoliticized. They may participate in periodic elections under the eye of local state servants; however, their interest in the economy and the polity is largely defensive. Their goal is merely to preserve their livelihood, with as little contact with the state authorities as possible. Whether in urban or rural settings, a secure if modest income and traditional habitations and culture are their requisites.

The elites in such states, by contrast, are highly politicized. The chief executive therefore is in a situation where he or she must broker among highly active elite segments. These commonly include traditional oligarchs, new professionals, and military/bureaucratic elites. Traditional oligarchs are generally strong supporters of the state; they usually depend on ownership of land, and while they have traditionally enjoyed the support of the state, they have also controlled their own networks of patronage and coercion. New professionals are the products of the introduction of modern systems of education, law, medicine, and communication. Engineers, journalists, lawyers, doctors, teachers, and businesspeople, they are characteristically rooted in urban settings and have strong contacts with international business and culture. If one adds skilled workers to these groups, they constitute the bulk of the urban middle classes.

The military/bureaucratic elites constitute the arms of the state. However, they are a force unto themselves with their own interests. They may support the old oligarchs, the new professionals, or the chief executive in the event of policy or financial conflicts. Or they may be rendered impotent by internal splits and corruption. Their loyalty to the chief executive varies, for that loyalty too depends on the workings of the patronage system. In short, neopatrimonial states rely on the support of a diverse assemblage of elites, themselves often divided, to maintain authority over a largely depoliticized population.

Such states can be quite resilient as long as the ruler's patronage seems likely to remain a major source of continued power/prestige to their supporting elites. However, they are also quite fragile. This is because unlike monarchies, which have a presumptive traditional legitimacy, and military and party regimes, which rest on strong institutions with corporate identity and resources, personalist regimes have no broader legitimacy. Their stability rests entirely on what the personalist leader can do for his followers. Moreover, because they have no strong institutional basis, they are prone to succession crises; typically the personalist leader will try to devolve power to a family member, typically a son. If the leader should run short of resources, due to a financial crisis, or if the leader's family and inner circle of cronies starts to exclude the wider circle of professional and military/bureaucratic elites from rewards or become too predatory on businesses, the leader can readily lose the loyalty of society's elites. Should the populace rise from its normally depoliticized state and be spurred to mobilize by hardships or anger at the regime's behavior, the leader may suddenly be deserted by the elites on whom he had relied and find himself adrift and forced to step down or flee. The Shah of Iran, the Somozas in Nicaragua, the Diem regime in South Vietnam, Díaz in Mexico, Marcos in the Philippines, Batista in Cuba, Chiang Kai-shek in China, Mobutu in Zaire, and Suharto in Indonesia are examples of chief executives who typified this pattern.

International influence also often plays a major role in the maintenance and vulnerability of such regimes. Over a decade ago, I wrote about this vulnerability in these regimes, noting the following for Marcos in the Philippines, the Shah in Iran, and Somoza in Nicaragua:

> U.S. policy eventually weakened neopatrimonial regimes in three ways. First, overdependence on the United States was encouraged. A massive flow of foreign and military aid often precluded the need for a foreign executive to build a domestic base. Instead, the resource flow encouraged the executive to continue to play the game of selectively dispensing or withholding patronage resources.
>
> Second, overidentification of the chief executive with U.S. aid irritated elites and provoked nationalist opposition to the regime. In the eyes of many elites and popular groups, opposition to the chief executive became synonymous with opposition to the United States and with asserting national self-determination.
>
> Third, while the United States sought to increase the dependence of the chief executive on U.S. aid, it also sought to impose domestic policies that weakened the executive—limits on coercion, greater political expression for professional elites and skilled workers, meaningful elections, and restrictions on corruption. All of these are necessary steps in the democratization of regimes; however, these steps also undermine the power of a dictatorship. U.S. policy thus sought inherently contradictory objectives; choosing neopatrimonial rulers as allies and seeking to support their regimes meant that the overriding goal of U.S. foreign policy—encouraging democratization—was incompatible with keeping these geopolitical allies, for democratization would undermine the rulers that the United States claimed to support.
>
> U.S. policy thus swung back and forth between its contradictory goals. Initially, the United States would support the neopatrimonial rulers with arms and money, while giving only lip service to the goals of greater human rights, political freedom, and democratization in these

states. Later, when the ruler's abuses of power became too visible, the United States would demand that neopatrimonial rulers take action to pursue democratization. These policy swings precipitated disasters by putting neopatrimonial rulers in an impossible position—if they enacted liberalizing reforms, they undermined the basis of their rule; if they did not enact such reforms, they lost the U.S. aid essential to maintaining the patronage that supported their rule. Moreover, such policy swings not only guaranteed that the neopatrimonial rulers would falter, but they also reduced the credibility and influence of the United States with opponents and likely successors of the regime. In times when the United States seemed satisfied with lip service regarding protection of human rights and democratization, the United States came to be viewed by domestic elites and popular groups as an insincere and untrustworthy advocate of popular rights and national self-determination. Thus, in the event that the executive faltered, successor elites were unlikely to view the United States favorably, either as a mediator for succession or as a continuing ally.

Goldstone 2003, 74–75

Although I wrote this as a description of US policy toward the Shah of Iran and the Somoza regime in Nicaragua in the 1970s, it is equally accurate in describing US policy toward the Mubarak regime during the early 2000s. Thus we see both how little US policy had changed and how similar Egypt's prerevolutionary state characteristics were to those of earlier neopatrimonial regimes that were overturned by revolutions.

Quite a number of the authoritarian regimes in the MENA region had devolved into personalist regimes by the late 2000s. This can be seen in the dominance of a single individual who operates above any formal institutions and tends to have marginalized the military, depoliticized the populace, and concentrated affairs in the hands of family members and cronies, oftentimes explicitly seeking to create a familial succession. This describes the regimes of Salih in Yemen, Qadhafi in Libya, Assad in Syria, Ben ʿAli in Tunisia, and Mubarak in Egypt.

Given the critical role of resources in sustaining neopatrimonial regimes, we should expect that oil revenues would make a difference to them as well. Here we find considerable variation among the personalist regimes, just as with the region's monarchies. Yemen and Syria are not major oil producers, but oil contributed a significant source of revenues to the regimes, especially in Yemen, where over 70 percent of government income comes from oil (Index Mundi 2012). In Egypt, by contrast, oil is a small part of the economy, and oil income is almost entirely offset by state subsidies on fuel, thus providing little or no net revenue to the regime. Similarly, oil represents only a sliver of GDP (about 5%)

in Tunisia. Libya is the major outlier among the personalist regimes, with vast oil revenues forming the base of the economy and providing the regime with substantial resources.

If we examine the course of events in the personalist regimes, we see that all show a similar pattern. As the combination of high unemployment, spikes in food prices, withdrawal of state subsidies, a youth surge, media penetration, and elite disgust at ever more narrowly concentrated corruption all contributed to growing popular mobilization and protest, the support of the regimes swiftly crumbled. In Tunisia, where Ben 'Ali's wife and her family had become not only notorious for egregious corruption but also widely hated by the elite for their growing predation on private business, and where the army had long been marginalized, the spread of popular protests soon left Ben 'Ali with no one to defend him. In Egypt, Mubarak's plans to install his son Gamal as his successor were widely resented by the military (who had provided Egypt's leaders for more than half a century). In addition, Gamal's circle of associates was reviled for enjoying outsized economic gains while much of the populace suffered from unemployment and stagnant incomes. When the populace came out into the streets in many cities in unexpectedly large numbers and workers undertook massive strikes, all to demand Mubarak's departure from office, Mubarak, like Ben 'Ali, found that the army would not defend his rule against protestors.

The main difference between Egypt and Tunisia in their subsequent trajectories was due to differences in the role of the military in these societies. In Egypt, where the military had long dominated politics and still played a major role in the economy, Mubarak's departure set the stage for a power struggle among the military, the Islamists (both the Muslim Brotherhood and Salafi parties), and other elements in society. The outcome was polarization between the military and Islamists, with the military winning out and oppressing all other groups. In Tunisia, where the military was smaller, and the officer cadre was a professional and nonpolitical group, the post–Ben 'Ali power struggle involved mainly the Islamist party (Ennahda) and representatives of various civil society groups. There, the Islamists and secular civil society groups were eventually able to agree on a new constitutional regime that was broadly inclusive, and so far appears to be the only fairly democratic regime to emerge in the region.

In Libya, Yemen, and Syria, events began similarly, but the consequent trajectories and outcomes of protest were not as simple, because of both the different resources of the regimes and international intervention. In Libya, when the population of the eastern portion of the country moved from protest to open revolt, the professional military drew back to their barracks, refusing—as in Tunisia and Egypt—to defend a corrupt dictator and his family who were plundering the country. Yet because of his accumulated funds gathered from years of oil exports,

Qadhafi was able to fund in essence a private army, made up of mercenaries from other African states and special "family" brigades under the direct command of his sons. These forces allowed Qadhafi to retain control of the capital and the western portion of the country and to plan a counterattack to recover the eastern provinces. His plans were only halted by the external intervention of NATO forces, which first halted his advances and then slowly destroyed his military capabilities. As it became increasingly clear that international forces were set on preventing Qadhafi from keeping control of Libya by force, the desertion of his former followers—mercenaries, tribes, southern Berbers, and state officials—increased in pace, just as we would expect in a personalist regime that holds power mainly because people have confidence in it as a source of future rewards.

In Yemen, similarly, when popular protests mounted against the regime's corruption and nepotism, the army split and President Salih was forced to negotiate, and eventually to leave the country and surrender his position. However, his oil-fueled patronage network was only partially sundered, and he has been able to return to the country and still exert influence from behind the scenes through his kinsmen. Yet international intervention has played a role here too: Yemen has become a base for al-Qaeda in the Arabian Peninsula (AQAP), and the United States has sought greater freedom to attack AQAP with drones, which has been granted by Salih's successor, President Hadi. With such a strong shift in US support away from Salih, who had previously enjoyed US protection, and toward President Hadi (Mohammed and Lange 2012), it seems likely that Salih will find his support much diminished and he will remain cast out of power. However, the regime has been so weakened by continued infighting that Houthi rebels—who unlike al-Qaeda, were not targeted by US attacks—have been able to move into the capital and dictate terms to Hadi's regime.

The Houthi rebels have displaced Hadi's forces from much of the country. Yet because the Houthi are a non-Sunni sect, the government of Saudi Arabia wants to prevent their coming to power on their borders and thus has used air power and troops in an effort to reverse the Houthi advances and restore the Hadi regime's authority. A long civil war appears to have begun, dividing the country, with no easy ending in sight.

In Syria, the regime had sufficient oil revenues to reward its backers when large parts of the mainly Sunni population engaged in urban revolts—again spurred by high unemployment, blatant corruption, and stagnant wages—against the Assad regime and its core of Alawite military officers and officials. It used those resources to retain support in the core urban areas of Damascus and Aleppo, and to send its army against the urban revolts in other regions. Or it did, until Europe cut off oil imports from Syria. Since then, Syria has faced an increasingly violent civil war that has spread to both Damascus and Aleppo, and taken large portions of northern and southern Syria out of the regime's control, with unknown but significant defections from its military joining the revolt. Several different opposition groups—most notably the Islamic State—now control territory in Syria's northern, southern, and eastern regions.

Yet international intervention again nuances the story. Iran has been vigorous in its support for its fellow Shi'a-ruled ally, providing arms, intelligence, advisors, and financial support, even providing fighters from its partner the Lebanese Hezbollah to fight for the Assad regime. Russia too, desiring to maintain access to its naval facility on Syria's Mediterranean coast and to keep its one remaining ally in the region, has been steadfast in support of Assad, providing advanced weapons, troops, and air strikes against his opponents.

It is common in revolutions for the breakdown of order to encourage the emergence of radical, ruthless, and ideologically driven groups who struggle against moderates to seize power. The Jacobins in the middle years of the French Revolution, the Bolsheviks in the Russian Revolution of 1917, and the Mao-led communists in China in the 1930s are familiar examples. In Syria, DA'ISH (or the "Islamic State") has similarly emerged, and extended its reach into Iraq. DA'ISH is a harshly conservative Islamist group, which seeks to create a new Caliphate that emulates the expansionist and orthodox state created by the Prophet and his followers. DA'ISH has combined this ideology with the most modern tactics and tools, including suicide bombings and internet postings of ritual beheadings, along with tapping numerous financial resources from oil sales to extortion, to build an effective, coercive military state.

DA'ISH's extremist ideology and terror tactics, spread both in the Middle East and abroad, have made it many enemies. Yet in Syria Assad has focused mainly on fighting the moderate opposition, while Iraq and Iran have been more interested in sustaining Shiite regimes than in teaming up with Sunni forces to attack DA'ISH. Turkey remains reluctant to support Kurdish groups fighting DA'ISH, for fear that Kurdish gains will promote autonomy or independence efforts by Kurds within Turkey, while Saudi Arabia's military has been bogged down in the civil war in Yemen. Western powers have carried out only air strikes against DA'ISH for fear that engaging ground troops would leave them embroiled in a long war similar to that the United States endured in Iraq and Afghanistan. DA'ISH's enemies thus have been divided and restrained. As a result, DA'ISH seems likely to remain a potent ideological and military force.

In short, the single best key to where regimes in MENA have been overturned or faced massive rebellions is where personalist regimes have arisen. In contrast to the monarchies, which all have either survived with reforms or even become counterrevolutionary, the personalist regimes have all crumbled—with the partial exception of Syria, although Syria's al-Assad regime has lost control

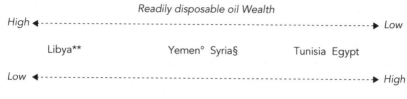

Readily disposable oil Wealth

High ◀--▶ Low

Libya**   Yemen° Syria§   Tunisia Egypt

Low ◀--▶ High

Ease and Speed of Regime Collapse

**Collapse hastened by major intervention by NATO

°Collapse slightly hastened by intervention by the United States

§Collapse delayed by favorable intervention by Russia and Iran

FIGURE 4.2 Personalist regimes in the "Arab Spring".

of much of its country and population, and has survived in large part because of external intervention from Russia and Iran. Events in the personalist regimes have generally unfolded as in prior revolutions, with civil wars (Libya, Syria, Yemen), military counter-revolutions (Egypt), and the rise of radical groups imposing terror (DA'ISH) all emerging. Only in Tunisia, with its much more developed pre-revolutionary civil society and professional and labor organizations, have events (so far) unfolded more like the democratic transitions of 1989 in Eastern Europe.

Among these regimes, the relative ease with which they were overthrown depended on the availability of oil revenues and the impact of international actions. The variation in the personalist regimes and their trajectories and outcomes is shown in Figure 4.2.

The Rest of the Region

It has seemed odd to many that the Arab states not yet mentioned—Lebanon, the Palestinian Authority (PA), Iraq, and Algeria—were hardly touched by the wave of protests that erupted in the "Arab Spring". After all, again we find the same general conditions that prevailed elsewhere in the Middle East: young and underemployed populations, stagnating living standards, and highly corrupt regimes. Yet except for a few minor public protests that quickly petered out, these states showed little in the way of upheaval (Lynch 2012). To be sure, there was a major conflict in Gaza, but that was started by rocket attacks by the Hamas organization, not by popular protests against local authorities.

This too can be explained by a focus on the state, rather than on the conditions behind popular protests. The countries where the "Arab Spring" had its impact were monarchies and personalist regimes. In both types, the broader populace had been largely depoliticized and passive under the heel of corrupt and authoritarian regimes for decades. The "Arab Spring" was a call to become actively political, to reclaim dignity through action and protest against authoritarian regimes that had been passively accepted for too long.

Yet this was not the situation in the remaining states. All of these—Lebanon, the PA, Iraq, and Algeria—had only recently been convulsed by mass uprisings and civil wars against their regimes. The Cedar Revolution in Lebanon, the multiple intifadas in the PA, the sectarian and anti-American war in Iraq, and the Islamist civil war in Algeria were all still fresh in memory. Given these massive uprisings, the populace in these nations did not need to act to reclaim their dignity.

Quite the reverse: these major conflicts had led to so many deaths, and to new or reinforced regimes, that people in these countries knew they could gain little simply by popular protests. Lebanon, the PA, and Iraq had become flawed partial democracies, far from truly free but also not the simple dictatorships that prevailed in other states. In Algeria, a corporatist military regime prevailed, reinforced by major oil wealth. The situation in these countries was so different, from the perspective of the character of their states relative to monarchies or personalist regimes, that it should be no surprise that they were hardly touched by the "Arab Spring".

From Mobilization to Political Opportunity Structures and Beyond

The popular accounts of the Arab Revolts, which stress rising prices and other grievances, a youth bulge, and access to social media are, often without realizing it, harking back to the group mobilization theory of Charles Tilly (1978). Tilly argued that aside from grievances, social protest needed conditions supporting group mobilization, and mechanisms for organization, to succeed. Tilly's view was later supplemented by the work of Doug McAdam and his coauthors (McAdam 1982; McAdam, McCarthy, and Zald 1996) studying American social movements, who developed the multidimensional political opportunity structure approach. McAdam and his colleagues argued that in addition to conditions favoring mobilization, protest success required an "opportunity structure" consisting of a state that was vulnerable and a narrative or cognitive view that provided protestors confidence that they could succeed. The exact components of opportunity structure have been much debated (Gamson and Meyer 1996; Goodwin and Jasper 1999; Goldstone 2004; Tarrow 2011) and expanded to include multilevel opportunities and shocks to social action fields (Fligstein and McAdam 2012).

Most of the work on political opportunity structures has analyzed protest in democracies, whether in Europe or America, where the flexibility of political structures and the diversity of actors has made it difficult to pin down the precise elements that made for "opportunity," and instead led scholars to point to multiple mechanisms behind social movements' emergence and the trajectories and outcomes of their protest efforts (McAdam, Tarrow, and Tilly 2001). However, for autocratic regimes—or at least those of MENA in the early 21st century surveyed in this essay—it seems we can narrow down the key elements of political opportunity to a few.

It is clear from this empirical study that the key factors determining opportunities for protest, and the subsequent trajectories and outcomes of protest, were the *kind of authoritarian regime*, the regime's *financial resources* as related to state-controlled oil and/or natural gas production, and the balance of *interventions from the international system*. These factors acting in conjunction seem to have decisively shaped the field of regime–protest interactions. Indeed, the relative simplicity of authoritarian regimes, with a single focus of power, makes it easier to identify these specific factors as crucial, as compared to the more complex shifting fields of political parties, local and national elected leaders, other autonomous elites, and more specific cause-oriented social movements typical of protest in democracies.

For state-centered theories of revolution (Skocpol 1979; Goldstone 1991; Goodwin 1997), a common observation is that while grievances are widespread and commonly found across different countries and different social groups, the emergence of large-scale protest is rare, and its success is rarer still. In this approach, the crucial feature determining protest trajectories and outcomes is how the dynamics of protest are shaped by the resources and actions of the regime and international system. The Arab Revolts of 2011 exemplify these relationships perfectly, allowing us to explain, with parsimony and reasonable accuracy, across a wide region with similar mass grievances and mobilization, why some regimes were swept away while others survived, and why some reformed while others remained unchanged.

PART II

Processes and Trajectories of Contention

5

The Drivers of Diffusion

COMPARING 1989, THE COLOR REVOLUTIONS,
AND THE ARAB UPRISINGS

Valerie Bunce

WHY AND HOW do waves of popular protest against authoritarian rulers
travel from one authoritarian regime to others in the same region? Thus far, the
answers to this question have usually been based on the analysis of one wave—for
example, 1848 in Europe or the more recent cases of the collapse of communism
in the Soviet Union and Eastern Europe from 1987 to 1990, the color revolutions
in postcommunist Europe and Eurasia from 1996 to 2009, and the ongoing Arab
uprisings (see, for example, Weyland 2010; Brown 1991; Stokes 1993; Bunce 1999;
Beissinger 2002; Forbrig and Demes 2007; Bunce and Wolchik 2011; Lynch
2011; but see Bunce and Wolchik 2013; and Weyland 2014).

The purpose of this chapter is to compare the three recent waves with one
another and thereby develop a more rigorous assessment of mechanisms that support the cross-national diffusion of popular challenges to authoritarian rulers.
I evaluate in particular the role of the two drivers that figure prominently in the
literature on diffusion. One is demonstration effects, or the argument that the
establishment of an innovative precedent in one site leads sympathetic observers in other sites to recalculate the potential for change and emulate that precedent. The other is transnational networks, or coalitions among international
and domestic actors that develop, apply, and transfer a particular innovation.
While the first driver is largely structural and rests in large measure on unintended influences associated with the introduction of an innovation, the second
driver is largely agency-based and presumes a much more orchestrated process.

As we will discover, both drivers played a role, albeit to different degrees, in
1989, the color revolutions, and the Arab uprisings of 2011. Thus, we do not have

to choose between these rival explanations of what propels the spread of popular mobilizations against authoritarian rulers among states. At the same time, however, the inability of the two drivers to answer certain questions, in combination with some patterns that emerged in our analysis of the three waves, leads us to identify a third driver that has not received any attention in the literature. Thus, in the early stages of these waves, whether they took place in the communist, postcommunist, or Arab world, the dynamic moved to a pivotal case that was much better positioned in comparison with the "early riser" to redefine the repertoire of contention and to broadcast popular uprisings to a much larger swath of the region (see Beissinger 2002, for the terminology). In this way, "one small revolution"—as Robert Kaplan (2011), assuredly to his regret, characterized the Tunisian uprising on the eve of the eruption of large-scale protests in Egypt—becomes a much more ambitious geographical project (and on regional effects on diffusion, see, for example, Hurrell 1995; Mainwaring and Perez-Linan 2005, 2014).

We begin our analysis by mapping out the theoretical terrain of this study. In particular, we define diffusion, highlight its key characteristics, and summarize the literature on what drives this dynamic.

Diffusion and Its Drivers

We can begin our analysis by defining diffusion, which is the transfer of an innovation—for example, a new product, policy, institution, or repertoire of behavior—among multiple units, such as enterprises, organizations, and countries. What is distinctive about diffusion, therefore, is that it is a horizontal dynamic; that is, one where similar changes in a group of units occurs, not because each one faces similar problems and opportunities, but, rather, because the units interact with one another. What this typically means in practice is that innovative precedents set in one site increase the likelihood that these precedents will be adopted in other sites. As a result, diffusion is responsible for sponsoring new and similar developments that take on the distinctive pattern of clustering over time and across space (see, for example, Beissinger 2002; Givan, Soule, and Roberts 2010; Bockman and Eyal 2002; Weyland 2010; McAdam 1993; Wehnert 2005; Strang and Soule 1998).

What drives this process of serial emulation? While this is an issue for all diffusion processes, it is particularly important for the waves of interest in this study. This is because there are so many compelling reasons why popular uprisings in authoritarian regimes should not take place, and, if happening to occur, should "stay put." Here, I refer, for example, to the formidable constraints on collective action in general, and in authoritarian regimes in particular, and the elaborate and tested strategies that authoritarian rulers have developed to pre-empt rebellion, whether by mass publics or by members of their ruling circle (see, e.g., Alimi 2009; Bunce 2014; Koesel and Bunce 2013). In the face of large-scale popular threats to their rule, moreover, democratic leaders have also been known to deploy similar strategies for demobilization of the citizenry. This "blurring" of the boundaries between types of regimes in difficult political times is an issue that is addressed in greater detail in the introduction to this volume.

The literature on diffusion has identified two drivers that have been present in diffusion processes, irrespective of types of regimes or types of challenges to the status quo. One is demonstration effects, which refers to the ability of an innovation introduced in one site to lead actors in other sites to become more optimistic about change and to model their actions on the behavior of their counterparts in the trailblazing case. While a seemingly straightforward process, especially as it has usually been applied by scholars to waves that have already taken place and thereby appear relatively effortless, demonstration effects depend in fact on the presence of some stringent preconditions. This is especially the case, more-over, when we focus on the spread of popular protests against authoritarian rulers. One precondition is that the outbreak of protests at the beginning of the dynamic must be viewed by citizens in neighboring countries as successful and relatively low risk—or at the least much less risky and more likely to succeed than observers thought prior to the establishment of the precedent. Otherwise, why experiment with emulation? A second condition is that the ensemble of innovative actions is viewed by potential adopters as relatively amenable to cross-national transfer. Thus, if the approach is too demanding in terms of its requirements, the actions are unlikely to invite outside observers to join the process.

The third condition for demonstration effects is that potential emulators must believe that their local situation bears important similarities to the contexts within which the initial protests erupted and succeeded. Turning once again to the case of popular uprisings against authoritarian rulers, we would expect that cross-national diffusion is more likely to occur when countries share, for example, a common culture; types and extent of popular grievances; political and economic systems; and/or historical experiences. Indeed, the importance of such cross-national similarities and the ways that they facilitate the drawing of instructive lessons for future action help explain why cross-national diffusion dynamics, whatever the innovations involved, tend to be phenomena describing the behavior of neighboring countries, countries located within the same region, or countries located in different regions that, for historical reasons, such as colonialism and culture, are nonetheless connected to one another, albeit less in a geographical sense (Weyland 2014). However, there are important constraints on the power of cross-national similarities, especially with respect to the spread of popular protests against authoritarian rulers. Some authoritarian leaders are more popular and/or more willing and able to co-opt challengers and to use force than others. Moreover, in part because of the strategies that authoritarian regimes have used to stay in power and oppositions have crafted in order to survive in difficult political circumstances, citizens can quite understandably view oppositions in negative ways; that is, as unpatriotic, corrupt, incompetent, and, therefore, unworthy of support. Why would citizens, as a result, take on the risks associated with supporting the opposition? In addition, in authoritarian regimes that rely on patronage (which is usually the case—see the chapter by Goldstone in this volume), citizens who decide to join protests must be willing to forfeit the benefits they receive from the regime for the unknown benefits that they would gain from a new regime. Finally, strong national identities can prevent citizens from modeling their actions on the disruptive behavior of citizens in other regimes. As Anthony Marx (2005) has persuasively argued, nationalism is always an exclusionary, as well as an inclusionary political project. It draws boundaries between states (and often within them) that are usually based on claims of difference and uniqueness. Both characteristics inhibit citizens from treating precedents set in other countries as lessons that should inform their future behavior.

Studies of the spread of new international norms and neoliberal economic ideology from the West to "the rest," however, have introduced a second mechanism that can drive diffusion: transnational networks (see, for instance, Bunce and Wolchik 2011; Keck and Sikkink 1998; Tarrow 2005; and Bockman and Eyal 2002). This term refers to the role of national and international actors who, for reasons of values, interests, and expertise, design an alternative to the status quo, form coalitions to promote that alternative, and collaborate with each other to diffuse these new ideas and practices among sites. Such coalitions can be formal or informal, governmental or nongovernmental, and they often grow as they travel by bringing in new recruits. As with demonstration effects, moreover, so in the case of transnational networks there are factors that encourage and impede the operation of this driver. On the one hand, international economic and political-military assistance often requires expanded contacts between international and national nongovernmental organizations, and such contacts can signal a tolerance for pluralism that reduces tensions between authoritarian regimes and opposition groups. Moreover, building on the earlier point about the power of similarities among countries in encouraging emulation, we can suggest that, just as transnational networks are more likely to develop and grow in contexts featuring neighboring countries and/or countries that share a number of traits, so key players within these networks can define their mission as one that applies to a group of countries that they see as similar to each other. In this way, it can be suggested that "neighborhood" effects can be built into why and how transnational networks promote their innovations. On the other hand, fears of popular unrest can lead authoritarian rulers to insulate their citizens from the threats posed by transnational networks by, for example, exerting greater control over state boundaries and orchestrating campaigns in support of both nationalism and the international norm of state sovereignty. In this sense, there are some limits to the power of transnational networks to diffuse change across national boundaries precisely because of the visibility of this mechanism in contrast to demonstration effects. That recognized, however, prudent authoritarian rulers take defensive action, whether the driver behind diffusion is demonstration effects or transnational networks.

With these drivers and their limitations in mind, we can now turn to an overview of each of our waves and an assessment of what drove them. We begin with 1989.

1989 and Demonstration Effects

The mass protests that led to the fall of communism began in fact in two places: the Soviet Union in 1987, when popular fronts in support of perestroika arose and proliferated in the Russian and Baltic republics (a process that was encouraged by Gorbachev in his struggle to reform the Soviet system) and Slovenia (a republic with Yugoslavia), when a student movement formed that, by entering the forbidden zone of criticizing the military, took on both the Yugoslav state and the regime (see, for example, Bunce 1999; Glenn 2001; Joppke 1995; Stokes 1993; Beissinger 2002). Protests then broke out in Poland in the fall of 1988 and culminated in an unprecedented development: the convening of a roundtable between the opposition and the Party that took place in the early months of 1989 and that created a transitional regime with some liberal features. However, semicompetitive elections held in June 1989 led, by August of that year, to an unthinkable development: the formation of an opposition-led government that then laid the groundwork for a rapid transition to democracy. The Polish roundtable, therefore, was the first case in 1989 where popular challenges to authoritarian rule led to regime change.

The Polish precedent, coupled with the considerable loosening of strictures on political change in Eastern Europe as a result of the Gorbachev reforms, was powerful enough to lead in the late summer of 1989 to a roundtable in Hungary. Here, there was more detailed planning for a democratic future, including plans (that were subsequently implemented) to hold fully competitive elections in the following year. In the fall of 1989 (after the two roundtables had concluded), massive protests then broke out in East Germany, which were then followed by similar developments in Czechoslovakia. Protests, albeit smaller, then erupted in Bulgaria, Romania, and Albania. At the same time, the protests within the Soviet Union and Yugoslavia continued as well.

How important were our two drivers in the 1989 wave? There is little doubt that demonstration effects played a critical role in propelling the spread of popular challenges to communist party rule. In particular, *all* of the key components of demonstration effects, as outlined earlier, were in place: (1) the establishment of successful and low-cost precedents by early risers; (2) the development of portable approaches to challenging authoritarian incumbents, and; (3) the existence of important similarities between the trailblazing cases and other regimes in the region. Central to all of these developments, of course, were the actions of the Soviet leadership. It was not simply that Gorbachev encouraged the rise of popular fronts in support of perestroika (in part because he was gaining little traction with his reform agenda); supported the pathbreaking Polish roundtable and even favorable stories of Lech Walesa in Soviet newspapers; chided the hard-line East German and Romanian regimes (both of which, in contrast to other regimes in the region, regularly censored his speeches) before protests broke out in them; refused to support the East German regime when the Hungarian government allowed the defection of East German tourists to the West at the end of the summer of 1989; and stood aside while massive protests erupted in East Germany, Czechoslovakia, and other countries in Eastern Europe (see, especially, A. Brown 1996). It was also that, in the early part of the wave, regimes did not use force to defend themselves. This was largely because control over such actions resided in Moscow, not the capital of each of the Eastern European countries—though this was not true for Albania, Romania, and Yugoslavia, and this was precisely why these three transitions involved violence.

However, the role of the Soviet Union in these processes should not be reduced to a "silver bullet," given the importance in the 1989 dynamic of the two other factors that encouraged demonstration effects. One was the clear evidence provided early in the process that the model was both successful and transferable. For example, just as the initial protests within the Russian and Baltic republics spread quickly to the Caucasus as well, so the Polish roundtable approach moved rapidly to Hungary. Here, however, we need to highlight the contrast between these two forms of challenges to communist party hegemony. With respect to the first factor: during the communist era there had been in fact a number of dress-rehearsals of antiregime mobilizations, especially in Yugoslavia, Poland, and Hungary and, to a lesser extent, Czechoslovakia, East Germany, and Romania. These prior rounds of protest did not just produce in the first four countries in particular a ripened opposition and in the first three more pluralist and less politically and economically invasive communist parties but also, more generally, familiarity with the protest model, including its geographical design, such as the focus on large squares and the capital cities (see Kenney 2002; and note the similarities to Egypt, as Patel [2012] has noted). At the same time, Poland and Hungary featured ideal conditions for the invention of a new model, the roundtable, because of their distinctive combination of economic crises, large and well-defined oppositions, and liberal communist parties.

Finally, as the arguments already made suggest, it was relatively easy in the Soviet Union and Eastern Europe for citizens in general and oppositions in particular to find the developments in the "early risers" highly relevant to their own situations and therefore highly instructive insofar as their calculations about future actions were concerned. While one can debate how meaningful the concept of geographical region is as a result of variations within and among the countries sharing it, one would be less likely to convene such a discussion when the region at hand was the Soviet Union and Eastern Europe (see, for example, Mainwaring and Perez-Linan 2005, 2014). Obviously, there were substantial differences in the cultures of the countries making up the region. However, the communist experiment had homogenized the region in critical ways. As argued by Zvi Gitelman (1974) 15 years before the collapse of communism, the Soviet bloc was in fact ideally configured to support cross-national diffusion, whether of approaches to, say, economic reforms or the propensity to challenge authoritarian rule (and see Bunce 1999). This was because of the existence of unusually similar political-economic systems throughout the region as a result of Stalinization; the political-economic and military integration of the region as a consequence of membership in the Council for Mutual Economic Assistance and the Warsaw Pact; and the role of the Soviet Union as the enforcer of the bloc's boundaries, the guarantor of local communist party rule, and the key provider of markets and energy. These similarities and the dependence of the Eastern European regimes on the Soviet Union, moreover, had already been demonstrated before 1989—for example, following the death of Stalin the reactions of the Soviet Union to the spread of protests from Czechoslovakia and East Germany in 1953 to Poland and Hungary through 1956. Finally, precisely because of these factors and the facts that the Soviet Union was hegemonic in Eastern Europe and the latter provided early evidence of the limitations of the Soviet political and economic model, the Soviet Union and Eastern Europe were ideally configured to encourage protest and its movement across state boundaries. The communist experiment, in short, alienated citizens while lowering the "national fences" that in most regions contain the spread of change.

Before we leave the discussion of similarities among the communist regimes in the Soviet Union and Eastern Europe and the ways in which they supported cross-national diffusion, however, we need to note another commonality that is less structural in nature and that, interestingly enough, will reappear in the analysis that follows of our other two waves. This is the fact that all of the countries that made up the communist region in 1989 were either governed by new leaders who were still in the process of consolidating their power (the Soviet Union, Albania, and Czechoslovakia) or very long-serving leaders who were likely to leave power in the near future (East Germany, Romania, Bulgaria, Poland, and Hungary). As studies of communist politics and, more recently, of the postcommunist region and other parts of the world have demonstrated, succession periods, whether involving elections or other means of selecting leaders, are strongly correlated with regime change and the outbreak of political protests (Bunce 1981; Bermeo 2003; Pop-Eleches and Robertson 2015; McAdam and Tarrow 2010; Trejo 2012).

Transnational Networks

Transnational networks also played a role in these events, but not one that was as paramount as demonstration effects. This was largely because of three factors. One was the relative absence of technology that could facilitate cross-state connections among publics and among dissident groups in the Soviet Union and Eastern Europe. Another was that, with the exception of Yugoslavia and to a lesser extent Poland and Hungary, the communist version of authoritarianism prevented not just contacts with the West, but also cross-border contacts among opposition groups and ordinary citizens. Finally, there was no outside actor that could enhance in any consistent manner the ability of protest communities to challenge these regimes by, for example, transferring resources and ideas to them or facilitating their connections with one another. Most obviously, the Soviet Union would not play that role. However, the United States also refrained from such actions, in part because of the inconsistent support of the United States for democratic change at this time and in part because of its desire to promote stability by accepting Soviet control over Eastern Europe.

These constraints on the formation of transnational networks notwithstanding, there were nonetheless several developments during the last decade and a half of the communist experiment in the Soviet Union and Eastern Europe that began to lay some of the groundwork for the rise of transnational networks that supported opposition to communist party rule. One was the Helsinki Process, and another was the formation of various international groups supporting an end to or at least a slowdown in the arms race. In both cases, collaborations evolved between local oppositions and their external supporters (Bunce 1999; Evangelista 1999; Thomas 2001). For example, the Helsinki Process generated the formation of groups within some of the countries in the region that monitored human rights and that served as a launching pad (and a protective cover) for the consolidation of national dissident communities, especially in more repressive regime contexts in the region. Another factor that facilitated the rudimentary development of transnational networks in the region prior to the collapse of communism was growing contacts in the second half of the 1980s between national dissident communities located in the "softer" regimes in the region (especially Poland and Hungary). These contacts, like those supported by Helsinki and the antinuclear movement, involved exchange of information and discussions of goals and strategies. They also led dissidents (especially the Czechoslovaks) to define their goals in regionwide terms, including advocacy on behalf of oppositions operating in more repressive regimes in the region, such as Romania. At the same time, it is important to note that the rise of Solidarity in Poland in 1980 had exerted important influences on opposition development throughout the region, including the Baltic States (Vardys 1983).

Finally, in the first half of the 1980s, US foreign policy began to undergo significant shifts—shifts that in fact built on a similar rethinking of US policies that had taken place during the Carter administration, but that had been countered by the Soviet invasion of Afghanistan in 1979. These changes in the direction of actively supporting democratic change in authoritarian regimes occurred in part because of the lessons drawn from two events that challenged the value and the future of US alliances with dictators: the popular mobilization against Marcos in the Philippines in 1986 and the mobilization against the Pinochet government in Chile in 1988. A key component of this shift was the founding of the National Endowment for Democracy, the International Republican Institute, the National Democratic Institute, and the Free Trade Union Institute—four nongovernmental organizations (but funded by US taxpayers) that were committed to supporting democratic change in authoritarian regimes (and see Domber 2008).

Just as these networks were very loose and always under threat, so the resources provided by the United States were limited. As a result, it is fair to conclude that demonstration effects, far more than transnational networks, played the key role in diffusing popular challenges to communist party rule in the Soviet Union and Eastern Europe.

The Color Revolutions

We can now turn to the second wave of interest in this chapter: the diffusion of the color revolutions from 1990 to 2009 (see Bunce and Wolchik 2011; Forbrig and Demes 2007). This diffusion dynamic began in Bulgaria in 1990, where the opposition, despite substantial external assistance, failed in their mission to defeat the communists in the first competitive election held in that country after the purported "fall" of communism. Six years later three key developments took place that laid the groundwork for democratic change: a united opposition in Serbia led unusually large-scale and long-lasting protests that contested the official claim that regime-backed candidates had won the local elections; protests erupted in Bulgaria, which paved the way for new elections that the opposition managed to win; and the opposition in Romania came together and finally succeeded in defeating the communist incumbent. This subregional hothouse of political change, no doubt encouraged by the fact that these three countries bordered one another, laid the groundwork for the next stage in this diffusion process. This was the Slovak election in 1998, where the opposition did not just unite (as it had in the other countries), but also, with the help of the international democracy assistance community, carried out a remarkably sophisticated campaign to win power that rested, for example, on such electoral innovations as encouraging young people to become more active in politics, forging close ties between opposition parties and nongovernmental organizations (NGOs), and conducting ambitious voter registration and turnout drives.

The Slovak model, which was strongly influenced by opposition efforts along similar lines in the Philippines in 1986 and Chile in 1988 (and see the chapter by Sznajder in this volume), was then adopted by oppositions in a series of other countries in the region, where it either succeeded, as in Slovakia, in replacing authoritarian leaders with leaders of the opposition (Croatia, Serbia, Georgia, Ukraine, and Kyrgyzstan) or failed to do so (as in Azerbaijan, Armenia, and Belarus). There were several reasons for these contrasting outcomes, but the most important one was the impact of successful precedents on the calculus of oppositions versus regimes in neighboring countries. Thus, as the wave progressed, while oppositions increasingly underestimated what the model required in order to succeed, authoritarian rulers, coding these developments as existential threats, went to increasing lengths to preempt these kinds of popular challenges to their rule. Beginning with the Serbian presidential election in the fall of 2000, moreover, the model was amended, because of a very repressive political context, to include significant mobilizations after the election to force the authoritarian incumbent to admit defeat. This was precisely the approach that was used subsequently in Georgia, Ukraine, Kyrgyzstan, Azerbaijan, Armenia, and Belarus.

Drivers of the Color Revolutions

To what extent do our two drivers of diffusion explain the spread of the color revolutions? There is little doubt that demonstration effects played some role in the spread of these electoral innovations throughout postcommunist Europe and Eurasia. For example, based on interviews conducted by myself and

Sharon Wolchik with opposition groups, it is clear that the early precedents set by the electoral defeats of authoritarian incumbents or their anointed successors encouraged opposition groups in other countries to focus on elections as a key site for political change and to adopt some of the strategies that the oppositions in, say, Slovakia had used to wrest power from Vladimir Meciar. However, the case for demonstration effects is weaker once we turn our attention to the other components of this driver of diffusion; that is, the portability of the model and similarities among countries within the region. It is hard in fact to make a case that the electoral model moved with ease and in effect "by itself" from Bulgaria, Romania, and Slovakia to other countries in the region. This is because oppositions in this part of the world had never used such strategies to win power and therefore could not build on past practices. At the same time, the Slovak model was far more demanding in what it required of oppositions, civil society groups, and ordinary citizens than was the case for either the protest or roundtable models of 1989. While implemented by local actors, therefore, the electoral model required the assistance of transnational networks.

It is also hard to make the case for strong similarities among the regimes that became sites for these electoral challenges—or at least similarities to the degree that we found for 1989. For example, after 1989 there was no Soviet bloc. Thus, the regimes and states in the region that emerged from the rubble of communism had no common ideology or political or economic system. Moreover, even if we focus specifically on the participants in this wave, which have been commonly termed competitive authoritarian regimes, we find again significant variation—for example, levels of regime repression, the extent of electoral competition, the size and influence of the opposition, and the age of the state. These and other distinctions meant that the kinds of cross-national similarities that had created the optimal conditions for hosting a regionwide wave in 1989 were absent in the case of the color revolutions.

In contrast to 1989, as a result, the most important mechanism driving the diffusion of the color revolutions was the role of transnational networks. These networks were composed of members of the US (and to some extent European, especially in Slovakia) democracy assistance community, local oppositions (including parties and NGOs), and "graduates" of previous rounds of these electoral confrontations who then took their experiences and expertise to new theaters of operation. These networks were responsible, first, for inventing the electoral model by drawing in part on the experiences of opponents to the Marcos regime in the Philippines and the Pinochet in Chile in the second half of the 1980s (see Bunce and Wolchik 2011). However, the role of this transnational network went further. It also involved implementation of these changes on the ground in each of the countries that participated in the diffusion process and the transfer of the model from one country to others in the region.

There were two reasons why transnational networks were so important to the diffusion of the color revolutions. One was that, as already noted, the model was very complex, and its application, as a result, depended on extensive training as well as the infusion of resources. At the same time, removing authoritarian leaders from office in the second wave was a more difficult proposition than it would immediately appear. A competitive authoritarian regime is typically a moving political target that inhibits the ability of publics to crystallize evaluations of the regime and of oppositions to converge on a common set of strategies. A key goal of this electoral approach, therefore, is to unite a fractious opposition and to convince a public skeptical about the prospects for change and the opposition's willingness and ability to promote change to switch political sides and to do so publicly.

Second, there was no equivalent after the collapse of communism to an external actor, such as the Soviet Union, that was in a strong position to influence regionwide developments. As a result, the game of politics in the communist era was different than it was in the postcommunist period. Under communism, for example, there was no debate about who the enemy was; the relationship of publics to the regime was remarkably similar among the states that made up the region; and there was a consensus in many countries, especially in Eastern Europe, around opposition to the regime. By contrast, none of these arguments apply to competitive authoritarian regimes (Levitsky and Way 2010). While admittedly vulnerable because they tolerate regular and competitive elections (albeit on an uneven playing field), these regimes endure because of their ability to muddy the struggle for power.

The Arab Uprisings

The final case of diffusion addressed in this study is the ongoing antiregime mobilizations in the Middle East and North Africa (MENA) (see, for instance, Patel, Bunce, and Wolchik 2014; Lynch 2011). This process began in Tunisia with the self-immolation of a street vendor at the end of 2010—an action that led quickly, much to the surprise of virtually all observers, to the rise of large-scale protests that moved from rural areas and smaller cities to the capital, Tunis, and that succeeded very quickly in forcing Ben 'Ali to change his address to Saudi Arabia. The Tunisian precedent prompted a few individuals in several countries in the region to also set themselves on fire, though without setting in motion the same dynamics. However, once large-scale protests erupted in Alexandria and Cairo and succeeded in ending the long rule of Husni Mubarak in Egypt, popular mobilizations against authoritarian rulers then spread to Bahrain, Yemen, Libya, and Syria, while encouraging smaller-scale and more short-lived actions in Morocco, Algeria, Oman, and Jordan. As in 1989, street actions, rather than elections (though the Egyptian opposition had experimented to a limited degree with this approach in 2010), as in the color revolutions, served as the venue in this wave of popular challenges to authoritarian rule. Like the earlier two waves, moreover, the repertoires publics used to challenge authoritarian leaders also changed early in the MENA wave. Thus, the Egyptian approach—for example, the focus on central squares in large cities and the naming of protest days—became the model that instructed sympathetic actors in other countries in the region.

As with 1989, so in the case of the MENA uprisings demonstration effects seem to have been critical for propelling the spread of contentious politics (though this interpretation might not withstand the test of more detailed study). First, the precedent set by the early riser—Tunisia—carried the important lesson that even long-serving and, for that matter, very corrupt and repressive dictators could be removed from power quickly and with surprisingly little violence. The role of social media, as well as Al-Jazeera, in covering these events, moreover, ensured that this lesson was communicated in stark ways throughout the region. Second, the Tunisian model at least in its most general form—that is, the use of popular protests that were based on widespread anger about unemployment and corruption that escalated easily to demands for leadership and regime change—was one that could travel easily to the rest of the region. Finally, while Tunisia presented an unusual profile for the region with respect to the limited political role of the military, the homogeneity of the population, and its relatively progressive social policies, it nonetheless seems to have encouraged publics and oppositions in other countries to draw some similarities between that country and their own (see, for example, Alexander 2010; Bellin 2002; Rutherford 2008; King 2009). Here, I refer, for example, not just to the shared concerns about corruption, unemployment, and the other costs of being governed by long-serving and repressive leaders who lacked accountability to their citizens but also the ties forged by a common regional language and historical experiences during the Ottoman Empire and after its collapse. These commonalities, plus similar political and economic systems as a result of the Nasser project and pressures from the international financial community to liberalize the region's economies during the 1970s, were particularly easy to perceive in the case of the Arab republics—which is one reason why the wave has concentrated so much on them. Moreover, as with 1989 and most obviously with the color revolutions, we also see a role in this wave for upcoming succession crises, as in Tunisia, Yemen, Libya, and especially Egypt (where Mubarak had been preparing his son to succeed him). The final three countries also featured, despite their status as republics, plans by the leader on the eve of the protests to pass power on to his son. While not to the extent that we found for the Soviet Union and Eastern Europe in 1989, because of the absence of a regional power on the order of the Soviet Union and greater diversity in political and economic regimes, the MENA was nonetheless a region that seemed to be relatively well suited for hosting, once an early riser appeared, the cross-national diffusion of popular protests against authoritarian rulers.

At the same time and also like 1989, it appears that transnational networks played a less pivotal role in driving the MENA dynamic. There is some fragmentary evidence that the Egyptian and the Tunisian opposition cooperated with each other prior to the onset of the wave; that Serbian youth activists who played a pivotal role in the defeat of Milosevic worked with the Tunisian and Egyptian oppositions during the 5 or so years leading up to the confrontations with Ben 'Ali and Mubarak; that European Union support for civil society also facilitated cross-national contacts among activists; and that the US democracy assistance community had provided some support for the development of the Egyptian opposition in particular (see, for instance, Rosenberg 2011, and Brooks and Teodorovic 2011).[1] However, it is hard to judge at this time the scale and impact of these international efforts. Moreover, it seems unlikely, especially in view of the focus of the challenges to authoritarian leaders on the streets rather than the ballot box and the ways in which the former built in important ways on past opposition efforts, that the MENA uprisings were driven by the efforts of a fully formed and highly influential transnational network.

Unpacking the Waves

One can argue, therefore, that one reason why these improbable waves materialized was that both drivers were in place and reinforced one another. However, some questions remain. Why were the early risers—that is, the countries where the wave began—so successful at encouraging diffusion, given the fact that they were in some important ways different from so many other states in their region? In particular, why would challenges to authoritarian rule in Tunisia (with its homogeneous population, its well-defined state, and its apolitical military), Hungary and Poland (with their distinctive profile in the context of their region of reform communists, large oppositions, and economic crises), and, finally, Slovakia (with its strong opposition and its prior success in winning power) have been able to play the role of encouraging citizens and oppositions in so many nearby countries to follow in their footsteps?

At the same time, how can we explain the fact that all three waves involved a transition very early in the dynamic from one innovative approach to challenging authoritarian leaders to a different ensemble of actions that subsequently held sway across the region? Thus, in 1989 the roundtable was replaced by popular protests in Eastern Europe, and in the color revolutions the Slovak model was amended to include postelection protests. Finally, while youth played a key role in Egypt as well as in Tunisia (as they had in most of the color revolutions), and while they were joined by older or established opposition groups and figures as the protests continued, the 18 days of Egyptian protests did not start with self-immolation, and they targeted, from the beginning, large urban areas (as opposed to rural areas in Tunisia) and the establishment of control over central squares (see Patel 2012). Moreover, the protests that took place in Egypt added the issue of ending emergency rule to the demands put forward by the opposition and built on past struggles in that country, such as those waged by the Egyptian Movement for Change (*kifaya*) and the April 6 Movement, and a large and increasingly active labor movement (Posusney 1997; el-Mahdi 2009).

These two nagging questions lead to a third one. While the case for demonstration effects is very strong for 1989, particularly given the evident similarities among these regimes and the role of the Soviet Union as their designer, defender, but ultimately, the key player in hastening their demise, it is less compelling when we turn our attention to the MENA uprisings. Regimes in this region were more varied than their Soviet bloc equivalents, and leaders of the MENA regimes had options for dealing with challenges to their rule that were not available to their Eastern European counterparts. Especially in view of the considerable constraints on the diffusion of protests, particularly in authoritarian regimes where neighboring elites can learn from dangerous precedents set elsewhere in the region, we must ask whether our two drivers provide a sufficient explanation of diffusion. Is there, in short, another driver that we have overlooked?

In our view, there is. Once we unpack these waves, we find a shift from uprisings taking place in regional backwaters—that is, Poland and Hungary in 1989, Slovakia in the color revolutions, and Tunisia in the Arab uprisings—to their eruption in countries that were more important in geopolitical terms and more similar in their politics to the other countries in the region (and see Patel and Bunce 2012; Patel, Bunce, and Wolchik 2014). Here, we refer to East Germany in the case of 1989, Serbia in the color revolutions, and Egypt in the MENA wave. These three cases were key to the creation of a diffusion dynamic because they showed that the precedent of popular challenges to authoritarian rulers could be transferred; recalibrated the innovation in ways that enhanced its portability; and demonstrated that even very repressive leaders with powerful international patrons could experience popular unrest and be removed from power.

Without this step in the process, we would argue, the wave might have become a "micro-wave."

When we apply this argument to 1989, we cannot help but be struck by the importance of the outbreak of protests in East Germany in the late summer and early fall of 1989. Poland and Hungary were the most obviously vulnerable regimes in the region, and this was the major reason why Gorbachev provided some support for the roundtables that were convened in these two countries. A logical question that could have been asked at that time, but that was in fact not posed, therefore, was whether challenges to authoritarian rule could erupt in other countries in the region that were less supportive of regime change— for example, countries that had fewer economic problems, more hard-line parties, and smaller and less experienced oppositions. Yet another constraint on the development of a diffusion dynamic was the difficulty of predicting what the Soviets would do if they were to confront cascading disarray in Eastern Europe. The Polish and Hungarian precedents, therefore, did not by any means furnish any guarantee—especially given the fact that the Soviets had intervened in Eastern Europe in the past and Gorbachev was facing significant unrest at home, little progress in economic reform, divisions within the party, and hesitant support from the West—that the Soviet leadership would tolerate significant challenges to communist party rule throughout Eastern Europe. A final obstacle to diffusion was the difficulty of transferring the Polish and Hungarian innovation—that is, the roundtable—to other countries in the region.

In all respects, East Germany filled the bill. It was on the front lines of the Cold War and in fact had many more Soviet troops within its borders than any other country in the region. It was, therefore, an unusually revealing test of Soviet intentions. Thus, while political change in Poland and Hungary was important, the uprisings in East Germany played the role of making the wave a wave—not just by demonstrating Soviet commitment to or at least tolerance of political change in Eastern Europe but also by showing that communist party rule could collapse in a hard-line regime and do so through protests in the streets rather than roundtables.

Serbia played the same role in the color revolutions. Like many of the competitive authoritarian regimes in the former Soviet Union, Serbia was a much more hard-line regime than Slovakia and Croatia, and it represented, as a result, a far more difficult test of what the Slovak model could accomplish. Second, the Serbian confrontation with Milosevic amended the Slovak model by adding post-election protests—a necessary ingredient for achieving victory in regimes where, as in much of the former Soviet Union, leaders regularly stole elections. Finally, the Serbian effort, like the East German demonstrations, was successful. And it was successful not just because of the careful deployment of the Slovak model and the addition of protests, along with substantial assistance from the United States (which had shifted its position from supporting to opposing the regime), but also because of the ways in which the Serbian political context resembled the politics of East Germany. In particular, as in East Germany in 1989, so a hard-line regime confronted a large and experienced opposition.

A similar interpretation can be offered of the MENA wave and the role of Egypt. Egypt was, in fact, a logical country to follow in the immediate footsteps of Tunisia, in part because, while different from one another in certain ways as already noted (for example, the role of their militaries), these two countries had nonetheless a great deal in common with respect to the structure and evolution of their political economies (see, for example, Waterbury 1983; Richards and Waterbury 2008; Rutherford 2008; King 2008; Brownlee 2002; Perkins 2004). In addition, like Tunisia as well and unusual for countries within the MENA, Egypt had well-defined state borders, a strong national identity, and a relatively homogeneous population in ethnic and religious terms (see, for example, L. Anderson 1987; Cook 2011). Egypt, far more than Tunisia (especially under Ben ʿAli), moreover, had a rich history of political protests and strikes (especially in the few years leading up to 2011). This is a factor that also figures prominently in the chapter by Karen Rasler in this volume. Like East Germany and Serbia in the earlier waves, therefore, Egypt under Mubarak was a repressive regime facing off against a ripened opposition.

Like the other two key cases, moreover, Egypt contributed two key developments that increased substantially the likelihood that a possible wave would become a real one with significant geographical reach. First, Egypt demonstrated to the region that the Tunisian precedent of bringing down a dictator could travel and succeed. Second, the Egyptian dynamic built on the model first developed and applied in Tunisia, but amended it in ways that, as discussed earlier, made the Egyptian efforts innovative, successful, and highly infectious.

Conclusions

The purpose of this chapter has been to provide an answer to a question that lies at the heart of all studies of diffusion. What drives the spread of an innovation from one site to others? I addressed this issue by comparing three waves of popular mobilizations against authoritarian rulers—that is, 1989, the color revolutions, and the Arab uprisings—and assessing the role of demonstration effects and transnational networks in propelling the spread of these uprisings across state borders. Several conclusions were drawn. First, regional influences can encourage cross-national diffusion in the particular sense that, when states within the same region share similar cultures, experiences with the international system, patterns of interactions between regimes and citizens, and political-economic systems, they are more likely to support the cross-national spread of change. Second, rather than one driver winning this "tournament," both of them seemed to have contributed to the cross-national spread of popular challenges to authoritarian rulers. Third, the importance of these drivers seemed to vary, none-theless, among our waves. While demonstration effects were the most important in 1989 and the Arab uprisings, transnational networks served as the dominant driver in the color revolutions. Finally, once we unpacked each of these waves and recognized the inability of our drivers to provide a fully satisfactory explanation of why these uprisings spread, we discovered a common phenomenon that has not received any attention in the literature on diffusion. That is the transfer of the process early in the wave to a key case that revised the innovation introduced by the early riser and that, because of these changes, certain characteristics of the country, and the success of these efforts, enabled the key case to broadcast these innovations to a much broader swath of the region than would have other-wise been the case. Thus, the puzzle of how popular uprisings can diffuse among authoritarian regimes can be solved by pointing to the existence of three drivers that in our waves at least worked in concert.

These conclusions in turn set an agenda for future research. Here, I would highlight several questions that are worthy of further inquiry. One is whether the type of innovation of interest matters with respect to the drivers it seems to require, if diffusion is to take place. One could hypothesize, for example, that innovations that challenge the political status quo in a fundamental way, such as the ones of interest in this chapter, need all three drivers—that is, demonstra-tion effects, transnational networks, and pivotal cases—for diffusion to proceed, whereas less disruptive innovations might be less demanding to the point that they could specialize in one of these mechanisms. At the least, it is important to assess the extent to which popular uprisings against authoritarian leaders will diffuse across national boundaries only if all three drivers are present—an issue that suggests adding other waves, such as 1848, to the analysis. Another issue is whether some regions are more hospitable to the spread of popular upris-ings against authoritarian rulers than others, because, for instance, they feature sharper discontinuities among member countries in terms of their cultures, his-tories, political systems, and the like. Two good examples of plausibly diffusion-resistant regions are Southeast Asia and sub-Saharan Africa—in direct contrast to Europe and Latin America (Bunce 2012). Finally, this analysis has said very little about the relationship between mechanisms of diffusion, on the one hand, and the efficiency and effectiveness of diffusion, on the other. Are some mecha-nisms, for instance, better at expanding the number of countries that join the wave and, furthermore, achieving the goals of the uprising?

Note

1. An interview I conducted with Ivan Marovic in Belgrade in spring 2005 also revealed (considerably before the Arab uprisings) that there had been contacts between members of the Serbian youth movement, Otpor, and oppositions in Tunisia and Egypt. Moreover, a similar claim was made by another leader of the organization, Srdje Popovic, in a presentation in SAIS, Washington, DC, April 2011.

6

Double Legitimacy Crises and Dynamics of Contention in Ethnic Democracies

Gregory M. Maney

TILLY AND TARROW (2007) note the existence of segmented composite regimes where groups occupying different power positions possess unequal citizenship rights. Ethnic democracies constitute a specific subset of this type of regime, where different ethnic groups possess unequal citizenship rights (Smooha 1990; Rouhana 1998; Peleg 2004; Yiftachel 2006; Howard 2012; Ndlovu-Gatsheni 2012). The possible effects of ethnic democracies on the dynamics and trajectories of contention remain largely unacknowledged and understudied.

In this chapter,[1] the term "minority group" is used in the sociological sense of being less powerful. It is possible for an ethnic group to constitute the majority of a society's population, but still be a minority group in terms of power relations. Using the first Palestinian Intifada as a case study, Alimi and Hirsch-Hoefler (2012) argue that ethnic democracies impact the dynamics of contention by creating distinct and shifting structures of political opportunity and threat for movements based in dominant and minority groups. The first Palestinian Intifada, however, may be an exception in that similar regimes do not experience similar dynamics of contention. To explore this possibility, I examine a case of contention in another ethnic democracy; specifically civil rights contention in Northern Ireland between 1963 and 1972. Like Alimi and Hirsch-Hoefler, I find that the regime type influenced levels and forms of contention used by authorities, challengers, and their opponents. Unlike the authors, I find that changing perceptions of political legitimacy explain the dynamics of contention in ethnic democracies more than preexisting bifurcated structures of political opportunity. Unionist authorities suffered a double legitimacy crisis, leaving them susceptible to challenges emanating from both minority and dominant groups. This dual crisis stemmed from strong ethnonationalist identities and ideologies as well as widespread yet contradictory discourses on democracy. Both minority- and dominant-group-based ethnonationalist movements took advantage of discursive opportunities to challenge the legitimacy of authorities and their responses to contention. Moreover, these discourses helped to explain variations in the forms of contention used by different actors as well as over the course of an episode of contention. The findings suggest the need for greater attention to the symbolic cultural effects of regime types on the dynamics of contention.

Recent events in the Middle East suggest that this is a topic in need of further exploration. Several of the recent uprisings have taken place in societies with large ethnic minority groups (in the sociological not demographic sense), including Egypt, Iraq, Lebanon, Libya, Syria, and Yemen. Minority groups have played roles in several movements (e.g., Shiites in Bahrain and Yemen; Coptic Christians in protests that led to the removal of the Muslim Brotherhood government in Egypt; Sunnis in post–Saddam Hussein's Iraq, Lebanon, and Syria; the Berbers in Libya; and the Hashid tribal federation in Yemen). Moreover, most instances of regime change have involved establishing ethnic democracies. For example, in Egypt, the secular Mubarak regime was overthrown and replaced by an elected government of the Muslim Brotherhood that quickly passed a new constitution widely regarded as favoring Sunnis to the detriment of both Shiites and Christians. The government also turned a blind eye to violent attacks against both minority groups. Prior to the "Arab Spring", the Iraq War resulted in the ousting of a Sunni-based dictatorship and the creation of an ethnic democracy dominated by Shiites. Since December 2012, Sunnis have embarked on a major protest campaign demanding greater political rights and access. This movement has been eclipsed by ISIS—an armed insurgency to establish Sunni-based ethnocracies in Iraq and Syria. Trends toward ethnic democracies in the Middle East warrant a closer examination of the relationship between this regime type and the dynamics of contention.

The analysis highlights the interplay between regime type and symbolic cultural factors in shaping the forms, dynamics, and trajectories of contention; the dialogical, "see-saw" character of constructions of perceived regime legitimacy by activists in dominant and minority-based movements; and the greater challenges that ethnic democracies face in responding to minority-based insurgency compared to other regimes; particularly in the context of high historic levels of ethnonationalist contention.

Symbolic Bases of the Dynamics of Contention

Drawing on the concept of legitimacy to explain the dynamics of contention allows us to go beyond highly questionable assumptions of transparent political opportunity structures and universal rational actors with perfect information. As an emotion and value-laden, interpretive concept, legitimacy is readily linked with other symbolic cultural concepts that explain the dynamics of contention in terms of moral shocks that motivate opposition to authorities. As illustrated in Table 6.1, I theorize that three symbolic, cultural factors play critical roles in shaping the dynamics of contention—collective identity, ideology, and discourse. In ethnic democracies, these factors often converge to create a double legitimacy crisis that leaves authorities susceptible to challenges emanating from large segments of both minority and dominant groups.

Table 6.1 Cultural Factors Contributing to the Double Legitimacy Crisis of Ethnic Democracies

Social Location	Cultural Factors		
	Ethnonationalist Identities	Ethnonationalist Ideologies	Democracy Discourses
Minority Group	• Rejection of the State • Boundary making	• Plural, republican conception of citizenship • Systemic inequalities	• Civil rights (and majority rules if numerical majority)
Dominant Group	• Loyalty to the State • Boundary policing	• Monocultural conception of citizenship • Minority privilege/ dominant group victimization	• Majority rules (or civil rights if numerical minority)

Double Legitimacy Crisis and Contention

Authorities strive for legitimacy—popular consent to their rule as reasonable, fair, just, and in the interest of society (Mann 1986; Barker 1990). The more a government and its policies are regarded as legitimate, extra-institutional challenges are perceived as being superfluous. Conversely, the more the government and its policies are regarded as illegitimate, extra-institutional insurgency is perceived as necessary and productive.

Ethnic democracies suffer from low levels of legitimacy in the eyes of those members of minority groups holding strong ethnonationalist identities. The rejection of these regimes forms the primary basis of group affiliation and commitment. It is the main marker that differentiates group members from nonmembers. Exclusive responses by authorities and opponents to nonviolent protests for equal citizenship rights are likely to reinforce physical, relational, and symbolic group boundaries that are at the core of strong collective identities (Taylor and Whittier 1992; Maney and Abraham 2008/2009). By strengthening ethnonationalist identity, these responses further delegitimate authorities.

Framing instances of repression of nonviolent protests in ways that evoke moral shock (Jasper and Poulsen 1995) delegitimates authorities. Such framing also contributes to the experiential commensurability as well as the empirical credibility of skepticism about the possibility of equal citizenship rights for an ethnonationalist minority group (Snow and Benford 1992). By further delegitimating authorities, repression often backfires in that it expands support for and participation in minority insurgency (Hess and Martin 2006). It provides dramatic evidence that the citizenship rights cannot be obtained without the creation of a new State that represents and protects the minority group.

Moral shock is both predicated on and enhanced by a pluralist, republican ideology regarding citizenship (Flynn 2000). This ideology asserts that all subjects of the State should have the same rights and obligations regardless of class, ethnicity, gender, or other social markers. While emanating from at least the French Revolution, it has gained traction, particularly after World War II and the attendant rise of a modernization ideology that eschews familial and ethnic ties as a basis of social solidarity in favor of functional interdependence based on complex divisions of labor.

While the United States has generally been treated as a liberal democracy, in terms of citizenship rights for minority groups, it historically has been and arguably remains a racialized ethnic democracy. International media coverage of civil rights contention in the United States mostly drew on plural, republican conceptions of citizenship (Layton 2000). As a result, the coverage presented protestors with discursive opportunities (Koopmans and Statham 1999; Ferree 2003; McCammon et al. 2007) to generate considerable moral pressure on ethnic democracies to grant equal citizenship rights to minority groups. A failure to meet the reasonable, fair, and just (as framed) demands of protesters would threaten the legitimacy of authorities for those with whom civil rights framing resonates.

If exclusive responses (e.g., repressive) to minority-based movements delegitimate authorities, what about inclusive responses (e.g., concessions and recognition)? Whereas with other regime types inclusive responses to minority-based movements may enhance the legitimacy of authorities, members of minority groups with strong ethnonationalist identities are more likely to doubt the sincerity of authorities. Ideologically, those who are conscious that they are structurally disadvantaged and systematically oppressed are also more likely to question the sincerity and substance of inclusive responses by authorities. They assume that if the inclusive responses were to alter the balance of power to such an extent that they would permit the minority to dismantle the current regime, then these responses would not be granted in the first place. Such assumptions hedge against the institutionalization and extra-institutional demobilization of minority dissent.[2]

In sum, symbolic, cultural factors gravitate against inclusive responses by authorities enhancing the legitimacy of regimes in the eyes of members of ethnonationalist minorities. The same, however, cannot be said of many in dominant ethnonationalist groups who, because of their collective identities, ideologies, and discourses, often view inclusive responses by authorities as illegitimate.

Ethnic democracies have been conceptualized as regulated spaces of domination with social boundaries primarily delimited by ethnic and national markers (Barth 1969; Olzak 1983; Abraham 1995; Maney and Abraham 2008/2009; Abraham and Maney 2012). These boundaries create strong ethnonationalist identities among both dominant and minority groups. By blurring these boundaries, minority-based movements demanding equal citizenship rights threaten to unravel ethnic democracies. As such, they activate identity-based boundary policing by members of the dominant group. Members of the dominant group opposing minority-based protest movements view themselves as the custodians or guardians of place and protectors of the nation. Initiatives to use space in new ways that support the claims of less powerful groups are actively resisted as acts of territorial aggression (ÓDochartaigh and Bosi 2010).

Oppositional movements police physical boundaries in two ways. First, they pressure authorities to take actions that restrict minority uses of public spaces. Second, members of oppositional movements engage, both individually and collectively, in threats, intimidation, isolation, marginalization, and violence against participants in public protests and other members of the minority inhabiting public spaces. These acts are especially likely if the protests occur in spaces constructed as having ethnonationalist significance.

Certain ideological orientations encourage the informal policing of social boundaries. The belief that members of the dominant ethnonationalist group are victims, on the one hand, and members of the ethnonationalist minority group and their allies are villains encourages participation in oppositional movements. Minority groups are believed to be abusers of space, services, and "rights" of legal and cultural citizenry. As such, demands for citizenship rights by the minority are seen as jeopardizing the citizenship rights of the majority. In a context where collective identities are primarily defined by either support for or rejection of the legitimacy of the State, a willingness by authorities to make concessions to civil rights demands is perceived as an abandonment of regulatory responsibilities, victimization of law-abiding citizens, an injustice, and a betrayal of the public trust.

By inverting social inequalities, this ideological orientation delegitimates efforts to accommodate minority-based movements. Dominant group members are portrayed as disempowered, disenfranchised, and victimized. Minority group members are viewed as politically powerful, dangerous, manipulative, and appropriating what is not rightfully theirs. As seen with the mass internment of Japanese Americans during World War II, such beliefs can contribute the exclusion of minorities (Petonito 2000). Such beliefs can also lead to the labeling of those in the dominant group who are supportive of minority demands as naïve or traitors to the nation.

The credibility of assertions of dominant group victimization is reinforced by defining the nation in cultural terms. In contrast to a plural, republican ideology, a monocultural ideology constructs membership in the nation in terms of common culture such as shared language, religion, sports, folktales, legends, myths, and narratives about a shared past and shared future (Flynn 2000). Through this prism, recognition and protection by authorities of those who are not part of the common culture is a violation of the nation-state "social contract" whereby the State, in both its boundaries and practices, should be coterminous with one nation and one nation only. To retain legitimacy in the eyes of those with this ideology, the health and well-being of the nation depends on the vigilant and systematic exclusion of minority groups by authorities. Sharing power with an ethnonationalist minority would undermine the logic and integrity of the nation-state. Whereas class-based states can incorporate elites from multiple ethnic groups, ethnic states can only incorporate elites from the ethnic group that controls the state.

In contrast to the republican underpinnings of civil rights framing, another widely circulating discourse helps to legitimate ethnic democracies in instances where states represent ethnic groups that constitute the majority of the population, namely the discourse that constructs majority rule as normative democratic practice.[3] This discourse provides opportunities to frame inclusive responses by authorities to minority-based movements as violations of the will of the people.

Dominant group–based opposition to minority-based movements contributes to minority-based rebellion in two ways. First, those viewing reform-oriented protest movements and inclusive responses to protests as threats to the nation and democracy will likely respond in violent opposition (Beissinger 1998; Tilly 2002). Second, opponents of minority-based movements attempt to pressure authorities to shift their strategies away from inclusion and more fully toward reliance on exclusion. When the dominant ethnic group segment of civil society is strong relative to authorities, reforms are likely to be halted if not reversed, while repression aimed at the challenger movement becomes more sweeping and intensive. Vigilantism and the renewed denial of political and civil rights produce higher levels of support for rebellion within the minority group by further delegitimating the State and reinforcing the belief that social justice for the ethnic minority group requires a change in territorial status (e.g., Tejerina 2001). For these reasons, I expect mixed responses by authorities to a minority-based movement in an ethnic democracy to give rise to intensive dominant group vigilantism and high levels of state repression against the movement, contributing to armed minority rebellion.

Comparing Ethnic Democracies to Other Regime Types

The double legitimacy crises often facing authorities in ethnic democracies encourage heavy contention (i.e., intense, extensive, violent, and protracted), especially if the primary participants are ethnically based. What then is the relationship between legitimacy and contention in other regime types with multiethnic populations?

Because of their power-sharing arrangements and guarantees of political and civil rights to all ethnic groups, consociational democracies possess what Weber (1922) referred to as rational-legal authority. Given that rational-legal authority is becoming hegemonic in the Gramscian sense, consociational democracies often have higher levels of legitimacy relative to other regime types. Equal protection and recognition of different ethnic groups along with open access and multiple institutional avenues for redressing grievances is likely to contribute to perceptions of rule and rulers as being reasonable, fair, and just. These structural components of consociational democracies provide discursive and other symbolic opportunities to rulers to enhance their legitimacy by promoting a pluralistic ideology, an inclusive national identity, and a republican conception of citizenship. Higher levels of legitimacy encourage an emphasis on institutionalized forms of contention. Monocultural conceptions of citizenship and majority rules discourses, however, can undermine the legitimacy of consociational regimes among ethnic groups who constitute the majority of the population. Nonetheless, high levels of political access encourage an emphasis on institutionalized forms of contention.

In contrast, authoritarian regimes lack these structural and cultural opportunities to gain legitimacy. Legitimacy in these regimes is more likely to come from two other sources—what Weber (1922) referred to as traditional authority and ethnic patronage. During the "Arab Spring", secular authoritarian governments were more susceptible to widespread, intensive protests and demands for regime change than royal monarchies (see Goldstone's chapter in this volume). Tying ruling arrangements to religious, tribal, and/or familial leadership over successive generations enhances the legitimacy of autocratic regimes. Secular, military dictators in the region did not possess this advantage and, instead relied on what Weber (1922) referred to as charismatic authority as a source of legitimacy along with strong military institutions convention-bound to safeguard the ruling elite.

Even authoritarian regimes possessing legitimacy derived from tradition are, nonetheless, under increasing challenge with the global rise of democratic discourses. Accordingly, authoritarian regimes in multiethnic contexts are likely to use ethnic patronage as a source of legitimacy. Preferential resource allocation and formal cultural recognition to certain ethnic groups encourages those groups to cooperate with the regime even if the regime is headed by a member of another ethnic group. While generating some legitimacy in the eyes of beneficiaries, this patronage may or is likely to alienate excluded ethnic groups. When segments of dominant ethnic groups seek to democratize authoritarian regimes, they are likely to find allies in ethnic minority groups. Nonviolent protests are likely to be responded to with military force, typically resulting in rioting and armed insurgency in the aftermath. In the absence of external military intervention and assistance, movements led by dominant ethnic groups are less likely to engage in armed campaigns given state patronage (Goldstone 2014). Ethnic minorities who challenge autocratic regimes on their own are likely to experience high levels of repression and backlash by the dominant ethnic group(s). Having theorized the role of legitimacy in contrasting dynamics of contention in different regime types, civil rights contention in Northern Ireland is presented as a case to illustrate the effects of a double legitimacy crisis on the dynamics of contention in an ethnic democracy.

An Ethnic Democracy in Western Europe

Northern Ireland is distinct from most other Western European societies both in its neocolonial status and in that ethnonationalism constitutes the primary basis of mass mobilization. Between its establishment in 1921 and the assumption of direct British rule in 1972, the State of Northern Ireland can best be described as an ethnic democracy. From its inception, the State witnessed conflict between the mostly Protestant, Unionist majority of the population supporting a political union with Great Britain and the largely Catholic, Nationalist minority seeking the reunification of Northern Ireland with the other twenty-six counties of the island of Ireland.

A deep desire to ensure the retention of British links coupled with a recalcitrant, irredentist opposition produced political and economic institutions largely controlled by, and favoring, the Unionist majority. Through gerrymandering the boundaries of political districts, granting multiple votes to business owners (who were predominately Unionists), and excluding non-rates payers (who were disproportionately Nationalists) from voting in local elections, Unionists retained political control in areas where they constituted only a minority of the population such as in Derry/Londonderry (herein Derry). Unionist-dominated local councils, in turn, allocated public housing along sectarian lines, often selectively rewarding their loyal constituents while maintaining gerrymandered majorities by denying Nationalists housing in areas where Unionists only held a slim majority of votes. On both the local and central governmental levels, Unionists disproportionately filled top civil service positions.

Nationalists felt the full brunt of their second-class citizenship status in the area of law enforcement. The Special Powers Act of 1922 gave the Northern Ireland Minister of Home Affairs virtually unlimited powers to censor publications, to outlaw political organizations, to ban public assemblies, to search premises without warrants, and to detain suspects without charge for indefinite periods of time. The government frequently invoked the Act to suppress non-violent political activities by Republican (militant Nationalist) political organizations. Given its overwhelmingly Unionist composition, the Northern Ireland police force, the Royal Ulster Constabulary (RUC), enforced the provisions of the Act with particular zeal. As a part-time auxiliary to the RUC formed during the early 1920s to establish the Northern Ireland state by force of arms, the Ulster Special Constabulary or "B Specials" were notorious among Nationalists for using excessive force and engaging in pogroms.

The civil rights movement in Northern Ireland, together with its supporters abroad, challenged the second-class citizenship status of the Nationalist minority without raising the issue of partition. The movement demanded fundamental changes in public housing allocation, the electoral system, and policing. Unionist authorities responded to the movement with a mixture of repression and promised reforms addressing civil rights demands. The movement itself combined with promised reforms resulted in a violent backlash from the hard-line Loyalist segment of the Unionist population. Vigilantism, mounting repression, and the slow pace of reforms, in turn, led to the renewal of an armed Republican campaign for Irish political reunification.

A Double Legitimacy Crisis in Northern Ireland

An examination of a wide array of data sources reveals a double legitimacy crisis that influenced the dynamics of contention in Northern Ireland between 1963 and 1972.[4]

Symbolic Politics of Inclusion and Early Civil Rights Contention, 1963–1967

Early civil rights contention in Northern Ireland emerged at the same time as Unionist government officials were signaling a desire to improve ethnic relations. Appointed Northern Ireland (Stormont) prime minister in 1963, Terence O'Neill embraced a modernization ideology. His administration sought to modernize industry and infrastructure as well as to rationalize government administration through processes of standardization and consolidation. To O'Neill and his supporters, the success of this project required the cooperation of all segments of society in the pursuit of improved socioeconomic conditions.

Bolstered by the growing ecumenical movement, O'Neill held publicized visits to Catholic schools and spoke openly of "building bridges" between the two communities. The prime minister also issued a public statement expressing condolences at the passing of Pope John XXIII. In another unprecedented move, O'Neill met more than once with Taoisigh (prime ministers of the Republic of Ireland). Intended only to promote functional cooperation between the two governments on matters of mutual economic interest, the meetings, nonetheless, suggested a thawing of the cold war between Unionists and Nationalists.

While signaling inclusivity, these policies were viewed with skepticism by many members of the minority who were unimpressed with O'Neill's "politics of the grand gesture" (Moloney and Pollak 1986, 121). Founded by middle-class Nationalists, the Campaign for Social Justice (CSJ) was established on January 17, 1964, "for the purpose of bringing the light of publicity to bear on the discrimination which exists in our community against the Catholic section of that community representing more than one-third of the total population" (1964 pamphlet titled "Why Justice Cannot Be Done: The Douglas Home Correspondence"). In contrast to the O'Neill government, they argued that industrialization and infrastructure were being developed along sectarian lines (e.g., "Londonderry: One Man, No Vote," dated February 19, 1965).

The CSJ was not alone in being critical. Speaking in parliament, Republican Labour Party cofounder and Stormont MP, Harry Diamond, said of the prime minister:

> Let him discard from his mind completely the idea that people are morons, that they are impressed when he appears at a civic week or the unveiling of a tablet or the opening of a school or one of the many other functions which are normally the concerns of mayors and chairmen of urban councils.... There are certain fundamental steps which must be taken. An integrated community can be built only if there can be established in the minds of the minority a feeling that practical steps are being taken. The minority do not want appeals for trust or speeches full of sweet phrases which leave the position as it was.
>
> House of Commons Proceedings, *Hansard*, p. 1553, July 11, 1967

Based in Great Britain, the Connolly Association used civil rights frames in lobbying British politicians to intervene in Northern Ireland affairs. In 1962, the Republican organization published "Our Plan to End Partition," arguing for a movement to abolish repressive, undemocratic Stormont laws. A 1964 article in their newsletter the *Irish Democrat* stated that the situation in Northern Ireland "Is the exact parallel of the Negro question in the United States, for in that country, the freedom of the people as a whole is dependent entirely upon the emancipation of the coloured people" (Dooley 1998, 46). Civil rights framing proved highly effective in generating moral pressure on the Unionist government, which felt compelled to respond publicly to the lobbying and media campaign in Britain. On April 24, 1967, the paper of record in England, the *Times*, published an article titled "Electoral System Weighted against Catholics; Ulster's 'Second-Class Citizens'." Prime Minister O'Neil's defensive response in a letter to the Editor reveals his government's vulnerability to civil rights demands:

> [A]lthough reform does indeed take a long time—and is in fact a process which is never at an end in any community—no one should assume that reforms in Northern Ireland are not in progress. As an example, university

and plural voting in elections to the Northern Ireland Parliament are being abolished, and we will be setting up a permanent impartial boundary commission to keep electoral boundaries under review. Again, a most exhaustive re-examination of the functions, areas, and financing of local government is now under way, and this is likely to lead to far-reaching reforms in that area.

In the same letter, O'Neill drew on majority rules discourse to discourage British government intervention in Northern Ireland affairs:

But there really is no acceptable or truly democratic alternative to letting us find the solution for our own problems. Stormont is, after all, a democratically elected Parliament, and no solution which is imposed upon the majority of the population could fail to provoke greater evils than it would solve. . . . Certainly this is not the moment for an ill-judged intervention in our affairs. As I said at the beginning, the long history of Anglo-Irish relationship warns that such an intervention may produce effects which no one can foresee.

While most Nationalists dismissed the significance of the inclusive policies of the O'Neill administration because of the low level of legitimacy of the State, many Unionists did not. The ecumenical movement threatened to blur social boundaries between Protestants and Catholics. Some Loyalists (militant Unionists) policed these boundaries. Beginning in 1959 the Reverend Ian Paisley led the charge. Upon the death of Pope John XXIII in 1963, condolences were issued by the Presbyterian Moderator, the Church of Ireland primate, the Governor of Northern Ireland, and the Northern Ireland Prime Minister. The day after his death, the Union Jack at City Hall in Belfast was lowered to half-mast. The Reverend Paisley led a march protesting these gestures. During a speech in Ulster Hall, Paisley stated, "This Romish man of sin is now in hell" (Moloney and Pollak 1986, 111). The speech was followed by a march of 500 people to City Hall. Bans on such marches and the jailing of participants only deepened the conviction of protesters that the government was betraying Unionists and paving the way toward a united Ireland.

Efforts to increase economic cooperation across the border also presented opportunities for boundary policing. A meeting took place between Northern Ireland Prime Minister Terence O'Neill and Taoiseach Sean Lemass in April of 1966. According to a police report of the meeting, "Paisley again seized the opportunity to preach hate against the Prime Minister and members of the government and accused them of selling Ulster down the drain. He objected in the strongest terms to any form of appeasement or collaboration with the government of the Republic of Ireland. He called Mr. Lemass a gunman and a murderer, and an enemy of Ulster" (RUC Headquarters, "Political Incidents in Northern Ireland from 17th April, 1966"). A few days later, Paisley addressed 1,000 at an Ulster Hall rally denouncing "the O'Neill-Lemass conspiracy." During his speech, he made the following comment about O'Neill: "He is a bridge builder he tells us. A traitor and a bridge are very much alike for they both go over to the other side." (Moloney and Pollak 1986, 120). Symbolic cultural factors that contributed to the delegitimation of the O'Neill government in the eyes of many Unionists also laid the groundwork for the dynamics of contention that ensued with mass civil rights mobilization.

Caught in the Middle: Authorities' Responses to Mass Civil Rights Mobilization, 1968–1972

The Unionist government soon found itself in a quandry. On the one hand, responding repressively to civil rights protesters and ignoring their demands would risk British government intervention, alienating moderate Unionists, and intensifying minority-based mobilization. On the other hand, allowing the protests to proceed and making concessions to the civil rights movement would risk intensified backlash among hard-line Unionists.

The Stormont Minister of Home Affairs banned the proposed route of the second mass civil rights march in Northern Ireland to be held in Derry. On October 5, 1968, 250 police officers waited for the demonstrators. The RUC County Inspector, William Meharg, read out an order prohibiting the parade from going through the walled city. Signaling the police's intentions, the Inspector urged that "those who were unconnected with the parade, especially women and children, should go home" (William Craig speaking on behalf of his resolution introduced to the Stormont Commons, October 16, 1968; *Hansard*, 70, no. 17, p. 1016). Two hundred yards into the march, the RUC blocked the street. In response, the protesters sat down and listened to speeches. According to one observer, "the police broke ranks and used their batons indiscriminately on people in Duke Street ... the District Inspector in charge used his blackthorn with needless violence" (McKinney 1998, 12). Officers then deployed water cannons, blasting not only the marchers, but also journalists covering the event. Trapped from both the front and behind, some of the demonstrators made their way to the Craigavon Bridge, where water cannons again knocked them down. Finally reaching the end of the bridge, a contingent of participants held a meeting where they decided to disperse and complete the march at a later date. As they departed, the police were still wielding their clubs. Eighty-eight persons were injured severely enough to go to the hospital—77 marchers and 11 police officers (Arthur 1974, 28). As a sign of things to come, rioting in Nationalist areas broke out later that evening in both Derry and Belfast. As a result of clashes between the RUC and residents, an additional 20 people were hospitalized.

A review of Stormont cabinet documents from the period suggests some reasons why authorities responded repressively to the march. By jeopardizing social stability while providing opportunities for political gains by elites who supported them, Loyalist protest groups effectively pressured authorities into responding repressively to civil rights mobilization. To many Unionists, the civil rights movement represented a serious threat to Northern Ireland's political ties with Great Britain. Republican (militant Nationalists) involvement cast an ominous, dark shadow over civil rights activities. In the words of one outspoken opponent, "the civil rights movement was seen as a Trojan horse or stalking horse for Republicanism" (author's interview with Clifford Smyth). A prominent official in the Orange Order at the time and later its leader, the Reverend W. Martin Smyth, stated that: "discrimination was not the main concern of the civil rights movement. Many in the movement were Republicans" (author's interview).[5] The threat to public order posed by promised Loyalist confrontations with civil rights marchers convinced even moderate cabinet ministers of the wisdom of first rerouting civil rights marches away from predominantly Unionist areas and then of banning such marches all together. Efforts by the police to enforce these policies resulted in the use of physical force against civil rights protesters.

If repression and countermobilization in an ethnic democracy are related to the degree to which minority-based protests are perceived as illegitimate, then one would expect an attempt by Nationalists and their allies to march through Derry to receive a very hostile response. The planned route included the Diamond—a square at the center of the walled city where Loyalists successfully repelled an invasion by the Catholic former King of England James II and his Catholic Nationalist supporters in 1688. The image of Nationalists symbolically taking over a location central to their mythology horrified many Unionists both within and outside the government (Moloney and Pollak 1986, 157). Organizers of the march deliberately selected a route that they knew Unionists would not accept. In a society whose territorial status was contested deeply, the lead organizers recognized that Unionists would never accede to Nationalists' "occupying" the Diamond (author's interview with Fionbarra ÓDochartaigh). One of the main organizers of the march, Eamon Melaugh, hoped that sight of the blood of those peacefully protesting social injustices would "tear the apathy out of the people of Derry" (author's interview with Eamon Melaugh). In keeping with this expectation, the police acted forcibly to protect prominent physical and symbolic boundaries.

This boundary policing backfired on authorities, increasing bystander and third-party sympathy for and participation in the civil rights movement. By the time the first mass marches took place in 1968, British politicians were already familiar with civil rights frames being applied to Northern Ireland affairs. On October 3, 1968, the CSJ sent a letter to Harold Wilson asking for the British prime minister "to provide protection for us in exercising our basic democratic right in participating in the civil rights march in Derry on Saturday" (The *Irish News*, October 5, 1968, p. 1 " 'Rights' March Goes Ahead as Planned"). On the same day, the Campaign for Democracy in Ulster held a conference attended by 50 delegates at Blackpool, England. During his speech to delegates, Republican Labour Party MP from Belfast, Gerry Fitt was quoted as saying that "trouble might break out on Saturday night at a civil rights march in Derry and he intended taking six (British) MPs with him from London to see if the police allowed the March" (*Belfast Telegraph*, October 3, 1968, " 'Civil Trouble' Warning by Fitt").

Members of British Parliament made credible, influential eyewitnesses for journalists. John Ryan, MP for Uxbridge, England, reported seeing "a woman, aged over sixty, having her spectacles removed by a policeman before being hit on the head by a baton. She was not one of the demonstrators. He saw children, covered with blood, being carried into a cafe" (*Irish Press*, October 7, 1968, untitled). Film footage taken by a Raidió Teilifís Éireann (Republic of Ireland public broadcasting company) television crew was broadcasted throughout the world. Coverage in the British, Irish, and international media drew on civil rights framing, which elicited a stream of letters expressing moral outrage at the actions of authorities and sympathy for the protesters and their demands.

Years of lobbying using civil rights framing combined with televised coverage had an effect on the British prime minister, Harold Wilson. During a debate in the British Parliament House of Commons, Labour MP and Campaign for Democracy in Ulster member Paul Rose asked Wilson whether he would transfer control of the RUC to the (British) Home Secretary. Unionist MP and Grand Master of the Ulster Orange Order, Captain Lawrence Orr, objected to Rose's question as "a slur on what is probably the best and finest police force in the world' (Wilson 1976, 671). According to his autobiography, Wilson responded, "I say to the honorable and gallant Member that he is entitled to his view on the matter he has just expressed. . . .. Up to now we have perhaps had to rely on the statements of himself and others on these matters. Since then we have had British television" (ibid).

Soon thereafter, British Prime Minister Wilson requested a meeting with Northern Ireland Prime Minister O'Neill to discuss what had transpired. Taking place on November 4, 1968, the meeting featured the most forceful threats of

British intervention to date along with attempts to bolster O'Neill against hard-liners. Wilson used virtually verbatim framing developed by the Campaign for Democracy in Ulster to justify British concerns and possible intervention:

> During the discussion, I made clear our determination about the urgent reforms which were required.... Only speedy reform could avert irresistible pressures for legislation at Westminster—under the rights explicitly reserved by Section 75 of the Government of Ireland Act 1920—intervening in Irish affairs; none of us wanted that.
>
> Wilson 1976, 672

Under threat from the British government, the Northern Ireland cabinet decided to go ahead with concessions to some civil rights demands. O'Neill announced a series of reforms on November 22, 1968. The company vote in local government elections was to be eliminated. The Londonderry Corporation and Rural Councils were to be replaced by a government-appointed commission to carry out the Londonderry Plan for housing and employment. Local councils were mandated to develop points systems for the allocation of public housing. Collectively, these measures tacitly recognized the illegitimacy of local councils with gerrymandered Unionist majorities. The reform package of November 1968 also included an agreement to the effect that "as soon as the Northern Ireland [government] consider this can be done without undue hazard, such of the Special Powers as are in conflict with international obligations will as in the past be withdrawn from current use" (Untitled cabinet document dated November 22, 1968). On April 22, 1969, O'Neill announced his acceptance of the civil rights movement's demand for one-"man," one-vote in local government elections. The next day, the Unionist Party Council voted 28 to 22 to accept the change. In October of 1969, on the basis of the recommendations of an independent inquiry, the Northern Ireland government announced the disarming of the RUC and the disbanding of the B-Specials.

Nationalist reactions to these promised reforms were a mixture of cautious optimism and outright dismissal. The executive boards of the two main civil rights coalitions in Northern Ireland (the Derry Citizens Action Committee [DCAC] and the Northern Ireland Civil Rights Association [NICRA]) welcomed the announcement of a series of reforms. While demanding further reforms, they, nonetheless, declared a moratorium on civil rights marches as requested by authorities. From December 9, 1968, through most of March of 1969, both coalitions abided by the moratorium.

For those activists prioritizing the immediate advancement of a united, socialist Republic of Ireland, however, the moratorium was unacceptable.

Members of the New Left belonging to the DCAC, the Derry Labour Party, and People's Democracy (PD) vowed to continue marching. Most of these activists believed that Stormont could not be reformed and that political destabilization held the key to achieving their objectives. Accordingly, they supported the continuance of marching. On December 9, 1968, a large People's Democracy meeting decided to call off a planned march to Belfast City Hall scheduled for December 11, 1968. In a subsequent, smaller meeting when most students were on winter break, PD members also affiliated with the Young Socialists pushed through a motion to hold a march from Belfast to Derry in early January. Eoin Sweeney explained the rationale for the motion:

> All were going for at least one common reason: a reaction against the evasive platitudes with which O'Neill and his men tried to pass the can for his own misdeeds ... in marching we felt that we were pushing a structure (that contained the seeds of great violence among other things) towards a point where its internal proceedings would cause a snapping and a breaking to begin.
>
> Arthur 1974, 40–41

Along with the majority on the NICRA executive board, DCAC leaders Ivan Cooper and John Hume opposed the "Long March," fearing the violence by Loyalist mobs that did, in fact, take place (Akenson 1973). On the night of the day when the march ended, part-time members of the police force known as B-Specials rioted through a Republican area of Derry known as the Bogside. Two water cannons were used along with repeated baton charges. Windows were broken and doors smashed down to beat and kick anyone in sight. The *Sunday Press* reported that 200 people were injured with at least 89 hospitalized. The incident resulted in the erection of dozens of barricades to keep the police out of the Bogside. Violent opposition to civil rights protests resulted in the reinforcement of physical, relational, and symbolic boundaries between Unionists and Nationalists. For participating members of the PD, "the march to Derry exposed to the world the old realities ... concealed behind the 'new face' of unionism" (People's Democracy 1969).

The old realities reflected widespread perceptions among members of the dominant group that the promised reforms posed grave threats to the Union. The result was increased mobilization not only against the civil rights but also the government itself. After attacking participants in the long march with rocks, bottles, Molotov cocktails, iron bars, and cudgels, members of the Loyal Sons of Ulster led by Major Reginald Bunting marched to the Diamond, where they staged a trooping of the British flag. Paisleyites continued to violently attack civil rights demonstrators throughout Northern Ireland. Civil rights demonstrators, in turn, became increasingly violent, hardening polarized ethnonationalist identities in the process.

There was also mounting parliamentary and electoral opposition to "O'Neillism" within Unionist ranks. In January of 1969, 13 Unionist backbenchers met in Portadown to publicize their differences with O'Neill and call for his removal. The following month, the Northern Ireland prime minister called a snap-election. O'Neill was elected on a minority vote; his majority in the Bannside over Paisley was only 1,414 on a total poll of 16,400 votes. British Prime Minister Harold Wilson described the narrow victory as "a shattering blow to his authority" (Wilson 1976, 674).

On April 23, 1969, Unionist Party MPs and Senators voted in favor of one-"man," one-vote in elections in Northern Ireland. Among those voting against the reform was James Chichester-Clark, who resigned as minister of agriculture in protest at the timing of the announcement. He said the decision "might encourage militant Protestants even to bloodshed" (NICRA 1978, 20). Less than a week later, Chichester-Clark succeeded O'Neill, who resigned as prime minister. With the assistance of O'Neill supporters, Chichester-Clark defeated another opponent of reforms, Brian Faulkner, by a vote of 17 to 16 votes. One of the prime minister's first official acts was to declare amnesty for all protest-related offences since October 5, 1968. The Reverend Ian Paisley and Major Ronald Bunting were released from jail. Those who attacked civil rights marchers as they entered Derry were not prosecuted.

The move signaled a major shift in authorities' responses to the civil rights movement as a result of grassroots Unionist pressure and countermobilization. While the years of 1968 and 1969 featured efforts by the O'Neill government to accommodate the Nationalist minority, the following two years were characterized by delays and backtracking on promised reforms. Despite the pledge to abide by the principle of one-"man," one-vote, the government continued to postpone local elections. In 1970, Chichester-Clark's successor as Northern Ireland Prime Minister, Brian Faulkner, announced the postponement of local elections until 1972. The government steadfastly refused to consider the "franchise issue" until it completed a review of the local government structure. As a result, beyond Derry, local councils with Unionist majorities in areas with majority Nationalist populations remained unaltered. Progress on implementing promised reforms in the allocation of public housing by local councils similarly slowed.

In terms of policing, rather than restricting the provisions of the Special Powers Act, Stormont invoked the law to intensify repression primarily targeted at Nationalists. In July of 1970, under the Act, the government used British troops to enforce a curfew in a Republican (militant Nationalist) area located in West

Belfast. On August 9, 1971, the government again used the Act to intern hundreds suspected of involvement in the Republican movement, including prominent civil rights activists. Of the 340-plus individuals interned on that day, all but two were Nationalists. Detainees were held in jails or camps without charge or trial, with some being interned for over a year. Regarding the police force, the government rearmed the RUC shortly after disarming them. Moreover, the British military unit formed to replace the B Specials accepted a large number of former B Specials. Former Specials also formed "gun clubs" in order to keep their weapons.

While restoring some legitimacy to the government in the eyes of some Unionists, these policy changes further alienated many in the Nationalist minority. By 1972, many Nationalists believed that events had come full circle. Speaking of an anti-internment march in late January of 1972 at which 13 demonstrators were killed by British paratroopers, the official history of the Northern Ireland Civil Rights Association reads:

> 20,000 marched down William Street demanding an end to internment, the introduction of proportional representation, the complete abolition of the Special Powers Act, legislation to guarantee the rights of all political groups including those opposed to the existence of the state, an end to discrimination, the establishment of an impartial and civil police force. . . . They were demanding the same rights as those who were batoned off the streets of Derry in October, 1968, and now, four years later they were met not with batons but with bullets, and when the guns were silenced the thirteen lay dead. Brian Faulkner and Edward Heath had given their response to the demand for civil rights.
>
> NICRA 1978, 35

In the face of Unionist violence and waning reforms, a large section of the Nationalist population concluded that social justice could only be obtained through an armed struggle to politically reunify Ireland. In the words of the future leader of Sinn Féin, Gerry Adams (1986, 34):

> The civil rights movement had been looking for democratisation of the state, but the state had made abundantly clear the fact that it would not and could not implement democratic reforms. The movement had placed its demands on the state; it had not demanded the abolition of the state, nor a United Ireland. Now, however, with the reaction of the

state and the intervention of the British army, the constitutional question had come to the fore and the whole existence of the Six County state stood in question.

Civil rights protests effectively became a subsidiary component of armed rebellion.

Discussion

An examination of civil rights contention in Northern Ireland between 1963 and 1972 supports Alimi and Hirsch-Hoefler's (2012) proposition that ethnic democracies exhibit dynamics of contention that are specific to that regime type. This study, however, also makes it clear that the dynamics were more effects of a double legitimacy crisis than of a preexisting bifurcated political opportunity structure. As such, the case suggests the need for a theoretical and methodological shift toward symbolic-cultural factors influencing the dynamics of contention.

The contradictory logics of representing and protecting the collective identity, aspirations, and interests of one ethnic group while, at the same time, guaranteeing equal citizenship rights to others with opposing identities, aspirations, and interests presents deep strategic dilemmas for authorities (Jasper 2004). On the one hand, exclusive responses to demands made by minority-based movements delegitimate the regime not only in the eyes of the minority population, but also in the eyes of international public opinion. On the other hand, inclusive responses to minority demands delegitimate authorities in the eyes of many in the dominant ethnic group. Mixed responses by ethnic democratic regimes radicalize and intensify both minority and dominant group mobilization against authorities. In short, they reflect and reinforce a double legitimacy crisis.

More research is needed to assess the external validity of the findings presented here. Future research could also assess expected variations in relative legitimacy and contention across regime types, controlling for other relevant, contention-related factors such as the extent and type of external intervention, levels of deprivation, and the presence or absence of military occupation and settlements.[6] In particular, the threat and reality of British government intervention on behalf of the Nationalist minority suggests that a state's degree of dependency on other states, international governmental organizations, and foreign investors affects how authorities respond to minority-based movements. Highly autonomous states may be able to avoid double legitimacy crises by engaging exclusively and effectively in repressing minority-based movements (see Alimi and Meyer chapter in this book).

Table 6.2 Legitimacy of Authorities and Dynamics of Contention: Application of Conceptual Framework to Specific Cases of Ethnonationalist Contention

Cases	Regime Type	Social Location	Legitimacy	Contention
Lebanon	Consociational Democracy	Majority ethnic group	Medium	Light
....	Consociational Democracy	Other ethnic group(s)	High	Light
Israel/Palestine, Northern Ireland	Ethnic Democracy	Dominant ethnic group	Low	Heavy
Egypt (Mursi), Iraq, Israel/Palestine, Northern Ireland, Syria	Ethnic Democracy	Minority ethnic group(s)	Low	Heavy
Egypt (Mubarak)	Authoritarian	Dominant ethnic group	Medium	Medium
Bahrain, Libya, Yemen	Authoritarian	Minority ethnic group(s)	Low	Heavy

Political developments arising from the "Arab Spring" lend preliminary support for the comparative framework presented above (see section "Comparing Ethnic Democracies to Other Regime Types"). As Table 6.2 shows, variations in the dynamics of contention are consistent with expectations derived from a conceptual framework that links relative levels of legitimacy among parties occupying different social locations to regime type. Unlike civil rights contention in Northern Ireland and the first Palestinian Intifada, concessions building on previous policies have led to the demobilization of prodemocracy protests in authoritarian regimes such as Jordan, Kuwait, Oman, and Saudi Arabia. In none of these cases were the protests organized along ethnic lines. The absence of ethnic-based cultural factors described in Table 6.1 allowed the regimes to enhance their legitimacy through reforms.

In one authoritarian regime where demonstrations were organized along ethnic lines (i.e., prodemocracy demonstrations by the Shiite minority [sociological] against the Sunni-led regime in Bahrain), contention continues to intensify despite government concessions and a major crackdown on protesters. Rioting has become more frequent, and the Shiite population appears to be arming itself. This unfolding of heavy contention over time can, in part, be explained by the low level of legitimacy of the Bahrain regime in the eyes of Shiite insurgents, who either want an ethnic democracy of their own or are dubious about the possibility of transition toward a consociational democracy.

Due to authorities' low levels of legitimacy in the eyes of dominant *and* minority ethnic groups, transitions to ethnic democracies in Egypt, Iraq, and Lebanon have been accompanied by intensifications in ethnic-based protests and armed insurgencies. Unlike ethnonationalist contention in an authoritarian context (e.g., Bahrain), these three cases involve substantial vigilante and/ or paramilitary violence by those affiliated with the dominant ethnic group(s). More systematic, comparative research in the Middle East and other regions is needed before any firm conclusions can be reached. Nonetheless, the preliminary analyses presented here highlight the need to recognize the critical role of symbolic, cultural factors in shaping the dynamics of contention.

Notes

1. The material in this chapter is based on work supported by the National Science Foundation (2010; SES-0958743).
2. This is not to say that such beliefs are universal among members of ethnonationalist minority groups. See, for instance, Maney (2012). Nor are such beliefs always accurate, as seen in the case of South Africa.
3. As Table 6.1 suggests, ethnic groups who do not possess full citizenship rights and constitute the majority of the population can draw on majority rules discourse to delegitimate the state.
4. For detailed information regarding data sources, see Maney (2000).
5. Named after William of Orange—the Dutch-born Protestant who defeated the army of Catholic King James II at the Battle of the Boyne in 1690, the Orange Order is the largest fraternal Unionist organization in Northern Ireland. Catholics are not allowed to be members.
6. This framework should not be construed as suggesting that one regime type will always possess the same level of legitimacy or the same dynamics of contention. There are differences in legitimacy and contention within a regime type as well as variations over time in the legitimacy of any single regime (e.g., Goldstone 2014). Moreover, contention itself can result in the transformation of regime types, as the "Arab Spring" amply demonstrates.

7

When Repression Fails to Backfire

MOVEMENT'S POWERS, STATE'S POWER, AND
CONDITIONS CONDUCIVE TO INTERNATIONAL
INTERVENTION

Eitan Y. Alimi and David S. Meyer

WHY DOES AUTHORITARIAN repression of popular contention *sometimes* promote international intervention? Dissident groups generally try to attract outside intervention when they are in danger, of repression or just losing, but do not always succeed. Their capacity to attract outside intervention has long been treated as a central factor in shaping the outcome of contentious episodes. Although the problem of figuring out what makes activists' appeals for extranational involvement generate helpful responses across regime types has received significant academic attention, persisting variability in international responses to ostensibly similar cases warrants rethinking existing explanations.

In authoritarian states, where rulers can deploy and rely on the major institutions of social control more fully and effectively, dissidents can rarely mobilize sufficient domestic support to change a regime. They are dependent on mobilizing outside forces to alter the balance of forces in a conflict. For the less powerful in a battle, success is contingent on turning the audience into participants in the conflict (Schattschneider 1960). Authoritarians exercise social and political control of media and the military to prevent transmission of reports and images that might provoke outside intervention. Dissident movements do whatever they can to undermine that control, often by staging dramatic public protests, daring dictators to overreact, thus dramatizing their political (and moral) failings. Horrific and violent repression can thus be the precursor for outside intervention that might, activists hope, ultimately result in a different (and better) government.

There are no simple formulations here. Repression does not always backfire; outside military intervention does not always produce desired outcomes, nor is it always necessary to produce some kind of regime change. In this chapter, we mean to draw attention to one factor that has surprisingly received little treatment in the literature and that, we argue, enhances understanding of the conditions under which dissidents' efforts to promote international intervention may work and also generates additional insights into variation in the degree of international intervention. Analytically invested in a political process framework, we argue that examining the political opportunity structure (POS) each *state* faces and presents dissidents—or relative power as captured by each state's degree of exclusivity and autonomy vis-à-vis other states—can help explain the vastly different outcomes in extranational response to popular dissent.

To this end, we begin by reviewing some of the existing explanations for the possibility of international intervention, and assessing them in light of the recent wave of popular contention in the Middle East and North Africa (MENA), particularly the cases of Libya, Syria, and Egypt. Next we develop a theoretical framework to account for those underlying conditions that make movements' success in inviting international intervention more likely.[1] We then provide evidence from the three cases, and conclude by assessing the generalizability of our explanatory framework, for which purpose we bring illustrative evidence from additional non-"Arab Spring" cases.

Why Powerful Outsiders Sometimes Come to Help

Consideration of the importance and difficulties of activists operating across borders in attracting international intervention from supranational institutions dates back to at least Keohane and Nye (1973) and extends deeply within international relations (Miall et al. 1999). A long-standing debate continues between those who stress moral motivations (normativists) and those who stress interest-based motivations (instrumentalists/realists) either against or in favor of international intervention within the framework of the UN (Gholz, Press, and Sapolsky 1997; Slim 1997; Rieff 2000; Fearon and Laitin 2004; Roberts 2004). Unfolding in the context of the UN-mandated collective enforcement of peace and security (Moskos 1990; Findlay 2002) and the more recent 2005 consensus over the international "responsibility to protect" (Weiss 2012), this debate surfaced most meaningfully in the context of the Gulf War of 1991 (Coleman 2007) and resurfaced again in the context of the MENA popular insurgencies.[2]

Since the late 1990s, scholars of contentious collective action and social movements have devoted increasing attention to the issue, with particular focus on the relations between challengers and the state. Social movement scholars have advanced the notion of the "multilayered" nature of POS, and have sought to conceptualize and theorize on the move of contention from the national to the international level and back (McCarthy 1997; Rothman and Oliver 1999; Keck and Sikkink 1998; Della Porta, Kriesi, and Rucht 1999; Meyer 2003; Sikkink 2005; Tarrow 2005; Bob 2005; Armstrong and Bernstein 2008; Alimi 2009).

Particularly influential has been Keck and Sikkink's (1998) "boomerang model," which goes beyond the instrumental/normative structural divide to incorporate agency into the analysis. Facing hostile state authorities, activists engage in informational political exchanges with transnational advocacy networks, whose members engage their own states in pressuring the blocking state (1998, 13). Those outsiders can constrain authoritarian regimes concerned about external legitimacy or resources and/or they can bring international legitimacy and resources to local actors. Subsequent analyses, including refinements of the "boomerang model" (Risse and Sikkink 1999; Sikkink 2005), have noted that reaching and activating a broader audience is difficult and that authoritarian regimes can block efforts by activists to get their messages out; effectively, powerful repressive states, by controlling the flow of information, can work to prevent the boomerang from crossing their borders.

But activists have a range of approaches and resources for getting the word out—and states can employ a range of social control strategies. In some instances, to be sure, repression fails to backfire and activists' efforts bear little fruit, with no international intervention of any kind; yet even when repression does backfire and intervention is the case, we find a range of possible responses: from rhetorical support to formal recognition; from condemnation of the regime to threatening or actually initiating diplomatic or even economic sanctions; and from covert or overt military sales to actual peace enforcement via military intervention (Findlay 2002; Coleman 2007). These scenarios are a powerful reminder of (1) the differences in both scope of claim-making and contentious repertoire between social movements and the interest groups (Keck and Sikkink 1999; Tarrow 2005) and (2) the varying space of action and political opportunities state authorities enjoy in regional and international arenas.

Indeed, in the cases of the recent episodes of popular contention across the MENA region, we saw activists appealing to supranational authorities for aid in combating authoritarian rulers. Of the numerous cases that make up what has been termed the "Arab Spring", the Egyptian, Libyan, and Syrian cases stand out most remarkably in terms of the striking differences in dissident groups' capacity to invite international intervention. In all three cases we have witnessed a fairly high level of similarities with respect to those *necessary* conditions scholars have identified and suggested (e.g., high death toll and international nongovernmental organizations, or NGOs, working along with domestic groups to cope with local blockage). Nonetheless, in Libya, Colonel Qadhafi's efforts at violently quashing an indigenous rebellion led to effective military intervention from abroad that ousted Qadhafi and facilitated the consolidation of a new leadership. In Syria, an equally powerful insurgency against Assad's regime provoked repression at least as violent, but at this writing has only generated limited and indirect support for some of the rebel groups. And, in Egypt, President Husni Mubarak tried to repress a domestic insurgency, undermining support from his own military, yet fell without outside intervention.

The "Arab Spring" and International Intervention

In a matter of a few weeks following the self-immolation of a Tunisian grocery vendor, revolutionary efforts spread at a previously unimaginable pace. The sympathy protests that erupted, to be sure, were met with intense repression, which backfired and led protests to spread north and to the urban areas, culminating in army defection and forcing Tunisian president Ben 'Ali to flee. Inspired and encouraged by the rapidity and the relative ease of the Tunisian revolution, Jordanian, Egyptian, Algerian, Yemenite, Bahraini, Libyan, Syrian, and other MENA dissidents took to the streets to topple their own (predominantly neopatrimonial, autocratic—see Goldstone's chapter in this volume) rulers in what became an unprecedented regional cycle of contention.

On top of the similarities among the disparate contentious episodes in numerous MENA countries, in terms of widespread popular discontent, means of mobilization, and security forces repression, there also were apparent dissimilarities expressed in the claims made, modes of coordination (as conceptualized by Diani and Moffatt in this volume), scope and intensity of protesting and rioting, and trajectories and outcomes. One additional facet of those "similarities in dissimilarities" concerns the attempts by activists in most of the rebellious societies to invite international intervention, on the one hand, and the resulting variability in terms of the degree of intervention, on the other (see Table 7.1).

Nowhere was such variability more apparent than in the cases of Libya, Egypt, and the still-raging case of Syria. In all three cases, insurgents deliberately sought to attract international intervention. In Libya, we witnessed a military intervention on the part of UN/NATO in support of the rebel camp; in Egypt, we witnessed a case of effective diplomatic intervention; and in Syria, the relentless attempts at attracting international intervention on the part of the dissident

Table 7.1 Overview of Motivational and Advocacy Work Data

Country/Measure	Libya	Egypt	Syria
Time Period	**February 15, 2011–March 19, 2011** (military intervention)	**January 25, 2011–February 11, 2011** (nonmilitary intervention)	**March 18, 2011**—(covert nonmilitary, limited support to opposition in early 2012)
Death[i]	February 21: 445–595 March 18: around 1,000	January 31: around 500 deaths February 11: 846	April 14, 2011: 200 September 2011: 1,900 September 15, 2012: 32,611 March 2013: over 72,500
Injury[ii]	February 2011: hundreds injured in the battles of Benghazi March 2011: 1,932	January 29: 1,500 February 11: 5,500	End of April 2011: hundreds injured in Dar'a July 28–29, 2012: nearly 7,000 injured in Damascus fighting March 2013: around 137,000
Internal Displacement[iii]	December 2011: 154,000	None	June–September 2011: 156,000 July 2012: 1,500,000
Refugees[iv]	February 2011: 100,000 March 2011: 300,000	None	April 2012: 73,000 January 2013: 569,000

I/NGO[v]	African Center for Democracy and Human Rights Studies; Cairo Institute for Human Rights Studies; International Federation of Human Rights—to name only a few	International Medical Corps; Institute for War and Peace Reporting; Doctors without Borders—to name only a few	Syria Justice and Accountability Center; Violations Documentation Center in Syria; Friends of Syria—to name only a few

[i] Reuters, January 31 2011; Daily News Egypt, January 31, 2011; Human Rights Watch report, 2011; http://web.archive.org/web/20110423023923/; http://www.haaretz.com/news/; international/government-fact-finding-mission-shows-846-killed-in-egypt-uprising-1.356885; http://www.washingtonpost.com/wp-dyn/content/article/2011/02/25/AR2011022501021.html; http://www.bbc.co.uk/news/world-africa-12636798; The Christian Science Monitor quoting Ban ki-Moon, March 18 2011; Reports of Amnesty, OHCHR, UN population, etc., cited in http://www.economist.com/blogs/dailychart/2011/07/arab-spring-death-toll; UN report: http://www.ohchr.org/Documents/countries/SY/Syria_Report_2011-08-17.pdf; Human Rights Watch report 2012; UN report: http://www.ohchr.org/Documents/countries/SY/Syria_Report_2011-08-17.pdf; http://www.strescom.org/briefings/daily-round-ups/item/356-db15092012.html.

[ii] http://www.crisisgroup.org/en/publication-type/crisiswatch/crisiswatch-database.aspx?CountryIDs={B915F536-D27C-4FAC-A808-06B2551C8ADB}&StartDate=20110101&EndDate=20110401; http://www.smh.com.au/world/gaddafi-forces-retake-towns-near-capital-20110302-1bejx.htm; Human Rights Watch report, June 2011, http://www.hrw.org/sites/default/ files/reports/syria061webwcover.pdf; Syrian Network for Human Rights, http://dchrs.org/english/File/Reports/27-02-2013_Facts_And_Figures_SNHR_Report_En.pdf; http://www.strescom.org/briefings/daily-round-ups/item/650-db14313.html.

[iii] http://www.unhcr.org/cgi-bin/texis/vtx/home/opendocPDFViewer.html? docid=50f95f7a9&query= Arab%20Spring; UNHCR Update No. 29 http://www.unhcr.org/4df9cde49.html.

[iv] For mid June 2011. See: UNHCR Update No. 29 (http://www.unhcr.org/4df9cde49.html); http://www.foreignpolicyjournal.com/2011/06/28/arab-spring-refugees-the-cost-of-war/; http://www.jpost.com/MiddleEast/Article.aspx?id=272399; UN refugee agency, cited in *Ha'aretz*: http://www.haaretz.co.il/news/world/middle-east/1.1917678.

[v] University of California Berkeley's search engine (http://www.lib.berkeley.edu/doemoff/ govinfo/intl/gov_ngos.html).

camp have thus far led to a brutal civil war with initially limited international engagement.

Although systematic data is hard to obtain, figures relating to instrumental, humanitarian, and advocacy network aspects of the Egyptian, Libyan, and Syrian cases suggest that existing explanations can provide only a partial account of variation in international response. Extensive horrific casualties in all three cases generated very different responses and outcomes. In terms of the instrumental motivations about disruption and power, here measured by internally displaced person (IDP) and refugee rates (see MacFarlane and Weiss 2000), it is evident that despite this being a nonissue in the case of Egypt we nevertheless witnessed international intervention. Concerning the role of international and local NGOs, here, too, the data offer little help.[3]

Multilevel Structure of Political Opportunities, State's/Movement's Powers, and International Intervention

The political opportunities framework promises explanatory leverage on the expansion and outcomes of contention by directing attention to the world outside a social movement and to the development of conditions conducive to international intervention. Scholars of social movements and contentious politics have explored how favorable or unfavorable changes in the POS may encourage (or not) protest (Tilly 1978; McAdam 1999; Kitschelt 1986; Meyer 2004). Seeking a more dynamic and agency-focused treatment of POS, Tarrow (2011) has suggested greater attention to the role of activists in coping with the inherently shifting and volatile nature of political opportunities. To navigate a dynamic set of political opportunities and to mold political conditions to their purposes, activists make choices about specific tactics, the organization of their mobilizing structures and resources, and the ways they frame their actions in a way that would resonate with potential supporters, domestically as well as internationally. Activists pick strategies given their perceptions of the possible, which are generated by the relational fields among movements, countermovements, publics, and authorities at various levels (Goldstone 2004).

Keck and Sikkink's (1998) "boomerang model" offers a helpful way of understanding how activists can navigate a resistant state authority. Adopting a relational approach, according to which interests and values are mutually constitutive and shaped within interactions, the authors argue that the weaker parties in a conflict seek to mobilize additional, often more powerful, outside actors on their behalf. Local activists work with outside advocacy networks that have access to extranational institutions and engage in efforts at persuasion, socialization, and pressure. These coordinated campaigns build primarily on informational and symbolic politics as a way to gain attention and call on outside international actors and parties to exert pressure on the "blocking" state and to hold its authorities accountable to universal principles, values, and norms (16).

Several scholars have worked to expand and refine Keck and Sikkink's framework. For some, the concept of transnational activist networks fails to distinguish between the various forms of noninstitutional actors, which may differ in the nature of their challenge to, and relations with, institutional politics and in their dominant mode of contention. When mass-based contentious politics is the case, blockage can take the form of outright repression (Tarrow 2001b, 2005). Relatedly, Keck and Sikkink pay little analytical attention to the agency of state authorities and the constraints and opportunities they face in regional and international arenas. Local activists who challenge the state and engage in contention may confront systematic outright repression, which may persist and even lead to the crackdown of the opposition despite "high degree of openness of international institutions to the participation of transnational NGOs, networks, and coalitions" (Sikkink 2005, 156) operating on behalf of the locally oppressed.

This means paying attention not only to the openness of (or access to) international institutions to claims made by nonstate actors but also, and more importantly, to other inherently relational aspects of POS: *divided elites* and *influential allies* (Tarrow 2011, 165–66).[4] Extended from the domestic to the international level, the concept of divided elites refers to how divisions among members of supranational institutions may provide greater maneuvering space and leeway for locally challenged states; concomitantly, the concept of influential allies refers to the prospects for mobilizing outside actors who can intervene or prevent international intervention (Tarrow 2005).

Attending to divided elites and influential allies helps assess the stability of states' ruling alignment, which is not simply a function of intrinsic economic or military *strength* but, more typically, a function of power and influence acquired and maintained by interaction. That is to say, it is contingent on the larger regional and international structures of political alliances and networks in which a state is nested, based on interests, values, norms, or prejudices and forms of economic and security interdependence (Rothman and Oliver 1999; Maoz 2011). Although it would be wrong to speak about authoritative powers in the international arena in sovereignty terms, it would be equally erroneous to think about states' conduct as constraint-free, and this holds true regardless of a given state's economic and military strength. Even a state possessing unconventional weapons (e.g., Pakistan) or a highly demanded resource (e.g., Saudi Arabia's oil) would play defense, forming alliances and joining supranational institutions as a way to establish or to preserve its maneuvering space (e.g., North Korea's Mutual Aid and Cooperation Friendship Treaty with China).

This logic holds across a range of regime types. Even in liberal democracies, under certain conditions or with regard to certain issue domains (e.g., prisoners' rights during intense security threat) local activists may face blockage and look for help outside the state. The blocking authorities, in their stead, may seek to preserve their maneuvering space by relying on their alliance system or even improving it.

In authoritarian regimes, however, which offer movements no meaningful access to the policy process and where the latter must always anticipate and plan for repression (Boudreau 2004), activists are indeed likely to seek international venues for making their claims. Regime incumbents, in their stead, look not only to the character and size of the dissident coalition, but also to the likely support they can find or pressure they may face regionally and internationally in assessing their own personal opportunities and constraints, in power or not (Nepstad 2011b; Ritter 2015; Swed and Weinreb 2015). The few regimes that care little about international legitimacy (e.g., Saddam Hussein's Iraq, Ne Win's Myanmar) pay a social and economic price for their indifference (Alimi and Hirsch-Hoefler 2012).

Authorities and movements then, make judgments about the varying and dynamic POS they face at different levels of authority. The specific nested configuration of the various POS at any given time, and its relative tightness or looseness, suggests a great deal about a regime's stability and space of action and, in turn, a movement's prospects for succeeding in inviting international intervention (Meyer 2003; Rothman and Oliver 1999). These structures are themselves nested within larger regional as well as international environments that constrain or facilitate particular kinds of political opportunities for state authorities.

To see how this nesting affects the range of possibilities and responses available to state authorities, we can examine its tightness or looseness along two related dimensions (Meyer 2003). Reconnecting with the notion of divided elites, the first structurally focused dimension is *exclusivity*, by which we mean the degree to which a state is constrained by claims made by larger institutions in which it is nested. Keeping in mind that almost all states are embedded within a maze of ties and interdependence, it is important to examine the existence of other nesting institutions with competing (at times countering) claims to those of other nesting institutions on matters of policy. It follows then that we should not only distinguish the exclusivity of claims nesting institutions have on a particular state, but also the maneuvering space a nested state has within a larger institution. Reconnecting with the notion of influential allies, the second agency-focused dimension is *autonomy*, by which we mean the degree of wiggle room or "slack" a state has within the larger institutions in which it is nested. When thinking about autonomy, and keeping in mind that almost all states have some value for other states, it is important to examine the diversity of alliances a given state has and the centrality of its allies. Exclusivity and autonomy are, of course, interrelated. Additional nesting institutions can create more slack; states constantly act to improve their position within the nesting institutions and rely on influential allies and capitalize on differences and conflicting interests between larger institutions as a way to preserve or improve their maneuvering space.

Broadly speaking and for analytic value and utility, combining the two dimensions allows identification of four nested configurations of a regime's stability (see Figure 7.1) as they pertain to those underlying conditions that make a movement's success in inviting international intervention more likely.

The first nested configuration is *low exclusivity/low autonomy*. In this fairly uncommon configuration, the state's relative power is low and we can expect repression to backfire and conditions conducive to dissidents' success in inviting international intervention are favorable. This is expected because a state's lack of integration with any one nesting institution coincides with absence of influential allies to rely on. In addition to the case of Libya and the UN Support Mission on the side of the National Transition Council (discussed in what follows), we also observed a similar scenario in the case of Somalia during the early 1990s, with UN and other supranational institutions (e.g., Arab League, Organization of Islamic Conference) operating on the side of the rebel forces against remnants of Mohamed Siad Barre's military regime.

The second nested configuration is characterized by *high exclusivity/low autonomy*, whereby a given state is exceptionally dependent on nesting institutions either economically or militarily or both, and has low levels of wiggle room as a result of little diversity in its system of alliance. In this scenario intervention, when occurring, is likely to take a nonmilitary, diplomatic form, yet nonetheless

		Autonomy	
		Low	High
Exclusivity	Low	Military Intervention	No Military Intervention
	High	Effective Diplomacy	Condemnations and Sanctions

FIGURE 7.1 Nested configurations and types of intervention.

effective and binding, as was the case with Marcos's Philippines and the UN/ United States during the mid-1980s and, as we discuss below, with Mubarak's Egypt.

The case of Syria, (like, e.g., the Chechen War of independence against Russia during the second half of the 1990s or the more recent Ukraine popular contention against Russian-backed Yanukovych's government [to which we return in the conclusion]), illustrates the third nested configuration, characterized by *low exclusivity/high autonomy*. In this configuration, states are less dependent on one particular nesting institution on matters of policy and maintain a diverse system of alliances with powerful allies, all of which reduces the likelihood of repression to backfire, and activists' efforts to invite intervention will result in condemnation at best.

The fourth and last nested configuration is characterized by *high exclusivity/high autonomy*. Here, a given state is tightly integrated within larger nesting institutions with little if any competing claims with respect to policy issues, and yet enjoys the support of powerful allies as guarantors against international intervention. As the case of Israel and the Palestinian movement has repeatedly demonstrated, the best activists can aspire for are international sanctions or "soft-power" diplomatic initiatives.

In what follows, we illustrate how the first three nested configurations apply to the cases of Libya, Egypt, and Syria, respectively, and how they enhance understanding of the conditions under which dissidents' effort to promote international intervention can have an influence. We return to the fourth nested configuration in the conclusion.

A Note on Data and Its Usage

In addition to the vastly growing body of research and writing on the "Arab Spring", and primary and secondary sources and materials on each state's foreign relations and alliance system, the analysis of each case relies primarily on two types of data as measures of each regime's relative power. Specifically, we rely on International Monetary Fund (IMF) data on direction of trade (DoT) between states, export as well as import, and Stockholm International Peace Research Institute (SIPRI) data on transfer of arms (ToA) between states, again inclusive of both export and import.[5] In both sets of data, we cover a period of 10 years (2001–2010) and allow for up to 10 partners to be included. Although the DoT data includes military goods (e.g., ammunition, vessels, vehicles, and aircraft) as part of the overall estimate of trade value between states, the ToA data has two important advantages. First, compared with DoT, ToA provides a refined and more comprehensive measure of arms trade. Second, unlike DoT, the ToA data is aimed at reflecting the value of weapons according to the unit production cost rather than the financial value of the transfer. Combining the two datasets to measure a regime's military power has the advantage of offering a more comprehensive picture, because each relies on different sources (primarily governmental sources in the case of IMF data and primarily nongovernmental sources in the case of SIPRI data).[6] Combined with information about a given state's regional and international system of alliances, these measures suggest a great deal about a given regime's nested configuration both in terms of exclusivity (i.e., the existence of competing claims) and autonomy (i.e., the diversity and centrality of allies). The analysis below draws primarily on the DoT data,[7] with additional reference to the ToA data.

Nested Configurations and International Intervention

Mubarak's Egypt, Qadhafi's Libya, and Assad's Syria faced ostensibly similar challenges, yet differed markedly along a few clear dimensions that help explain their different trajectories. We can reduce these differences to an explanation of why, despite dissidents' efforts in each case to invite international intervention, the outcomes were strikingly different. From a nested institutions perspective, we should examine the relative power of each state along the related dimensions of exclusivity and autonomy, and how variations in this regard contribute to our analytical leverage regarding differences in international response.

Libya: Low Exclusivity/Low Autonomy

Slightly over a month after the massive protests in Libya began on February 15, 2011, the UN Security Council voted in favor of forming a NATO-led no-fly zone over Libyan airspace. Resolution 1973 of March 17 followed extensive and indiscriminate bombings of Libyan air forces on rebel strongholds—which took the shape of the National Transition Council (February 27)—with rapidly growing numbers of casualties as well as IDPs and refugees fleeing the country to bordering and nearby states. Preceding the UN vote, France recognized the NTC as the legitimate government of Libya. Reinforced by an intensive international campaign on the part of various advocacy organizations, the UN sided with France in recognizing the NTC as the government of Libya (Bhardwaj 2012) and the Human Rights Council in suspending Libya's membership. The imposition of the no-fly zone quickly expanded to NATO engagement in limited air raids on Qadhafi's forces and, later in September 2011, consolidated as the UN Support Mission in Libya.

Although not as isolated as during the 1980s, Libya still represents a case of exceptionally low exclusivity. Qadhafi purposefully isolated his country both regionally and internationally, embracing an unrepentant and defiant policy vis-à-vis outside actors, including the UN, the Arab League, and other African institutions (Eljahmi 2006). No wonder that when concerns were expressed by the UN in the face of the skyrocketing death toll, and pressures were exerted by bordering state members of the UN regarding the waves of refugees (HRW Report 2012, 442), Qadhafi not only rejected them, but also continued with his brutal crackdown on the opposition. It is telling that when Resolution 1973 was considered, only a few members expressed a faint and mostly symbolic objection and abstained from the vote; there were no competing claims made by any other regional or international institution. Not only did the African Union and, most notably, the Arab League support intervention (in fact the Arab League decision prompted the Security Council one) but also the reservations expressed by Russia and China revolved mostly around the depth and scope of the operation.[8]

Examining Libya's autonomy in terms of economic and military value adds an important layer to our understanding of why NTC forces were successful in promoting international intervention. The DoT data on Libya's value, both as supplier and consumer of goods to and from other states, presented in Figure 7.2 and supplemented by the ToA data (see Appendix), offers valuable insights.

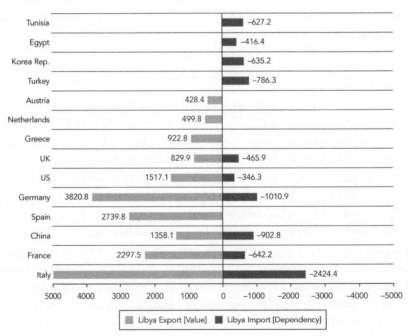

FIGURE 7.2 Libya's economic and military partners, 2001–2010 (avg.).
Source: IMF Direction of Trade Statistics. Figures are rounded, based on US$ million.

Qadhafi's Libya controlled valuable economic assets (most notably oil and gas) and capitalized on them financially to maintain some degree of diversity. Over time, however, given the declining diversity of partners and their centrality, Qadhafi's Libya enjoyed less wiggle room. It is clear that Italy captured the lion's share of Libya's export and import and that, despite a noticeable drop in both dimensions following 2008,[9] the situation was relatively stable over the years. To illustrate, comparing Libya's average import value from Italy with China, for example, reveals a striking difference: Libya's import from Italy amounts to $2,424 million compared with $903 million from China. Of course, Italy is an influential ally; as a long-standing, important member of NATO (albeit not nearly as important as the United States, when it comes to the relative portion of deployable forces, or even Turkey, for that matter) and based on the colonial ties between the two states, Italy might have had an interest in playing the role of guarantor against intervention. Yet, from Italy's perspective, the crisis in Libya posed a major national security threat that pushed it to fully support and promote intervention (Kashiam 2012). Despite concerns over the loss of a major supplier of gas, it seems that the far graver concern Italy faced related to the waves of thousands of Libyans fleeing the country and seeking refuge on Italian soil.[10] Given the exceptionally low figures in the ToA data, one could hardly speak of any meaningful military ally; when compared with Egypt and Syria, the low value of weaponry unit production cost transferred from and to Libya seems to further reinforce the low levels of autonomy Qadhafi's Libya had.

Egypt: High Exclusivity/Low Autonomy

The Tahrir Square–based popular dissent in Egypt, which began on January 25, 2011, and ultimately brought about the fall of Mubarak, provides an instructive example of how a state's nested configuration of POS, characterized by high level of exclusivity and low level of autonomy, sets the conditions under which repression may backfire. Taking off in what became known as the "day of rage" with tens of thousands of Egyptians taking to the streets and demanding the end of Mubarak's decades-long rule, the Egyptian popular revolt quickly resulted in a ruthless repression and a coordinated effort on the part of local and international advocacy groups to invite international intervention. The early stage of the contentious cycle witnessed a wavering international response with occasional international denunciations and concerns regarding the brutal policing. By the end of the second week, and especially by the United States, these concerns turned into explicit pressure and calls for Mubarak to step down. On February 11, 2011, Mubarak resigned and handed power to the Supreme Council of the Armed Forces.

One of the clearest and most instructive observations in the Egyptian case related to the high exclusivity of NATO's claim for influence, which, when eventually made, was swift and effective. Mubarak's Egypt was not isolated from either regional or other international actors, and the brewing contention showed no signs of developing a refugee and IDP-related emergency situation. The undeniable geopolitical value Egypt presents for many states may help explain why we observed no unwavering consensus within the UN parallel to that of the Libyan crisis. Moreover, with few exceptions (e.g., Iran), most states, while expressing concerns over the cumulative evidence of severe military police repression, were nonetheless at least initially interested in seeing Mubarak regain stability.

Yet, ever since the early 1970s, and increasingly following the peace treaty with Israel of 1978–1979, Egypt's dependence on Western economic and military support has been so high that, once these states' leaders made it clear that Egypt's stability trumped the survival of the Mubarak regime, the government lost elite support and fell in short order. On top of the immense economic benefits Egypt gained as a result of siding with the United States and the EU, perhaps the most central dividend included Egypt's entry into NATO as a major non-NATO Ally member. This status grants valuable military benefits, but in this case, it has come to mean that the Egyptian military is completely under the influence of NATO (NCAFP 2012). When pressure from Western powers began to mount, as was the case with the German minister of finance's announcement from early February 2011 to stop all weaponry export and to cancel those already approved,[11] the army deserted the president (Frisch 2013, 188).

The exceptionally tight nesting within NATO and its exclusivity of claim with respect to the Egyptian turmoil is reinforced by the relatively low degree of autonomy the Mubarak's Egypt enjoyed economically and militarily. As seen in Figure 7.3, the most noticeable finding relates to the prominent place occupied by the United States and by EU countries (most of whom are NATO members) among Egypt's economic and military partners (Pace 2012). Egypt's fairly high diversity of economic and military partners is subsumed by the fact that most are limited to the West and the most central of them is the United States, whose role in setting the tone in NATO is undeniable.

At first glance, the presence of China and, to a lesser extent, Russia (see Appendix), among Egypt's economic and military partners may seem surprising. But China's relative importance in Egypt's economy is dwarfed by the role of the United States. That China's relative portion grew over time,[12] and arms transfer value with Russia exceeds that of the United States during 2010, should not be overrated. These developments indicated the mounting tension inside Egypt between the military establishment and the attempt of the heir-to-be, Gamal Mubarak, to weaken it and to diversify the country import policy, which,

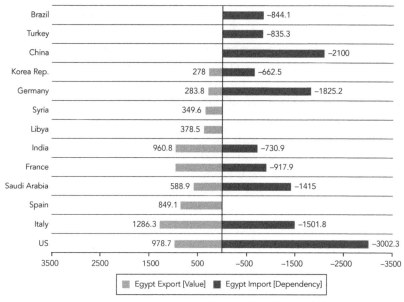

FIGURE 7.3 Egypt's economic and military partners, 2001–2010 (avg.).
Source: IMF Direction of Trade Statistics. Figures are rounded, based on US$ million.

as noted, was only partly successful (Frisch 2013). One could plausibly assume, then, that had the situation in Egypt demanded actual intervention and involvement of other supranational institutions, Russia and China would have taken a more active and assertive role in the events (other than concerns for the safety of Russia citizens located in Egypt for example[13]). Given the tightness of Egypt's nesting configuration and the exclusivity of claim NATO had, this was not the case, all of which stands in sharp contrast to the still-raging situation in Syria.

Syria: Low Exclusivity/High Autonomy

We approach the still-unfolding case of Syria with appropriate caution. Nonetheless, the first stages of the Syrian revolt provide ample evidence in support of the third scenario of the conditions conducive to international intervention. Compared with the Libyan and Egyptian cases, the Syrian revolt began in the small and relatively unknown city of Dar'a and took a longer time to spread and to consolidate. A series of skirmishes during early February and March 2011 instantly met with harsh repression, aggravated the city population, and prompted even larger demonstrations. With more explicit demands for the downfall of the Assad-led Ba'athist regime voiced and symbolic acts of defiance taken (e.g., tearing down the statue of Hafez al-Assad and a billboard of his son), repression hardened, only to be met by an unabated, wide-spread, and daring uprising, which gradually deteriorated into a bloody civil war (Leenders 2012). But the most striking difference between the Syrian case and the Egyptian and Libyan ones concerned the lack of international intervention. It is not that the situation in Syria was less dire. The struggle in Syria has produced steadily rising casualties and massive numbers of IDPs, with torrents of refugees. The Syrian National Council consolidated its position in early summer 2011 and worked in systematic collaboration with regional and international advocacy groups to invite international intervention, but no collective and coordinated international intervention took place. When foreign intervention began in April 2012, it took the form of limited and semicovert supply and training, mostly by individual states (Chatham House 2012; Bhardwaj 2012).

Examining the characteristics of Syria's nesting configuration generates valuable insights as to why repression has failed to backfire in the case of Assad's authoritarian regime. To understand the international paralysis despite vocal denouncements by various regional states (e.g., Turkey, Iraq, Jordan), it is critical to take into consideration the continuing disagreements and discords between various supranational nesting institutions with regard to Syria. When the UN claim on Qadhafi's regime was made, it was met with little opposition by regional and international players; the exclusivity of NATO's claim on Mubarak was so high that it amounted to effective diplomatic intervention. But in the case of Syria, any claim was met by a counterclaim. Between the fall of 2011 and summer 2012, three Security Council initiatives to draft resolutions, ranging from sanctions to actual military action under Chapter VII, were undermined by Russia and China, who wielded veto power as permanent Security Council members (IISS 2012). Even though Syria is not a member of either the Russian-led Collective Security Treaty Organization or the Chinese-led Shanghai Cooperation Organization, alliances designed to counter the influence of the United States and NATO in central Asia, it enjoyed their consistent patronage.[14] This reflects Syria's high value to both Russia and China and the long-standing trade agreements and defense treaties between the countries, a system of alliance in which Iran also has a vital role (ibid.; Rafizadeh 2012; Magen 2012). Both Iran and Syria are Russia's close partners in the region, as central military and economic customers, with Syria also having several other added values, such as providing Russia with a naval resupply base in the seaport city of Tartus (IISS 2012).

However, as seen in Figure 7.4, the value of Assad's regime is not limited to Russia, China, and Iran. The valuable geopolitical strategic position Syria represents to many states affords it relatively high autonomy and, consequently, more wiggle room for the regime. This is also reflected in the diversity of economic and military partners, inclusive of both Western and Eastern ones, and the lack of

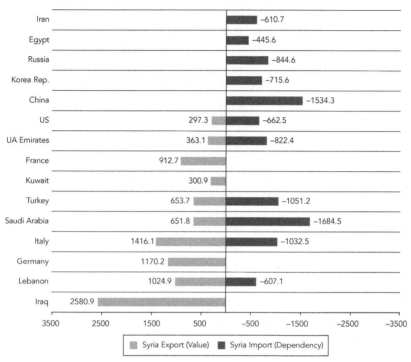

FIGURE 7.4 Syria's economic and military partners, 2001–2010.
Source: IMF Direction of Trade Statistics. Figures are rounded, based on US$ million.

heavy reliance on any one single major state. For example, the fact that Syria has been a central supplier of goods to Iraq may help explain why the latter has refused to vote in favor of the Arab League's sanctions motion of November 2011.[15] While Saudi Arabia, a prominent import partner, supported the sanctions (and Turkey too, although only as observer), Syria was still able to rely on other import partners. Nevertheless, the increasing reliance on chemical weapons by Assad's regime has generated important changes in this regard. Although Syria's powerful nested configuration initially prevented international military intervention, the developing civil war could erode the regime's position in relation to other states. As we emphasize, a state's nested configuration, opportunities, and constraints are dynamic.

Beyond Authoritarianism and the "Arab Spring"

By paying attention to how activists use their powers to externalize their struggle, scholars of social movements and contention have advanced our understanding of why sometimes interest-based and/or moral-based considerations are not

enough to attract international intervention on the part of supranational powers. As these cases suggest, there are times when even the most vibrant and savvy
dissident leaders fail to mobilize outside support. The striking differences in
international response to the cases of Libya, Egypt, and Syria provide a powerful
reminder of what has long been a relative neglect in social movement scholarship: the tendency to overlook the strategic role of authorities as a proactive agent
in contention. Examining the POS and the constraints that challenged states
face in relation to a larger international configuration of actors advances understanding of those conditions conducive to international intervention.

We cannot close without addressing briefly three unfinished agendas: a
nested configuration of "high exclusivity/high autonomy," a more dynamic
model that captures shifting alignments, and applicability of our framework
to nonauthoritarian cases. The Palestinian national struggle against Israeli rule
(a.k.a. the first Intifada of 1987–1992) is a useful case for addressing the first two
agendas. Despite conscious, well-orchestrated, and systematic efforts on the part
of Palestinian activists and representatives early in the uprising, efforts that capitalized on a harsh Israeli crackdown and steadily growing numbers of casualties
and internally displaced Palestinians, the best Palestinian activists could accomplish amounted to threats of international sanctions and "soft power" diplomatic
initiatives. Later, around 1990–1991, international pressure was consequential in
bringing Israel to the negotiating table with a joint Jordanian-Palestinian delegation in Madrid 1991 for the first time in the history of the conflict. Nonetheless,
it is telling that Prime Minister Shamir's rightwing coalition was able to prevent
the participation of an independent Palestinian delegation or Yasser Arafat, to
continue Israel's settlement policy, and to stall the peace talks to the point of
rendering them ineffective.

From a nested configuration perspective, Israel's changing wiggle room can
be explained, in part, by changes in its autonomy and exclusivity. During the
run-up and into the first few years of the Intifada, Israel enjoyed an impressive
diversity of economic and military partners with a fairly balanced export/import
ratio. In fact, like Syria, Israel faced low exclusivity of claims, partly as a result of
the United States's countering of claims made by the UN. Israel's nested configuration of "low exclusivity/high autonomy" changed later on to one of "high
exclusivity/high autonomy." This was the result, inter alia, of its integration
within NATO as a major non-NATO Ally in 1989 and the combined effect of
the developing crisis in the Gulf in late summer 1990 and the unsettling bloodshed in the Temple Mount in October 1990.[16] These developments engendered a
meaningful shift in Israel's nested configuration of an alliance system, with the
United States working closely with the Soviet Union to link the Iraqi and Israeli
issues, and exerting unprecedented pressure on Israel to declare its willingness

to participate in an international peace conference. Much like Assad's efforts at strengthening Syria's autonomy (e.g., initiation of a gas deal with Iran and Iraq as early as May 2011), the heavy pressure on Israel pushed Shamir's government to improve its autonomy. In the context of weak economic performance and sky-rocketing external national debts, Shamir's government not only strengthened ties with preexisting trade partners (e.g., India, Turkey, Mexico, South Africa), but also formed new diplomatic ties and opened new trade partnerships with China, Honduras, Bulgaria, and Czechoslovakia, to name only a few. The fact that some of these partnerships were facilitated by the actual fact of Israel's pro-peace stance should not lead us to overlook the importance of recognizing the proactive role of state actors both in responding to changes in the structure of their system of alliance and in structuring them.

Finally, we have argued that it is important to consider the multiple contexts in which contention between challengers and state authorities is nested. But how well does our framework translate to other sorts of regimes, not only composite or hybrid ones like Israel, but also more democratic settings? Obviously, dissidents in nondemocracies operate in higher-risk environments and face more severe obsta-cles when they challenge authorities. As noted, however, democracies are capable of repression as well. The conflict in Ukraine provides another illustration of how a challenged state's nested configuration should be considered when assessing the capacity of dissident activists to mobilize international intervention.

Ukraine declared independence in the wake of the Eastern European wave of democracy movements and disintegration of the Soviet Union. But the new democracy was still in tight orbit around Russia, with considerable public sup-port for continued relations with Russia and Russian dominance of a series of corrupt governments and, more significantly, a corrupt and very weak economy (Peisakhin 2013); in 2013, more than 40 percent of Ukraine's trade was with the nations of the former Soviet Union. Although the share of Ukrainian trade with the EU grew, approaching 30 percent, Ukraine represented less than half of 1 percent of Europe's trade. Thus, for both financial and strategic reasons, Ukraine was much more tightly nested in Russian dominance, with President Viktor Yanukovych's government enjoying relatively high autonomy and facing fairly low exclusivity of Western claims, thereby constraining the reforms avail-able to Ukrainian dissidents.

Activists at the grass roots had long pushed the Ukrainian government to create more autonomy for them to make claims and more wiggle room for their government to innovate, by capitalizing on prior Western policies and developing closer economic and military ties to the EU and NATO (Beissinger 2013; see also Bunce's chapter in this volume). In November 2013, however, the Yanukovych government abandoned a trade agreement with the EU, under financial and political pressure from Russia. Activists took to the streets immediately, demanding first a reopening to the West, and in short order, Yanukovych's ouster. Facing large and disruptive demonstrations and occupation of Kiev's Independence Square (Maidan), Yanukovych tried to crush the opposition through both legal initiatives and police brutality, which resulted in heavy casualties, yet only stiffened the opposition. Its leaders tried to mobilize support from Western powers in their struggle. Similar to the Syrian case, despite the undeniable interest among Western powers and institutions in intervention and the ever-growing number of casualties, the systematic efforts on the part of opposition leaders to mobilize international involvement were largely unsuccessful. Although Western governments have expressed rhetorical support for the reformers in Kiev, and even tried to promote a UN resolution following Russia's annexation of Crimea, they were unwilling—or unable—to do much more.

In late February 2014, facing intensifying and spreading deadly clashes, Yanukovych negotiated an agreement with activist leaders to hold new elections, restrict presidential powers, and restore an earlier constitution. Activist leaders, however, could not enforce the quiescence of their own supporters, who took control over key sites throughout Kiev. The already impeached president, surely fearing for his own safety, left Kiev for a sanctuary in Crimea, the eastern Russian-speaking portion of the country, which was even more tightly nested in Russian dominance (and which was unilaterally annexed in March), while the western part of the country was dominated by a newly elected government and president as of May 2014, and allied with the West. This configuration of power helps explain why Russia has been able to maintain great, almost exclusive, influence over Ukraine's fate: it first blocked or discouraged other powers from effective intervention and then, when this turned out to be insufficient, became more deeply involved in the conflict and unilaterally and outside the UN framework, intervened and promoted the country's split.

The utility of the nested framework we have advanced for explaining the cases we outline above and a range of other cases, should lead us to think about the various levels of authorities that enable and constrain both dissident activists and the state they challenge. Taken together, this should result in more accurate, if not always more optimistic, appraisals of a challenging movement's influence.

Acknowledgments

This chapter is an expanded version of an article published in a special issue of the *Swiss Political Science Review* on the "Arab Spring". Earlier versions were presented in panels at the International Studies Association meeting in Toronto 2014, and the American Sociological Association meeting in Chicago 2015. Useful comments came from participants in both panels as well as from Jack Goldstone, Robin Wagner-Pacifici, Vincent Boudreau, Avraham Sela, and Yitzhak Brudny, for which we are grateful. Special thanks go to Alon Burstein for assisting us in data collection.

Appendix: SIPRI Arms Transfers Data

Libya

Arms figures are at constant (1990) prices, based on US$ million.

Arms Import	2001	2002	2003	2004	2005	2006	2007	2008	2009	2010
Russia						13	13	13		15
Italy						2	2		23	6
France								3	3	3
Arms Export	**2001**	**2002**	**2003**	**2004**	**2005**	**2006**	**2007**	**2008**	**2009**	**2010**
Pakistan				113	113		10	14	14	10
U.A. Emirates							18		18	18
Zimbabwe			16							
Namibia		11								
Chad								3		

Egypt

Arms figures are at constant (1990) prices, based on US$ million.

Arms Import	2001	2002	2003	2004	2005	2006	2007	2008	2009	2010
USA	815	480	348	459	535	539	464	186	106	249
Russia		60	60	60	145	60	85		8	367
China	18	67	88	88	21		35	35	35	35
Montenegro						71	109			
Germany (FRG)	10	24	122							
Netherlands							42	70	26	
Finland	1	2	6	6		68				
Austria		79								
Ukraine					26				26	26
France										

Arms Import	2001	2002	2003	2004	2005	2006	2007	2008	2009	2010
Arms Export	—	—	—	—	—	—	—	—	—	—

Syria

Arms figures are at constant (1990) prices, based on US$ million.

Arms Import	2001	2002	2003	2004	2005	2006	2007	2008	2009	2010
Russia	8	25	25	5	15	26		46	73	268
North Korea	20	20	20	20	20	20	20	20	20	
Belarus			24					172		
Iran						54		40	45	45
China Mainland										20
Arms Export	2001	2002	2003	2004	2005	2006	2007	2008	2009	2010
Lebanon/Hezbollah						3			20	20

Notes

1. Two points of clarification: The analysis is limited to cases of *collective* intervention by international institutions/organizations, most critically, the UN. Those few cases of international intervention outside the UN Security Council or framework (e.g., Korea 1950 or Iraq 2003) are seen here as exceptions that prove the rule. Additionally, we focus on the political opportunity structure of the challenged states, and less on the opportunity structures of those states that are part of a given international institution.

2. See *Ethics and International Affairs*, volume 13, March 1999, and volume 25, 2011. For an approach that questions the divide between interests and norms, see MacFarlane and Weiss (2000).

3. Regardless of the number of local NGOs, dissidents in all three cases enjoyed the active support and involvement of myriad of regional and international NGOs and other advocacy groups and coalitions. For a list of local NGOs, see http://www.wango.org /resources.aspx.

4. A third aspect is *shifting alignments*, which deals with the volatility and instability of political alignments. Given our focus on one particular configuration at one specific time juncture, this aspect is excluded from the analysis. We discuss this aspect in the conclusion.

5. Respectively, see http://www.imf.org/external/about.htm and http://www.sipri.org/databases /armstransfers/background/coverage.

6. Two points are worth noting. First, although it is unlikely that incorporation of data on small arms will have any bearing on the overall, broad patterns we are interested in here, future research would benefit from including this type of data. The second point relates to a possible discrepancy between export and import values of trade partners in the DoT data (e.g., Egypt and Libya), which is likely the result of failure or refusal of a given government to report on certain goods. Here too, there is little reason to believe the overall pattern would be different.

7. The detailed DoT data is available on request.

8. See UN special report: "The 'Arab Spring' at the United Nations: Between Hope and Despair," http://www.cihrs.org/wp-content/uploads/2012/06/UN-en.pdf (accessed May 19, 2013).

9. Export to Italy dropped by some 50 percent after 2008 and import from Italy by some 15 percent.

10. See ABC News, "Libyan Crisis Could Spell 'Disaster' for Italy," http://www.abc.net.au/news/2011-03-03/libyan-crisis-could-spell-disaster-for-italy/1965818 (accessed May 19, 2013).

11. *Ha'aretz*, February 7, 2011.

12. From 513 million in 2001 to 6,643 million in imports.

13. http://en.wikipedia.org/wiki/International_reactions_to_the_2011_Egyptian_revolution (accessed May 26, 2013).

14. Dadan Upadhyay, "CSTO Emerging as an Alternative to NATO," *Russia and India Report*, January 10, 2012, http://indrus.in/articles/2012/01/10/csto_emerging_as_an_alternative_to_nato_14134.html; accessed on May 31, 2013, 18:21.

15. *New York Times*, "Isolating Syria, Arab League Imposes Broad Sanctions," November 27, 2011, http://www.nytimes.com/2011/11/28/world/middleeast/arab-league-prepares-to-vote-on-syrian-sanctions.html?pagewanted=all&_r=0 (accessed June 1, 2013).

16. It is noteworthy that the United States supported a condemnation motion of Israel in the special meeting of the Security Council of late October 1990.

8

Understanding Dynamics, Endogeneity, and Complexity in Protest Campaigns

A COMPARATIVE ANALYSIS OF EGYPT (2011)
AND IRAN (1977–1979)

Karen Rasler

The Case for Complexity

The systematic study of nonviolent civil resistance campaigns (or more simply protest campaigns) is now quite popular among political scientists. This new interest is likely to be due to the success that such campaigns have had in bringing down autocratic regimes and paving the way for possible democratic transitions. For instance, there were the East European and Asian revolts in the 1980s and 1990s (East Germany, Czechoslovakia, Philippines, and Serbia), the color revolutions in the 2000s (Yugoslavia, Georgia, Ukraine, Lebanon, and Kyrgyzstan), and more recently, the "Arab Spring" revolts in 2011 (Tunisia, Egypt, Libya, Syria, Bahrain, Jordan, and Yemen), and European and Latin American revolts in 2013 and 2014 (Turkey, Ukraine, and Venezuela).

Despite the effort of sociologists and political scientists who have studied these and other nonviolent protest campaigns, we have little consistent information about how and why they lead to successful outcomes. Key findings indicate that successful civil resistance campaigns that lead to regime change depend on factors such as: (1) nonviolent varied and innovative protest tactics, (2) large numbers of diverse protesters, (3) military and/or security force defections, (4) repression and backfire effects, (5) diffusion, and (6) international support.

Unfortunately, we can also find cases of protest campaigns where some or all of these characteristics were present but their outcomes were not associated with regime change or significant political reforms.[1]

Why such disparate results? One reason is that the emergence and outcomes of protest campaigns are difficult to predict, largely because the mobilization of participants is a highly "endogenous and contingent process" (Beissinger 2011, 27). More precisely, each protest campaign is the result of a mobilization process that involves a "highly interdependent set of actions and reactions" among multiple governmental and nongovernmental actors. The interrelationships among these actions and reactions is what produces the evolutionary, dynamic characteristics of protest campaigns. So, indeterminate factors involving elements of spontaneity, critical mass, bandwagon, adaptive learning, and diffusion processes shape and transform transgressive contention during protest campaigns. Therefore, identifying fixed causal linkages is difficult given the "radical unpredictability of contentious interactions, the contingency of their outcomes, and the path dependence of these interactive sequences" (Koopmans 2004: 29).

The Advantages of a Mechanism-Process Approach

In light of this complexity, how do we study protest campaigns? I contend that the "mechanism-process" advanced by McAdam, Tarrow, and Tilly (2001) in *Dynamics of Contention* is an ideal approach for understanding protest campaigns as "dynamic, endogenous and complex" phenomena. These authors argue that protest campaigns can be dissected into "relational mechanisms and processes." While relational mechanisms "alter the connections among people, groups and interpersonal networks," processes reflect large-scale political contentious actions. The theoretical goal is to identify which mechanisms, alone or in combinations with others, shape the onset, the evolution, and the outcome of political contention under specific circumstances. The aim is not only to understand the dynamics of protest campaigns but also to find salient features that can be generalized to other protest campaigns.

In keeping with this strategy, this chapter undertakes an analysis of the intersections between three relational mechanisms and three processes of political contention in the Egyptian (2011) and Iranian (1978–1979) cases. These relational mechanisms are attributions of similarity, social appropriation of mobilizing vehicles, and government "carrot and stick" policies. They will be linked to the broad contentious processes of mobilization, multisectoral coalition formation, and scale shift. Why these two particular cases? First, both episodes ended with protesters successfully ousting their leaders (Mubarak in Egypt, Riza Shah Pahlevi, of Iran). Second, they occurred over 30 years apart, which downgrades the transnational role of demonstration and diffusion effects as important causal factors in the emergence and outcomes of protest campaigns. Third, both protest campaigns occurred in semiauthoritarian political systems whose state leaders faced little threat from elite divisions, weak repressive capacities, or the withdrawal of international support from strong allies. Therefore, the absence of shifts in macro political conditions or political opportunity structures that could have undermined these leaders' survival cannot explain the onset of these protest campaigns. Instead, greater explanatory leverage is obtained from understanding the role of dynamic processes in these paired cases.

Political Opportunity Structures in Egypt (2011) and Iran (1978–1979)

Both campaigns began in the context of stable political opportunity structures. Social movement scholars argue that revolutionary situations emerge when there are macro environmental changes, usually associated with state weakness that may encourage domestic actors to mobilize against the regime. Structural shifts encourage rebellion because opponents perceive that the likelihood of success in achieving their goals increases with collective action. If shifts also signal that governments are less likely to repress collective action, opponents are equally likely to seek collective action to redress their grievances.[2]

The strongest arguments against the presence of political opportunity shifts are made by Holmes (2012) for the Egyptian case and Kurzman (1996, 2004) for the Iranian campaign. Holmes maintains that the Mubarak regime did not face deep divisions or the loss of traditional allies inside and outside of the government (including the military) prior to the uprising. Moreover, Mubarak had diverted enormous investments toward upgrading the state's repressive capacity, which doubled the size of the internal security apparatus over the previous two decades. Instead of expanding political openings to the opposition, Mubarak, through fraudulent elections in 2010, restructured the Parliament to expand his power and pave the way for his son, Gamal, to succeed him as president. Finally, the United States was a constant source of support for Mubarak before the uprising and remained so until the final stages of the protest campaign. Therefore, structural shifts that would have signaled state weakness failed to materialize. Instead, Holmes (2012) argues that key features of the mobilization process were most responsible for the campaign's success: the resilience of protesters in the face of state violence, their ability to establish "liberated zones" and "popular security" organizations that replaced security forces in key urban areas throughout Egypt, and the diffusion of their efforts to labor and civic strikers who crippled the economy in the final stages of the campaign.

As for the Iranian case, Kurzman (2004) also maintains that there were no serious political openings extended to the opposition in 1977, and the United States had not withdrawn its support from the Shah despite his record of human rights abuses.[3] There were also few serious elite divisions in Iran prior to the uprising. Meanwhile, the repressive capacity of the Iranian government was high, and the military was a willing actor in repressing opposition groups prior to and during the early stages of the protest campaign and remained steadfastly in support of the regime until the very end of the campaign (Kurzman 1996, 157).

Kurzman argues that the key factor in escalating the momentum against the Shah from 1977 to 1979 was the public's realization that the protesters were growing in both numbers and strength. People joined the uprising when they perceived that the likelihood of success in ousting the Shah was high even in the presence of severe repressive crackdowns by the regime. Their willingness to join the campaign was largely influenced by their expectations "that sufficient numbers of like-minded collaborators" would also participate (Kurzman 2004, 131).

In a nutshell, macrostructural shifts did not accompany the onset and expansion of the protest campaigns in either the Egyptian or Iranian cases. Rather, the dynamic endogenous processes of political contention were more critical factors. In particular, three central processes in both cases were the mobilization of the opposition, the formation of a multisectoral coalition among the opposition, and the scale shift in the breadth and scope of the opposition.

Processes of Political Contention: Mobilization, Multisectoral Coalition Formation, and Scale Shift

According to Chenoweth and Stephan's (2011) analysis of 80 cases of nonviolent protest campaigns, military defections from the regime to the opposition was the single most important influence in their success. Yet, in the Egyptian and Iranian cases, the military only played a significant role at the end of these protest campaigns *after* the emergence of antiregime mobilization, dissident coalition formation, and protest diffusion. In actuality, the military's defection (or military paralysis in the Iranian case) was contingent on these earlier processes of political contention. Therefore, to understand successful campaigns, we need to understand how and why processes of political contention evolve to the point that military leaders confront the decision to defect or stay in their barracks. The answer to this issue is likely to reside in understanding the sequence of mobilization, coalition formation, scale shift, and the "relational mechanisms" that link them. To this end, the analysis that follows focuses on identifying these mechanisms in both the Egyptian and Iranian protest campaigns.

But first, the concepts of mobilization, coalition formation, and scale shift need to be defined. Mobilization is the activation of resources available to groups for collective claims-making. In this instance, the critical resource in protest campaigns is the number of people participating in demonstrations and protests (Tilly and Tarrow 2007, 217). Mobilization then fuses with the emergence of a multisectoral coalition, which links the participation of protesters, as well as groups and organizations, from more than one class or social sector, such as students, teachers, farmers, clerics, peasants, workers, and urban slum dwellers. Mobilization and coalition formation then join with scale shift, which is the diffusion of contentious actions to new geographical sites and actors. In the Egyptian and Iranian cases, these processes played a significant role in affecting the military's behavior at the end of these protest campaigns.

Relational Mechanisms: Attribution of Similarity, Social Appropriation of Mobilizing Vehicles, and Government Carrot and Stick Strategies

Relational mechanisms, according to McAdam et al. (2001) alter the relationships among dissidents, rulers, ruling elites, and even external actors that support transgressive contention. Relational mechanisms appear during—not prior to—protest campaigns. Hence, they are intimately connected to the evolving dynamics of political contention. In addition, mechanisms that activate political contention are mutually reinforcing and have combinatorial influences on contentious processes.

In this analysis, three relational mechanisms are analyzed in the Egyptian and Iranian protest campaigns. The first one is "attribution of similarity," which is associated with the successful efforts of dissident entrepreneurs who "frame the claims and identities of different actors as sufficiently similar to each other to justify mobilization and coalition formation" (McAdam et al. 2001, 334). For instance, Egyptian activists focused on police brutality, while Iranian dissidents stressed the state's repressive policies. The second relational mechanism is the "social appropriation of mobilizing vehicles" or the successful actions of political groups who seize old or form new networks and/or institutions for the purpose of coordinating collective actions and strategies with previously inert populations (McAdam et al. 2001, 47). In the Egyptian case, the effective use of the new social media was a crucial instrument in generating two different processes of

Table 8.1 Two-Way Linkages between Mechanisms and Processes in the
Egyptian (2011) and Iranian (1978–1979) Protest Campaigns

Relational Mechanisms

Processes of Contention	Attributions of Similarity	Social Appropriation of Mobilizing Vehicles	Government "Carrot and Stick" Policies
Mobilization	X	X	
Multisectoral Coalition	X	X	X
Scale Shift		X	X

contention—coalition formation and scale shift. In the Iranian case, it was the mosques that played a crucial role in disseminating and coordinating information and strategies of resistance (Kurzman 2004). The last mechanism for consideration is the government's "carrot and stick" policies of repression and accommodation. In an attempt to contain transgressive political contention, government actors will extend superficial concessions at the same time that they repress activists with the use of force, only to face backfire effects that escalate protests (Rasler 1996).

The interrelationships between the relational mechanisms and the processes of political contention in both cases are depicted in Table 8.1. The analytical narrative that follows focuses on explaining how each mechanism is related to one or more of the processes of contention in the "mobilization—multi-sectoral coalition formation—scale shift dynamic."[*] The goal is to demonstrate how similar mechanisms and processes drive the trajectories of protest campaigns in two different periods and places.

Application of a Mechanisms-Process Approach to the Egyptian Protest Campaign

Attributions of Similarity: The Role of Police Brutality on Protest Mobilization and Multisectoral Coalition Formation

The widespread dissatisfaction with police brutality was a unifying theme that brought large numbers of protesters to the streets on the first day of the Egyptian protest campaign. By the start of the uprising on January 25, 2011, there was not a single segment of Egypt's political and economic society that had not been touched by police brutality. The primary institution involved in this brutality was the Interior Ministry.[5]

The Interior Ministry's police presence was ubiquitous in the everyday lives of Egyptians: police issued passports, drivers' licenses, birth and death certificates; vetted political and academic appointments; monitored workplace environments; and mediated labor–management disputes. In addition, the police supplemented their wages by organizing the drug trade; collecting tributes from taxis, bus drivers, and shopkeepers; or setting up "loan shark" and protection rackets (Amar 2011; El-Ghobashy 2012, 24–25).

A semiautonomous organization within the Interior Ministry, the Central Security Services was responsible for monitoring and infiltrating political opposition and civil associations. This police force, over 30,000 personnel, became notorious for its policies of detaining and torturing dissidents. In 2010 alone, there were approximately 17,000 detention centers.[6] One estimate is that the Central Security Services had an army of approximately two million informers: one for every 40 Egyptian citizens (Shatz 2010).

Finally, the Interior Ministry and Central Security Services outsourced coercion to street thugs by paying and training them to use sexualized brutality in order to punish and deter female and male protesters alike. These "police-connected" thugs also harassed wealthy citizens for money, molested women on crowded streets, terrorized shopkeepers and small business owners, and tortured those who refused to submit (Amar 2011; Kandil 2012, 196).

Consequently, violence permeated the relationship between the police and Egyptian citizens, who developed a profound hatred of them, and it proved to be a unifying force in encouraging large numbers of people to demonstrate peacefully in their opposition to it (Amar 2011). In fact, photos and video tape of the brutal death of an Internet café owner, Khalid Mohammad Sa'id, at the hands of local police in Alexandria in 2010 were posted on the Internet and used to mobilize protestors in what started out to be an antipolice rally on January 25, 2011, celebrating National Police Day (Amar 2011). The central organizing theme of the rally was "We Are All Khalid Sa'id."[7]

Social Appropriation of Mobilizational Vehicles: The Role of Social Media in Coalition Formation and Scale Shift

This relational mechanism refers to the challenger's ability to create or utilize organizational contexts or tools that can be transformed into instruments of contention (McAdam et al. 2001, 47). In the Egyptian revolt, the effective use of the new social media was a crucial instrument in two processes of contention: coalition formation and protest diffusion.

Dissident entrepreneurs stitched together a multisectoral coalition by using Facebook, Twitter, and YouTube to make broad appeals and formulate strategies of collective action. The use of these media had three effects. First, it aided collective action by lowering information costs and enhancing coordination strategies (Howard and Hussain 2011). Second, it brought about a "cascade of messages" that helped raise people's expectations for success (Howard et al. 2011). Third, the regime's attempt to shut down the Internet had an unintended backlash effect that brought many more participants to the streets (Hassanpour 2014).

Regarding the first effect on political mobilization, Howard and Hussain (2011, 39–40) maintain that Facebook provided a logistical infrastructure for the initial stages of the Egyptian protest. For instance, Google executive and Internet activist Wael Ghoneim set up the "We Are All Khalid Sa'id" Facebook page, which documented the death of the Internet café owner at the hands of the local police. The web page would become a virtual forum for protest against police brutality and human rights violations. Facebook followers eventually totaled over 500,000, as users posted photographs, videos, and lists of the names of corrupt police officers. After the Tunisian uprising, youth activists used the Facebook page to announce a massive demonstration in Cairo on January 25, 2011, during the National Police Day holiday protesting police brutality. More than 85,000 followers confirmed that they would participate (Bhuiyan 2011, 15). The "We Are All Khalid Sa'id" Facebook page allowed activists to build solidarity around shared grievances and to identify collective political goals (Howard and Hussain 2011, 42).

Meanwhile, coordination during the January 25 street protests was facilitated by Twitter and cell phone text messages between and among activists and their followers in order to amass large numbers of protestors in Tahrir Square in Cairo (Khamis and Vaugh 2011). These strategies were played out in other Egyptian cities and towns. Youth activists were also careful about directing large crowds to attend protest sites in working-class neighborhoods not only to mobilize wider numbers of participants but also to highlight the connection between their living conditions and the political environment. As one young activist, Amr Salah, said, "We needed to make the connection between liberty and bread to attract broader support" (Jensen 2011).[8]

The second important impact that the new social media had was its role in influencing people's expectations for success (Howard et al. 2011). Empirical evidence on messages sent in Egypt via Twitter and blog posts show that there was a spike in online revolutionary conversations that often preceded major protest events on the ground. In-country Twitter traffic peaked on the day that street protests reached into the thousands and then peaked again during the last days of Mubarak's reign. Much of the twitter traffic and blog posts dealt with political change. Meanwhile, twitter traffic inside and outside of the North African region increased substantially, especially after Tunisia's president, Ben 'Ali, resigned. Much of the twitter traffic produced a cascade of messages across the region that centered on themes of "freedom, liberty, and democracy" and raised public expectations that political uprisings could be successful (Howard et al. 2011).

Finally, a new study by Hassenpour (2014) shows that the Egyptian government's decision to shut down the Internet, which had its full impact on January 28, increased the dispersion of the protesters across Cairo and overwhelmed the number of police forces. In short, "there were too many protests in too many places" (Hassenpour quotes local blogger, 2014, 20).[9] Dispersion of the protest action occurred because the lack of cell phone coverage and Internet connection forced Egyptians who were worried about their friends and family members to join the crowds in the streets to find out about them. As more people entered the streets for face-to-face communications, the uprising swelled and became more decentralized, which made it harder for the Egyptian government to control and repress it. Equally important, Hassenpour (2014) maintains that as risk adverse bystanders interacted with protesters, new links between activists and potential participants were established, which aided the mobilization of new recruits and the diffusion of protests to new sites.

In sum, these new technologies played an important role in creating networks across families, neighborhoods, mosques, and other local civic associations, rather than the typical political associations or parties. They were especially important in sustaining wildcat strikes as rank and file workers coordinated their own lines of formal leadership and union support independent of their traditional union leaders, who had been co-opted by the regime. Hence, the digital technologies made it possible for workers, who had been traditionally insulated from other sectors of the economy, to coordinate their wildcat strikes with workers from a variety of different settings as well as protesters. The result was a broad-based coalition that transcended sectoral and class divisions (Johnston 2011, 16).[10]

Government's Carrot and Stick Policies: Backfire Effects on Increasing Scale Shift

"Carrot and stick" policies refer to a government's attempt to demobilize protesters by offering a combination of limited concessions coupled with repression. The government's strategy is to appeal to moderates to go home with the future expectation that their demands will continue to be met while leaving the radicals in the streets. This divide-and-rule strategy is designed to break down the

multisectoral coalition with the intention of separating the protesters and easing the dispersal of the remaining protesters.

However, this is a strategy that could misfire, because the combination of concessions and a government crackdown can have a *backfire effect*. Concessions (especially superficial ones) signal to protesters that the government is weakening and capable of being pressured to provide deeper reforms. Therefore, challengers are likely to expand their demands while sustaining and increasing their opposition. If these concessions are combined with a government crackdown, the situation becomes highly combustible. More precisely, a government crackdown in the midst of protester activity can incite the participation of bystanders—which in turn can escalate the scale and scope of the opposition. This backfire effect occurs when governments miscalculate the level and range of sympathy that the protesters have garnered among the rest of the population. Therefore, *a shift in the scale of the protests* occurs as collective actions are emulated by other groups across different geospatial locations. Moreover, new forms of collective action may emerge and spread as well, as illustrated by the civic and labor strikes that occurred in the later stages of the Egyptian campaign.

This sequence of "carrot and stick" policies, backfire effects, and scale shift occurs in the context of two prearranged events scheduled on January 28 and February 1, 2011. On the first day of the campaign, January 25, 2011, a rally was organized by prodemocracy activists, and other youth groups linked to opposition political parties, labor rights associations, and the Muslim Brotherhood. They also announced the sites and time of the demonstrations on the Internet and Facebook.

By the evening, tens of thousands of protesters made it to Tahrir Square in Cairo along with thousands of demonstrations that also occurred in Alexandria and other major Egyptian cities. By the second day, however, the government began to crack down on these demonstrations. Riot police used tear gas and water cannons along with thousands of thugs wielding knives and sticks against the protesters. By the third day, January 27, the government had shut down the Internet and text-messaging services, which connected Egyptian businesses, banks, Internet cafés, schools, embassies, and government offices. In response, the opposition groups called for a "Day of Anger" demonstration after Friday prayers on January 28, largely in reaction to civilian deaths due to police brutality.

By the end of the day on Friday, January 28, after bloody battles over several hours long and hundreds of civilians dead, the outnumbered police force retreated and army tanks rolled into the streets of Cairo. Similar actions occurred in Suez, Alexandria, and the towns and small cities of the Nile Delta. By the end of the evening, 365 citizens had died and another 5,000 were injured. The police lost 32 personnel and reported 1,079 injuries. Meanwhile, 99 police stations and

3,000 police trucks were burned throughout Egypt, including the National Democratic Party headquarters in Cairo (El-Ghobashy 2012, 38). During this period, neighborhood groups that had defeated the police established citizen governance committees and citizen patrols to protect their residential areas from looters.

The *diffusion* of collective action between January 25 and January 27, 2011, and across different locations in Cairo and elsewhere (and especially in the neighborhood areas unused to such displays) "emboldened Egyptians who revised their calculations of what was possible and reduced their uncertainty about the consequences of action." It broke down the divisions between different groups, forcing the regime to confront them simultaneously when "for thirty years, it had done so serially" (El-Ghobashy 2012, 33).

On January 29, Mubarak appeared on state television and announced political concessions: (1) the dismissal of the cabinet, (2) the appointment of a new vice president; and (3) a change in the prime minister. According to El-Ghobashy (2012, 38), if Mubarak's offer had been extended four days earlier, it would have been a shrewd move. However, the cabinet reshuffle proposition only "sharpened the population's apprehension of imminent victory, spurring them to stay out doors and demand nothing less than the ouster of the president" (El-Ghobashy 2012, 38–39).

By January 30, 2011, the coalition of protesters expanded to include the wider membership of the Muslim Brotherhood and secular opposition groups (including Mohammed El Baradei) who demanded Mubarak's resignation. Subsequently, protest organizers appealed for a "million-man march" in Cairo on February 1, and the army publically announced that it would not use force in the demonstrations.

As expected, on February 1, between 250,000 and a million protesters filled the streets in Cairo as Mubarak announced in another television address that he would not run for reelection in 2011 and that he would reform two articles of the constitution that would ensure this. On February 2, government-organized attackers armed with guns, knives, machetes, pipes, brass knuckles, and tear gas canisters entered Tahrir Square and attacked protestors, accelerating a new round of demonstrations in the days to follow. Six hundred people were wounded and three killed in the day's battle (International Crisis Group 2011, 10–13).

From February 3 to February 6, 2011, an "uneasy and unstable détente" emerged between the protestors and the regime, as both sides struggled to find a strategy to break the impasse. As the regime initiated discussions with political groups on February 6, Tahrir Square protest leaders worried about losing their momentum and that splits within their ranks about political concessions would encourage people to leave the streets. They were aware that protestors were getting weary and wanted to get back to work after weeks without working. In an effort to regain lost momentum, they successfully escalated their protests in the forms of "strikes and joint actions with other political and labor groups" (International Crisis Group 2011, 10–13).

On February 7, 2011, thousands of workers joined wildcat strikes in parts of the country that had been untouched by the protest movement. Wildcat strikes occurred in wide sectors of the Egyptian economy: public electricity, communications, sanitation, railways, bus, and oil. Doctors, lawyers, and pharmacists joined in as well, along with workers in state-owned companies. Workers pressed for higher wages, fairer working conditions, a minimum wage law, and free trade unions. By February 9, between 250,000 and 300,000 workers were estimated to be participating in some form of work disruption (Bishara 2012, 96–97). By February 10, there were demonstrations that amounted to millions of people all over Egypt. Strikes by industrial labor and civil servants diffused to include education, energy, agriculture, transportation, the ports, and the state-owned press (El-Ghobashy 2011, 4–5). In short, the uprising had shifted from public spaces like Tahrir Square to everyday workplaces (Holmes 2012, 406).

On February 10, Mubarak made another televised speech announcing additional concessions.[11] However, he refused to step down formally. Strikers and protesters alike stayed in the streets, and on February 11, the new vice president Omar Suleiman announced Mubarak's resignation and that his powers had been transferred to the military.

To put it briefly, the regime's strategy over the course of the protest wave involved a "carrot and stick" approach that combined violent repression, both official and unofficial, with limited concessions in an effort to "peel off" parts of the opposition. The slow, frequently piecemeal forms of concessions that Mubarak offered over the course of the 18 days undermined the government's survival. Protest leaders viewed these concessions as encouragement that they were close to toppling Mubarak, and they pressed harder for their central demand. However, a broader segment of the protesters might have been swayed to go home if a "contrite" Mubarak had offered substantive concessions early in the protest wave. Meanwhile, Mubarak's use of indiscriminate violence also backfired as outraged demonstrators increased in numbers in its aftermath (International Crisis Group 2011, Report No. 101: 6–7).

Scale Shift and Military Defection: The Pivotal Role of Civic and Labor Strikes

The timing between scale shift and the decision by Egyptian military leaders to withdraw their support from the Mubarak regime was closely connected.[12]

The first scale shift occurred between January 25 and January 28, 2011, when thousands of Egyptians marched to, then occupied and eventually defeated the police to gain control over, Tahrir Square as well as public spaces in outlying provinces. Yet, another scale shift occurred on February 8, with the onset of widespread public and private sector strikes. These strikes paralyzed the economy and probably led to the military's decision to defect (Beinin 2011, 194).

Three explanations have been advanced to explain the timing between the military's defection on February 10 and the widespread civic strikes between February 8 and 10. Gelvin (2012, 80) maintains that the timing may have been coincidental but more likely, the military calculated that the strikes made Husni Mubarak's political position untenable.[13] Frisch (2013, 187–88) and Kandil (2012, 315) indicate that the military, after being politically sidelined for many years, saw the civic uprising as an opportunity to reassert its position and protect its political and economic interests. Finally, Amar (2011) and Sallam (2011) argue that the labor strikes encouraged the military generals to intervene because the economic costs were too high for themselves and the Egyptian economy as a whole.

In short, the outcome of the Egyptian protest campaign was military defection and the resignation of Husni Mubarak. This discussion shows that an understanding of the timing of defection and the successful ouster of Mubarak needs to take into account the sequence of contentious political processes from mobilization to multisectoral coalition formation and scale shift and the underlying relational mechanisms responsible for them.

Application of a Mechanisms-Process Approach to the Iranian Protest Campaign

Attributions of Similarity: The Role of Repression in Protest Mobilization and Multisectoral Coalition Formation

Unlike the Egyptian revolt in 2011, where the acceleration of mass mobilization occurred quickly, the Iranian protest campaign (starting in late 1977) unfolded more slowly as the opposition movement expanded beyond a core of Islamic religious students to one that would include all segments of Iranian society. By late summer 1978, the movement became "viable" in the minds of many Iranians outside of the core circle of Islamic militants. As the demonstrations increased in size and scope over a 12-month period, average Iranians perceived that the anti-Shah movement was likely to bring about change, and this perception of success fueled more participation (Kurzman 2004, 136–37). The one recurring theme that unified Islamic radicals, students, scholars, and bazaaris in these demonstrations were the slogans "The Shah Must Go" or "Death to the Shah" (Sazegara and Stephan 2009, 190–91).

According to Kurzman (2004, 132–37), government repression during the protest campaign was the most important motivating factor behind people's protest activism. Kurzman's interviews with activists during the campaign reveals that participants became outraged with a series of security crackdowns that ended in civilian deaths and injuries. Many of these crackdowns came on the heels of demonstrations that were organized to occur at the end of a 40-day religious mourning period. With each successive crackdown and more civilian deaths, Islamic militants mobilized increasingly larger numbers of demonstrators protesting the repression. Over time, these demonstrations included participants across a wide segment of Iranian society. This 40-day mass mobilization cycle, which began with a military crackdown at a Qom seminary in January 1978, contributed to a bandwagon effect by the fall of 1978, as more people "lost their fear" of repression and had high expectations for success.

Social Appropriation of Mobilizational Vehicles: The Role of Mosques in Mobilization and Coalition Formation

For over 25 years of autocratic rule, the Shah had removed or eliminated secular political parties and other nongovernmental organizations. Nationalists and communist movements were crushed; trade unions were infiltrated by SAVAK, the secret police; and the press was strictly censored (Bayat 1998, 144). However, the clergy faced less repressive exposure, had more autonomy, and possessed a strong institutional capacity with over 10,000 mosques, religious centers, and seminaries. These institutions were linked by religious leaders in every town and village (Bayat 1998, 144). This mosque network would eventually be mobilized to coordinate antigovernment demonstrations and strikes among the general public. It would also provide sanctuary for the revolutionaries, distribute scarce food resources, ensure neighborhood security, and in the last 2 days of the campaign, provide arms to the opposition. Finally, young Islamist activists would use the network to unify Muslim intellectuals and clerics around the leadership of the Ayatollah Khomeini (Sazegara and Stephan 2009, 192).

However, the activation of the mosque had not occurred prior to the protest campaign. According to Kurzman (2004, 49) the mosque network "had to be commandeered before it could be mobilized." As the protest campaign emerged in 1977, politically cautious religious leaders controlled this network to the exclusion of younger, more militant Islamists. A majority of these nonrevolutionary clerics preferred reforms rather than the overthrow of the Shah through activist tactics. Consequently, these radical clerics and students appropriated the network through three strategies that were designed to persuade the moderates or non-revolutionary clerics that opposition to the revolution would be more costly than their support. The first strategy that the radicals used was to challenge and embarrass senior clerics publicly, forcing them to take revolutionary positions. Second, as radicals engaged in protests, the regime used severe repression to contain them, which subsequently "radicalized" moderate clerics who earlier had distanced themselves from the protests. Finally, radical clerics threatened moderates that an image of acquiescence in the presence of widespread protests would be costly to their public reputation and even treasonous. Nonrevolutionary clerics soon found that they were losing their support to younger, more aggressive radicals. Kurzman (2004, 48) reports from a SAVAK record that moderate clerics joined the radicals in order to protect their own position among their followers.

The appropriation of this mosque network was complete by the end of August 1978. At this point, clerical radicals were able to lead and coordinate protests throughout Iran with tens of thousands of participants (Kurzman 1994, 66–67). Moreover, they were able to expand their opposition beyond core Islamists to include bazaaris, liberal oppositionists, and leftists under the leadership of the Ayatollah Khomeini. This alliance was manifested on September 4, 1978, in what was initially planned to be a religious demonstration in Tehran involving about 14,000 people. Instead, the demonstration expanded to include 200,000 to 500,000 marchers. Similar demonstrations occurred throughout the country. Three days later, on September 7, 1978, another march brought even greater numbers of demonstrators to the streets in Tehran (estimated to be hundreds of thousands larger than the September 4 march), and by the end of the day a new slogan calling for the establishment of an "Islamic Republic" was invoked (Kurzman 2004, 65). The protest campaign would peak in December 1978, with millions of people across Iran demonstrating in support of the Ayatollah Khomeini.

Government's "Carrot and Stick" Strategies: Backfire Effects on Increasing Scale Shift

A quantitative analysis of the effects of Iran's carrot and stick strategies over the course of the protest by Rasler (1996) shows that the combined effects of repression and concessions subsequently fueled an increase in the numbers of demonstrations throughout the major cities of Iran. At the beginning of the protest campaign in 1978, the government employed a bloody crackdown on radical clerics protesting an inflammatory story about the Ayatollah Khomeini in Qom on January 9. Government security forces fired into the protesters, which resulted in deaths numbering less than a dozen but rumored throughout Iran to be in the hundreds. Unfortunately for the government, this event generated a cycle of protests throughout Iran's major cities, known as "doing the forty-forty" (Sazegara and Stephan 2009, 191). Islamic radicals transformed a traditional religious custom of commemoration on the 40th day of mourning into massive demonstrations in the aftermath of the Qom event. When the government confronted these subsequent demonstrations with violence, more deaths ensued and another round of 40-day antigovernment demonstrations commenced. These confrontations between security forces and the protesters fueled an escalation in the number and diffusion of participants throughout Iran.

In August 1978, in an effort to dispel the demonstrations, the Shah appointed a reform-oriented prime minister, Sharif-Emami, who met with top opposition leaders of the clergy and liberal political organizations. Sharif-Emami made significant concessions—some of which involved free elections, tax concessions, press freedom, and civil rights guarantees.[14] Despite these reforms, the number of demonstrators continued to swell. At the same time, the content of the demonstrations changed from a defensive protest against earlier killings to an offensive attack on the Shah and his rule. The opposition now perceived that the Shah was vulnerable and weak (Parsa 1989, 211–25).

Consequently, Islamist clerics called for even larger demonstrations around the themes of "Death to the Shah" and "Khomeini Is Our Leader." By September 7, 1978, hundreds of thousands of protesters were in the streets joined by the bazaaris, liberal oppositionists, leftists, and Islamists. One day later, the Shah declared martial law in Tehran and other cities. In Tehran, several thousand protesters entered Jaleh Square, ignoring martial law orders to disperse. On a day that would later be known as "Black Friday," army units opened fire and clashed with protesters, killing at least 89 people (Sazegara and Stepan 2009, 194).

In the aftermath of the "Black Friday" tragedy, the Islamists shifted tactics to call for nationwide strikes and work stoppages. Between September and November 1978, members from every sector of Iranian society had held work stoppages, including oil workers, journalists, transportation workers, customs officials, and power plant and bank employees. The oil workers' strikes had the most serious effect on the Iranian economy, because oil was the government's chief source of revenue. Within 2 weeks, Iranian oil exports had dropped from more than 5 million barrels a day to less than 2 million (Sazegara and Stephan 2009, 194).

As the opposition expanded both in scale and scope, the Shah launched another major crackdown. In November 1978, he fired his new prime minister and appointed a military government. With martial law declared, tanks and armored vehicles entered cities and towns across the country to stop future demonstrations. The army took control of the media, arrested opposition leaders, and forced the oil workers to return to work (Parsa 1989, 222–28).

Concurrently, the Shah made conciliatory gestures designed to pacify the public in a televised speech, apologizing for the repression and promising to transform the regime into a constitutional monarchy (Kurzman 2004, 106). As for the new military government, its leaders lacked the will to confront the demonstrators with force, especially because the Shah was indecisive and reluctant. The result was state paralysis, as the opposition was too large to repress. Thus, the Shah's attempt to repress in the short term while supporting longer-term reforms was unsuccessful in demobilizing the public.

On December 10–11, 1978, more than "10% of the country marched in anti-Shah demonstrations" in Tehran and other major cities throughout Iran. In Tehran alone, estimates range from 1 to 4 million people marching against the Shah in Tehran, while another 6 to 9 million people marched in other cities (Kurzman 2004, 122). By January 1979, the Shah and the military government ceded control to remaining moderates; the Shah left the country, and in February 1979, the Ayatollah Khomeini arrived in Tehran.

Scale Shift and Military Paralysis

The "Black Friday" massacre on September 8, 1978, forced the Islamic revolutionaries to pause briefly in order to calculate their next course of action. At this point, Ward (2009, 214) argues that the government mismanaged an opportune moment to reassert its control. Instead of applying consistent pressure against the activists in the aftermath, the government pursued an inconsistent policy between repression and compromise. At times, the Shah coupled a strategy of military confrontation with concessions, which unintentionally solidified the opposition and undermined the Shah's credibility (Ward 2009, 215). At other times, the Shah ordered security forces to fire only into the air unless they were attacked, and then dismissed unpopular security officials in order to appease public demands (Ward 2009, 215). The Shah's mixed strategy increased the inability of security forces to make decisions at the local level. As a result, the security forces vacillated between inaction and harsh responses—an inconsistency that emboldened the radicals to mobilize their followers. When the military appeared resolute, opposition leaders became more cautious, but they constantly probed for signs of weakness and acted boldly when they were convinced that the army and police would not retaliate (Ward 2009, 214–16).

After the Black Friday massacre, Iranian military leaders had serious doubts about the Shah's willingness to keep power. Yet, internal divisions among the various military units stymied the efforts of the generals to seek a unified response. Instead, Iranian generals continued to look for strong leadership from the Shah, which they failed to get even when he appointed a new military government, as it lacked new powers that would help them implement martial law more effectively (Ward 2009, 215–16).[15]

Meanwhile, Islamic radicals engaged the military directly, extending invitations to join the demonstrations and issuing religious edicts and threats to encourage conscripts and professionals alike to defect. In addition, radicals included soldiers' grievances in their demonstrations, highlighted the class differences between officers and conscripts, appealed to the soldiers' religious obligations on behalf of the opposition, and engaged them peacefully during their demonstrations with flowers in rifle barrels and garlands on tanks (Ward 2009, 217).

Eventually, Iran's soldiers increasingly sympathized with the citizenry in the streets. The result was that enlisted personnel either deserted in large numbers or disobeyed orders to fire on demonstrators. By the end of 1978, Iranian officers, frustrated with their senior leadership's inaction and the reliability of their troops, either retired from their service or sat on the sidelines. According to Ward (2009, 217), desertions and absenteeism increased from 100 to 200 per day in early 1978 to more than 1,000 each day by the end of 1978. Meanwhile, Islamic militants or their sympathizers had penetrated military units at all ranks. After the Shah's departure on January 16, 1979, and the Ayatollah Khomeini's arrival on February 1, 1979, the joint staff of the Iranian armed forces declared that the military would "remain neutral" in disputes between the Shah's regime and the public (Sazegara and Stephan 2009, 185).

Conclusion

Since protest campaigns are endogenous and complex episodes of contention, the case is made for a greater commitment to understanding the dynamics of political contention that occur in the course of these campaigns. Our theories need to incorporate causal "relational" mechanisms that can be found in a "mechanism-process" approach advanced in the *Dynamics of Contention* (McAdam et al. 2001). The paired comparisons of the Egyptian (2011) and Iranian (1977–1979) revolts is meant to demonstrate the utility of understanding these cases in terms of the role that recurring causal "relational" mechanisms played in the evolution of political contention. In both cases, three crucial "relational" mechanisms (the attribution of similarity, the appropriation of mobilizing vehicles, and "carrot and stick" government strategies) contributed to the expansion of broad political processes of mobilization, coalition formation, and scale shift—all of which were key features of both protest campaigns. While complexity hinders our ability to theorize about patterns and outcomes across protest campaigns, a mechanism-process approach offers a potential solution to increasing our search for limited generalizations.

Acknowledgments

I thank the scholars at the Workshop on Protest Politics, Democratization and Political Change held at the Hebrew University, Jerusalem, Israel in 2012, the PIPES (Program on International Politics, Economics and Security) at the University of Chicago, and the Political Science Department at Arizona State University in 2014 for their constructive comments at various stages of this research.

Notes

1. Space limitations preclude the opportunity to include or provide a breakdown of the entire protest campaign literature. However, these results are found in Chenoweth and Stephan's (2011) cross-national study of 80 cases of nonviolent protest campaigns.
2. Shifts in political opportunities are associated with: (1) liberalization or political reforms by the state that opens the door for mobilization, (2) divisions within the ruling elite that encourage defections to the opposition, and (3) international pressure that weakens the state's ability to repress the domestic opposition.
3. Although President Jimmy Carter had promised to restrict foreign aid to governments that relied excessively on violent state repression during his presidential campaign in 1976, he did not extend this threat to Iran and in fact praised the Shah for his leadership, the stability of his regime, and his strong domestic support in a speech in Tehran in January 1978 (Kurzman 1996, 158).
4. There is little space to discuss the interconnections between the processes as well as those between the relational mechanisms.
5. Over these 10 years, Mubarak increased the number of security departments and swelled the police force from 150,000 personnel in 1974 to more than a million in 2002, a 21 percent increase. By 2011 the number of police personnel was approximately 2 million (Kandil 2012, 192).
6. Kandil (2012, 194) reports this figure and cites human rights organizations that document torture rituals among male and female detainees: they were blindfolded, handcuffed, stripped naked to their underwear, beaten with sticks or batons, and subjected to electric shocks and stress positions.
7. Ghonim (2012) posted the photos and video tape on a Facebook page, which quickly amassed hundreds of thousands of readers and sympathizers. The January 25th day of antipolice protest was organized via this Facebook page.

8. Social media networks also allowed for instant, on-the-ground reports that activists could use to adapt their mobilization strategies to both overwhelm and avoid security forces (Idle and Nunns 2011, 19–21). The new social media helped to "turn individualized, localized and community-specific dissent into a structured movement with a collective consciousness about shared plights and opportunities for action" (Howard and Hussain 2011, 41).

9. More precisely, Hassenpour quotes Peter Bouckaert, emergencies director of Human Rights Watch, on January 28, 2011.

10. This chapter rests on the argument that the new social media was a tool used by activists to facilitate their efforts to spread their message and coordinate protesters actions. It does not make the argument that the media was a cause of the Egyptian revolution, nor that it was a primary factor for the success in the resignation of President Mubarak.

11. Mubarak offered to transfer some of his presidential powers to his vice president and said that he would reform six and possibly more articles of the constitution.

12. An explanation of the loyalty shifts in the Egyptian Army also requires an understanding of the United States's role in influencing the military's behavior but there is little detailed information, other than that the United States signaled its opposition to a repressive crackdown (Kandil 2012).

13. Gelvin (2012, 87) reports that experts estimate that the military controls anywhere from 5 to 40 percent of the economy, and according to the International Monetary Fund (IMF), the military oversaw about 50 percent of all Egyptian manufacturing by 2011. Frisch (2013, 187) also makes the case that the military's threat perceptions crystallized in 2008, when a wave of working-class demonstrations broke out in the industrial towns of the Egyptian delta in reaction to imports from China and elsewhere. The strike wave encouraged high-ranking officers to believe that Gamal Mubarak's neoliberal economic policies would threaten not only their own interests but also the interests of Egypt as a whole.

14. He also reintroduced the Islamic calendar, released many of the high-ranking clergy imprisoned since 1975, closed down 57 gambling casinos, dismissed more than 30 SAVAK officers, abolished the post of minister for women's affairs, and set up a Ministry of Religious Affairs.

15. Milani (2011) indicates that the Shah's inconsistency and indecisiveness during this period was due to his deteriorating physical and mental health and chemotherapy for lymphoma. On the other hand, Milani also acknowledges that the Shah failed to perceive the true nature of the antigovernment opposition's demands and discontent, preferring to rely on flawed, conspiratorial interpretations. As the opposition expanded and deepened, the Shah became more indecisive and looked for signs of support from the United States, which failed to provide clear, precise instructions.

PART III

Between Contention and Transition

9

Regime Transitions, Antidictatorship Struggles, and the Future of Protest in Democratizing Settings

Vincent Boudreau

THE "DYNAMICS OF contention" (DOC) research program contributed significantly to the study of social movements and protest in many ways, among them by indicating how we might appreciate and grapple analytically with contingency (McAdam, Tarrow, and Tilly 2001). That capacity has had wide implications and promises powerful benefits in the analysis of what many call democracy movements. Two particular benefits emerge most clearly. First, in ways that theorists of revolutions would appreciate, the DOC program revises earlier tendencies to define episodes of mobilization and struggle by their ends (Goldstone 1980). Mobilization processes are contingent phenomena with a variety of endpoints, and can turn on any number of critical junctures (before which turning, we cannot really describe the action as revolutionary, democratic, or reformist). Second, democracy may not be a defining objective of so-called democracy struggles, but something that emerges from the interaction of people interested in a whole range of different things—in state power, in revenge, in avoiding arrest, in ending human rights violations. Democracy and democratization may be an established movement goal from the outset or a kind of provisional settling point reached in the course of struggle (Zavadskaya 2013).

If democracy is a contingent, rather than inherent objective of struggle, it probably requires analysis in light of ongoing, historically rooted contentious processes—and patterns of democratic consolidation (that most optimistic

204 BETWEEN CONTENTION AND TRANSITION

phrasing) require the attention of contentious politics specialists no less than that of democracy theorists (Hamayotsu 2011; Rivera 2002; Salman 2007). A host of questions follow. If democracy movements do not always begin in the search for democracy, what happens to other interests or orientations mobilized into the struggle? After the transition, what factors influence movement trajectories? Do all activists accommodate themselves to new political rules and objectives, and if so, with what consequences (Ozler 2009)? Will revolutionaries still pursue state overthrow? In unlocking the role that contentious politics plays in democratic transitions, one needs to look both backward and forward from the transitional moment to identify how patterns of struggle carry on to eventually help define relationships between a citizenry and the new system's emerging institutions.

What of the new system itself? Have conceptualizations of democracy helped or hindered our understanding of how social movements interact with emergent democratic or hybrid regimes? Many describe democracy, once established, as a naturally preferred and so politically inevitable system, hampered in the end mainly by coordination and communication problems (Fukuyama 1995). Others see it as mainly self-regulating, designed around processes that domesticate recalcitrants toward political moderation via electoral competition (Feng 1997). But the idea of democracy as an automatically stable resting place is a thin fiction, primarily because it treats threats to democracy as exogenous to the democratic process. Accordingly, theorists (particularly those writing for a policy audience) caution against a hard-line backlash, but imagine that democratic procedures, properly organized and supported institutionally, would cool passions and resolve conflict (Hunter 1998; Savun and Tirone 2011). Guided by such assumptions, democratization efforts have too often impatiently pursued early elections and the construction of strong civil society organizations, even in hotly contested postconflict settings.

Core democratization policies respond to much of what motivates activists—a desire for a fair political system, demands that basic rights be protected, and some interest in transitional justice—but little in the substantive programs that also motivate protest (that is, programs to redistribute wealth or to change the ideological content of government). But if all manner of activists find themselves in democracy struggles, and the relationship between activists and democratizing goals is contingent, we should examine how differently positioned activists struggle against authoritarian regimes, how processes of struggle influence activist collectives, and how movement organizations interact with one another and with the emerging political order. We should consider democracy as a mode of political competition, rather than an encompassing movement goal. We must then ask how activists are likely to engage that mode of competition and what relationship will emerge between demands that establish the parameters of politics—the new rules and institutions that are the architectural substance of a democratization process—and the content of politics.

Some analysts regard social movements as more or less epiphenomenal to democratization processes driven by elite realignment, defection, and contestation (Kennedy 2010; Przeworski and Limongi 1997). Even when democratization theorists bring mass mobilization back in, they often treat it as a contributing factor to elite efforts (O'Donnell and Schmitter 1986; although, for a critical contrasting view, see Tarrow 1995). Social movement theorists often ask about factors that allow movements to "succeed" in their democratizing objectives, but assume that the democracy movements they select to study pursue democracy (Reid 2001; Slater 2009).

What would an approach that marries the two perspectives look like? It would, I think, seek to explain how mobilization processes *create* prodemocracy activists and how processes of regime fragmentation *create* democracy advocates among regime actors. It would examine the interests and relationships that become linked together in movement formations during the struggle and find out what happens to them during the transition. It would, in short, acknowledge the centrality of social movement processes in the larger transition and make relationships between democratization programs and other movement programs (e.g., socialism, land and labor movements, religious fundamentalism, and even antidemocracy) an explicit object of study.

This chapter develops an approach to these questions by using two Southeast Asian cases with which I am quite familiar as a foil to look (in less detail) at two cases from the "Arab Spring". My broad reflections on transitions in Indonesia and the Philippines will serve to generate some framing questions and to set up comparisons with the Tunisian and Egyptian cases. My objective at this point is less to answer questions than to raise them and to call attention to some important avenues for broader comparative analysis. I begin to theorize in-transition contention by situating it in different modes of antidictatorship struggle, different processes of regime transition, and different efforts to constitute a postdictatorship government.

These abridged accounts distinguish between two elements of the democratization process: efforts to write new political rules and the use of democratic institutions and procedures in substantive political competition. Both elements influence, and are influenced by, the social ties and political positioning of activists and movement organizations. Regarding the formation of democratic institutions and procedures, I ask how participatory and sustained the process was. Of the competitive use of democracy, I examine how new political modes change activists' social and political relationships. In relation to both, I examine how a dynamic closely associated with the DOCs program (brokerage) shapes how legacies of struggle carry forward to transition politics.

A Note on Brokerage

The DOC research program argues that the best way to study contentious politics is through the examination of dynamics that concatenate into contentious processes in a broad—yet not infinite—variety of ways. The work occasioned some early confusion, from supporters and critics alike, around the role that these dynamics should play. Some sought to develop an exhaustive list of dynamics—or called analysts to task because the list seemed exhausting and open-ended. Early exposition of the approach suggested that key payoffs of the program would concentrate on different sequences of dynamics in the analysis of contentious processes. Here, I elaborate another of the DOC program's comparative promises: that we can learn important lessons about episodes of contention by asking about dynamics that take place differently across settings and with different consequences. I will ask these questions of brokerage, one of the more frequently cited dynamics of contention identified by McAdam, Tarrow, and Tilly (2001). Investigating brokerage allows us to examine how the social fabric of social movements rise and fall. Those looking to describe and explain brokerage direct our attention to the activity and location of those who connect activist sites and collectives together. The activity of brokers and the geography of brokerage occurs in most movements of any scale, and so sighting it in any case should not excite much curiosity. But who brokers are, how they link different groups together, and how durable those connections turn out to be will deeply matter and should suggest significant comparisons and contrasts among cases.

Dynamics of Contention in Three Arenas: The Stylized Accounts

In this section, I adopt a path-dependent approach to the two Southeast Asian narratives, asking what legacies of struggle carry forward to influence post-transition politics. The accounts emphasize elements of contention highlighted in this chapter's introductory pages: the weight of social relationships on movement politics, the influence of transitional contention in driving movement actors into new alliances or out of old ones, and the sequencing and impact of efforts to construct and use democracy. The accounts that follow look at three different periods in the process: the antidictatorship movement, emphasizing how it peaks as a democracy movement; the transition, with particular weight given to how it reshuffled political and social relationships; and the subsequent construction of a new governing system.

Antidictatorship Movements in the Philippines and Indonesia

Several important elements constitute what we may call the Philippine antidictatorship movement template that took shape after the declaration of martial law in 1972. Activists built movement organizations as parts of a long-term, state-replacing initiative, differentiated along a left–right continuum by explicit ideological commitments. Across that spectrum, activists developed sector-specific programs (i.e., for farmers' groups, labor unions, student or youth organizations) and functionally differentiated organizations (mass and cadre groups, nongovernmental organizations [NGOs], party chapters, and sometimes armed wings) for each, integrating the whole complex into a struggle for state power. Full-time movement organizers brokered and maintained the relationships embodied in these organizations, and that brokerage occurred mainly within the formal party-movement-insurgency structure.

The dynamics of the Marcos dictatorship allowed these organizations to flourish. The regime conceived of itself as a modernizing political force, with a natural appeal to an emerging urban middle and upper class linked to industrial activity rather than the plantation agriculture of the traditional elite. Anticommunism and the argument that development required authoritarian control underpinned the regime's hopes for an elite-backed constitutional authoritarianism. This strategy required the state to allow space for bounded urban protest organizations and campaigns—demonstrating to the urban middle class the arrangement's liberal possibilities. Periodic regime crackdowns pushed these advocacy organizations toward the radical flank, repolarizing things, and creating connections between armed and formally legal movement formations. In time, cycles of liberalization and crackdown contributed to the growth of a larger and larger organized antidictatorship apparatus, holding together a broad range of constituent-differentiated demands within their state-replacing agenda (Thompson 1995).

This pattern had three consequences that are important for our present purposes. First, more or less formal and fairly stable social movement organizations developed steadily over the course of Marcos regime. Part of their stability and formality consisted in explicit ideological commitments, long-term strategies to restructure social and political relationships, and a stable membership system connecting mass constituencies to the network via specific sectorial demands and programs (Jones 1989; Abinales 1996). Second, these movement organizations attracted elite allies who were also displaced by Marcos, some of whom joined or led movement formations, others of whom worked closely with movement forces during the transitional period (Thompson 1995). These elites, in turn, could mediate between movement groups and later defectors from elite business, social, and political circles. Third, in consequence of both of these factors, movements approached the transition as an opportunity to constitute themselves into a new regime, and as we will see, became deeply involved in that process. To gauge the distinctive consequences of these three factors, consider the contrasting Indonesian case.

Save for several exceptional separatist insurgencies, Indonesian activists, following the bloody elimination of the communist party in 1965–1966, never developed anything resembling Philippine organizational formations, because the regime specifically proscribed and repressed activist organizational formations (Boudreau 2004; Aspinall 2005). Rather, the Indonesian activist pattern (or, modes of coordination, to use Diani's conceptualization—see chapter in this volume) contained the following main elements: First, while Philippine movement organizations were long term and formalized, Indonesian groups were more typically emergent, informal, and small. Even comparatively organized Indonesian legal aid associations never produced mass organizations, and student-led NGOs avoided base-building activity in favor of research, discussion, and case-specific advocacy (Eldridge 1989; Yayasan Lembaga Bantuan Hukum Indonesia 1998). Second, Indonesian activists never developed integrated, multisectoral programs for governance, and never conceived of themselves as candidates to wield state power. To the extent that different activist collectives were brokered together—and for the most part they were not—the effort advanced via the work of public intellectuals to encourage a discourse about democracy and reform (Al-Chaidar, Saharasad, and Rachman 2000; Njotorahardjo 2003). But over the course of the Suharto regime, these connections were loose, short term, and produced very little organizationally. Indonesian activism had very little in the way of an organizational apparatus, and so very little in the way of social relationships between activists and mass constituencies.

The Indonesian regime managed challenges to its authority with a combination of legal prohibitions, targeted crackdowns, and veiled threats that invoked the 1965–1966 anticommunist violence. The regime depended on a larger and more powerful bureaucracy than Marcos controlled, with the formidable Indonesian military more firmly at its core. It was only over time, when an aging and more divided Suharto regime launched modest liberalization efforts to disperse its critics, that activists had the opportunity to situate their dissent in more robust organizational settings. Student councils grew more political, and NGOs built small and localized followings (McRae 2001). Muslim organizations made less tentative forays into political advocacy, and dissidents appropriated the previously tame PDI (Partai Demokrasi Indonesia) and made it a more robust opposition vehicle (Alfian 1989; Aspinall 2005). Despite these stirrings in its final decade, however, the Indonesian state under Suharto masterfully scattered its opponents and cut off protest, and so the sharpest tensions in the authoritarian edifice were within the government, rather than between government and an activist network.

Many differences set the Indonesian and Philippine experience apart from one another, but I wish here to highlight two. First, the involuted and organized Philippine movement structure, in which movement leaders and cadres attempted to develop stable relationships with their mass bases, contrasts to an underorganized Indonesian activist sector that had few long-term individual or organizational members. Second, the ideologically explicit differences among Philippine movement networks had no real parallel in Indonesia. In part, of course, this was a function of the lower level of Indonesian organization—less organized movements perhaps need less in the way of explicit ideology. But it also reflected the postpoliticide Indonesian context, in which any formal ideology carried the stain of subversion, and the subversive tag carried the threat of extermination (Anderson and McVey 1971; Hunter 2007).

For the purposes of questions raised earlier, these differences are consequential in several ways. Philippine movement organizations had to approach democracy in relationship to both what it promised politically for long-term movement goals and for what resources it could produce for mass bases. Even organizers who saw democracy as sharply limited needed to think about what reforms might keep mass members in the game. Indonesian activists, precisely because they operated outside of powerful organizations, carried no such social obligations into the transition. Moreover, even as Philippine activist organizations formed a democracy movement of exceptional breadth and evocative power, each network had explicit ambitions for themselves that threatened to trigger zero sum competition with others. Unified prodemocracy protests thinly disguised a tradition of rivalry among movement networks. In Indonesia, while general suspicion existed between secular and Islamic movements, and between different Islamic networks, they had not the same sense of sharp and organizationally embodied rivalry. Both differences would be important going forward.

Finally, both the Philippine pattern of moving from strategic to tactical goals (evident, for instance, in the articulation of sectorial programs within the larger state power agenda) and the class basis of most movements' ideologies meant that Filipino activists could, and did, engage in a kind of alliance-building, scaling up and down for their demands (Rodan and Hughes 2012). While, for instance, movements might not agree on modes of struggle or the particular nature of the regime they wanted to build, they could ally on broad and more general projects like land reform and democracy—and so could both move from particular to general political expressions and back again in ways that facilitated flexible coalition building. In Indonesia, these revisions were beyond the experience of most activists both because they were not allowed to work at the organizational scale of the coalition, and because, for them, class-based ideology was not a permitted expression, having been effectively eradicated in the 1965–1966 murders. Not only were Philippine movements more organizationally developed, therefore, but also they had a greater capacity for maneuver and alliance.

Two Transitions

Both the Indonesian and Philippine governments fell in an upsurge of protest following a protracted crisis that began with some economic shock, and generated protest, repression, and escalation to a regime-ending crisis. In both countries, formerly reliable regime allies began to call for reform, and in the end, trusted military officers delivered an ultimatum that led to the executive's withdrawal. Nevertheless, important differences exist in the relationship of these events to Indonesian and Philippine activist positioning during the transition and afterward.

Economic shocks (some self-inflicted and some exogenous) and dramatic human rights violations triggered anti-Marcos mobilizations that swelled the ranks of the organized movements and placed them in interaction with a new wave of less organized protests. In light of this upsurge, movement groups began to work together in coalition projects of unprecedented breadth. From 1983 to 1986, centrist mobilization was so sustained and powerful—appropriating so many established civic and religious institutions—that state violence proved unable to clear the political center but instead provoked alternating patterns of polarization, brokerage, and mobilization (Thompson 1995). Rather than ushering newly activated dissidents *into* established movement groups as they had once done, brokerage processes increasingly occurred *between* existing groups and new, more moderate and programmatically limited democracy advocates, many of whom were late of the regime itself. As we will see, somewhat similar brokerage shifts lay at the heart of Egypt's spike in January 2011 mobilization. In Egypt, however, brokerage was comparatively ephemeral and served mainly to draw the Muslim Brotherhood into a movement previously led by more secular and liberal youth activists—rather than cementing ties between activists and defecting regime elites. Indeed, as shown in Rasler's chapter in this volume, interorganization links remained at the level of loose and weak coalitional ties and were carried out mostly via information and communication technologies (ICTs).

This shift had two immediate consequences. First, the pivot point for conflict between the regime and the movement shifted sharply to the political center—from an earlier conflict between state-replacing left revolutionaries and authoritarian stability to one between regime supporters and those advocating a more open and transparent political process. Second, this shift extended key sites of brokerage to outside of stable movement formations. While organizers inside the ideological/sectorial/insurgent formations continued to build and maintain their internal social relations, organization leaders increasingly linked their capacities and activities to newly mobilized and largely unorganized democracy advocates. In this process, movement organizations downplayed many existing modes of struggle (armed insurgency) and political demands (basic transformation of the structures of economic and political power), substituting instead demands for free and fair elections, the protection of key rights, and a participatory process to reconstitute representative government. Importantly, this mobilization process moved the movements' internal social arrangements, including demands for the substantive redistribution of power and wealth, into the broad democracy coalition.

The Marcos regime succumbed to a people-power movement in which a vast number of fairly conservative and elite actors had, in the heady days of the struggle, positioned themselves as "revolutionaries" and had even taken positions in underground movements (Abinales 1996). In the months and years that followed, this would all get sorted out—but for the time being, the broad people-power coalition *was* the new government, with ex-Marcos officials, human rights lawyers and activists, and members of the elite political opposition all involved. Movement leaders had the opportunity to develop close ties with members of established political families (Eaton 2003) and could also insert some of their most important reform agenda items into the general narrative of the day. Everyone—even those who owned haciendas—accordingly talked about the necessity of land reform. All—including those who had private armies—raised the banner of human rights. The movement laid claim to a role in government, but to do so, placed many from traditional political and elite families—latecomers to the antidictatorship movement—in the forefront (Abinales 1996).

Importantly, in the aftermath of the deeply fraudulent election that briefly returned Marcos to power, more moderate groups prepared electoral protests, but armed formations of the communist left, having boycotted the elections, positioned themselves to lead a military phase of the struggle. But the rapid escalation of protest, military defections, and the Marcos regime's resignation alleviated the need for an armed assault on the dictatorship, and strengthened the hand of those who embraced more peaceful tactics and moderate politics. One may well ask, with an eye cast to the more prolonged and violent transition in Libya (and the Syrian civil war), about the possible impact of a longer armed transition in the Philippines. It likely would have positioned more militant movements more centrally in the new dispensation. Because the transition occurred through peaceful modalities, it elevated the standing and power of groups with scant capacity to fight. But things could well have been different.

From early 1986, the transition progressed in several stages. First, until July 1987, President Aquino exercised special executive powers under the framework of a transitional revolutionary government, which allowed her to govern by decree—but she used these powers with extreme caution. In the middle of 1986, a constitutional commission that originally spanned the political spectrum (though some members of left organizations walked out) produced a document that passed in a popular referendum early the next year. The 1987 constitution went into effect that July, on the day when those elected in the first post-Marcos polls took office, thus ending the revolutionary period and the president's special executive powers. In these various stages, the unity forged in the democracy struggle among different activist groupings survived, and they largely worked together (Boudreau 2001).

For our purposes, there were three key outcomes of the transition. First, movements retained strong connections with their mass bases, although the transition did little to resolve the specific demands that brought farmers, workers, and other poor and working people to the movement. Second, because procedural debate and discussion regarding the constitution came up first in the transition, differences among the various movement strands did not prevent them from all supporting the constitution or from working together for its ratification. The campaign to pass the constitution featured activity by a range of activist coalitions representing the full movement spectrum, but the largest three were a liberal to left social democrat grouping, a social democrat to popular democratic coalition (further to the left of the first), and a popular democratic coalition that included social democrats on the right flank and some national democrats (associated with the Maoist insurgency) on the left. Finally, the movement's central place in the transition and in the discussions that followed meant that from the very beginning, elections were seen as a venue for movement activity (and military action and specialists in the exercise of violence were more marginal) even if the first exercise swept a coalition of administration/people-power candidates into office.

The Indonesian transition bore some resemblance to the Philippine protests of 1986, but the differences are more significant. The eventual regime-ending events followed a paralyzing financial crisis and extraordinary external pressure, both of which triggered broad but largely uncoordinated social mobilization (with a significant food riot component) strong fragmentation within the regime, and more assertive advocacy from prodemocracy forces (Schulte Nordholt and Hoogenboom 2006). Public intellectuals in prodemocracy circles often called on government actors or soldiers to lead the democracy process in the name of the Indonesian people. Street demonstrations that began as uncoordinated protests against basic commodity price increases eventually focused on actions like the denunciation of the postelection cabinet that included many Suharto family members and cronies—criticism that resonated with excluded members of the polity who lost out when Suharto circled the wagons to fend off pressure for a transition (Aspinall 2005).

Days before massed and (eventually) exuberant student-led protests occupied the national assembly complex to initiate a final confrontation, security forces attacked student demonstrations, killing several people. The murders triggered a wave or rioting and violence that left perhaps 1,500 people dead and shook the old regime to its very core. Behind the scenes, factions of the Indonesian military squared off against one another, and though they eventually resolved their conflict, things teetered on the brink for several days—until Suharto resigned and his vice president took power. Student protests continued as the post-Suharto regime moved toward more liberal and democratic practices, but the movement that gathered that day never clearly formed a coherent network, nor did students welcome participation from other sectors of Indonesian society (McRae 2001). Most importantly, activists never parlayed their role in the transition into any position (qua movement) in the new government.

Brokerage patterns in Indonesia differed from those we identified in the Philippine case. Laboring under organizational restrictions, Indonesian brokers typically operated at a fairly small scale, often *within* organizational sites appropriated by the movement (such as the opposition PDI). Crucially, brokers often were veterans of Suharto-era political parties and bureaucratic networks, rather than activists, and never connected activists to elite dissidents or government defectors on so large a scale as occurred in the Philippines (Hadiz 2008). Movement activity helped spur on reformers in government, but Suharto's departure left everyone else in power and did little to reposition activists—either individually or in their networks—to within government. The key brokers of the New Order period remained in place, politically important, and largely disconnected to such activist collectives as existed.

Consequently, while Suharto grew more isolated over the course of the regime crisis, those who drew away from him never coalesced in an oppositional pole. Rather, an initially tentative—and socially quite limited—gulf emerged between Suharto and his critics: Secular elements in the military grew estranged as the president drew closer to Muslim organizations and networks in government, and formerly supine political parties grew a bit more critical and combative

(Chandra and Kammen 2002). Economic downturns in 1997–1998 polarized relations between authorities and a more restive and ungovernable society—but activists operated in light of (and in some fear of) that polarization rather than as its agent. Finally, regime fragmentation did not typically drive a core of reformers toward the movement. Worried members of the parliament, the Golkar Party, and the military forced Suharto's resignation because they were concerned about succession, economic collapse, and social stability: Few embraced movement demands for a limited military role in politics or a new constitution. Hence, the dynamics of Indonesian contention did not give rise to an activist-led coalition against the regime, as we observed in the Philippines, but instead stretched between the government and challengers from within the polity. Mobilization pressures were sufficient to drive Suharto from power, but left few distinct legacies for activism in the post-Suharto period.

Nor did the post-Suharto period build stronger relationships between Indonesian activists and those in power. Unlike in Manila, where an extended and broadly inclusive process to write a new constitution emerged, changes in the Indonesian framework for government took place via discrete (though sometimes quite bold) constitutional amendments, often, however, without broad participation. At key moments and decisions, such as the late 1998 debate over whether the military would retain its reserved seats in parliament or its political functions, protest exerted substantial influence. But in the main, the process was a governmental affair and emerged via the decisions of elected officials and a string of constitutional amendments (Dagg 2007). Hence, while agreement on and activity to advance procedural democratic reform helped forge and preserve activist unities in the years after Marcos left, these discussions did not long involve Indonesian activists, and many soon concentrated on the specific demands of particular advocacy agendas. Nor, of course, did Indonesian activists have the broad ideological framework or organizational apparatus that allowed Filipinos to place the demands of farmers, workers, youth, and ethnic minorities on the same platform.

One singular moment demanding particular attention, because of its parallels and divergences with Egyptian events, stands out in this process of government-driven reform. Elected as the first post-transition president, Abdurahman Wahid, more popular known as Gus Dur, came to office as the leader of one of the largest Islamic social organizations and one involved in the reform process, the Nahdlatul Ulama. Wahid inherited the debate over what the scope of the Indonesian military should be. Two questions were at issue: whether the military should retain its dual political and security roles (and the reserved seats in otherwise elected legislative bodies) and what to do about prominent military rivals, such as Armed Forces chief Wiranto.

Eventually, Wahid moved decisively, ending the military's political role, abolishing the allocation of legislative seats to the military, and removing Wiranto from his post. Although the Wahid presidency ended several months later in a contentious impeachment process, the moves were not reversed or even seriously challenged. Many argued that the military's involvement in East Timor violence and its failures to adequately respond to the tsunami in Aceh undermined the institution enough to allow the move (Editors 2000). It marked a key moment in the government-driven process of early, post–New Order reforms, and stands in stark contrast to Egyptian events, in which President Mursi progressively attempted to strip the military of its powers and then was removed in a military coup. Many elements distinguish the two cases from one another, including the comparatively higher standing of an Egyptian military dealing with terrorist threats in the Sinai and Hamas in Gaza. But Mursi's move against the military was also less decisive, and never cut into its budgetary or foreign policy powers—and so left the Egyptian armed forces fairly intact institutionally.

More generally, transition processes, combined with antidictatorship dynamics previously discussed, produced different consequences in Indonesia than in the Philippines. First, movement activists had very little in the way of obligations or organized connections to mass constituencies, and indeed only began talking about building such connections in the years that followed. Second, the absence of activist participation in constitutional discussions meant that the transition did nothing to close the gulf that existed between poorly organized activists and government officials (Slater 2004). Finally, because of the movement's general remove from formal politics—and a lingering sense that such politics, and particularly party politics, were not an appropriate venue for an activism that had long been characterized by patterns of moral witness—activists did not immediately embrace elections as an appropriate venue for their involvement, did not often form parties or endorse candidates, and tended to view the movement of individual activists into election work as defections from the cause (Tan 2002). Taking these points together, we can say that the Indonesian transition left activists with more freedom to explore what advocacy and organizing would mean, but little in the way of immediate social obligation, movement apparatus, or connection to political power. The contrasts with the Philippine case should be apparent.

Politics in the New Regimes

What seems most in need of explanation, in the comparison between the two cases, is how a well-positioned, programmatically sophisticated, and at least apparently unified Philippine movement failed to drive a more thorough democratization process. Indeed, a closer look at movement politics will reveal further puzzles, for over the past decade or two, Philippine movement organizations have campaigned for warlords and political clans in elections, been implicated in corruption scandals (Ufen 2012), sided with military coups, and in many ways failed to advance the movement agendas with which each came into the post-Marcos period. Despite Indonesian activists' organizationally and politically weaker passage into the democratic period, the procedural elements of the Indonesian democratic system grew stronger in the years that followed, and activist groups (if not fully consolidated movement networks) have become more stable advocates for substantive reform. The reform impetus remains weak, and Indonesian activists are still more likely to leave a movement for a political career than to position their movement as an actor in elections. And, the key criticisms leveled at Indonesian democracy (that it has been a largely money-driven insiders' game, and that government too seldom responds to public need) are consistent with the way activists were positioned relative to the government. But Indonesian movement groups have been far less implicated in allegations of corruption, and have strengthened (albeit slowly) their political position ever since. To the extent that we can attach some movement role in the forging of a strong democracy, the deterioration of Philippine democracy over the last decade stands in stark contrast with the elevation of that in Indonesia. What accounts for the difference?

In seeking an answer, consider the dynamic of brokerage discussed earlier. Movement engagement with the Philippine constitution-writing process meant that their substantive demands, for land and labor reform, the protection of human rights, and the removal of US bases, found their way into the document. To push for substantive inclusions, movements demonstrated for broad and universal policy reform (land reform, labor reform, a new human rights code) in some of the country's largest demonstrations in its history from 1988 through 1990. Movement organizations jockeyed with one another for position, but their broad coalitions held and channeled rivalries into common efforts. In that process, social relationships between movements' political leadership and their mass bases survived—as did reciprocal obligations embodied in those relationships.

In the 1990s, two changes occurred in the political landscape that deeply influenced the dynamics shaping activism. First, the newly elected legislature had passed sweeping universalistic reforms on virtually every important social and political reform agenda (Thompson 1996; Aldaba 2002). The new laws were unprecedented in their breadth, but were so broad as to ensure that implementing activity would determine whether they would have any real effect and for whom. As the policy conversation moved to matters of implementation, movement organizations sought to name their leaders and allies to bodies set up by the different executive agencies, and to use those positions to determine how measures like the Comprehensive Agrarian Reform Law would be implemented and what communities would be its most immediate and direct beneficiaries. As the policy process moved from universalistic conceptualization to particularistic implementation, the broad movement coalitions dissolved and particularistic, often patronage-seeking connections emerged between movement groups and those in power (Magadia 2003).

Second, and later that decade, a range of new electoral laws came into effect that established the "party list" system—a set of 50 reserved seats for "cause-oriented" electoral parties: Any party running on the party list could win (only) three of these seats, and could ally with parties running in the larger, unrestricted electoral contests, but could not run candidates in them. Under this system, movement engagement with the electoral process became an intramural competition; to increase leverage over one another and garner resources, activist parties were driven to ally with, and endorse, traditional and elite-driven parties running in the larger competition (Choi 2001; Holden 2009). As with the shifting policy dynamics, electoral competition influenced activists away from collaboration in the construction of ideologically consistent electoral politics to a competition that produced ideologically anomalous alliances between movement collectives and old style politicians, many with links to the Marcos regime. Activists nevertheless undertook these alliances because they seemed to enhance movement power and could produce resources and political access necessary to satisfy mass base needs. In both policy and electoral realms, then, activists began more often to prioritize selective benefits and political positioning over efforts to secure the universal implementation of reforms or longer-range political goals. Soon, movement networks could reliably be brought into the service of established political parties in their disputes with one another, and activists grew circumspect about advocacy that risked criticizing those allies (Quimpo 2005).

In what ways does the evolution of Philippine activism in the transition period build on earlier legacies? Three matters come to mind. First, strong social relationships between movement leaders and mass constituents survived into the new dispensation. These ties made activist leaders important brokers in the electoral system, but also ensured that movement leaders would need to find ways to satisfy those bases. Second, newly formed links between politicians and activists (a direct consequence of the geography of polarization in the late Marcos years) rendered electoral politics more accessible for movement activists and provided contacts for overtures about political endorsement, alliances, and the exchange of resources for mass support. Third, because the democracy movement was but a stage in a longer and more fractious history of interactions among movement networks, connections across movement streams were fairly brittle. Together these factors made broad movement unities less and less likely, and after some initial efforts to develop broad center-left political parties, activists concentrated on the party list elections and established electoral and political alliances with professional politicians. In this process, the broad left movement died away, yielding to a politics with less consistent ideological moorings or clear political orientations.

Compare the Indonesian case. Indonesian activists, having no strong ties to mass base constituencies, did not encounter tradeoffs between policy advocacy and securing benefits for members. Less grounded organizationally, they were also more able to pursue a style of work that concentrated on research, writing, and argument—and less on the mobilization of mass politics. Moreover, Indonesian activists did not operate within any large activist front and did not need to work to maintain those broad unities (Boudreau 2009). For both reasons, in the years following the transition, they concentrated on building small activist collectives, often in local, rather than national arenas, and began talking about building new skills and frameworks (Antiov, Brinkerhoff, and Rapp 2010). Activists typically steered their movements away from electoral politics, for the transition process had not placed them among professional politicians, and activists did not, in any event, hold the kinds of social or material resources that would make them attractive electoral brokers or campaign operatives (Tan 2002). Activism and advocacy began much closer to the ground, and built upward but slowly. Progress toward reform more often emerged via local programs to train policy or mediate sectarian tensions, rather than via national advocacy programs, and a decade into the new dispensation, activists were only beginning to formulate an approach to policy reform—although these efforts, like most movement activity, were fragmented rather than the product of broad or unified action.

While falling short of a full account of the transitions, these comparisons indicate some key areas of research by concentrating on several core dynamics, such as brokerage and polarization. Brokerage does not merely put people on the streets—it may also establish sets of social relationships that ramify into the future. Who is brokered into new relationships, by whom, and with what consequences for the political positing of both brokers and those they connect is consequential. Similarly, identifying patterns of polarization (rather than the mere existence of a polarized political situation) can help predict how movements are likely to be positioned. The fact that Philippine activists brokered together prodemocracy coalitions in a situation polarized between regime supporters and opponents outside the government helped ensure that activists would be central to the new regime, but would also have new and powerful relationships with established politicians outside of any activist or reform tradition. In contrast, despite the economic polarization of Indonesian society during the 1998 crisis, the key brokers of the Indonesian democracy movement existed within government, and pulled together anti-Suharto sections of government and the military alongside the leaders (only) of opposition parties and moderate social groups. In this sense, Indonesian activists—despite their key role in final antiregime demonstrations—were the beneficiaries of the coalitions brokered together (rather than brokers themselves or key participants in the brokered coalition). Not surprisingly, therefore, activists were more peripheral after the transition.

The impact of brokerage however, was also modified by new institutions that could either strengthen or undercut the relations bequeathed by the transition. The new institutions of Indonesian democracy were essentially consistent with the pattern of social relationships of the transition: established political and organizational professionals had the political inside track, and activists, while capable of pressuring government at key moments, remained outside the polity and immersed in more local and limited politics. Emergent Philippine institutions, in contrast, disrupted the social relations of the transition, and one might almost venture to guess that the party list system (suggested in the new constitution but fully designed in subsequent legislation with less powerful movement representation) sought explicitly to dismount activist networks that accumulated power in the struggle against Marcos by pitting them against one another (Quimpo 2005). Hence, while activist relationships forged in the anti-Marcos struggle shaped early post-transition dynamics, new political and social arrangements also influenced those dynamics and require explicit study.

Another important lesson from the comparison is that people and constituencies brokered into a prodemocracy movement bring their social and political agenda with them. Where brokerage is ephemeral and those social and political obligations less established or complex, the agenda for procedural reform may be separable from that of substantive social and political reform. In Indonesia, procedural reform was largely taken up by government officials (prodded at key moments by student protests) while social reform fell more to activists' more localized and nationally uncoordinated efforts. The two were less separable in the Philippines, because activists operated within stronger movement organizations with established political programs. Because these relationships were not disrupted as activists passed through the transition, the entire approach to reform combined procedural matters and those of more substance. During the early open moments, substantive elements of the reform agenda found expression in some provisions of the 1987 constitution—calling for land and labor reform for instance—but also manifest themselves in the early policy campaigns. Later, they emerged as part of the electoral engagement strategy of movement groups.

There may be no way to predict precisely how movements will respond to contact with an electoral system—or with the other institutions of an emergent democracy. But the foregoing also gives us a clue about how movement histories and transition dynamics might inform the matter. The social ties within Philippine movement organizations pressured activists to deliver resources to mass members. Unities forged among the different movement strands were weak and vulnerable, as we have seen. But the existence of a complex movement goal and ideologies seems also consequential here, because these ideologies also produced strategies of struggle with long- and short-term goals (as indeed the struggle for democracy was a tactical departure for some of the originally revolutionary movements). The interplay of long- and short-term strategies, however, meant that decisions to support a particular candidate, even if ideologically dissonant, could be tolerated provided it occasioned a plausible promise of positioning activists for greater success in the long-term struggle. Without that kind of longer-term ideological perspective, Indonesian activists typically did not distinguish tactical from strategic objectives, and so needed to "balance the books" (politically and morally) at the end of each political act; guided by such calculations, most activists rejected participation in electoral politics for at least a decade after the regime change. Filipinos also broadly understood electoral politics to be compromised and compromising, but also saw them as a means to an end.

Middle East Comparisons and Some Conclusions

Stepping back slightly from the details of the two cases, we may identify a more general but essential difference between them that is instructive for broader comparisons. In the Philippines, intramovement competition was at first postponed in efforts to build antidictatorship coalitions and then to construct a new constitution. Still, different activist groups viewed the antidictatorship struggle as tactical elements in a fight to control the new regime. This means that the question of political power hovered over all of the other conversations, and reemerged fiercely with elections and movement participation in them. In Indonesia, pressures for reforms had a more autonomous logic and dynamic, if a less comprehensive organizational or rhetorical expression. Demands for elections, for the rule of law and an end to corruption dominated the transition process, and in the aftermath many activists returned to the local advocacy campaigns—for they did not have fully developed countervailing programs for new regimes, lurking below the surface of their advocacy. If but loosely organized, therefore, activists in Indonesia were seldom pitted against one another in elections, and so voting did not work so corrosive an effect on their movements. Indonesian activists *lost* many of their number to electoral parties or government service (shifts in activity that Filipinos would have more likely regarded as movement *advances*). But the movement organizations, if less driven to national power, were also more able to retain a critical and autonomous stance, at least insofar as the transition has thus far progressed.

How do we account for these differences? Examining the relationship between the two aspects of transition—efforts to establish democratic political processes and to use democratic processes to choose leaders and make decisions—helps us begin. To put the matter in crude, preliminary terms, democratization involves both a collective effort among all democratic forces to rewrite the political rules to ensure a participatory politics *and* the implementation of those rules in a competitive process (often among different elements in the prodemocratic forces) to make political decisions. On the one hand, movements for democracy often pull together broad coalitions of diverse actors, committed to democratic reform as an end in itself. Certainly elements of that program, such as the respect for human rights or governmental transparency, have occupied core positions in many reform programs. But we can expect many elements of these programs to *not* reduce to democratic reform alone, and so activists and analysts have often puzzled over how to balance engagement with and support for an open-ended (electoral) process against a desire to secure specific outcomes (including power). Since prodemocracy movements almost inevitably contain diverse interests and perspectives, comrades in that struggle are likely to drift toward opposition to one another in contests over power—although they may need one another, and so more easily coalesce, in the effort to construct systems. This suggests that the sequencing of these two processes will matter for transition paths.

From this standpoint, the Indonesian and Philippine transitions differed from one another in the proximity and sequencing for the two aspects of the democratization process. Indonesian activists were largely absent from the process by which the new rules were drafted (in the sense that no broad constitutional assembly was ever called, and most key changes took place in rather closed government sessions). While constitutional changes alternated with early elections, the distance that movements stood from the process meant that they were not strongly eroded by political competition—though they did remain a rather minor political force. The new democratic institutions were designed and fought over by political professionals, and if the system produced weak substantive reforms, the changes in the power structure were not so great as to provoke a reaction from, for instance, the military.

In the Philippines, the sequencing of collaboration in institutional design and then competition under the new rules meant that things were rockier—that competition would produce more in the way of constitutional crisis and continued contention. It also meant that movement organizations were often pulled further and further away from their advocacy programs by the quest for power (Quimpo 2005). But enough had been accomplished in the construction of the democratic system to drive political processes back toward at least a formal adherence to the constitution following periodic departures from it, and despite more frequent violence against those who most challenged the status quo (Holden 2009).

What about cases in which the construction of the system and competition within that system are more simultaneous affairs? Egypt and Tunisia provide an opportunity to think through the consequences of such circumstances. In each case, considerations of both sequencing and brokerage determine what kinds of social and political pressures impinged in the transition process, and ultimately whether or not short-term democratic institutions were equal to that pressure. Brokerage matters because its scope and durability helps determine who had access to core political processes, and what demands they brought to that process. Sequencing matters because it influences whether processes of institutional design and of competition took place simultaneously or not. Together, who was involved and what they involved themselves *in* explains a lot about how the transition played out.

In this regard, two elements of the Tunisian transition seem most important. The first is the movement of contention from the small provincial towns that initially rose in protest to larger ones. The self-immolation of Tunisian fruit vendor Mohamed Bouazizi set off a wave of sympathy protests that diffused spatially (rather than across any organizational connections), expressing the fundamental frustration of a people living in economic hardship and insecurity. Only after several days did the protest spread to the city, and when it did, it was by virtue of the involvement of new, more organized activists, concentrating their attention and anger more precisely on questions of democracy, due process, and the rule of law. The General Tunisian Labor Union (UGTT) and the Lawyer's Syndicate had networks connecting the country to the urban centers and played important coordinating and mobilizing roles, but the lawyers' group in particular concentrated on procedural demands. Importantly, while organizationally central to the final, urban-based confrontation with the regime, neither organizational network had the kind of fully realized political program that the Egyptian Muslim Brotherhood brought to the broad movement—nor did they broker into the transition a full slate of mass alliances that would shape a post-reform policy agenda. Hence, the Tunisian transition elevated people more interested in working through a process of constructing a new government than in securing power for themselves (although, instructively, the most organized of the opposition groups were most eager to fast-track elections) (Miller, Martini, and Larrabee 2012).

The absence of a movement organization with electoral ambitions in Tunisia was more in evidence when electoral exercises began and people started to use the new institutions to compete for political power. The transitional process produced an upsurge of new parties, none of which could dominate the pending election. The broad and poorly organized High Commission for the Realization of Revolutionary Goals moved less swiftly when compared with the Egyptian military or the Egyptian Muslim Brotherhood—but that very slowness opened space for a conversation that separated the design of new representative institutions from the use of those institutions in competitive elections. In fact, the full process of constitutional revision took place in several rounds, punctuated by elections. Over the course of those rounds, a separation emerged between a class of politicians running for office, and a group of democracy advocates concentrating more on the design of a fair system (this dynamic was similar to what we observed in the Indonesian case, but stands in contrast to Philippine events).

Hence, the competition for power eventually occurred in a context that was not dominated by any force and in which the design of the system was not intended to privilege one group over others. The transition positioned activist voices and collectives in a closer relationship to power—but because their formations were so fragmented (coordinated by, rather than organized into the dominant networks of the transition) the switch to electoral competition retained an essentially pluralist cast. Moreover, in time the political class that produced most election candidacies was dominated by politicians (many returning from exile) rather than activists. That is, the combination of who was brokered into the transitional coalition (activists without strong mass bases, concerned mainly with process) and the sequencing of institutional design and electoral competition produced a separation between the former and the latter—leaving adequate space for the emergence of a system that was viewed as procedurally fair and has consequently emerged, at least at this writing, as the one apparent success story of the transition.

Two things mark the Egyptian transition as different from that which we see in Tunisia and more similar to Indonesian events. The first is that the newly empowered activist brokers in Egypt were able to build only ephemeral links between different constituencies. Early on, activists in different networks linked secular youth, labor, and Muslim Brotherhood organizations together, but these links did not last long and were mainly based on ICTs. Egypt's Muslim Brotherhood formed part of a broad coalition with early rising groups such as the April 6th Movement (allied with labor groups) and "We Are All Khalid Sa'id" (initially a Facebook community established by a Google executive). These links helped coax an initially reluctant Muslim Brotherhood old guard into demonstrations initiated by secular activists, and the resulting surge unseated the regime (Clarke 2014). A few short weeks later, however, the Muslim Brotherhood had formed a new alliance with the post-transition military, and this left secular activists isolated and vulnerable (Cole 2011). That is to say, while secular and process-minded activists were brokered *in* to the transitional power arrangement in Tunisia (as also happened in the Philippines) they were brokered *out* of those circles in Egypt.

At various points, leaders of different movement organizations, and even military officers, were important conduits connecting elements of the movement. At the same time, to the extent that electronic media like Facebook and Twitter played important roles connecting different groups to one another, that connecting work seems to have produced little political capital of any duration for new brokers after the transition. With fewer stable brokers to displace, organizations with strong, old-fashioned organizational capacity (the Muslim Brotherhood and the military) moved easily to power, shouldering aside activists who were less organizationally connected.

Here we find the second key difference between these two cases from the Middle East and North Africa: the relative size and institutional heft of Egypt's Muslim Brotherhood—because that bulk positioned the organization to assert its substantive interests early in the transition. Muslim Brotherhood activists brokered *into* post-transition power arrangement in Egypt had a fairly clear field—while activist collectives were diverse and individually small in Tunisia (and, as we have said, more interested in procedural reform than substantive power). Not only, therefore, did Egypt's Muslim Brotherhood have the capacity to dominate the first elections but also it quickly turned that victory into an effort to promote substantive change informed by the claims and orientations embedded in its organizational fabric. We saw something quite different in the Philippine case, where activists also were brokered into a post-transition arrangement. Here, however, the arrangement involved relationships with established political elites—and soon enough placed them in competition with other activists. The internal diversity of the activist complex diluted any one group's drive to power in the Philippines, and alliances with conservative political groups watered down the change agenda. In Egypt, no secular activist network, or existing political class, could stand against the Muslim Brotherhood. The military did pose some challenge initially in that first election, but not enough to dilute the Muslim Brotherhood's eventual victory. Egypt's Muslim Brotherhood contested elections from the outset, and had a clear, agenda-driven ambition for state power (Faris 2009). When President Mursi assumed office, the Muslim Brotherhood was already long unmoored from its erstwhile allies in the anti-Mubarak movement and would soon come in conflict with its short-term military allies. In combination, the near simultaneity of institutional design and competition, on the one hand, and the relative bulk and strength of the organizational interests (the Muslim Brotherhood's) brokered into the transition sets Egypt apart from other cases.

Here, we find a kind of puzzle that reflects on the whole case set. In each dyad—that in Southeast Asia and that in the Middle East and North Africa—movement organizations that enjoyed the most immediate influence in postregime collapse politics soon ran into trouble (although the Philippine and Egyptian stories are different). Strong early success in Egypt, and the conflation of procedural reform and competition for power, led to overreach and backlash. Less success and greater separation between procedural reform and substantive competition helped Philippine activists establish a reform voice in post-Marcos politics—but protracted contact with electoral politics and more intensive substantive competition eventually took a corrosive toll. In both Tunisia and Indonesia, activists were less immediately influential in competitive politics after the transition—with Indonesians effectively brokered out of post-Suharto arrangements, and those in Tunisia more involved in procedural matters. In both cases, however, democratic institutions, and so perhaps the longer-term prospects of activist leverage on the political system, seem to have been correspondingly stronger than in cases that seem to have initially strengthened activist capacities.

These brief comparisons yield no clear causal relationships, but they do suggest a number of questions that one might ask to figure out how processes of struggle can shape a post-transition dispensation. In particular, my analysis suggests that we should ask questions in a number of key areas concerning movement engagement with the new political system.

First, what is the relationship between movement organizations and the general electoral activity of pulling voters together? To answer, we must consider both the strength of activist connections to mass actors (strong in Egypt and the Philippines, weaker in Tunisia and Indonesia) and the extent to which activist groups were key contestants in electoral politics (as opposed to having been more involved in establishing fair processes). This second consideration will reflect both the impact of brokerage processes during the transition on movement groups' proximity to political parties, and the separation or simultaneity of reform processes and those affecting the substantive distribution of power. In respect to this question, Tunisian and Indonesian reform processes seem most separate from substantive competition of the reform agenda, Egyptian cases least so, and those in the Philippines on a trajectory that took them from great separation early in the transition to virtually none at all by the mid-1990s.

Second, a set of institutional questions are suggested by these considerations. When movement groups do undertake deep involvement in substantive and competitive political processes like elections and policymaking following a transition, how are their demands aggregated, and by what logic are they directed into the political system? That is, what is the nature, strength, and coherence of the social relationships brokered into new political processes, and what institutional structures direct them? To what extent does the logic of movement engagement with the new system overwrite the old logic of anti-dictatorship struggle, and what strains does that shift put on the movement's internal social relationships?

However one approaches these questions, they will most likely yield insights into different processes of struggle, rather than tight covering laws linking antecedent conditions to consequences and outcomes. But figuring out how movements make, and are made by, popular contention and transition processes should provide us with some good guesses about where they will stand within an emerging democracy.

10

Chile's Winter of Discontent

IS PROTEST ACHIEVING DEEPER DEMOCRATIZATION?

Mario Sznajder

THE RECENT CYCLE of protest in Chile that began in 2011 did not challenge the democratic system, nor did it challenge the neoliberal model. Rather, it strived toward reform that would widen the GINI bottleneck of the country for the benefit of those wanting to become the new middle classes. Chile's 2011 "winter of discontent" is a useful case for demonstrating how popular contention not only acts as a "voice"—to use Hirschman's (1970) term—for those who expect much from the socioeconomic model but do not see their expectations being realized but also, and in parallel, shapes the public agenda by placing issues essential to the country's socioeconomic model at the center of the public democratic discourse. These issues include redistribution, taxation, the quality of services and of education at all levels, and the need to reform the balance between the functioning of free markets and policies of state intervention—better laws and regulations as well as redistributive taxation and state financing of the needs of the weaker sectors of society—in a democratic way. Thus, in Chile, a mostly nonviolent cycle of protest is trying to solve the contradictions produced by the socioeconomic model inherited from military rule and the consolidating democracy of the country.

In many ways, Chile poses no exception. The use of this socioeconomic model in societies characterized by deep socioeconomic gaps was meant to impose a certain kind of "economic rationalization" in which the individualistic ethos characteristic of neoliberalism has been implanted in parallel to the establishing or recreation of political democracy. This process amplified a deepening contradiction between the economic and political regimes and has brought about the reemergence of popular contention with the purpose of ensuring the growth of social mobility, as one of the main results of the above combination. The dual model of political democracy and a free market economy has characterized Chile and other Latin American countries in their "third wave" of democratization (Huntington 1991; Hagopian and Mainwaring 2005) since the 1980s. In this kind of democratization scenario, the possibility of promoting greater economic inclusion and social mobility as a response to the rising demands of the excluded and less mobile sectors of society in the context of an open (democratic) public sphere becomes a reality. In the process of democratization, the public concern for the interests of all sectors, as well as the economic and political articulation needed to generate resources and legal provisions to make inclusion and mobility effective, have only shown mixed results. In the case of Chile, the issue is larger than the spillovers from the dictatorial period to the transition to democracy. The socioeconomic model imposed by force under military rule still exists, with very little change, a quarter of a century after the beginning of democratization. Even in the cases of long-term successful application of free market policies, inclusionary and exclusionary trends have functioned in parallel. If poverty is reduced, the socioeconomic gaps are augmented. In situations of this kind, inclusion becomes relative and related to the capacity to generate upward socioeconomic mobility. A growing socioeconomic gap, coming in parallel to the rise of socioeconomic expectations—especially in the lower-income sectors of society—appearing when growth and employment stand behind the decrease of poverty, generally works against the rising expectations of this less privileged segment of society. Though a series of governments have recognized these problems and introduced policies for confronting them, successful results have been scant.[1]

In what follows, I provide a short summary of and historical background to Chile's "winter of discontent," and then analyze the cycle of contentious transition according to the nature of the tension between the economic and political dimensions; the forms, claim-making, and goals; and the outcomes. The concluding part of this chapter not only steps back to assess the broader meaning and significance of that specific cycle of contention in terms of future trends and developments but also puts the Chilean case in comparative perspective. Here, in addition to pointing to an insightful resemblance between the Chilean and the Israeli protest summer of 2011 (analyzed in depth in Talshir's chapter, in this volume), mostly in terms of the link between the economic and political dimensions, I offer a comparative analysis of the Chilean experience with that of Jordan before and during the "Arab Spring."

Chile's Winter of Discontent

In May 2011, a wave of student mobilization, encompassing both university and high school students, began the largest and longest wave of contention in Chile since the return to democracy. Although the protest centered on education, the range of demands was wider. Basically, the leaders of this wave of protest challenged the existing socioeconomic model as a whole, demanding reforms, mainly in the educational system, such as increasing the tax rates in order to finance the education reform. In essence, however, the demands represented a general adherence to the combination of democracy and free markets that had characterized Chile since 1990.

If before 1970 and especially during Allende's government, protest was of a revolutionary character, demanding deep structural changes, in the period under discussion, the reformist character of protest in Chile was rather clear, even though the demand for free education may seem "revolutionary" for the supporters of free markets and privatizations.

Various reasons are behind the change in the political culture of protest in the country. The first is strongly related to the trauma the country suffered under authoritarian military rule and the massive human rights violations (Roniger and Sznajder 1999). This generated both a twofold sensitivity about preservation of democratic rule and respect of human rights, on the one hand, and insensitivity and growing apathy about the functioning of party politics, on the other. Nonviolent demonstrations, a maximization of the impact of the new media—especially Internet means, novel ways of demonstration, and much social activism, both through nongovernmental organizations (NGOs) and intersectorial coalitions, characterize the modern nonpartisan mobilizations.

Lack of confidence in traditional politics and the political parties was compounded by a system of constitutional guarantees, authoritarian enclaves—that is, the need of special majorities to reform the 1980 Constitution and main legislation granting special rights to the minority, and the binominal electoral system granting virtual veto power to minority elites. Thus, the preservation of the socioeconomic model implanted under military rule, which was favored mostly by the richest minority segments of the population, has been ensured. The model could not be changed by regular party politics, by political negotiations, or by force, especially because the armed forces were the guarantors of the 1980 Constitution and the socioeconomic model it supported.

Moreover, the socioeconomic reforms that began in 1975 have been in place for about four decades and are closely related to Chile's macroeconomic success and modernization. These reforms have affected—even at the individual level—the majority of Chileans. Privatization of health, pension funds, housing, education, mining, transportation, basic infrastructures, and every possible sector have created clusters of interests that link individually the absolute majority of the population to the private sector. The shrinking size of the state—both as an employer and provider of social benefits—has placed the vast majority of the population in the realm of free markets, decreasing the formal and political meaning of citizenship in favor of a mixture of formal citizen and *homo oeconomicus*. Thus, in an individually based society in which the socioeconomic gaps have grown in parallel to expectations and upward mobility, active market participation has become central for most of the population. Only those that can afford it are likely to protest, but very few will endanger their place in the market—losing a job, a business opportunity, or earnings—in order to protest. The norm of Chile's democratic/free market system (political/socioeconomic system) has come to achieve prominence through earnings rather than through social and political activism.

In a certain sense, this explains the composition of protest groups nowadays. The largest demonstrations were manned by students (university, high school), while other sectors (mining, industrial, indigenous, ecologist, peripheral, and even *lumpen proletariat*) joined in various forms and circumstances. The leading participation of students' pre-*hominem oeconomici* can last long, and partially confront the government, municipalities, and police. The incorporation of extraeducation demands of other sectors widens the legitimacy of the protest, transforming it into a large social phenomenon. Still, the language of reform rather than of revolution, with which demands were framed, allowed the political classes to support, reject, or to negotiate them, still in terms of representative democracy.

The Historical Background

The Chilean case is especially interesting for two main reasons. First, Chile experienced the earliest radical neoliberal reform in Latin America. Second, in spite of ups and downs and contrary to other countries, Chile maintained and continues to uphold neoliberalism.

Indeed, the economic model adopted under military rule has survived, remaining nearly impenetrable to change, throughout the transition to democracy. As a matter of fact, it has been part of both the transition to democracy and of democratized Chile in the last quarter-century.[2] Moreover, under democratic rule, and successive governments of the *Concertación*—the center-left coalition that opposed Pinochet and ruled Chile from 1990 until 2010—the neoliberal economic model has thrived even more than it did under military rule. As a matter of fact, Chile is globally perceived, in the last two decades, as a successful combination of a consolidating working democracy and an efficient and an advancing prosperous economic model.[3] In spite of all the shortcomings associated with repressive military rule, the governments of the transition to democracy have preserved the economic model imposed under dictatorship.

A large percentage of Chile's population today has been born in a country with a free market economy. Most of the Chileans today have not experienced any alternative to this economic model. Yet, we may ask whether this has transformed Chile into a country "inhabited by the *homo oeconomicus*," a country guided solely by individual self-interest. The answer is negative, and the 2011 wave of protests and the demands presented constitute a solid proof.

A forceful application of the free market model—as had taken place in Chile under military rule—created a double impact: First, the people that change but lose in the process nonetheless become part of the model. They may be social and political enemies of the model but will still work within it, because no plausible alternative is available. Second, rising tensions are then transmitted to the public sphere, generating long-term distrust in the system as a whole—not only in the free market but also in the social and political framework that enabled it—even if the new model is relatively successful, because of the gap between the expectations it creates and its capacity to "deliver." These tensions are assuaged in periods of rapid economic growth, but in times of economic crisis, the loss of trust in the model may generate waves of protest in which grievances coming from different sectors will be brought together.

The Political Culture of Protest in Chile

In the last 40 years the political culture of protest in Chile shifted from one of highly mobilized, yet polarized elites and masses—culminating in the Popular Unity government of Allende (1970–1973)—to one of almost total social and political demobilization and polarization during the military rule (1973–1990). Still, as mentioned above, military rule was contested in various ways, including violence.

Despite heavy-handed repression and systematic targeted killing, during military rule, waves of protest were frequent in Chile, waged against Pinochet and the armed forces in various forms. This included armed resistance to military rule in various periods during the 1970s, days of civil protest in 1983 (during the second economic crisis), a serious attempt to assassinate Pinochet (1986), and massive *cacerolazos* (pot-banging demonstrations) in various periods between 1973 and 1990 (preceded by the same kind of demonstrations as were held against Allende's government). The transition to democracy and its consolidation thus can be seen as period of relative calm, marked by labor strikes and some sectorial protests.

At the end of military rule there was a shift toward plebiscitary and electoral mobilization, combined with an electoral system that preserved certain levels of block polarity. The blocks of parties are the alternative center-left and center-right coalitions that have governed Chile since the transition to democracy in 1990 and until today. At the same time, political veto rights were granted to the minority and generated increasing levels of political apathy and a decrease in formal political participation—registering/voting—especially among the younger generation in the period of democratic consolidation (1990–2014).[4] Although freedom of expression, reunion, association, and parliamentary representativity existed and functioned as regulatory mechanisms, and macroeconomic success alleviated unemployment, misery, and poverty, Chile was accumulating internal pressure. An interesting point is that the center-left *Concertación* governments that ruled the country between 1990 and 2010 achieved a high level of political stability, despite increasing socioeconomic pressure generated by the growing income gap. As Taylor argued (2002),

> The "improved political situation" constitutes the success of the *Concertación* governments in containing social struggles through a reinvention of neoliberalism within the context of electoral democracy. In this respect, that the rapid growth of the Chilean economy occurred immediately following the transition from dictatorship to electoral democracy was particularly well received by the IMF, World Bank and the US State Department, who, during the 1990s, have been anxious to promote globally a combination of neoliberalism and highly-elitist institutional relations similar to that of post-1990 Chile. (72)

Nonetheless, sectorial protest continued as a long historical trend in Chile's sociopolitical landscape throughout this period, at time reaching higher levels and visibility, as was the case with the Mapuche Indians, or over ecological issues, excessive governmental centralization, and other issues. Another expression of popular discontent took place during 2006, first between April and June and then, in September-October of the same year, when high school students carried out the Penguins Revolution—*Revolución de los Pingüinos*—which got the name from the school uniforms in use in the country's high schools.[5] The students demanded the revocation of the education laws enacted under military rule, more autonomy, and free transportation to and from school. Most of those demands were accepted by President Bachelet in June 2006, and although there was a subsequent attempt to resume the protest, it waned away. In 2009, the reform law, which had been enacted by military rule (LOCE: Ley Orgánica Constitucional de Enseñanza—Organic

Constitutional Law of Education (of Teaching)) in the last day of military dictatorship (March 10, 1990), was replaced by a new General Education Law, perceived by most of the students in the country as inadequate and mostly cosmetic.

Tensions between Economy and Politics: A Contested Transition

The success of Chile in developing into a modern economy within the framework of democracy has not been free of flaws and shortcomings. Although political democracy seems to have consolidated in Chile, alongside neoliberal reforms, it is a peculiar kind of democracy based on dual societies and characterized by declining participation.

Chile is a country with a population of over 17,620,000 inhabitants (2013). In 2010 more than 6 million Chileans were employed and earned wages. From a socioeconomic point of view, Chile has developed huge income gaps between the richest and poorest section of its population. The Gini coefficient for Chile in the late 2000s was 0.52, and in 2013—according to World Bank data—it reached 0.50, still the highest among the OECD countries.

Dividing the country into three categories of earners of monthly wages, we find out that 6,000 (0.1% of the wage earners) earned above $12,000 US per month; 40,000 (0.7%) earned above $4,000 US per month and 120,000 (2%) earned a monthly wage of above $2,400 US per month. All the rest (97.2%) earned less than the latter. In 2000, the Chilean income ratio between the highest and the lowest 10 percent—or deciles—was 27.8 to 1. This trend has not been reverted throughout the 2000s.

This simple data is closely related to the political narratives about the middle classes and the benefits they should enjoy from different governments the majority elect to speak in their name. In Chile, it is claimed that the "middle classes" enjoy policies such as tax cuts—in our case study, especially tax exemptions that could alleviate their education expenditures, or, in another instance, lower taxes on gasoline. The problem is that all these tax benefits favor the highest 10% income earners, who are clearly part of the upper classes. The redistribution bias—in favor of the upper income segments—is related to the lack of regulation for lobbying groups, the opacity of parties' financing, and the general public's (and many politicians') lack of knowledge of the quantitative data hidden beyond the general and popular concept of the "middle classes."[6]

Another problem to consider is that although it is true that poverty has been seriously reduced since the late 1980s, not only has the socioeconomic gap widened but also the share of the national income earned by the lowest quintiles of Chile's society has been reduced as well. In spite of the efforts of Bachelet's government to redistribute, Chilean poverty statistics in 2009 show that the absolute numbers of the poor and the indigent have grown by nearly 10 percent compared with the previous statistics of 2006. This renders problematic the qualitative-quantitative dimension of political rhetoric about the "middle classes," as a widening GINI and increasing poverty become a real menace for those politically and symbolically presented as "middle classes."[7]

Another factor, generally disregarded, is the imbalance between Santiago and the rest of the country. Chile is a unitary country divided into administrative regions, and the political power center is still in Santiago, in spite of the fact that the parliament (*Congreso de Chile*) has operated in Valparaiso since 1990. Santiago enjoys the highest concentration of capital, income, population, culture, institutions, NGOs, and political activity in the country. Decisions of all kinds, especially political decisions, are made there, and it is clearly the center of Chile's public sphere. This fact has generated historical tensions typical of center–periphery relations, especially because the sources of wealth of the country—mining, agriculture, forestry, fisheries, and even industry—are found elsewhere or in the peripheries of Gran Santiago. This explains also why during the last waves of protest, although demonstrations took place in various parts of the country, the main thrust of the protest was in Santiago.

In addition to these factors, it is important to note the lack of political recourse in terms of political party representation. Ideologically speaking, most political parties in Chile have converged and blurred their platform differences due to the constitutional authoritarian enclaves and the very peculiar electoral law that brought about the formation of electoral blocks. This has produced less ideological parties and electoral blocks centered in the presidential candidate. Political channels for the resolution of social problems related to the above mentioned reforms have also been obstructed by institutional authoritarian enclaves the also fostered impunity for perpetrators of serious human rights violations during military rule. This kind of obstruction has also maintained the "sacralization" of private property and economic liberal values, granting the political minority, constituted as a political block, veto rights on major reforms. Most of the authoritarian enclaves were removed through a series of reforms to the 1980 Constitution, which took place in 2005, at the end of Ricardo Lagos's presidential term, and the binominal electoral law is being reformed. The pressures generated by the mechanism of defense of the legacy of military rule have generated the social and later political pressures needed for its own undoing.

The neoliberalization of the state economy and technocratization of political mediation that accompanied it have led to a disconnection between party militants and social activists at the grassroots level, where ideology is still strong in some communities. Expectedly, declining trust in politics, representative institutions, and formal representation have pushed a growing number of people who favor democracy to look for other venues and find them in protest, while rejecting electoral politics.

Closely related to the continuing unresponsiveness of the political system, and the public disillusionment that comes with it, is ever-growing and widening political apathy. In Chile, this phenomenon is most prevalent among both the young and poorer sectors of the population. An analysis of electoral results shows that between 1988, the time of Pinochet's plebiscite, and the presidential and parliamentary elections of 1997 the percentage of accumulated abstentions, void and blank votes, rose from 4.8% to 31.4% (Olavarría 2003; Toro 2007).

Finally, Chile's educational system not only epitomizes the above-specified tensions between politics and economy but also reinforces them. The problems of Chilean education are many but can be subsumed under what we could call an educational GINI: the socioeconomically stronger sectors of Chilean society enjoy the best high school and university education available, while the weaker sectors struggle to get education in far lower quality high schools and universities. The fact that Chile's PISA (Programme for International Student Assessment) results are second to last among OECD countries (the last being Mexico)—is indicative of the problems of uneven quality of the education. It is also one of the most expensive education systems in the world—only in the United States do students pay proportionally more than in Chile. Most of the education system is private and receives low subsidies. At the university level, the student population is nearly one million. Although universities, according to reforms during the military rule, were meant to be nonprofit corporations, at present most universities are private, with only 21 (12 public and 9 private, most of them Catholic universities) receiving some subsidies.

Forms of Contention: The Dynamics of the 2011 Protest Wave

The income gaps, difficulties faced by redistribution policies, and massive privatization of education carried out under military rule generated an explosive situation that flooded the public sphere of Chile with protest in 2011. The forms employed in the 2011 wave of protest, while resembling much of previous waves, were nonetheless novel and unusual in many respects. These new forms were less the result of generational differences or new means (e.g., information and communication technologies, or ICTs), and more the result of deepening and

sharpening of those aforementioned tensions between the political and economic regimes and, consequently, the authorities' response.

The trigger for the higher education–driven wave of protest in Chile was an
attempt to change the statutes in one of the private universities—*Universidad
Central de Chile*—related to the Christian Democratic Party—such that it
would have allowed that institution, according to the students, to become an
openly for-profit enterprise. The timing of the protest initiative was far from
being coincidental. Every May 21, the president of Chile is due to make his speech
in parliament presenting an account of his administration—the equivalent to
the US state of the nation speech. Some days before the 2011 speech, the Students
Confederation of Chile called for a march in Santiago that brought together
15,000 university students, trying to influence the presidential agenda on education. Students prepared another demonstration, and this time it included university and high school students. A third demonstration by the students, on June
1, 2011, took the form of a general strike of the education sector supported by
the state employees union, the teachers union, and rectors of two universities.
After this event, the Students Confederation allowed the unions of students in
each university freedom of action. This resulted in strikes in 17 universities, six
of which were occupied by their students. The snowball effect expanded to high
schools, and a large number of these were occupied by their students. Joaquín
Lavín, the minister of education, called on the students to disoccupy the schools
and to enter in negotiations with the government.[8]

Later in June, demonstrations took place in Santiago. The first encompassed
a few thousand high school students together with striking copper miners and
ended with a clash with *Carabineros* (Chile's police). The second was the largest
demonstration since the end of dictatorship, encompassing nearly 100,000 participants and spreading to Valparaiso, Concepción, and other urban centers in
Chile, mobilizing around 200,000 protesters. At this stage, students of private
universities and the teachers union joined the demonstrations. The third episode involved primarily high school students and led the minister of education
to present a set of proposals, which were rejected by high school and university
students alike. On the last day of June, demonstrations took place all around
the country, mobilizing about 400,000 participants. The center of Santiago was
paralyzed by a huge number of protesters that filled the main thoroughfare of the
city.[9] The students assaulted the headquarters of the Socialist Party of Chile and
of the UDI—*Unión Democrática Independiente* (the strongest right-wing party)
in an attempt to involve the political leadership (of both government and opposition) in the crisis. At the same time, high schools were occupied by students. At
the beginning of June, three occupations took place. By the end of June, nearly
600 schools were already occupied.

The pressure exerted by the intensifying and rapidly broadening protests was partly successful, forcing President Piñera to present a set of government proposals to solve the crisis. The governmental proposals, made public on all national TV channels, were rejected by the students' leadership and, moreover, criticized by the leaders of the political opposition (center-left *Concertación*). The presidential settlement proposal, called GANE (*Gran Acuerdo Nacional de la Educación*)—the acronym meaning is WIN, in Spanish—led the students union to organize a team of representatives, together with the high school students union and the teachers union, supported by unions of small entrepreneurs, copper miners, administrative education employees, and an organization of indigenous students, to elaborate a counteroffer.[10]

Meanwhile, clashes with the police were increasing in size and violence. In July 2011, a mass-scale demonstration took place at the center of Santiago, which turned out to be the largest of all the protest events, despite refusal on the part of the local authorities to grant it an authorization. Toward the end of the demonstration, violence erupted, which prompted the police to intervene forcefully and to detain 62 protesters. It must be pointed out that during the demonstration, small groups of hooded youngsters, not necessarily students and probably criminals, attacked the police with rocks and Molotov cocktails and destroyed property. The police reacted not only against those hooded youngsters but also against the demonstrating students and teachers, using large amounts of tear gas and irritating liquids fired from water cannons.

The crisis became political and deepened to such an extent that President Piñera had to make changes in his government, replacing the minister of education and the government spokesperson and making changes in the ministry of planning and the ministry of mining. Nonetheless, these governmental measures did little to alleviate the tension or to appease the protesters. In August 2011, protesters began to rely on barricades, an innovation that was met by even harsher repressive measures on the part of the police. The students union gave a 6-day ultimatum to the government, demanding better responses, and the spokesperson of the government rejected it.

When the government rejected this ultimatum, student leaders decided to try and broaden the challenge further by employing a well-entrenched and familiar protest repertoire: the *cacerolazo* (night pot-banging demonstration). Alarmed by the students' move and the broadening scope and intensifying level of the challenge, the police overreacted, and student protesters responded in kind. In early August, violence reached another peak, with 874 protesters arrested and 90 *carabineros* injured. Evidence of students' militancy and radicalism continued to accrue. Acts of vandalism against symbolic targets included, for example, an attack on *La Polar*, a retailer that was suffering from a credit crisis involving the embezzlement of millions of its card holders, which was sacked and burned. Additionally, on August 5, when President Piñera visited the mine San José, in remembrance of the beginning of the mining accident that left 33 miners buried for months, demonstrators disrupted the ceremony. Expectedly, the crisis reverberated internationally, leading the Inter-American Commission of Human Rights to denounce the government of Chile for forcefully curtailing the rights of free speech, association, and public demonstration in the country.[11]

The scope of the protest wave expanded further when, on August 9, a national strike was supported by both student unions and the *Central Única de Trabajadores* (Chilean main labor federation), as well as by another 42 sectorial labor unions, and was accompanied by marches carried out in various cities in Chile. Many demonstrators were detained, and 55 policemen were injured. The mounting clashes between demonstrators and *carabineros*, as well as increasing damages by hooded demonstrators, brought about parliamentary demands for investigation of the incidents. The result of parliamentary inquiries revealed that policemen, dressed as hooded civilians, infiltrated protest events and provoked violence and, in turn, harsh uniformed police reactions. They also revealed many instances of police violence while entering occupied education centers; facts availed by security camera recordings. Female students revealed that in one instance, after police detention, the students were forced to undress and were abused and repeatedly insulted by the police. Demonstration leaders, detained by *carabineros* and accused of violence, were "framed" and beaten, in some cases, until they fainted. By the end of August, the level of violence reached new peaks. In a matter of two days of clashes (August 23 to August 25) an estimated number of 1,400 protesters were detained and more than 150 policemen and some 53 protesters were wounded.

But it was not just the level of violence that saw new peaks; it was also the severity of violence. On August 25, during one of the *cacerolazo* demonstrations, the police shot to death a 16-year-old high school student, Manuel Eliseo Gutiérrez Reinoso. The police denied responsibility, yet under pressure from opposition politicians and human rights activists, an investigation was opened. The *carabinero* who fired the shot was found, one police general was removed, and the commander of *Carabineros de Chile* resigned. Later, during a national strike that took place October 18–19, a bus was burned by hooded demonstrators, and the minister of interior affairs applied the emergency law (*Ley de Seguridad Interior del Estado*) while confronting grave incidents in various cities.

First, various rounds of mutual accusations took place between the national and local authorities (including police commanders) and the student leadership about violence and acts of vandalism. These issues were widely publicized in the media, and the student leadership accused parts of the media of manipulating information against their movement by stressing acts of violence and vandalism and not showing the orderly and respectful aspects of the protest, or simply playing along with the government line by diminishing the importance and size of the protest or dismissing its most legitimate message.[12]

Another aspect of the protest in Chile was the novel strategies and means of protest the students used. Meetings were rapidly organized via Facebook and Twitter and were highly effective in the promotion and coordination of all kinds of protest actions. In addition to relying on known repertoires from previous waves of protest, student leaders and activists innovated in several meaningful ways. One such innovation was the practice of *flash mobs*, with music of their liking being played in various opportunities to symbolize the terrible state of Chile's education. On one occasion, in front of the Presidential Palace (*La Moneda*), students used the anniversary of the death of Michael Jackson as a "living death," a symbolic token of Chile's educational system. A symbolic suicide was presented in the main walking mall of the city of Santiago. The *Plaza de Armas* was the scene of a Lady Gaga–style dance performed by hundreds of students, calling for a better educational system.

Other types of tactical innovation included an 1,800-hour relay run in the center of the city from mid-June to the end of August, symbolizing the 1,800 million dollars per year needed to fund the costs of higher education of 300,000 students; the state of indebtedness of 4,000 university students was updated on a website created for that purpose and widely publicized; students of various institutions conducted hunger strikes; other students, responding to a call launched through the social networks, attacked official websites of the Ministry of Education and political parties, putting them out of service. Additionally, at the end of June a large group of students participated in a two-day public concert "in defense of public education," and in another form of protest, 3,000 students met at the central square in Santiago for a "kissing marathon" in favor of education. In a football match between the Chilean and Mexican national teams, taking place in Argentina in July, a giant flag with the slogan "Education: free, dignified and gratis" was displayed, but Chilean TV, broadcasting the match, did not show it.

Demands and Public Support

The students' demands could be summarized under the banner of creating a more egalitarian education system that would reverse the impact that privatization and other legacies of military rule have had on Chile's education system. General demands about a free, plural, and tolerant education combined with practical steps that could, so student leaders believed, deal with the differences of educational levels generated by underfunded public and municipal schools versus rich private institutions. Practically, the students demanded a large increase in public spending in education and freedom for the universities regarding the spending of funds allocated to them. They also wanted to change the educational scholarship and credit system, seen not only as another way of producing and perpetuating inequality but also as an unjust source of profit for private financial institutions. They demanded lower rates of interest and strong affirmative action for the lowest income segments of the students' population. Lowering matriculation fees and free public transportation, as well as state subsidies for institutions of technical and professional education were also part of the demands. Student's participation in the governing bodies of the universities (together with administrators and academics) completed the list of demands for higher education.

Other more specific demands were to enforce the law about the nonprofit character of education institutions, to ensure the right to academic education through the abolition of fees and the provision of free education, to reform the tax system in order to finance free public education, to nationalize copper mining, and to call for a constituent assembly in order to reform the 1980 Constitution. High school students' demands were similar, according to which the state should again undertake the funding responsibilities of the school system, which military rule had placed under the control of the municipalities.[13]

The system of political networks and influences used by the student's protest movement was based on alliances with other organized sectors—mainly workers unions, Mapuches and other indigenous groups, ecologists, and groups demanding decentralization and regional autonomy. All these combined to generate a crescendo wave of protest that enjoyed increasing levels of public opinion support while the popularity of President Piñera declined concordantly.

As can be seen in Figure 10.1 about protest and support for government, the data of which is based on a series of public polls conducted between May and December 2011, support for the protest rose inversely to the decline in popularity of the president of Chile, his minister of education, and the government's education policies and proposals. It seems that the interaction between the students and the government—and the government's reactions to massive student's mobilization and protest in its various forms—galvanized the protest. Police repression and violence, massive arrests, and the lack of substantial proposals by the government seemed to have helped to widen and consolidate the wave of protests in Chile in 2011. The protesters' leadership became widely popular and capitalized on all the above factors. Some of them acquired enough political capital to make the transition into formal representative politics and get elected to parliament in the 2013 election.

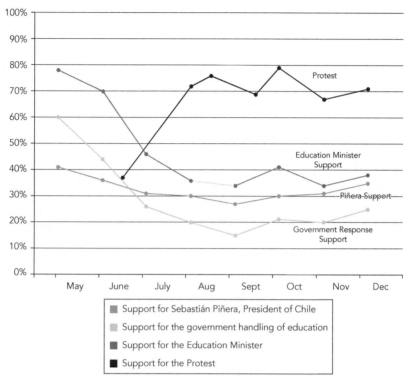

FIGURE 10.1 Graphic display of survey's results about the students movement in Chile 2011.

Encuesta del conflicto estudiantil (Encuestas Adimark, Encuestas La Tercera y Radio Cooperativa), in "Conflicto estudiantil en (Chile)." Retrieved November 18, 2013, from http://www.taringa.net/posts/info/15155705/Conflicto-estudiantil-en-Chile.html.

The public support the students enjoyed was related also to preexisting political apathy, declining legitimacy of politicians and political parties, and the new political style introduced by the students' protests. The students' protest was led by the youngest sectors of Chile's society that have shown growing apathy toward traditional politics and politicians. Most of the protesters were born after 1990, in the postdictatorial era, and have grown in a democracy shaped by the authoritarian constitution of 1980 and its safeguarding of the neoliberal socio-economic model and the political model of limited democracy. Still, the student leadership has posed demands for negotiation, centered on reforms of the educational and the state role toward this sector that, while far from the education minister's proposals they rejected, did not call for a revolutionary alternative. This is not to say that revolutionary calls were absent, yet these calls referred to long-term objectives and, more importantly, were rooted in practical claims and concrete goals. This is proved by the eagerness to negotiate that the leaders of the protest have shown during and after the large protests of 2011.[14] Furthermore, as Salinas and Fraser argue (2012), the socioeconomic model implanted in Chile not only served as a basis and, through accumulated debt and pressures, as a trigger for student mobilizations but also helped to develop the students' aspirations through expectations about improving income levels and social mobility and a better understanding of free market mechanisms and their limits (see also Belle and Cabal 2014).

More than any revolutionary objectives, the demands made by the student leaders reflected the will to widen the socioeconomic bottleneck created around the market effects of the education system. Indeed, about 70 percent of the students in the higher education system were first-generation university students, coming from the lower income segments, and in order to acquire university degrees they and their families basically mortgaged their economic futures. What student leaders called for was effective social mobility, high-quality education, and the ability to enjoy the benefits of market efficiency and openness—not as a transgenerational phenomenon but within the generation of those that graduate from the higher education system.[15]

Protest Outcomes

The fact that the protest produced changes in the government and two personnel changes in the post of minister of education, as well as casting a strong shadow of unpopularity on the political right-wing alliance, is a clear indication of its impact, an expression of what De Nardo called "power in numbers" (1985). Sebastián Piñera changed a government of technocrats for another controlled by the right-wing UDI, whose antileftist ideological commitments made it very difficult to find the needed compromises to solve the crisis.

The government supporters who attempted to present the protest as a return to premilitary rule polarization and its dangers failed. They failed because the large majority of Chileans, who sympathized with the students, support democracy and refused to perceive the students' movement and their demands as a menace to Chile's democracy. On the contrary, the protest was perceived as an act of legitimate participation in which large segments of Chile's youth played within the limits of the democratic game, in spite of their obvious electoral apathy and lack of belief in traditional politics. In other words, the students, as a large and transverse social movement, became central actors in democratized Chile—a democratizing force from below (Tarrow 1995).

Another important aspect of Chile's winter of discontent has to do with the acceptance, in the country's public sphere, of a general discussion about

the legitimacy of the model implanted under military rule and seemingly functioning efficiently—from an economic and a political point of view. Moreover,
it was seen by many abroad—in a Europe confronting serious problems about
financing higher education in a framework of economic crisis but also in Eastern
Europe, Asia, and Russia after the fall of communism and today in the Arab
world—as a model that combines sustainable levels of development with controlled democracy.[16]

The inclusive reaction of Chile's public sphere is a further indication of both
the depth of democratization and the democratic character of the students' protest. The political sector reacted also by discussing the problem, changing the
main actors—ministers of education—and trying to solve the problems posed
through a serious increase in the use of general parliamentary means—motions
and legislation—on this subject.

To be sure, media coverage played a central role in this process. Yet of equal
importance was a series of research articles and books written by intellectuals
from the social sciences, humanities, and law that bestowed scientific legitimacy
to the challenge on the political, cultural, and socioeconomic model of the country and the calls for change that were made by the student movement. A series
of books and studies have seriously analyzed the main problems of the educational system and strongly criticized both the segmental quality of education as
well as the economic problems the privatization of the education has generated.[17]
Moreover, the criticism of the impact of the privatization of education served as
a bridge for a general criticism of the free market as its functions in Chile. While
this line of thought existed throughout the military rule and the transition to
democracy, there is no question that the wave of student's protests has enhanced
it. Chilean researchers and intellectuals have been responding vibrantly by publishing works such as *El otro modelo* as well as *El derrumbe del modelo* by Alberto
Majol and a recent interview with Manuel Antonio Garretón (Chile's Social
Sciences National Prize 2007 and perhaps one of the best-known political sociologists in Chile and Latin America).

The main arguments in these publications are about the need to reform the
neoliberal socioeconomic model through changes in increasing taxation, redistribution, social rights, and regulation as well as the need to change the 1980
Constitution and the electoral system.[18] It is important to point out that the
main leaders of the *Nueva Mayoría*—New Majority, the center-left coalition
supporting Michelle Bachelet in the November–December 2013 presidential
and parliamentarian election—including Bachelet herself and Carolina Tohá,
the major of Santiago; Barbara Figueroa, the president of CUT (the main syn-
dical federation); and senator Ignacio Walker came to the presentation of *El
otro modelo* in July 2013. Moreover, the above-mentioned proposals presented by

Chilean social scientists have been integrated into the political program of the New Majority coalition and Michelle Bachelet and addressed in all the political programs presented for the 2013 election.[19] In this sense, Chile's winter of discontent has produced a clear result by transferring social pressures to the public sphere through civil social action and, from there, into the political arena, as political programs to be implemented after the 2013 elections. This is a clear case in which the interactions of work in both directions evolve from social pressures into demands, protests, and articulated proposals that reach the central political actors, up to the level of programs.

Concluding Discussion and Comparative Perspective

The inner workings of Chile's democracy and its democratization process have lived through a process of contention and catalyzation that led the transition into a deepening of the discussion of the socioeconomic model of the country. Chile is a telling example of the claim that formal democratization generates further discussions about the level of democracy reached and that "transition to democracy" is neither a short nor a simple process. A change in the system of mandatory registration in the electoral lists for one of voluntary registration did not produce a decline in the political apathy of the youth and did not strengthen the electoral participation percentages.[20] A change in the binominal system may infuse new life into traditional politics. A constitutional plebiscite or the election of a constitutional assembly in order to change the 1980 Constitution enacted under military rule and acting, until now, as the guardian of the socioeconomic model implanted in the country, may even be a more radical solution. All the options may be executed democratically in the next presidential period, 2014–2018.

Good macroeconomic performance has produced the resources to finance a deep reform of the educational system, but in order to decide to allocate those resources, reform is needed and the crisis produced an ideological stiffening of the Piñera government, and the political supporters of the neoliberal model through personal and party changes. This in itself radicalized the political proposals and programs of the left political block of Nueva Mayoría, led by Michelle Bachelet, that took power in 2014. In order to decide to allocate those resources, reform is needed, and the crisis produced an ideological stiffening of the government and the political supporters of the neoliberal model through personnel and party changes. The most extreme supporters of a limited democracy based on a free market economy perceived the deep reform of the educational system as a prologue for the disarticulation of the structure that has provided serious macroeconomic gains and a large measure of political stability to the country.

Chile's wealth income distribution system and the educational structure seem to perpetuate a situation of wide income gaps and high stratification. During the first 20 years of democratization, the *Concertación* governments promised mobility through education and results to reforms introduced in the existing system. These promises have been only very partially realized or not fulfilled at all. During the presidency of Sebastián Piñera, when Chile's became again a right-wing ruled country, protest from groups historically associated with the left acquired a larger scope and magnitude and broadened to include issues and sectors well beyond education that also demanded serious reforms.

Although mobilized students and civil society in general have proven effective in promoting accountability, responses to demands, transparency, negotiations with the main political parties, and proposals by the government (three sets of proposals), it is clear that the major decisions will have to be taken in the traditional political arena. No menace to Chilean democracy is visible in this crisis. On the contrary. The main student leaders of Chile's winter of discontent, Camila Vallejo, Giorgio Jackson, Gabriel Boric, Karol Cariola, and Francisco Figueroa, entered the political arena and became candidates for the Chilean parliament in the 2013 election.[21] The demand for reforms and better redistribution are legitimate in democratic terms, especially when they enjoy high levels of popular support.

Moreover, no large antisystem movement is visible. The issue of violence was, as discussed, two-sided and sometimes was provoked by the police force itself. Still, the vast majority of the protest actions were nonviolent. Chilean popular demands as represented in the students' protests were definitely more reformist than revolutionary but had shifted from quantitative—reduction of misery and poverty, through increasing employment and economic opportunities—to qualitative—real access to better quality higher education, social mobility, and resulting better income levels in order to allow the lower classes to become a real middle class.

If we examine the Chilean wave of protest in terms of the cyclical linkage among popular contention, regime, and transition, we may get some useful insights. A regime of limited democracy, as imposed by military rule of 1973–1990, has existed in Chile, through a process of partial dissolution carried out democratically and as part of the transition to democracy. The socioeconomic regime implanted in the same period has survived almost intact. Not only have the constitutional reforms enacted from 1989 to 2005 "opened" Chilean democracy from a rather limited model to a more pluralistic one, but also they have been propelled by different types of contention and protest during these years. The issue of whether the transition from military rule to democracy can end without replacing the military-imposed Constitution of 1980 is still open. Undoubtedly, however, the Chilean winter of discontent of 2011 and its sequels in the following years will have provided an important push in this direction. In this sense, the regime change and the transition process, established by the 1980 Constitution itself, engendered, through democratization and the detachment of the military in 2004 from Pinochet's heritage of human rights violations, a clockwise movement in which popular contention provided the fuel for democratic change while articulating the actions of civil society groups, led by the students' movement, into formal electionary and later, parliamentary politics. While under military dictatorship, the exit choice—in Hirschman's terms—generated a large wave of political exile, although protest and even resistance were present in Chile; under democratic conditions, the voice choice seems to be working.[22]

The development of the transition to democracy in Chile is interesting for many reasons, but perhaps the most important one lies in its incremental, albeit contentious, nature and moderation. In the 1990s, the first democratic governments had to cope with an extremely limiting constitution—the 1980 Constitution, enacted under military rule—but it was gradually reformed as democracy stabilized. There were various crises between the democratic government and the military, especially about the human rights violations legacy, and financial scandals related to Pinochet and his family that led to "negotiations" between the still powerful military and the elected authorities. Still, the mutual understanding of the importance of avoiding violence, grounded on the trauma of violent military rule, gradual political reforms, and economic and social stability coupled with growth and reduction of poverty within the inherited model, led to the depoliticization of the military and their slow but sure departure from Pinochet's political heritage, rabid anticommunism and the legacy of human rights violations. This kind of opening of the public sphere created space for demands about further reform and changes in the socioeconomic model that were mainly propelled through waves of student mobilizations and protest supported by large segments of the population. The dynamics of transition and contention have generated changes in the central actors and have opened spaces for further action and reform.

From Chile's experience we may conclude also that transitions to democracy, even when formally short (1988–1990) are long, contentious, and open-ended processes, both socioeconomically and politically. Transitions produce temporary arrangements in which social movements—preexisting or newly formed—play a central role. In Chile, the kind of democratization, imposed by military rule, generated a long political transition in which many constitutional reforms took place and the space for democratic discussion and protest was opened. The student movement has played a central role in reshaping the agenda of democratization, which, in fact, produced the winter of discontent and embodied a challenge to the inherited economic model. Most possibly, further reforms and changes will produce new needs and more pressures that will obligate the incumbent rulers to face further discontent, protest, and contention, and then a further reform of the models—political, economic, and social—as happened in the past.

Seen from this perspective, the case of Chile resembles that of Israel, specifically the cycle of contention taking place during summer 2011 (see Talshir, in this volume). Despite apparent and obvious differences between both cases, it is nonetheless possible to identify a similarity in how the tension between the economic and political realms shapes and is shaped by contention. Whether or not we are dealing with an inexorable link between the two realms (and the salience of such a link) and the extent to which it shapes the claims, issues, and targets of contention or is shaped by them is related, to a considerable degree, to the type of regime. As is taken up by Sela in the concluding chapter of this volume, whereas in the Israeli liberal democracy this seems to have had an influence on the targeting of business corporations and moguls, the monopolization and control of the economy by the authorities in authoritarian regimes surely has shaped the targeting of Chile's political leaders.

Finally, once examined through the prism of popular contention driven by and set against socioeconomic-related wrongs of a state-sponsored neoliberal economy and aimed at promoting greater democracy within a hybrid regime, and without overlooking apparent differences in initial conditions, it is possible to identify meaningful similarities between the Chilean and the Jordanian cycles of contention.

When the revolts in Tunisia and Egypt erupted, public protest in Jordan, which had begun several years before then, assumed growing scales, frequency, and intensity over issues of unemployment, worsening working conditions, rising food prices, and corruption. The Jordanian crisis was essentially rooted in the kingdom's lack of natural resources and constant need for foreign aid to maintain its bureaucracy, military, and other state institutions as well as to finance social and economic services. Historically, Jordan's financial needs were met by Western powers and oil-rich Arab monarchies, primarily Saudi Arabia. Nonetheless, by the late 1980s, a combination of plummeting oil prices, a growing gap between population and economic growth and shrinking foreign aid forced Jordan to turn to the IMF for financial aid. To meet the IMF's conditions, however, Jordan had to introduce economic reforms including broadening the tax base, reduction of subsidies, and privatization of state property (Itani 2013), adopting a model similar to the one imposed in Chile. Also similar to Chile, the neoliberal regime needed political reinforcement; in November 2009, in the face of mounting discontent and criticism, both outside and inside parliament, King ʿAbdallah II dissolved the parliament and appointed the neoliberal prime minister Samir al-Rifaʿi, of Palestinian descent (a meaningful move as discussed below), assigning him with implementing the monarch's vision without further delay.

During the previous two decades the political economy had changed profoundly as the state gradually retreated from its long-standing social contract with its citizens, the main benefactors of which were the East Bank indigenous population. Whereas half or more of Jordan's population is of Palestinian descent, East Bankers have historically dominated the state bureaucracy and security establishment, serving as the monarchy's protector and primary political base against both domestic and regional threats. For the East Banker, the social contract was thus far more than subsidized basic commodities provided to the whole population. Rather, the state maintained a comprehensive patronage system toward the East Bankers providing them social and economic security by absorbing them into the state bureaucracy and security establishment, including the armed forces, in return for their loyalty to and support of the monarchy. Hence, the consequences of the neoliberal policy—rising prices and decreasing employment opportunities—favored the Jordanian Palestinians who were already more integrated into the market economy, added yet one more source of tension to the already tense relations between East Bankers and Palestinians (Ryan 2002).[23]

The result was a direct attack on the authorities accusing them of a sell-out of Jordan to the Palestinians, with large sectors of East Bankers, urban retirees of the security forces and public service as well as tribal populations strongly protesting against the king's economic policy, signaling that their loyalty to the monarch was not unconditional (David 2010). On February 6, 2011, 36 tribal figures published an open letter against the corruption, warning the monarch that unless it conducted reforms Jordan might follow the Tunisian and Egyptian examples. Indeed, Jordanians were not indifferent to the waves of popular contention in bordering and nearby Arab countries, and raised a mixture of socioeconomic and political demands. Following a modest beginning on January 7 of a demonstration in a small town south of the capital, a week later the demonstrators moved to Amman. The participants in the demonstrations were initially young people and leftists, underlining their socioeconomic motivation. As the protest came to encompass additional political groups, Palestinian secular and religious groups alike, the demonstrations, the printed media, and public discourse in general, increasingly adopted slogans calling for reducing the powers of the executive authorities, primarily those of the security establishment and the king, and against the rampant corruption at all levels.

Ultimately, although a challenge to the regime as a whole was absent in both Chile and Jordan, with the majority of challenging groups and organizations in both countries seeking reforms, Chilean protesters, as discussed above, seem to have managed to achieve more than their Jordanian counterparts. It is possible to argue that the reason for the failure of the Jordanian cycle of contention to promote a more meaningful transition to democracy is found in long-standing social polarization between the two main population sectors (East Bankers and Palestinians), a feature that had little if any role to play in the Chilean case. This tension was reflected in lack of unity and even suspicions among the various Jordanian groups, which translated into failure at presenting a clear and common platform as well as capitalizing on and sustaining the surging and spreading wave of contention.

While this line of argument has merits, it falls short in at least three respects. First, the Chilean movement, while demonstrating higher level of unity, was nonetheless not free of dissenting voices among the various groups, as was the case with the Mapuche and the indigenous population more generally. Moreover, despite the aforementioned tension and lack of unity in the Jordanian movement, it is important to note that its expressions were felt mostly between the East Jordanian and the largely Palestinian Muslim Brotherhood, with hardly any discord with other organizations, and that even between the former two, the tension did not sharpen to the point of mutual infliction of damage.

Second, much of the tension between the East Bankers and the Muslim Brotherhood was shaped and influenced by the authorities' response and own strategy and tactics of coping with the domestic challenge. Several weeks into the consolidating wave of protest, the king announced two economic programs of aid worth of $550 million in the form of raising the subsidies on food and fuel and the wages in the public service, including pensions of the security sector. In addition, the king resorted to a familiar ploy of appointing a new government headed by Ma'rouf al-Bakhit, a typical East Jordanian figure with a long record of service in the security and diplomatic establishments and an opponent of the neoliberal economic policy (Vogt 2011). The appointment of a new government triggered the first major split in the reform movement's ranks. Whereas the Muslim Brotherhood and a small leftist organization, called the Popular Unity Party, sought to continue the protests, most members of another organization, called the Committee for Coordination among the Opposition Parties,[24] decided to give the new government an opportunity to make the required changes. Subsequent promises and symbolic gestures of reforms on the part of the king, however, ultimately brought about a lessening of tension within the opposition camp, as was the case, for example, with the formation of special committees in March and April 2011, assigned to study the needed reforms and to submit recommendations accordingly as well as to consider amendments in the constitution. None of the major recommendations was implemented.

Finally, it was the impact of unexpected developments across the border that further mitigated the pressure on the regime by the various opposition groups. Particularly, it was the developing civil war in Syria and the consequent taking flight of hundreds of thousands of refugees into Jordan, with its repercussions in terms of economic burden and inflating crime rate. These developments infused genuine concerns among the opposition groups lest their continued challenge deteriorate into internal strife and undermine the Hashemite monarchy's capability to continue and secure domestic stability. Chile did not experience this kind of regional menace and concern. The point to be made, however, is that whatever the differences between the two countries' experience of popular contention and regime type, theoretically meaningful similarities emerge in the context of the dynamics of contentious interaction between popular dissident groups and regime forces which, along with externalities, shaped and was equally shaped by the transition process.

Acknowledgments

I thank the Liwerant Center for the Study of Latin America, Spain, Portugal, and their Jewish Communities at the Hebrew University of Jerusalem, for its generous support of the research for this chapter.

Notes

1. According to Merrill Lynch (New York) Chile's GINI coefficient is located in the 0.55 to 0.59 range a near those of Brazil and South Africa—at the highest end of the scale. According to the OECD Social Indicators (2011) it is 0.503 (the highest in the OECD group), while the average OECD GINI is 0.31 (www.oecd.org/social/soc/ 47572883.pdf; retrieved November 15, 2013).

2. Formally, the transition to democracy in Chile took place between October 1988 (the plebiscite in which Pinochet's candidacy for the presidency was defeated) and March 1990 (assumption to the presidency of Aylwin, the first democratically elected president). Still, many will argue that as long as authoritarian political enclaves—such as the binominal electoral system—still exist, the transition to democracy is not complete.

3. For an informative and insightful analysis of this period, see Garretón (2012).

4. On the binominal electoral system, see Rahat and Sznajder (1998). On political apathy in Chile, see Olavarría (2003).

5. On the Penguins Revolution and the student protest in Chile, see Cabalin (2012).

6. On this issue see Eduardo Engel, "¿Dónde está la clase media?" *La Tercera*, April 25, 2012 (http://blog.latercera.com/blog/eengel/entry/donde_está_la_clase_media; retrieved November 15, 2013).

7. See, Eduardo Engel, "Encuesta Casen: ¿Qué sabemos y qué no sabemos?" *La Tercera*, August 9, 2012 (http://blog.latercera.com/blog/eengel/entry/encuesta_casen_qu%C3%A9_sabemos; retrieved September 13, 2012).

8. *Cronología de las Movilizaciones 2011*, Santiago: CESOC 2011 (http://cesocuchile. wordpress.com/especial-movilizaciones/cronologia-de-la-movilizaciones-2011/ ; retrieved November 18, 2013). This work contains the links to the written and electronic press dealing with the students demonstrations during the whole of 2011. The rest of the chronological description of the 2011 is based on the above links and information provided by CESOC.

9. "Multitudinaria marcha: 400,000 personas en todo Chile" (http://www.google. com/hostednews/epa/article/ALeqM5jou9vG6cw8KAq4ByDpnHgubowlxA?d ocId=1560320; http://www.elmostrador.cl/noticias/pais/2011/06/30/gigantesca-alegre-y-pacifica-marcha-copa-la-alameda-pidiendo-reformas-estructurales-a-la-educacion/; retrieved November 18, 2013).

10. "Piñera se refiere al tema de la educación en cadena nacional, dando a conocer el 'Gran Acuerdo Nacional por la Educación'" (http://diario.latercera.com/2011/07/06/01/contenido/pais/31-75400-9-pinera-lanza-plan-en-educacion-y-abre-debate-nacional-sobre-el-lucro.shtml (retrieved November 18, 2013).

11. "En víspera de marcha estudiantil: Manifestantes levantan barricadas en distintos puntos de la capital" (http://www.elmostrador.cl/noticias/pais/2011/08/04/en-vispera-de-marcha-estudiantil-manifestantes-levantan-barricadas-en-distintos-puntos-de-la-capital/; "Crónica de una ciudad sitiada" http://www.elciudadano. cl/2011/08/05/cronica-de-una-ciudad-sitiada/; retrieved November 18, 2013).

12. High schools and universities were de-occupied by the students toward the end of the academic year, during November and December 2011.

13. Following recommendations by UNESCO and the OECD, the students demanded a serious increase in the budget of education from 4.1 percent of the GDP to 7 percent of it. On this subject see a detailed analysis in *Reviews of National Policies for Education: Tertiary Education in Chile 2009*, Washington: OECD, The World Bank, April 2, 2009, 297–302 (http://www.oecd-ilibrary.org/education/ reviews-of-national-policies-for-education-tertiary-education-in-chile-2009_9789264051386-en; retrieved November 18, 2013).

14. Students attempted negotiations with the government of Chile and through the Congress on numerous occasions during 2011, especially on June 5, June 21, July 26, August 16, August 28, September 3, September 9, and September 12, 2011.

15. Interview with Andrés Fielbaum, president of the Students Federation of Chile—FECH—in Santiago, July 7, 2013. Fielbaum pointed out some important facts. The main slogans/goals of the students protest were, first, to put an end to profit making in higher education and, second, to achieve gratis universal education. He confirmed the hypothesis that the main block of protesters—students and nonstudents—strived to achieve a reform of the free market system that will

internalize redistributive and welfare criteria, while only a small minority envisioned revolutionary and structural replacement goals.

16. As an example, see Oscar Guardiola-Rivera, "Chile: A Model to Follow," *The Guardian*, October 2, 2013 (www.the guardian.com/commentisfree/2013/oct/02/chile-salvador-allende-coup-youth- protest-pinochet; retrieved on November 13, 2013).

17. See, for example, Fernando Atria (2012), which includes a prologue written by two central student leaders, Giorgio Jackson and Francisco Figueroa; Majol (2013); an interview with Gabriel Salazar (Chile's National History Prize 2006) and Maria Olivia Monckeberg (Chile's National Prize on Journalism 2009) in *La mala educación chilena* (http://www.youtube.com/watch?v=NEnBMkPfyts; retrieved November 14, 2013); and Meller (2011), in which the author, a distinguished economist, claims that the problem is not that owners of private universities profit from their investment and this is forbidden by the education law but the fact that higher education has been invaded by free market malaises, affecting the quality, heightening the costs, and generating huge debt levels. Also, see Urzúa (2012), who claims that higher education is positively correlated to social and economic mobility and higher earnings, and that in Chile all this is complicated by the uneven levels of the universities and debts generated by tuition costs.

18. See, Fernando Atria et al. (2013), Majol (2012), and Santiago Barassi, "Se perdió la legitimidad del modelo económico y social neoliberal," entrevista con Manuel Antonio Garretón, *El portal del Sur*, Octobre 16, 2013 (http://portaldelsur.info/2013/10/se-perdio-la-legitimidad-del-modelo-economico-social-que-se-llama-neoliberalismo/—retrieved November 14, 2013).

19. María José Ahumada, "Bachelet anuncia fin del lucro y gratuidad universal en seis años," *El Mercurio*, June 8, 2013 (http://www.elmercurio.com/blogs/2013/06/08/12445/Bachelet-anuncia-fin-al-lucro-y-gratuidad-universal-en-seis-anos.aspx; retrieved November 18, 2013).

20. The trend of political apathy/abstention continues. In the presidential and parliamentary national elections of November 17, 2013, the percentage of voters was 44 percent—6 million out of the total of 13.5 million. See "Bachelet y Matthei pasan a una segunda vuelta en la elección presidencial con menor participación," *El Mercurio*, November 18, 2013 (http://www.emol.com/noticias/nacional/2013/11/17/630270/ bachelet-no-logra-imponerse-en-primera-vuelta-a-matthei-y-me-o-se-queda-con-el-tercer-lugar.html; retrieved November 18, 2013).

21. Camila Vallejo ran as candidate of the Communist Party to Chile's lower house of Congress in a district of the South of Santiago. Giorgio Jackson was an independent candidate at Santiago Centro supported by the left. Gabriel Boric ran in Magallanes—the far South of Chile—for Izquierda Autónoma. Karol Cariola was a communist and Nueva Mayoría candidate for North Santiago. Francisco Figueroa ran for the Congress in Ñuñoa, South Santiago, as an independent

candidate. Most of them supported the candidacy of Michelle Bachelet for the presidency of Chile.

22. On Chilean political exile, see Mario Sznajder and Luis Roniger (2009, 229–43).

23. Contrary to the largely rural East Bankers, the Jordanian Palestinians—most of whom are descendants of the 1948 refugees and migrants from the West Bank— tended to settle in the cities, with their relatively better education and emerging middle class enabling them to hold a major segment of the private sector (see Itani 2013 for more on this aspect of Jordan's society and economy).

24. The "Committee" was established shortly after the signing of the Israeli-Jordanian peace agreement in 1994 to press for the abolition of the treaty.

11

The 2011 Israeli Protest Movement between the "Arab Spring" and the "Occupy" Movement

A HYBRID MODEL?

Gayil Talshir

The protest movement that began in Tunisia ... subsequently spreading to Egypt, and then to Spain, has now become global, with the protests engulfing Wall Street and cities across America. Globalization and modern technology now enables social movements to transcend borders as rapidly as ideas can. And social protest has found fertile ground everywhere: a sense that the "system" has failed, and the conviction that even in a democracy, the electoral process will not set things right—at least not without strong pressure from the street.

—JOSEPH STIGLITZ, *2011*

IN THE GLOBALIZATION OF PROTEST (2011) Stiglitz analyzes the social protest as a transnational reaction to the global economy, which produced worldwide social inequalities sending millions to the streets. It is the capitalistic globalization process that is at the center of his argument.[1] This chapter challenges Stiglitz's globalization thesis arguing, instead, that though there were influences, bonds, and certainly *activists beyond borders* (Keck and Sikkink 1998) there are at least two distinct types of phenomena that differ in claims and forms of collective action and therefore call into question the tendency to treat globalized protest as one general phenomenon: one archetype, the "Arab Spring" revolts, manifestly sending hundreds of thousands to the city squares claiming—in light of oppressive reaction—a meaningful regime change, and another archetype, the *Occupy* type in advanced democracies, mainly producing claims against growing social gaps using participatory democracy within the encampments that occupy public parks. However, I take Stiglitz's observation that it was not the economics, per se, but the political system that has failed, to be instrumental to understanding the depth of the recent waves of popular contention. Even if there are structural faults in globalization and neoliberalism, the way to challenge and address them is through the political realm. Thus, the "system" is not solely the global economic system nor electoral processes in general, but here again differs in different contexts: The political system that failed in the Arab world is the autocratic regime, whereas the system that produced capital and powerholder ties and the failures of representative democracies given the economic global crisis have caused dissatisfaction in the democratic world. This is not to overlook the differences among countries within each region, only to suggest that the political perspective is tied to the type of regime, nor that while the Arab revolts were usually of mass character, the Occupy type were colorful deliberative action of the few.

However, between these two archetypes—the "Arab Spring" and Occupy—there is also a hybrid one: one that in terms of popular contention was characterized both by mass demonstrations and deliberative tent cities. This model featured mainly in Spain, Portugal, Greece, and Israel. While Shalev (2013) is arguing that all pertain to the same, third kind of wide protest, close to what Kousis and Diani term "large protest events" (Diani and Kousis 2014), I maintain that the hybrid model should be seen as an expression of the crisis of democratic legitimation and analyzed accordingly. The first three are characterized by the crisis of the EU: the austerity measures inflicted on them by the dominant policy-givers in the corridors of Brussels due to the economic crisis is damaging the popular sovereignty of the nation-states and hence experienced as a political crisis on their behalf (Merkel 2013; Lapavitsas et al. 2010; Kousis 2012). If this is the case, Israel seemingly remains a sui generis phenomenon, both geographically and politically between these two models—the "Arab Spring" on the one hand and the Occupy movement in advanced democracies on the other. Is Israel a unique case? How does it fit into the picture? Why is it that only in Israel more than 400,000 people out of 8 million citizens roamed the streets in one night, side by side with intensive tent cities all over the country?

I argue that the 2011 wave of social protest should be taken within the crisis of democratic legitimation. That it is precisely the failure of the legitimacy of the existing system—be it autocracy or representative democracy—that failed and that in all four cases there was a claim about the democratic system that was being made within the context of a crisis of legitimation (Habermas 1975). Thus, it is possible to capture the particularity of the Israeli case, as well as others, without losing sight of cross-case similarities, by employing the crisis of legitimization framework, a framework developed with liberal democracies in mind, and yet is useful for understanding waves of popular contention in nondemoc-racies as well.

In terms of contentious politics, there is a popular challenge manifested in the claim professed by social protest groups against the political system—demanding more democratization and social change—be it against authoritar-ian or advanced democratic regimes. In this paper I take the two archetypes—of the "Arab Spring" on the one hand and advanced democracies-based Occupy on the other—and assess the comparability of the Israeli case along three dimen-sions: the economic agenda, the political claims, and the practices—and percep-tion—of democracy. I start with sketching the two archetypes and mapping them onto a general structure of social movements in particular and conten-tious politics in general. I then analyze the economic, political, and democratic dimensions of the social, with focus on the Israeli case, and discuss the par-ticular model of a "new politics" representative democracy, and the rejection of politics of identity that characterized the Israeli summer of discontent in 2011 and its surprising effects on the 2013 and 2015 elections.

Collective Action and the Structure of Politics

Popular contention is thus instrumental in challenging the political regime and set within the context of legitimation crisis. Given the different regimes of the popular challenges erupting around the globe in the same year, the analytical tools as well as the political opportunity structure should be clearly defined. One theoretical challenge facing researchers of collective action in face of the fifth, global wave of economic-based contention is to determine whether we are deal-ing with new social movements or contentious campaigns. While the latter were characterized, in contradistinction from one-time demonstration, petition, or mass meeting, as a continuous protest including several protest events encom-passing certain claims toward political decision makers (Tilly 2004, 4; Tarrow 2001a), social movements on the other hand, "involve continuous interaction between challengers and power holders" (Tilly 2003b, 23) and usually produce collective action in conflict situations, networks of informal communication, and shared collective identity (Della Porta and Diani 2006). Under these defi-nitions, the wave of protest in 2011—both in the Arab world and in advanced democracies—has certainly included demonstrations, marches, and public events, but went beyond that to encompass continuous—albeit diverse—forms of challenge to powerholders in conflict situations. While to determine whether in the different cases it was a full-blown new social movement on the make or a wave of protest is beyond the scope of this chapter, set to address the question whether Israel has produced a unique model of its own, it is still critical to situate the wave of protest within the contentious politics and opportunity structure.

What was the structure of social protest in the Arab world? Though the social unrest in Tunisia and the overthrown president, Ben 'Ali, were the precursor events, in the public mind the imagery of the "Arab Spring" is identified with the scenes from Tahrir Square (Kerton 2012, 302). That uprising, sending millions to the streets in pursuit of freedom, food, and work, facing the army and the regime, took the world, by and large, by surprise. Indeed, it was not predicted or expected and was the spark that ignited the social protest in other Arab countries and provided the symbols that enthused advanced democracies as well. However, some indications of these demonstrations were encapsulated within the workers strikes and marches taking place all over Egypt since 2005 (Abdalla 2012). This protest was not identified with official political forces, and demanded workers' rights and protection by the law. Due to the policy of Mubarak's regime, these workers social protest groups remain depoliticized, to avoid repression, and the different social movements remained on the whole disconnected among themselves. However, they were able to spread some hope that should they unite, they could put structural pressure on the regime (Abdalla 2012, 89). This was also expressed by the reforms that authoritarian and traditional regimes in the Middle East have chosen to lead of their own initiative—like in Jordan or Bahrain, in light of the revolts in other parts in the Arab world.

In contradistinction to the autocratic Arab world, the social protest in the context of the 2008 economic crisis is considered the fifth wave, one of consecutive waves of protest against neoliberalism and globalization since the late 1980s (Kousis 2012; Della Porta 2009). Still, the antiglobalization protest wave is one of the most widespread waves, with interesting national variations ranging from the *Indignados* in Spain to the Adbusters in Canada to the Occupy Wall Street in the United States, with numerous manifestations of the 99% and Occupy movement across the democratic world.

What was the background of the social protest in Israel? Crucially, in similar vein to the Tahrir Square events, there were no obvious precipitating signs for the width and depth of the social protest in Israel. In fact, apart from isolated events on Wadi Salib in 1959 and the Black Panthers in the 1970s, Israeli civil society has never seen a large-scale protest on socioeconomic grounds. Rather, the most populous protest were the antiwar ones against the Lebanon war in 1982, with 400,000 demonstrating against the Israeli army silent cooperation with the Lebanese Phalanges in their massacre of Palestinians in Sabra and Shatila refugee camps, protest against the high cost associated with the peace process with Egypt, and the intensive campaign against the disengagement from Gaza in 2005. The other demonstrations Jerusalem was acquainted with were the demonstrations for and against the status quos in state and religion relations. Thus, the Rothschild protest and the city tent movements that took hold of public squares in almost 20 Israeli towns took skeptical Israel—analysts, politicians, and activists—by sheer surprise.

As important as the roots of social protest in the two archetypes and our case study of Israel are, there is a major role played by the political opportunity structure in the different models. It is clear that for the Arab uprisings, most regimes being autocratic and nondemocratic, there was little chance of containment and gradual political change, though there were two major manifestations— reformist and revolutionary models. Those who desperately wanted to prevent the social unrest and had funding to do that used financial means to appease the protesters, as many of the Gulf countries did. Political promises were the solution in Jordan to curb the social unrest. However, in other countries there was little room for political maneuvering and the regime eventually changed—as in Libya and Egypt—or fell into a civil war, as in Syria. However, in advanced democracies the public sphere and the legitimacy of social protest led to the slim chance that a substantial political change would follow. In fact, as we shall later see, there was little partisan mobilization, and much of the effort was concentrated on declaratively creating an alternative political model—one of participatory democracy.

What was the political opportunity structure in the Israeli case? Most analysts take the protest as an expression of outrage toward the economic conditions, especially the high cost of living. This chapter argues that in the Israeli case the economic protest was crucially centered on distrust with the political system: its main claim, I argue, was to enable politics in which government acts in view of the common good and public interest and not according to sectorial politics of identity. The demand for clean, new politics in a party system highly fragmented would produce a stark choice for the activists: either to create an alternative participatory civil society, closer to the deliberative model in advanced democracies, or to join en masse institutional politics and try to influence policymaking from within. Thus, there was a political opportunity for change with a stark choice between civil society versus institutional politics options, a debate that was to tear the protest leadership from the inside. This choice is at the heart of my argument and is therefore the main issue in the concluding discussion.

"It's the Economy Stupid": Indeed? Three Models Considered

The central slogans of each of the archetypes of social protests—"Bread, Freedom and Human Dignity" in the Egyptian case, "99%" in the West, and "the People demands Social Justice" in Israel, all encapsulate deep economic resentment which indeed led most analysts to understand them as claims to change the economic redistribution in society. While Stiglitz (2011) and others have seen these as different manifestations of the same protest against the all-encompassing globalization process that imposed neoliberal economic superstructure, it is my argument that—despite the self-reported links between the activists of the different struggles—there were in fact crucial national variations and a strong distrust of the distinct political system that produced the economic hardships in the varied cases. Though the activists in the West related to the Tahrir revolution, despite the fact that in Israel the Spanish protest was an inspiring model (Schechter 2012), there were fundamental differences contrived from the different political structure and national agenda. I focus on the economic dimension in this section and analyze its political bearings in the next section.

Tellingly, one of the slogans of the workers' demonstrations before the January 25 movement in Egypt was "It doesn't matter whether or not Mubarak stays in power. What matters for us is our wage increase" (Abdalla 2012, 88). Yet the economic demands represented a spectrum of socioeconomic grievances, from pure hunger and self-subsistence, on the one hand, to the growing unemployment of noticeably educated middle classes and young people, on the other. The ousting of both president Mubarak and postrevolution newly elected president Mursi arguably suggests that both the regime change and the military-cum-civic uprising fell short of a social revolution—à la Skocpol, with substantial restructuring of the economic stratification in society and a move from a low-tech agrarian society to a form of postindustrial society. Economic hardship cannot be solved by more of the same, and a radical restructuring of the economic and political system is needed. This is true of most Arab societies, with thin middle classes, which are crucial for sustaining a democracy. The economic problems in the Arab world and especially in Egypt, are ones that sent the millions to stand against the canons and rifles, defending their dignity, liberty, and livelihood with nothing but shackles to lose. Thus, rather than protesting against the neoliberal global economy they demanded bread and work from their ruling politicians.

This is of course very different than the 99% movements, where the protest emerged in relation to the 2008 economic crisis but the claims were made mainly by educated middle classes, protesting against the growing gap between the first percentage and the rest of society and objecting to the political system that enhanced the role of economic tycoons generating growth without equality. This fifth wave of economic protest can even be traced back to the emergence of the new left in the 1960s and the demonstrations against Western imperialism, materialism, and cultural domination. Their contemporary manifestation, however, is placed strongly within the context of the failure of the dominant ideology since the 1980s—neoliberalism. The claims—against the virtualization of economics, the role of speculators in the markets, the dependency of the political decision makers on the economic elites, and the concentration of financial decisions in the hands of bureaucrats (in the European case) and international unelected corporations—indeed focus on the injustices of the global market system. As Stiglitz reminded us, even the most severe economic grievances have a political edge when talking about social change.

The situation in Israel is very different from these two models: First, the 2008 global crisis did not hit Israel as hard as other democracies, and certainly not as abruptly. Second, there was no apparent worsening or crisis that ignited the social protest in Israel. Third, socioeconomic issues were never the main battleground in Israel politics: Whereas most national democracies debated levels of intervention of governments in the free market as the prime ideological axis distinguishing between Left and Right (Bobbio 1996), the main contention in Israeli politics since 1967 was the issue of the Occupied Territories and the Israeli–Palestinian conflict. However, the 2011 social protest came within two interesting waves of civic phenomena: the first successful consumer boycott regarding cheese prices and a wave of strikes by the workers in the welfare, education, and health sectors. The analysis of these two phenomena is crucial to understand the economic demands—and later the political claims—of the protest.

The constitutive event of the social protest in Israel was the erection of a tent in the main square in Tel Aviv by a young woman, Daphni Leef, arguing housing prices have become unaffordable. This personal act was intensified when the municipality did not allow her to build her protest tent, which in the minds of her friends represented antidemocratic behavior of the ruling authorities vis-à-vis citizens (Shechter 2012, 32). The democratic dimension would later return, but the economic claim of high prices of living found sympathy in vast cohorts of the population. Indeed, one of the most imagination-capturing struggles was that concerning the price of cottage cheese, very popular in Israel; a consumer act involving 100,000 people signing petitions on the web and a consumer boycott finally resulted in the resignation of the executive director of the dairy company and the reduction in the prices of some milk products for a while. This consumers' action, very rare in the Israeli public domain, was crucial as it united both lower and middle classes. It was a concrete demand that encapsulated that something is wrong not just with the lack of competition and the concentration of power in Israeli economy but also with the support this model received from the political elites. It was also important that this petition was led by an ultraorthodox person—Itzik Elrov—thus breaking the bond of cultural segregation among different ethnic, national, and religious groups in Israel and generating a united struggle of all Israelis. The empowering consumers' struggle, on the one hand, and the identification with the claims of Leef concerning the continuous rise of housing in Israel, on the other, facilitated identification across wide segments of Israeli society.

However, a crucial contextualization of the social protest—often less emphasized—is its emergence in the midst of a wave of strikes and economic conflict between workers and the state: the social workers, the medical doctors, the teachers, the nonunionized workers, the lawyers, and the mothers' marches all expressed public dissatisfaction. These supposedly sectorial struggles for workers' conditions demonstrated several important aspects of the protest. First, the issues of these strikes were central to the future of the welfare state: health, education, social security, and housing. However, the question of whether it is government policy to dismantle the welfare state was never part of the public discussion—the framing of the strikes were as part of a labor disputes between the treasury and the unions. Second, the other main issue—the privatization of these fields, and the fact that a growing part of the social workers, teachers, and nurses are working for manpower companies under poor personnel contracts with little social rights—was also hiding in the wings of these strikes. It was especially prevalent in the case of the social workers, where the deal that the treasury reached with the unions did not apply to the vast majority of the social workers and only gave the appearance that the problem was solved. It exposed the system of outsourcing, which has become dominant in the last 30 years without any public discussion or parliamentary debate. The pervasive power in the hands of the top bureaucrats in the financial ministries was thus exposed. Third, the cost of education and health, public services previously provided by the state, became very high for middle-class families with children. Whereas there was no single economic crisis, the burden of the increase in cost of living, the rise in the prices paid for public services, and the relative stagnation of the salaries of the middle classes since the 1990s gave its signals and burst with the social protest of 2011. The best evidence for that is that in the first big public event on July 23, 2011, the speakers on the main stage in Tel Aviv included representatives of the different strikers—social workers, young medical doctors, and teachers.

Thus, the dwindling of the welfare state and the rise of the cost of living went hand in hand in the Israeli social protest, together with the claims against the lack of nonmonopolistic free markets, the concentration of capital in the hands of about 20 rich families that held pyramids of control—owning networks of supermarkets, banks and insurance companies, natural resources, media, telecommunication, and newspapers—thus exposing the interrelations between political and economic elites. For the first time in Israeli public discourse, the political focus was on a need for a fundamental restructuring of the economic system and its political nesting. Despite the fact that in terms of economic ide-ologies some of the protesters wanted less bureaucracy, less taxes, and a more free market to remedy these ills, and others wanted to reinstate the welfare state and a greater commitment of the state to its citizens, both these contradictory eco-nomic ideologies subsisted in the social protest side by side. This was not the case with the leadership and main backbone of activists, who were going through a socialization process, backed by close engagement of some academics, that eventually resulted in a strong position in favor of social democracy (Yona and Spivak 2012).

Thus, whereas the Arab world needed an economic revolution and dealt with issues of hunger and growing rates of unemployment, in the advanced democra-cies protests were waged against the global economic crisis and the injustices of neoliberalism and in Israel the disintegration of the welfare state and the grow-ing social gaps and cost of living were the main sources of discontent.

Economics-Cum-Politics: The Power System Exposed

The opening citation from Stiglitz emphasizes the failure of the "system" and the need for "pressure from the street" to push the established political realm into policy change. However, here again the nature of the system is different in each of the models we develop—and importantly it is the political system, rather than the economic one alone—that is at the heart of the protest.

For the Arab revolts, economic hardship produced claims to nothing less than a regime change in some and reforms in others. The slogans that connected bread with freedom and human dignity exposed the connection between autoc-racy and poverty based on unsustainable economic models and the yearning for the bond between democracy and prosperity; clearly, the lost "social contract" between the state and society was at the heart of the contention. The economic problems—in Libya, Egypt, Yemen, and Syria—are but a mirror to the fragility of tyrannies in the aftermath of the collapse of the Soviet Union as an alternative to democracy in the 21st century. As long as popular contention could be con-tained—due to redistribution of state resources in the Gulf countries or political reform in Jordan—the regime was saved for the time being, but clearly the main issue was to structure economics as intertwined with the political system. Thus, the unexpected claims for democracy and freedom—and the inability of the lib-eral camp to unite precisely because of the depoliticization it was coerced into by the oppressive regime (Abdalla 2012)—were perhaps the strongest impetus of the "Arab Spring".

A regime change was definitely not on the cards of the Occupy movement. Interestingly, it was often not translated into a direct challenge of the government in power, be it left or right, both because most governments have adopted a neo-Keynesian approach and because the context of the protest was a system larger than the national arena. Thus, the European Union was especially intrusive in the cases of Greece, Spain, and Portugal, as were the neoliberal forces of unelected economic institutions like the International Monetary Fund (IMF), the World Bank, the World Trade Organization (WTO), or the G-8 in terms of world dominance and their influence on people's lives (Stiglitz 2012; Diani and Kousis 2014; Della Porta 2009).

What was the political system against which the social protest in Israel took place? This is the main thrust of this chapter: to demonstrate that the economic protest and social upheaval were highly connected to a struggle for Israeli democracy and the move from politics of identity to policymaking in the public interest. Perhaps the most proficient speaker of that was Itzik Shmuli, the chair of the national student union and today a member of Knesset, the Israeli parliament, for the Labor Party who coined the term "the New Israelis." In the biggest protest event, held in Tel Aviv on September 3, 2011, with almost half a million people roaming the streets, Shmuli argued:

> Mister Prime Minister I know you are watching us now. I urge you to look closely: what you see now, the huge public that is here and all over Israel—is the public you do not know at all. It is not a public that is willing to accept what governments have decided on its behalf because "this is how it goes." Let us introduce ourselves: We are the new Israelis.
>
> Shmuli 2011a, *author translation*

In order to understand the concept of the New Israelis but also the position vis-à-vis the government and what the protest was, it is necessary to introduce if very briefly two main features of Israeli society as reflected in politics. For Israeli society is a highly multipolarized society with many social, ethnic, national, religious, and other cleavages (Horovitz and Lissak 1989). In fact, Israel scores one of the highest measures of tensions in the OECD countries, as Figure 11.1 shows.

This social structure is closely reflected in the party system, as Israel has one of the most representative systems in the democratic world (Figure 11.2). If we thus take Lipset and Rokkan's (1967) thesis about voters' alignments around social cleavages and apply it to those tensions relevant for this society, we could see the fragmentation of the party system in relation to its traditional social cleavages. This was not the case in the first generation of Israeli politics. In fact, 1948–1977 there was a one-party dominance, the Party of Eretz Israel Workers,

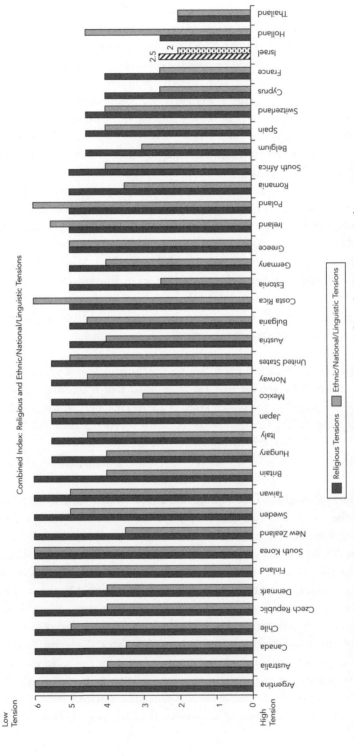

FIGURE 11.1 Combined Index: Religious and ethnic/national/linguistic tensions from the Democracy Index.

Source: Israeli Democracy Institute (2009, 39).

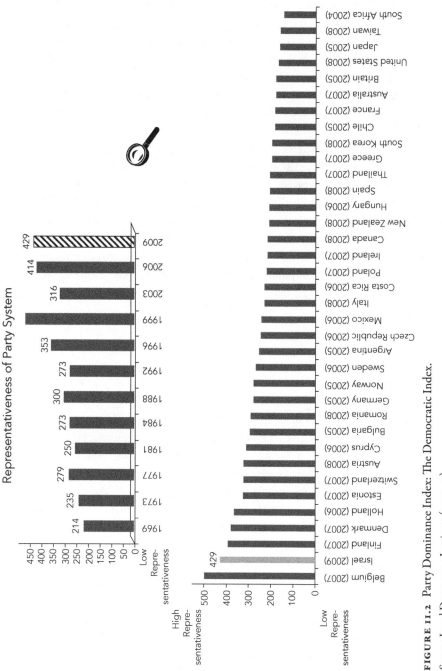

Representativeness of Party System

High Representativeness / Low Representativeness

1969: 214
1973: 235
1977: 279
1981: 250
1984: 273
1988: 300
1992: 273
1996: 353
1999: (no value label shown)
2003: 316
2006: 414
2009: 429

FIGURE 11.2 Party Dominance Index: The Democratic Index.

Source: Israel Democracy Institute (2009, 31).

Low Representativeness

Belgium (2007)
Israel (2009) — 429
Finland (2007)
Denmark (2007)
Holland (2006)
Estonia (2007)
Switzerland (2007)
Austria (2008)
Cyprus (2006)
Bulgaria (2005)
Romania (2008)
Germany (2005)
Norway (2005)
Sweden (2006)
Argentina (2005)
Czech Republic (2006)
Mexico (2006)
Italy (2008)
Costa Rica (2006)
Poland (2007)
Ireland (2007)
Canada (2008)
New Zealand (2008)
Hungary (2006)
Spain (2008)
Thailand (2007)
Greece (2007)
South Korea (2008)
Chile (2005)
France (2007)
Australia (2007)
Britain (2005)
United States (2008)
Japan (2005)
Taiwan (2008)
South Africa (2004)

MAPAI party of Ben Gurion, later becoming the Labor Party. Since 1977 a more European-like system has developed—with two dominant parties—Labor for the Left and Likud for the Right. But already in the early 1980s this two-block system began to fall apart as more and more ethnic, religious, and cultural groups gained electoral representation, so much so that in 2013, 34 political parties competed in the elections and 12 parties are represented today in the Knesset. Crucially, if in 1984 Labor and Likud still held together 85 out of 120 Members of Knesset (MK) seats, today they both (Likud without Israel Beytenu) control only 15 and 20 seats respectively.[2]

This representative party system, with a low 2 percent threshold, generated a political dynamics in which, to compose a coalition, the two dominant parties had to convince the centrist, ethnic, and religious parties to join it, and their votes would usually go to the potential coalition partner that would offer the most. This contest produced a much-despised politics of identity and became one of the dominant issues in the social protest: the attempt of the ruling parties to divide and rule, to give funds to the sectarian parties but not to pay attention to the demands of the main public, the middle classes who were obediently voting for the main parties. The interests of the majority of middle-class voters were ignored due to the coalition game; changing this was a crucial demand made by the social protest. In the main gathering of the protest on August 13, 2011, Shmuli voiced it thus:

> Good evening to all of you. Good evening to the soldier from Afula, good evening to the student in Jerusalem, good evening to her parents in Degania, good evening to the policeman from Beer Sheva, good evening to the teacher from Taybeh, good evening to the immigrant from Ariel, good evening to the pensioner from Netanya, good evening to the homeless from Holon. Good evening, Israel! This struggle encompasses many—far too many—problems of the Israeli society. Many audiences join in. The shared hardship strikes the high walls that were built in Israeli society and darkened its glory. No more Jews against Arabs; no more secular versus religious; no more leftists against right-wingers. The high cost of living takes a toll on us all.
>
> Shmuli 2011b; *author translation*

This quote is fundamental to understand the change that was sought: The imagined people addressed by Shmuli represent individuals from the periphery, not just the center: minorities—national, ethnic, settlers, and the elderly; most employed by the public sector—policemen, teachers; and also the disadvantaged groups—homeless, poor, and pensioners. In contradistinction to the politics of segregation—building on the main social cleavages he mentions—national, religious, and economic divides—Shmuli considers all these individuals as part of Israel, as the New Israelis. What is new is of course not their places of origin or workplace but their self-consciousness as new Israelis: as belonging to the same people—yes, the teacher from the Arab village Taybeh also—who form a new conceptualization of the concept of people as manifested in the main slogan of the Israeli protest: "The People Want Social Justice." This is not the Jewish people, the ethnocratic rule of the Jewish state,[3] but an Israeli people united in their demand to reinstate the alliance between the state and its citizens. Against politics of identity the leadership of the protest movement would urge time and again that governments should act in view of the public—not segregated—good.

The other crucial dimension here is solidarity: though this movement was characterized as a middle-class movement (Rosenhak and Shalev 2012), and the main parties that stood to gain from it in the 2013 elections—Yesh 'Atid and Labor—were both speaking on behalf of the middle classes, the leadership of the protest was very careful to try to harbor a relationship between the middle and lower classes. This was demonstrated by the division—and the attempts to overcome them—in the establishment of the tent cities. In Tel Aviv there was the Rothschild camp and the Jessy Cohen camp—the first highly bourgeois, the second a poverty neighborhood; in Jerusalem there was the Horse Park students' camp, the single mothers' camp in Independence Garden, and the homeless camp in Saker Garden: The leadership made special efforts to mobilize a cooperation and interclass solidarity. This was part of the aim to build a unitary Israeli identity, resistant to artificial divisions and groupings, to stand united against the government and to voice a demand for a different kind of politics. While the government reacted by trying to dub the protesters as radical anarchists, Sushi-eater bourgeoisies, and extreme leftists (Schechter 2012), the leadership was adamant about establishing tent cities not just in Tel Aviv and Jerusalem but also in Afula and Beer Sheva, in Arab villages and developmental towns (with varying levels of success), so much so that the government had to establish a public committee to act swiftly and consider the demands of the protest, the Trachtenberg committee (Committee for Economic and Social Change 2012).

Thus, a constitutive claim toward the powerholders was against the politics of identity and for the development of clear policy that identifies the public interest and acts in view of the common good of Israelis. While one side of this coin was a rejection of the institutionalization of identity politics in the party system, the other side was encapsulated in the wave of workers' struggles that we already discussed: the teachers, doctors, lawyers, social workers, manpower companies workers, and moms' marches exposed the lack of governability in the Israeli system. In all these instances it was not the minister responsible or the prime minister who conducted the negotiations, but the top bureaucrats of the treasury. Not once in the public debate did the ministers reveal their position: Are they for or against the privatization of the health system? Are they for or against outsourcing of social work? Are they for or against a voucher public education system? The lack of public discussion, the lack of a governmental clear position, the lack of a unitary policy measures emerging from a sound political ideology were at the heart of the demand for different politics. Yet, the "system" that was exposed was clearly a neoliberal one: "It is not a mistake, it is policy" was one of the most telling slogans of the protest in that regard. The claim was precisely that the government is hiding behind the back of its officials and does not put forward a policy while de facto dismantling the welfare state and changing radically the relations between the state and its citizens.

The main demands document, signed by all tent cities and 40 civil society organizations, some of which were established during the protest, reads as follows: "economic policy of unrestrained privatization empowering the free market. This policy is presented by its leaders and pursuers as an exact science and deterministic realism." Instead, the document demands fundamental change in the contract between state and its citizens in the spirit of the declaration of independence—"freedom, justice, equality of social and political rights regardless of religion, race or gender" (Forum for Social Justice 2011).

Note that the symbolic struggle is on the symbols of the state—the declaration of independence, the concept of peoplehood, the notion of Israeliness. The alternative sought by the protest movement is not voiced in social democratic or leftist terms but in terms of returning to the historical alliance between state and citizens as enshrined in the declaration of independence. It is to the struggle for Israeli democracy that we now turn.

The Struggle for Democracy: Between Representative and Deliberative Models

The political claim of the social protest in Israel, I argue, is to regenerate the common good pertaining to the public interest and replace the fragmented politics of identity. The concept of the "New Israelis" encapsulates in ideational terms the collective consciousness of the protesters vis-à-vis the party system and the ruling practices of the government over the last generation in Israeli politics. It is thus a struggle not just against the policies of the current prime minister or government but against the basic assumptions and rationales by which the system is functioning. But what is the model of democracy that the social protest is advocating?

Again, the two archetypes of the "Arab Spring" and the Occupy movement set a good typology against which the Israeli case can be considered. For it is clear that the contention of Arab protesters was with the regime itself, not just with this or that policy. The calls for freedom, human dignity, and democracy were clearly implying the popular struggle against an oppressive regime. Economics was just the tip of the iceberg, it is the rotten political system that needed to be replaced in Libya, Egypt, and Syria and other Middle Eastern states. As the unfolding events in Egypt have suggested, it is not merely elections that are at stake, but a genuine expression of the national movement of Egyptians that could change the direction of Egypt's society, economy, and politics. The masses in Tahrir Square possibly wanted not just Mubarak to be ousted from his presidency but also a transition away from autocracy to democracy. The demonstrations a year later, against Mursi, may have demonstrated that it was not just elections but the whole system at stake: parties with policy packages concerning national interest that the people demanded. The legitimacy of the personal elections thus did not provide the goods.

Thus, Arab societies have called for a transition away from autocracy and perhaps toward democratic regimes. Yet what was the model of democracy held by the protest movements in advanced democracies? Was it a protest call only? As Stiglitz claims, "The protesters have been criticized for not having an agenda. But this misses the point of protest movements. They are an expression of frustration with the electoral process. They are an alarm" (Stiglitz 2011). For him, within a representative democracy framework protest is a traditional tool to voice concern and raise issues to the agenda for the policymakers to address. However, observing the actual political behavior and modes of collective contention taken by the activists of the Occupy movement suggests otherwise. Indeed, as is sometimes the case with social movements, the best way to learn about their worldview is through analyzing their practices. In the Occupy movement, the disappointment with the established political system is encapsulated in the conscious adoption of participatory democracy, connected to a long tradition of antisystem protest of the Greens, the women's movements, and the World Social Forum (Smith and Glidden 2012). The participatory mode of action—including encampment in tents in the main city squares, general assemblies as a place of open decision-making, deliberative discussion including the hands sign symbols—that includes a number of coded gestures to imply agreement, applause, critique, etc. from the listeners by way of making them active audience, consensus building, and egalitarian participation in leadership—all epitomized an alternative culture of democracy. The main claims thereby made are against the representative nature of modern democracy—people should voice their own concerns, participate and get engaged, and not let others represent them; against the "cartelization" of party politics, particularly the close bonds of the economic and political elites; against the mediation of interests given "the march through the institutions" and taking into account not short-term policies but the silenced and disadvantaged groups as well as future generations. This participatory model has of course been criticized by activists and analysts alike arguing it is ineffective, accentuates self-selectivity of organized groups in the seemingly "leaderless" crowd, and fails to generate real dialogue with powerholders (Polletta 2002). However, far from merely "voicing discontent" and economic hardship, the protesters emphasize participatory democracy not just as means to voice concerns about globalization, as Stiglitz argues, but also, importantly, to express their criticism of the formal national political system and the minimalist model of representative democracy.

Thus, between regime-change toward representative democracy and participatory democracy, where does Israel stand? Starting from the social practices and political behavior, it is clear that Israel have adopted a double-edged strategy, whereby consecutive mass demonstrations built up the legitimacy of the protest in the streets reaching, at its peak, almost half a million marchers out of a population of 8 million. This was augmented by nearly 20 encampments of activists in tent cities in the public parks and squares of many Israeli cities. In these camps, all the repertoires of the Occupy movement, influenced by importation from the Spanish model in particular, were practiced (Schechter 2012, 42). As was argued at the outset, the hybrid model of intensive activist participatory democracy, mass demonstrations, and vast public support characterized Greece, Spain, Portugal, and Israel. Moreover, as already noted, the first three were highly involved with a democratic claim against the problem of national sovereignty by the policymakers and austerity measures at the EU level. The EU institutions and German-led decision-making override popular sovereignty of the individual states. However, what was the claim against Israeli democracy? Clearly, the context is very different.

On the face of it, the claim of regime change as the Arab type model is inapplicable here, as Israel is a functioning representative democracy recognized by Freedom House indicators as one of the advanced democracies in the world (Merkel 2012). Indeed, in terms of practices, the Israel activist scene has established an elaborated model of participatory democracy in encampments in Tel Aviv, Jerusalem, Ashdod, Zichron Yaacov, Mitzpe Ramon, Kiryat Shmonah, and many others. Each tent-city camp developed a unique civic culture, with distinct local activities, followers, and trends. Thus, the Kiryat Shmonah camp focused on local cooperation between the development towns, the kibbutzim, and students, focusing on open discussions and local action plans; the Jerusalem camp focused on generating the ideology of the whole activist scene in Israel, the document of demands, and the more mature social democratic agenda of the protest movement; Tel Aviv generated the most populous activist environment; the festival of local arts, graffiti, and roundtable discussions; and the public leadership of the movement. Crucially, beyond associations like the youth movements and student unions that were organized before the protest, an impressive number of new voluntary organizations—consumer action groups, political watch groups, and workshops for public knowledge—were established during the 2011 protest and were still functioning 5 years later. In Daphni Leef's words, "Our revolution is one of consciousness, standing for our rights. We do not want to replace the government but the rules of the game!" (Leef 2011). In terms of a model, the social protest has definitely produced a vibrant civil society with the explicit political role of generating critical public discourse in realms of economics, politics, and education (Talshir 2015).

Is it therefore clear that Israel falls in the Occupy model of participatory democracy, trying to establish an alternative to the representative model dominating Israel? In this regard, it is worthwhile to look at the hardcore of the leadership of the protest and see its choices. Shmuli, in the August 13, mass demonstration argued, "the leadership of the students is a reasoned voice and acts out of national responsibility . . . this country is dear to me, to all of us, more than to lead to a collision of the government and its people—in the elections each of us will act in accordance with his conscience but now we all share the obligation to generate real, deep and wide solutions" (Shmuli 2011b). What is at stake here, argue Shmuli and the leadership of the protest, is to do the right thing, to act responsibly, to develop policy plans for the public interest. Stav Shafir, another prominent figure in the protest and today MK for Labor explained that when she first got to the Knesset during the protest days and demanded that MKs work for the people, they did not understand what she wanted; she wanted to get into the parliament because, in her words:

> There is a chance to get people into the Knesset that will work for us . . . the discourse has changed. It was clear that the protest would not last forever, and it was clear technically, that in regard to change on the ground, revolutions are not something you do in democracy in couple of months but start processes that take years and demand compromises, otherwise you need to take the Knesset down by tanks. But on the social level there has been a revolution. There is no journalist or politician that does not relate to it today.
>
> Shafir in Esterkin 2012

Thus, "changing the rules of the game," in Leef's terms, was to generate a vibrant civil society, a critical public discourse, but also to change the way politics is performed and policy is being made in Israel: to move away from politics of segregated communities fighting for special funds to politics in the interest of the

public good, of putting forward clear ideologies, of coming up with policy packages and creating real social change. What they wanted, in short, was a functioning model of representative democracy rather than an alternative model of
participatory democracy. The Israeli protest sought to create a bond between
democratic civic culture and participatory civil society and an established party
system that would act on behalf of the people. In other words, they wanted to fix
the representative system rather than replace it.

Discussion: The Struggle for Israeli Democracy—A Hybrid Model?

The main argument in this chapter is that there is a connection between popular contention, economic grievances, and political regime change. The connection is expressed in terms of legitimation crisis. Though the 2011 wave of protest
was worldwide, it produced two quite distinct models in both of which there
were strong connections between economy and politics within the context of the
crisis of democracy. In contradistinction to Stiglitz's analysis, this wave was not
unanimously pointing against global neoliberalism, but had a strong national or
regional context within which the economic-cum-political demands needed to
be disentangled. While the "Arab Spring" was against the autocratic regime, and
the Occupy movement was a deliberative democratic attempt to protest against
the institutional forms of representative democracy and globalized economy,
between these two archetypes Israel has developed a distinct model of its own.
Table 11.1 summarizes the main features of our analysis:

The main feature of the "Arab Spring" protest was the national demonstrations calling for the voice of the people to be heard in politics, given the stark economic situation of hunger, mass unemployment, and lack of robust middle classes
and to call for social revolution more than a cosmetic change of leadership. The
main claim of the Occupy movement was against the cartelization of the politi-
cal-cum-economic global elites, which generate growing social gaps and infringe
on the sovereignty of states. In Israel the main claim for social justice was to
generate a political system in which real ideological differences are presented and
debated and policy packages offered to the people and governments act on behalf
of public interest, not the politics of sectorial communities. While the summer
of Israeli discontent has produced a vibrant civil society, giving rise to dozens
of new voluntary associations, nongovernmental organizations, and local initiatives in education, economy, society, and politics, together producing a network
of organizations with shared consciousness that positioned themselves against
the established political system, thus embodying the main conditions for the rise
of a new social movement (Della Porta and Diani 2006), its main achievements

Table 11.1 Three Models of Social Protest?

	"Arab Spring"	Advanced Democracies	Hybrid Model: Israel
Main Social Practices	Mass demonstrations	Activists encampments	Mass demonstrations + Activists encampments
Main Slogan	Bread, Freedom, Human Dignity	99%	The People want Social Justice
Economy	Against hunger and, unemployment, for economic relief	Against neoliberalism; against social gaps and inequality	Against cost of living; for welfare democracy
Politics	Politics on behalf of the people	Against globalization + cartelization of political and economic elites	From politics of identity to politics in the public interest
Democracy	Regime change to national democracy	Participatory democracy	Participatory civil society and a functioning representative democracy
Protest Results	Regime change	Voicing protest call	Changing social discourse and "New Politics"

were in transforming the social discourse, generating a critical and active social critique, and demanding "new politics" in the established institutions—parliament and government. Indeed, those parties that put forward a demand for new politics, acted in the name of the New Israelis, and vowed to work for the people were the great winners of the 2013 elections, despite the fact they did not profess a social democratic creed (Talshir 2015). In all three models popular contention worked through economic grievances to act for political change. In all models a question of legitimacy was at the heart of the debate. In terms of political change, the "Arab Spring" was the most daring one; the Occupy was most radical yet ineffective either in "overturning" the globalized economy or in promoting participatory democracy. In Israel the mass power of the demonstration produced an impetus for change leading the government, the new political parties, and the civil society organizations to adopt the themes of the protest, yet in reality there was little political change.

Distinctive to the Israeli case, we saw the tendency of the young protesters not to offer an alternative model of deliberative democracy but to try to "fix" Israeli representative democracy from within by joining—rather than just protesting—against it. Also, the government of Israel, in contradistinction to other past governments that have tried to simply avoid the protest, eventually formed a committee that held public hearings, and its deliberations were adopted as a governmental law and endorsed by the coalition parties when campaigning for 2013 elections. The government as well as its opposition were actually adopting the themes of the protest. And finally, the bearers of the protest into the election—some of the leaders who joined established political parties—were struggling between inclusive "New Israeli" parties advocating a universal welfare state, like Labor, and middle-class liberal parties advocating the economic interest of their class, like Yesh 'Atid. But both the national-religious right and the Left were attempting to speak in "New Israeli" terminology, and all parties—old and new—marketed themselves as the ultimate social parties in Israel (Talshir 2015).

How does the influence of the social protest on politics stand in comparison with the other hybrid models in the European context? While the indignados in Spain gave birth to Podemos, a political party that has since won the majority in Barcelona and Madrid, and the Greek movement gave birth to Syriza, which won state power through elections, the Israeli movement has influenced the party system in three distinct ways: First, the key players in the leadership of the protest—Shafir and Shmuli—joined the Labor Party and became dominant players in revitalizing the old Labor Party. Second, the spirit of the protest in connecting economic consumerist ethos with political critique contributed substantially to the rise of Yesh 'Atid Party, which in effect became the largest party in the aftermath of the 2013 elections (given that the Likud Beiteinu party was a conglomerate that fell apart shortly after the elections, going back to two distinct parties—Likud and Yisrael Beitenu). Third, it was also the use—or abuse—that the religious party Jewish Home did in trying to forge a spirit of Israeliness. They called it Israeliness but meant only the Jewish citizens, not the Arab ones, hence highly in contrast to the spirit of the social protest, which was inclusive and pluralist, a party which rose from 3 mandates to 15 in the 2013 elections. Yesh 'Atid and Jewish Home became the backbone of a short-lived government in 2013–2015, thus paradoxically transforming the party system but leaving out of the picture the authentic leadership, which found itself in the opposition. Those riding the wave of the protest were clearly making political history in Israel, transforming the discourse, the coalition partners, and the policy packages—thus making a difference, albeit a difference very distant from the agenda of the social protest. This coalition dissolved one or two issues that rose from the two "brother" parties—Yesh 'Atid's demand for 0 percent V.A.T and the Jewish Home demand to enshrine the national Jewish state law as a basic law. Consumerism instead of social justice, nationalism instead of democratic inclusion. The self-appointed vehicles of the social protest into parliament ended up manipulating the votes and creating an agenda removed from the main thrust of the protest.

However, one crucial perspective was overlooked in the 2013 elections: the crisis of the party system itself. If we do take the protest movement to demand ideology-cum-policy politics, big parties that act in the public interest and a decline of the identity parties, the elections constituting the 19th government have caused a dramatic breakdown of the party system. This is despite the attempt of the Likud to unite with Israel Beytenu, marking the disappearance of dominant parties and the rise of six medium-size parties instead. In terms of "fixing" the representative democracy, the social protest has produced the opposite effect, of a complete destruction of a two-block party system into diverse identity parties thus hindering governability. Nonetheless, taking social-cum-economic issues as the prime arena of the elections in Israel was a clear success of the social protest. The Right/Left divide, so conventional in European party systems, has for the first time played a role in Israeli politics. This divide between the neoliberals and the social democrats, is to expand in the 2015 elections into the reemerging two-bloc system—this time with consistency over economics, Israeli-Arab conflict, and collective identity issues, showing a slight advantage to the Rightwing with its national-cum-religious and neoliberal ideology. Given the unique position of Israel as a single developed democracy in the Middle East, the social protest has produced a hybrid model that is sensitive to Israeli political context and its problems. Whether this emerging democratic political culture, active civil society, and fragmented party system will in the long run actually constitute an answer to the crisis of legitimacy is yet to be seen.

Notes

1. For analysis of the global protest movement see Beissinger and Sasse (2012), Kriesi (2011), Smith (2011), Fuster Morell (2012), and Shepard (2012).
2. On the decline of the catch-all parties in Israel in comparative perspective, see Kenig and Kneplmann (2012).
3. For a useful debate on whether Israel is a liberal democracy or ethnocracy, in relation to the Arab minority, see Smooha (1990), Yakobson and Rubinstein (2008), and Yiftachel (2006).

Conclusion

THE ARAB REVOLTS IN COMPARATIVE HISTORICAL PERSPECTIVE

Avraham Sela

STIMULATED BY THE recent revolutionary waves in the Middle East and North Africa (MENA), yet consciously avoiding the assumption that MENA's contentious episodes constitute a distinct category, contributions to this volume have used social movement theory, and more specifically the contentious politics approach, in order to explain the emergence, unfolding, and outcomes of these events and to put them in a comparative perspective. As we have argued in the introductory chapter, similarities are found once moving beyond a focus on root causes/preconditions to explain why people rebel to focusing systematically on *dynamics* of contentious politics. That is, a focus on the processual, hyper-paced, emergent, and eventful features that popular contention, regimes, and transition acquire and, consequently, the intricate and indeterminate interrelation among them during cycles of contention.

Contributions to this volume have therefore used concepts and tools from the study of social movements and contentious politics to flesh out those similarities. Nonetheless, and consistent with our appreciation of the unique properties and traits of each case, our contributors have been attentive to how these "initial conditions" give rise to theoretically meaningful dissimilarities. Primary among these insights is the significance of regimes' political legacies and state–society relations as key factors shaping their initial response to contention, the impact of regionalism on cross-national diffusion of contention and political change, and the role of the military as a political player, arbitrator, or balancer in times of popular contention and transition.

This kind of similarities-in-dissimilarities reasoning and mode of inquiry has shaped the two complementing questions that have guided this volume: What can cycles of contention in other parts of the world tell us about revolts in the Arab world, and, equally important, what can the cycles of contention in the Arab world tell us about contentious politics more generally? Before discussing the contributions of the chapters of this volume in light of these two complementing questions and according to the three main themes/sections of the book—"Between Structure and Contention," "Processes and Trajectories of Contention," and "Between Contention and Transition"—it is useful to review some of the main strands of research of the Arab revolts and assess their strengths and limitations.

The Arab Revolts in Historical Perspective: The Strengths and Limits of Macro-Based Explanations

The Arab revolts provide an invaluable set of intriguing variations concerning the emergence, unfolding dynamics, and trajectories and, with some perspective, consequences, impacts, and outcomes of cycles of contentious politics. With partial hindsight and initial perspective, these variations loom large when evaluated in light of the abundance of works already published on the Arab revolts, where one can find a tendency to treat MENA states and societies as sui generis and to idealize the wave of popular upheavals as strides toward democracy. Yet, notwithstanding their undeniable commonalities (i.e., culture, demography, human development, social structures, and authoritarian regimes) the Arab states and societies are starkly different from each other in many other aspects such as history, geography and ecological conditions, economic resources, and level of *stateness*, or state-to-nation ratio (Nettle 1968; Miller 2006). This multifaceted diversity has indeed manifested itself in substantial dissimilarities among the Arab uprisings in their consolidation, regimes' responses to discontent, and the outcomes of state–society encounters.

That these dissimilarities were salient even among states of the same categories, such as regime type (Tunisia, Egypt, Syria, Yemen, and Libya vs. Algeria) or national wealth (most Gulf monarchies vs. Bahrain, Libya, Iraq, and Algeria), renders each of the Arab states a useful case study for a thematic comparison with non-MENA cases. At the same time, and without falling into the trap of "exceptionalism," given the obvious diffusion of the revolts across the Arab region within a short time period—to point out only one aspect of commonalities—it is equally important to respect and to explore those sources of similarities as a springboard for generating valuable theoretical insights.

Before delving into the volume's main theoretical themes and insights, it seems in order to discuss some of the main strands of works and their respective lines of explanation to the "Arab Spring" and put them in broader historical perspective. Doing this serves two complementing purposes. First, discussing prevalent explanations to the "Arab Spring" and placing them in broader historical context is useful for demonstrating both the value of appreciating the initial and structural preconditions of a particular case and the limitation of those works in terms of understanding similarities across apparently divergent cases as well as differences across apparently similar cases. Second, discussing the broader historical context of those structural/macro-based factors and preconditions that are case/region-specific facilitates an appreciation of those inductively generated theoretical contributions, which is discussed in the subsequent section.

With no one predicting the wave of uprisings and no immediate cause in sight to explain the eruption of Arab revolts, the vast body of works published since 2011 has largely focused on three intertwined sets of *underlying factors* that had been at work for several decades (Owen 2012; Noueihed and Warren 2012; Amin 2013; Ramadan 2012; Lynch 2014a). First is the accumulative impact of socioeconomic grievance and discontent of large segments of society following decades of rapid population growth and massive rural-to-urban migration, coupled with relatively slow economic growth; inflated bureaucracies with increasing unemployment and underemployment, especially of university graduates; rampant poverty; and youth bulge. In addition, the post-1973 oil boom and the migration of millions of Arab labor migrants from the poor countries to the oil-producing states coupled with economic liberalization accounted for a growing gap between rich and poor, especially in the labor-exporting countries (Tuma 1980). The economic liberalization adopted by hitherto highly centralized, non-oil-rich economies represented their long-term failure and increasing dependence on international financial institutions to cover their unpayable debts.

This aid, however, came with strings pulled by the creditors, who insisted on official commitment by the recipient states to introduce neoliberal economic reforms. Arab rulers were indeed reluctant to conduct full implementation of the required reforms due to experienced backlash of the masses (e.g., riots in Egypt in 1977 and in Jordan and Algeria in 1989) in response to drastic rises of basic commodities such as food and fuel. Nonetheless, consecutive cycles of international loans, followed by neoliberal reforms and social crises, left their unmistakable imprint on non-oil-rich Arab economies. The reforms gradually eroded the unwritten "social contract," according to which in return for public political obedience the state was to provide minimal social services, subsidize basic commodities at affordable prices for the poor classes, and ensure jobs and housing, especially for young people.

The above aspects of social and economic distress should be understood in the context of the rise of the "mass society" in the developing regions in the second half of the 20th century—a phenomenon well captured and analyzed by the Egyptian economist Galal Amin in *The Era of Huge Masses* (Amin 2003). Prominent attributes of the mass society are the rapid rural-to-urban migration, mostly to capital cities, creating overcrowded neighborhoods marked by poor social services and housing, exposure to modern media and consumer goods, high rate of unemployment, and youth bulge, the combination of which has created a highly explosive social reality. Rapid urbanization indeed leads to the emergence of varied types of informal networks that function as mechanisms of self-help, providing vital goods and services to the disoriented urban poor and mediating between them and the official authorities. Seemingly contributing to social and political stability, these nonstate networks can nevertheless become foci of resistance and, through the articulation and collectivization of grievances and discontent, may well transform into hubs of mobilization and engines of contention, a phenomenon particularly prevalent in Middle Eastern urban centers.[1]

In this social and economic reality, the growing gap between rulers and ruled boosted the rise of influential Islamist movements as organized frameworks offering the disadvantaged urbanized masses a convenient avenue for expressing a broadly shared sense of deprivation and alienation. Active participation in, and identification with, these movements became a default choice, especially among the impoverished urban lower middle class and underemployed youth. Committed to social concerns, mainstream Islamic movements absorbed much of the energy emanating from the indignant and frustrated masses, which further underlined the potentially contentious nature of these movements and their representation of social and economic grievances (Wickham 2002). Indeed, much of the history of state–society relations in the Arab states since the early 1980s reflects the ongoing efforts by the ruling elites to repress, co-opt, and restrict the growing influence of popular Islamist movements in their quest for appropriate parliamentary representation and spaces of operation and collective action. Precisely in view of the long history of political conflict and competing socioeconomic infrastructures between the state and Islamist movements, and the occasional contentious expressions it gave rise to, one would have expected the latter to have played a central if not leading role in the Arab revolts.

The second set of factors relates to the long-term personalized authoritarian regimes, headed by what Roger Owen has called "Presidents for Life" (2012) and authoritarian monarchs, facilitated by flexible exercise of diverse levels of political repression under a façade of political legitimacy based on constitutions, multiparty systems, and elections (Heydemann 2007). Beginning in the late 1970s, authoritarian regimes in Tunisia, Egypt, Jordan, Algeria, Morocco, and Yemen introduced measurable neoliberal economic reforms parallel to controlled political liberalization, including formal multiparty systems, elections, and more freedom of speech. The heavily controlled nature of this liberalization, nonetheless, may well have mitigated potential revolutionary tendencies, yet they also facilitated, as elaborated in what follows, the development of a more vibrant and critical public discourse through diverse channels of communication, thus encouraging more daring challenges to the regime years before the 2011 revolts (Costello et.al. 2015).

The combined impact of decades of the same ruling figures or their family-member successors, economic liberalization, and privatization by most non-oil-rich Arab states became ever more evident in the decade before the revolts erupted, with increasingly flagrant corruption of power at all levels. To these features, one should add abuses of human and political rights, privatization of public enterprises, and forging of the already limited model of political liberalization imposed on these regimes by Western governments and international financial institutions. A central manifestation of the personalized republican regimes was the intended "bequeathing the unbequeathable" (Amin 2013, 32), namely, preparing for succession of the incumbent presidents by one of their sons or another family member, as was applied in Syria in 2000 and seemed to be followed suit in Egypt, Tunisia, Libya, and Yemen.[2]

The highly centralized management of political and economic affairs enabled authoritarian rulers to cement their autocratic authority by developing political and economic forms of neopatrimonialism, including patronage networks of favorite social and political elite groups, clienteles, clannish relationships, corruption, and co-optation of political rivals—all of which blurred the boundaries between the public and private spheres. With the swelling ranks of Islamist movements and threat of jihadist groups, Arab rulers invested increasing resources in expanding their domestic security and intelligence agencies with broad, often pervasive apparatuses of repression, giving rise to a new elite group sharing similar interests with, and constituting a third party in, interconnected security-business-political elite networks. At the center of these networks were the presidents' family members and cronies, who usurped much of the common good and coalesced in ensuring the political survival of their system of power and mutual interests (Azmi Bishara, in Mustafa and Hamada 2012). Arab autocrats not only shared much of these practices of projecting political power but also learned from each other's experience in bolstering their presidential or monarchic domination (Owen 2012).

The above forms of authoritarianism and neopatrimonialism were largely facilitated by the prevalent model of *rentierism*, which has marked many Arab states since the late 1960s. Rentierism connotes the flow of large funds into states' coffers as directly earned revenues (e.g., of oil and/or gas production) or indirectly (e.g., foreign laborers' remittances or international aid)—that is, separately from domestic production—all of which effectively allow regimes to keep their constituencies under control without accountability to, or sharing power with them. The *rentier state* theory thus became a major explanation for the lack of regime change and democracy in the MENA states (Beblawi 1987; Chaudhry 1994; Schwarz 2008).

The third set of underlying factors focuses on the brazen gap between, on the one hand, a façade of political participation and limited freedoms of expression and assembly and, on the other, the cumulative impact of continued sense of marginalization and humiliation of myriad social groups and the quest, especially of the young urban generation, for genuine political freedoms, social justice, and economic security. Indeed, despite its emasculated and manipulated nature, the process of tightly controlled political liberalization conducted by most republican regimes as well as Jordan and Morocco, allowed the rise of opposition parties, the conduct of election campaigns, open critique of official policies, and in the cases of Tunisia and Egypt also the option of employing judicial procedures in the relations between citizens and institutions.

These new avenues of expression enabled social movements, political parties, labor unions, professional associations, human rights advocacy nongovernmental organizations (NGOs), and myriad social networks and regime opponents to criticize the regime's domestic and foreign policies and propagate their slogans and messages more freely and effectively in the public sphere. These changes were unquestionably facilitated, in fact enhanced, by the advent of new social media technologies and its increasingly broadening uses by young, urban, and educated men and women, many of whom were activists in various civil society NGOs and networks concerned with promoting human rights, education for democracy, and the environment. Especially since the mid-1990s, these NGOs enjoyed funding and guidance from Western governments and international organizations and agencies eager to build civil society agencies and export liberal norms and values presented in terms of universal ethics, peace, and prosperity.[3] While the extent to which years of Western efforts to help building a civil society made a difference is not clear, we may safely assume that many of the organizers of the demonstrations in Tunisia and Egypt were well connected to official EU and American agencies. In retrospect, scholars marked 2005—when Mubarak's succession by his son became a matter of public attention—as the beginning of growing critical discourse by the educated elite of social grievances—such as poverty, social inequality, and arbitrary conduct of the security services—through the printed media, movies, theater, poetry, and Internet blogs. Apart from reaching out and mobilizing many for collective action, the main contribution of the new social media to the developing spirit of protest is explained as providing an alternative and challenging forum of discourse to that of the regime. This was demonstrated in the labor strike of al-Mahalla al-Kubra workers of April 6, 2008, in Egypt, which in retrospect is seen as "training toward the revolution" (Mustafa and Hammada 2012, 28; Noueihed and Warren, 53; Ramadan 2012, 7–9).

Indeed, the Arab revolts represent a historical precedent in the role of information and communication technologies (ICTs) in their early phase of mobilization, carrying an important insight for any future study of contention. Beyond acting as outlets for expressing social, economic, and political grievances, the new information technologies and social media had a "democratization effect,"[4] providing social activists with effective means to enhance mobilization and refute the regime's media warfare against its critics and challengers (Mustafa and Hammada 2012, 28–30). Especially in the early weeks and months of the revolts, the new media played a crucial role in propagating the call for justice, dignity, and political freedoms both within and across Arab states as well as to the Western societies. These slogans provided different groups and sectors with a hitherto missing common "master narrative" with symbols and meanings capable of rallying masses around them in protest against the regime (Alexander 2011).

In addition to its ability to constitute virtual networks, indeed, an "imagined community," social media also played an important role in reaching out beyond state boundaries as attested by the "spillover effect" of similar patterns of mass protests traveling throughout the Arab world and bringing the news to the world public awareness despite the state attempts to block such communications. Equally important in rendering social discontent in the MENA countries universal during the first few weeks and months of 2011 were all-Arab TV networks, especially Al-Jazeera.

The liberal discourse of the early days and weeks of the Arab revolts apparently accounted for the impression or wishful thinking among Western governments and media commentators of the revolts as a genuine push toward democratization, prompting them to rethink the Arab world's image as exceptionally resistant to democracy or, at the least, a reason to review and criticize this pre-2011 widely held perception (Owen 2012, 153–71; Noueihed and Warren 2012, 16–21; Dabashi 2012, 65–69). For others, the revolts at least partly reflected the results of Western support along years in building Arab civil societies (Lynch 2014a, 11–12). The impact of these Western efforts on Middle Eastern societies is hard to determine, even though Tunisia and Egypt were very cooperative with the EU and took part in many joint projects, including the advancement of political reforms and human rights (Bicchi 2006; Boubakri and Lindahl 2009). Similarly, the impact of ICTs had its own limitations, being exposed to regime countermeasures such as blocking communication and arrests of bloggers. Most significantly, these technologies were no substitute to long-term mobilization and organized collective action.

Indeed, despite the emerging coalitions of social actors, including existing organizations with more or less autonomy, the revolts were largely leaderless, lacked clear and specific agendas, and were marked by divided identity along political and religious lines susceptible to exploitation by the incumbent regimes. Moreover, the Arab revolts did not draw on a particular philosophical thought (as, for example, the Sh'i revolution in Iran). Hence, the demand for democracy lacked clarity, reflecting disagreement on a specific model for attaining it (Bishara, in Mustafa and Hammada 2012, 10, 32).

With respect to Egypt, which epitomized much of the above-mentioned features, the eruption of demonstrations took place just a few weeks after the country had experienced a most blatant abuse of the parliamentary elections held in late November 2010. The results of the elections effectively eliminated the Islamic opposition's representation in the National Assembly for the first time in three decades, a representation that reached an all-time high proportion of 20 percent of the seats in the 2005 elections. The 2010 elections, taking place amid an unprecedented wave of brutal repression against the Muslim Brotherhood, including hundreds of arrests of the movement's activists prior to election day and turning over a court decision that invalidated the result in two dozens of electoral districts, prompted not only Western condemnations but also protest events, which coincided with, and were further encouraged by, the Tunisian demonstrations (Abdel Hamid 2011). It is noteworthy that following these elections the Egyptian sociologist, liberal thinker, and primary critic of the regime, Saad Eddin Ibrahim, observed that the regime's greed and flagrant forgery of the elections would be the "straw that will break the camel's back" (Ibrahim 2010).[5] Such a statement could be just as valid had it been said 10 years earlier. The point to be made is that our ability to foretell the moment at which discontent reaches the breaking point is practically nonexistent. Nonetheless, and especially in the context of the present discussion, it is instructive to recall Goodwin and Skocpol's important observation that, "Other things being equal, the narrower the regime, and the more repressive, the broader the coalition potentially available to be mobilized by revolutionaries" (1989, 496).

It is indeed ironic that despite decades of social and political turmoil, including mass uprisings and contentious episodes represented by social sectors (workers, students, and women) and ethnic groups, Western social scientists in recent decades held Arab societies as deferent to authoritarianism and resistant to democratization and political change (Bellin 2004; Anderson 2006). Recalling the frequent strikes of workers, political demonstrations stirred by opposition parties and grassroots networks in most Arab states both before and after attaining independence attest to the fact that despite decades of repression these societies maintained their agency in potential activism (Tripp 1998, 2014). And though authoritarian regimes had constantly advanced their control over societies by combining "stick and carrot" strategies rendering their image "robust" and unshakable (Heydemann 2007), Arab societies still manifested their rebellious potential throughout the decades before the 2011 revolts (e.g., Egypt's students' demonstrations of 1971–1972 and food riots of 1977; Syria's Muslim Brotherhood uprising 1979–1982; Jordan and Algeria food riots of 1989). In Gramscian terms, the growing distance between the ruling elites and their societies accounted for poor legitimacy and effectively weak states.

Indeed, regardless of the popular nature of the Arab revolts, their unprecedented scope, energy, persistence, and success in radically shaking hitherto "robust" authoritarian regimes (Bellin 2004), for many scholars and observers the reality against which the masses of protesters took to the streets was old news. In fact, at least two cycles of mass demonstrations and protests of political nature as well as against deteriorating social and economic conditions preceded those of 2011. In the eruptions of discontent in Lebanon (the Cedar Revolution) and Egypt (*kifaya*) in the spring of 2005, coalitions of diverse social groups and socioeconomic background took to the streets introducing new patterns and scope of mobilization (Bayat 2010). More recently, the world financial crisis of 2008 resulted in mass strikes and demonstrations, especially in Egypt and Tunisia and, to a lesser extent in Algeria, Jordan, Yemen, and other countries, with protesters complaining about high prices and low wages and aiming their rage directly against the rulers (Noueihed and Warren 2012, 24, 53; Vogt 2011).

Given all the above developments, why were there no cycles of popular contention of such magnitude before 2011? And why, if accepting arguments regarding regional similarities, did cross-national trajectories and outcomes (let alone transitions when unfolded) differ so strikingly? After all, each of the above sets of factors carried the impetus to rebel and conditions were ripe even in terms of ICTs and the quest for greater freedoms long before late 2010.[6] The point to stress is that a focus on grievances and discontent without looking into interactions and dynamics of contention provides us only with partial explanations at best.

The Arab Revolts in Comparative Perspective: From Theory to Empirics and Back

This part of the chapter is structured according to the three sections of the book: "Between Structure and Contention," "Processes and Trajectories of Contention," and "Between Transition and Contention." In relating to chapters from each section, I first summarize briefly the main contribution of each chapter as it pertains to the usefulness of concepts and tools from the study of social movements and contentious politics in identifying similarities between Arab and non-Arab cases. I then move on to discuss how the particularities of Arab countries help inform specific theories and models used in each section. As stated and demonstrated throughout the chapters, and as will be demonstrated in what follows, the organization of the book's sections and respective chapters is analytically useful for highlighting the interrelatedness among processes of popular contentions, regimes, and transitions, without this implying any clear-cut empirical distinction.

Between Structure and Contention

As noted in the introductory chapter, contributions to this section of the book have moved beyond a unidirectional line of research regarding the effects of structural factors and root causes on the impetus for popular contention—a line of research that tends to encourage a focus on the unique properties and traits of a single case—to probing how structural factors (writ large) shape and are shaped by popular contention. While unquestionably offering strong indicators of the willingness to rebel, structural factors, facilitative preconditions, and precipitating events offer poor analytical tools for the understanding of how cycles of popular contention consolidate. While not overlooking the role of macro and root conditions (and particularities of a given case or region), chapters in this section consciously refrained from treating them as causal forces and, instead, focused on how they are activated by, give rise to, and inform the specific interactions by the parties and actors involved. This more dynamic approach and mode of investigation has facilitated the identification of meaningful similarities between Arab and non-Arab cases in particular, and between authoritarian and nonauthoritarian regimes more generally.

Building on a recent trend in the study of social movements and contentious politics, one that calls for attention to the specific, case-particular way popular contention gets coordinated and takes shape (i.e., applying social movement as an analytical tool rather than as an all-fitting empirical entity), Diani and Moffatt's chapter demonstrates how such a less imposing approach is useful for making sense of the "problematic" of social movements also in some of the recent Arab revolts. Specifically, the authors show how the process along which the challenging collective actors in Egypt and Tunisia were formed, what they call "mode of coordination," was largely shaped by the separate and joint influences of three central elements of political opportunity structure: social cleavages, the role of local elites, and the level of repression. Repression, it goes without saying, figures prominently in authoritarian regimes, and MENA countries are no exceptions in this regard, both before and during the "Arab Spring". But, as Pilati's chapter reminds us—building on the cumulative knowledge in studies of social movements and contention—the effects of repression on mobilization are far from straightforward. What Pilati shows in her analysis of Nigeria and Zimbabwe is that in addition to examining repression in a more refined manner (e.g., levels as well as forms), one needs to also consider the powers of opposition groups in shaping repression. Specifically, it is useful to examine organizational structure adaptations that make it possible for opposition groups to sustain and, at times, increase the scope of contention mobilization—a dynamic she identifies as unfolding also in the repressive contexts of Saudi Arabia and Egypt and in the cases of migrant-based contention in the developing repressive contexts of Italy and Switzerland.

Focusing more closely on the side of authorities/regime's features, the chapters by Quaranta and Goldstone share a similar dissatisfaction with the line of argument regarding the role of structural/macro factors in explaining levels and forms of popular contention. Thus, for example, Quaranta's analysis of levels of protest participation offers support for the argument that the likelihood of engaging in demonstrations is higher when dissatisfaction with economic performance of a given regime is linked to high level of particular aspects of political opportunity structure, specifically distrust in political institutions. Whereas Quaranta's chapter centers on Latin American countries, Goldstone's chapter provides a broad comparative framework that seeks to account for the enormous diversity in terms of openings and scopes (but also of trajectories—see section "Processes and Trajectories of Contention") of popular contention out of what appears to be very similar fundamental conditions for mobilization across the MENA countries. The answer Goldstone's chapter offers, one that connects with the recent shift among scholars of social movements away from a movement-centric approach to one that brings in equal attention to the features of regimes, namely, their political opportunity structure, which largely rests on their authoritative style and characters; their financial resources; and their international contexts of opportunities and constraints. The Goldstone chapter's attention to regime features underscores the importance of distinguishing regimes from states as an analytical tool for the explanation of the unfolding and trajectories of contention in the MENA countries.

The following discussion addresses the issue of how regime features play out in contentious politics within a broader context of a state–society framework of relations. Employing this approach offers a more dynamic, nuanced, and intertwined relationship between these two realms and helps us to understand mobilization potential, authorities' responses, and types and modes of social organization and shows why quests for freedom, equality, and responsiveness should be considered especially under authoritarian settings.

State–Society Interface, Regime, and Consolidating Cycles of Contention

As argued previously, focusing solely on popular grievance and discontent is insufficient for explaining the emergence and consolidation of cycles of contention. The analyses of Arab/authoritarian cases in this section's chapters have also pointed to meaningful contributions to the theory. One outstanding contribution stems from a more fluid and dynamic approach to state, regime, and society boundaries and relationships attributed particularly to developing countries.

The contentious politics framework has unquestionably contributed to a more dynamic and interactive analysis and understanding of episodes of cycles of contention by moving beyond the previous movement-centric tendency and "bottom-up" orientation of scholars of social movements. It would be equally accurate to say, however, that a more developed treatment of authorities as proactive actors, both outside and inside social boundaries, as part of a less formalized and prescribed relationship between state and society is still lacking.

Indeed, increasing attention among comparativists to social revolutions outside the West engendered a move away from the structural dichotomy of "state" and "society," with their relative autonomy and capabilities defined in such terms as "weak" and "strong," and led to more hybridic approaches that underline the complex and interconnected relationships between state and society in Third World countries (Migdal 1988; Migdal, Kohli, and Shue 1994; Skocpol 1994). Closely related, research on the transitions to democracy in southern European countries in the mid-1970s and the growth of interest in the origins and processes of revolutionary changes in developing countries brought about an explicit distinction between *states* and *regimes*—though it remained fairly underdeveloped both empirically and theoretically until the early 1990s (Fishman 1990; see also Goodwin and Skocpol 1988, and Skocpol 1994).

Adopting a state–society approach can benefit the study of contentious politics in two meaningful ways. First, examining state–society relations might illustrate the level of dependence or independence of an organization, association, a trade union, or an ethnic community from the state and hence its ability to affect collective action. The significance of existing forms of organized social and political action as potential foci of mobilization thus directly applies to Diani and Moffat's comparison of the Egyptian Trade Union Federation with its Tunisian equivalent. While referring to both organizations as active instruments of mobilization, a closer look into their relations with the state would have identified their different levels of autonomy from the state and better explain their unequal opportunities and constraints (see Pilati's chapter in this volume concerning the Egyptian Trade Union Federation). Additionally, the weakly institutionalized and informal nature of most Arab state–society relationships strongly affect coalition building—a topic that has recently received greater attention. In sociopolitical settings where the lines separating society and state authorities are less clear, state practices and strategies that are meant to inhibit and thwart efforts at coalition building usually go beyond "channeling" mechanisms (e.g., segmentation of policy arenas and/or nonprofit tax status), as recently shown by Obach (2010), to include more obtrusive and duplicitous ones.

The result of long-term state repression of organized social action, as Pilati's chapter shows, is the emergence of informal and local networks as substitutes for formal organizations, thus largely denying the state of its preventive capability in this context. Such informality, marked by small groups, family and neighborhood connections, irregular face-to-face meetings, and mobile telephones, enabled the maintenance of social agency and diffusion of contention despite the government repression. Indeed, long before the Arab revolts, observers pointed to this informal type of social networks as a viable and effective social agency connected to urban unrest and political instability (Denoeux 1993).

Under such circumstances, and reconnecting with Pilati's chapter, it is not unlikely that some groups and organizations present no explicit policy or political agenda precisely because they adapt to a reality in which holding and promoting one would expose them to severe repression. This, however, does not prevent the expansion of contention, once begun by a given social group, into other potential aggrieved groups regardless of whether they share the same grievances and agenda. This, in turn, has clear implications for the effectiveness of popular contention and its ability to function as a coalition rather than a fragmented mass of protesting groups in subsequent processes of transition.

Indeed, the literature is divided over the impact of repression on opposition organizational development and mobilization for protest. It broadly stresses the leading role of organizational structures, such as trade unions, student associations, and political parties as islands of social agency and potential opposition to authoritarian regimes. Under repressive conditions, however, such organizations are susceptible to repeated intrusion, crackdowns, co-optation, and manipulation by the state—as exemplified by the Egyptian Trade Union

Federation—rendering almost impossible a substantial protest mobilization. This, however, could not stop grassroots initiatives of mobilization from gaining momentum through, among other things, adaptation of organizational structure, tactics, and goals.

Second, avoiding reference to the state as a given unit of analysis and investigating its interrelations with other actors and institutions, both formal (e.g., the military, political parties) and informal, enables a more refined understanding of a regime's response to, and maneuverability in the face of, protests and demonstrations. If states are generally conceived as the ultimate autonomous institution within a given territory and population, regimes connote the system of power relationships between ruling elite groups and society. In Third World countries, regimes often represent a system of rule and socioeconomic order led by a narrowly based ruling elite that employs state power to implement its objectives. While each state exercises a particular level of integration and relationship among state organizations within the ruling system, in Third World countries such integration is often poorly formalized, based on shifting alliances between the ruling elites and powerful social actors. In such cases, state organizations such as the military and judiciary may be marginalized and excluded from the regime, and yet they possess the ability to undermine the latter's legitimacy and even survival, especially under conditions of revolt or transition (Fishman 1990), as pointedly demonstrated in the case of Egypt during the 2011–2013 upheavals.

The distinction between state and regime in the context of the more general state–society framework warrants a clearer and more precise examination of the history and the nature of relations between state organizations and society (e.g., the extent of the military's embeddedness in society) and therefore provides useful tools for the analysis of the degree of autonomy maintained by the state. To a considerable extent, these multifaceted, case-specific relationships among state, regime, and society shape the particular responses of authorities to popular contention and, as a consequence, deepen our understanding of transition processes (as discussed in what follows and elaborated in section "The Military—Beyond Issues of Social Control").

Understanding the history and complexity of state–society relations of any given case is indeed necessary for explaining the fundamental diversities among Arab states in their forms of uprisings (or lack thereof), pace, dynamics, and the depth of challenge to the incumbent regime—indeed, how, when, and why Arab authoritarian rulers acted so differently in their response to domestic challenges: How critical were these initial responses to setting the tone and nature of the slogans and messages exchanged between state and society? To what extent were these responses, as well as the dynamics of the revolts, causally linked to state-to-nation ratio? What made "robust" authoritarian regimes, as in Tunisia and Egypt, collapse so quickly despite decades of repression and exclusion of political opponents? The answers to these questions are largely found in the state–society nexus and regime vis-à-vis society capabilities. Indeed, authoritarian regimes may be able to repress their challengers as long as they maintain a stable alliance with key social actors or, alternatively, a coherent administrative and coercive system. Let me elaborate on this point.

Due to poor political legitimacy, insufficient or distorted distribution of public resources, and conflictual, competitive, or partly nonexistent relations with societal actors, a postcolonial state is in fact less autonomous from and more at odds with its society, constituting a "state-in-society" (Migdal 2001, 47–52). In this model, the state is just one of many social players struggling to attain the hegemonic role of shaping a society's loyalties and collective identities and determining the governing norms and rules. State–society interactions thus function as a complex web of cultural and practical exchanges in which social players seek power and prestige amid shifting identities and loyalties. By employing and appropriating symbols and values that resonate with the populace, the state and alternate social agents compete for dominance in shaping the social order, articulating collective consciousness, and establishing a hegemonic structure of authority (Migdal 2001; Chambers 2002, 92–93).

Failing to establish social primacy through a state-led national identity, Arab regimes traditionally sought to entrench hegemony through all-embracing authoritarian rule, inflated bureaucracy, repressive police tactics, and manipulation of identity conflicts. However, because total state domination of deeply rooted identities, ideologies, and social structures is unfeasible, the resulting strategy was to strike a power equation that holds down potential social challengers through a mix of coexistence, co-optation, and coercion. The competition between the state and other social agents, in turn, manifests itself in repeatedly shifting alliances and "fluid loyalties" where social actors, including the state actors and organizations, work together against other social actors to maximize their respective gains (Migdal 1988, 27–28).

These patterns are quite evident in the Arab states that, lacking legitimacy and regularly challenged by strong societal structures-actors, have been labeled "over-stated" and "baseless" (Ayubi 1995, 4; Kelidar 1993, 315–39). Many of the Arab states represent diverse levels of alienation to the region's supranational and religious doctrines (i.e., Arabism and Islam), and even more so to local and primordial identities (e.g., familial, tribal, ethnic, confessional). Similarly, they represented various degrees of regime legitimacy and distance between state and society, which surfaced in many ways in the course of the Arab revolts.

Above all, the Arab revolts underlined the differences among Arab states in their levels of national coherence, institutional development, and state capabilities, all of which had a discernible impact on their response to contention and especially, as will be discussed later, on the politics of transition. Arab states indeed differ from each other in their preindependence history and tradition as politically and territorially integrated entities with centralized authority and collective identity (Harik 1990; Owen 2004). Hence, in Egypt and Tunisia, two states that are marked by long preindependence political history as relatively integrated entities, developed bureaucracy, and institutions, the military and judiciary were instrumental in maintaining a relative level of domestic control and continuous order despite the mass protests. In contrast, in Libya, Syria, and Yemen—traditionally divided along geographic and ethnic lines—the revolts revealed the absence of "statist" concepts of ruler and ruled alike as well as the fragile nature of the state as a self-imposed social and political organization claiming exclusive identity and uncompromising loyalty.

Indeed, even in the most developed and coherent states of Egypt and Tunisia, politics of identity played a significant role. Intrastate and societal divisions along religious (e.g., Muslim-Christian; Sunna–Shi'a), ethnic, regional, tribal, and secular versus Islamist lines were indeed apparent, weakening the overall potential of mobilization to contention. Thus, the deliberate avoidance of the Muslim Brotherhood from participation in the early demonstrations in Egypt—despite strong reasons to protest their political exclusion in the November 2010 parliamentary elections—and mutual alienation between them and the secular groups remained a major source of weakness of the Egyptian popular revolt. It not only divided the potential weight of contention and ability to form and maintain a coalition but also weakened the Islamists' bargaining position in their subsequent "pact making" with the military institution in the post-Mubarak transition process. Similarly, political competition among secular groups in Tunisia enabled the Islamic al-Nahda Party to take the largest number of seats in the National Constituent Assembly in the first postauthoritarian elections of October 2011. These features of the contentious nature of the politics of transition are discussed later.

Politics of identity also dictated the scope and nature of contention in Jordan revealing the ethnonational and socioeconomic cleavages of identity between Palestinian- and East-Bank Jordanians. Constituting a majority of the population, mostly urban and market economy oriented, the Palestinians seemed to have benefited from the government's neoliberal policy. In contrast, this policy hit hard the East-Bank Jordanians, the political backbone of the monarchy, vastly employed in the public sector, security establishment, and the military. As of 2010 East-Bank Jordanians expressed their socioeconomic grievances over insufficient wages of the public sector, rising food prices, working conditions, and corruption, with protests assuming growing scales, frequency, and vehemence against the government and the monarch.

The eruption of mass revolts in Tunisia and Egypt indeed inspired additional discontent led by mixed social and political groups. As in the case of Egypt's Muslim Brotherhood, the Jordanian Islamic opposition—largely identified with the Palestinians—did not join the early protests, apparently to avoid accusations by their East Jordanian counterparts of employing the economic difficulties to undermine the existing political order. In the following months, despite some efforts to mobilize masses to the demonstrations, and though Islamist activists did participate, the Islamist opposition did not play a substantive role and was far from dominating the protest (Vogt 2011). Already the first few weeks of the protests revealed the lack of a unifying framework and leadership capable of organizing the initially spontaneous contention toward an effective reform movement with a common platform. As in previous cases of contention, whenever Jordanian Palestinians' and East Bankers' political grievances could potentially converge over issues such as widespread desire for political reform, the state played on East Bankers' suspicions toward Palestinian political motives. East Bankers' appetite for political liberalization was thus limited by fear of empowering the majority Palestinian population at their expense.

The Arab uprisings also gave prominence to some aspects of regime structure and sustenance in the face of domestic and international challenges, especially the inherent weakness of personalist autocrats, such as Mubarak, Ben 'Ali, Qadhafi, and Salih. The inherent weakness of this type of regime was demonstrated in the rulers' lack of will and ability to reach out to major segments of the population and show interest in the latter's grievances; instead, they engaged in forceful repression, which proved detrimental or costly to the regimes of Tunisia, Egypt, Yemen, Libya, and Syria. It is in this context that the role of the military in contention became a crucial factor in shaping the trajectory of the cycle of contention—indicative of the analytical usefulness of distinguishing between state and regime, as discussed earlier. For example, compared to long-term marginality and scarcely social embeddedness of the military in Libya, the social embeddedness of the military in Egypt was surely an important factor behind the Armed Forces' support of the "people's will." I return later to the role of the military in contentious processes of transition.

Within this context of narrowly based personalized regimes, the attempts to establish dynasty-like systems of succession by Mubarak and Qadhafi, following Assad's precedent, further indicates their disregard of state organizations and focus on safeguarding the continuous survival of the ruling elite. This phenomenon should also draw our attention to the different types of social responses. Mubarak's intention to transfer power to his son Gamal was apparently one of

the reasons that the military leadership withdrew its support of the president
and turned against him shortly after the beginning of the mass demonstrations
(Piopi 1013). Hence, it was the strength and prestige of the military Leviathan
as a symbol of national unity and sovereignty coupled with the image of the son
as the epitome of the corrupt Egyptian elite that eventually prevented Mubarak
from realizing his plan. In the case of Syria, it was the Alawite minority's attempt
to safeguard its existential interests and those of its non-Alawite allies, cronies,
beneficiaries, and clients that dictated the succession of Hafiz al-Assad by his son
Bashar as sine qua non for maintaining the community's exclusive grip on the
reins of power (Tibi 2013, 127–29).

As mentioned previously, regimes' conduct in the course of the revolts primarily represented the cumulative symbolic and material resources as well as the
regime's bases of international support. This factor was quite salient in defining the responses of the poor vis-à-vis rich monarchies (Jordan and Morocco vs.
Saudi Arabia and Kuwait). While the former employed a preemptive approach
by reshuffling governments and promising political reforms, the oil-rich monarchies confronted with substantial contention, as in the Saudi case, repeated the
same strategy applied in previous crises (e.g., 1979 Shi'a riots) namely, pouring
generous funds onto potentially rebellious groups. Bahrain was the exception
among the Gulf oil monarchies. Facing a serious revolt of the Shi'i majority, the
Sunni ruling government entered negotiations with the protesters that ended
with brutal military suppression supported by Saudi forces.

Another set of factors determining regime responses to contention relates
to national coherence, institutional development, and state–society relations.
Evidently, the relatively responsive-preemptive reactions by Jordan (before and
after 2011) and Morocco to the early manifestation of discontent saved these
monarchies from more serious challenges. Contrarily, the almost immediate
use of brutal repressive force by the rulers of Syria, Libya, and to a lesser extent
Yemen, in response to initially nonviolent contention, represented these rulers'
narrow tribal-ethnic political and military basis and conduct according to the
"Hama rule."[7] From these rulers' viewpoint, any civil protest carried an une-
quivocal message of an existential threat to their power and the vital interests
of their families and ethnic or tribal groups, hence their immediate and excessively violent response, which soon deteriorated into total intrastate war (Owen
2012, 180).

To be sure, other factors also played a role in shaping the consolidation of
cycles of contention, such as the traditional/religious legitimacy ascribed to the
monarchs. On the other hand, the quick deterioration of Libya and Syria into
civil war, with clear division along geographical lines in Libya and ethnoreligious lines in Syria, clearly attests not only to poor legitimacy of the rulers and

their failure at, or deliberate avoidance of building national rather than factional coercive organizations, but also to these states' internal fragmentation and low state-to-nation ratio and lack of national integration despite over 60 years of independence.

Processes and Trajectories of Contention

If chapters in the first section of the volume have made the case for the necessary-yet-insufficient attention given to macro/structural preconditions and causes in understanding the emergence and consolidation of cycles of popular contention, contributors to the second section of the volume have made the open-ended and dynamic features of cycles their main focus. Precisely because cycles of popular contention are contingent, interactive, and conjunctural, which means that ideologies, action strategies, and goals of the various parties and actors involved are open to adaptation and negotiation, how cycles end is not a foretold story, and their eventual outcomes cannot be determined beforehand. Illustrating this point is the fact that demonstrators called for the dismissal of the ruler[8] only a few days after demonstrations had begun and in response to the use of indiscriminate violence by the incumbent regime forces (Patel, Bunce, and Wolchik 2014; Lynch 2014a). What this essentially means is that the emergent and open-ended features of cycles hold the promise for the identification of meaningful similarities in processes and trajectories of contention across regime types.

The four chapters in this section point to meaningful similarities between Arab revolts and non-Arab cases of various regime types, based on analysis of several processes and trajectories. Using two central mechanisms from studies of contentious politics—demonstration effects and transnational networks—to explain diffusion of contention, the chapter by Bunce shows how the operation of these mechanisms helps detecting meaningful similarities among three cross-national waves of popular challenges to authoritarian rule: the collapse of communism in 1989, the spread of electoral-based challenges to authoritarian rulers in postcommunist Europe and Eurasia from 1998 to 2005, and the 2011 MENA uprisings. The composite regime of Northern Ireland, deeply divided along ethnic and religious lines, serves Maney's analysis of the challenges posed to authorities by minority and dominant groups in the context of contradicting discourses of rights and democracy, what he labels a "double legitimacy crisis," in developing an analytical framework for comparing the Northern Ireland case with other cases, Arab and non-Arab. Accounting for the differences among Arab and non–Arab cases (e.g., Libya, Syria, Israel-Palestine, and the Ukraine) in terms of opposition groups' success in promoting outside intervention, Alimi and Meyer's chapter makes the case for the importance of examining not only the powers of opposition groups but also the powers of regimes in order to make sense of why repression of popular contention in the Arab revolts *sometimes* promoted international intervention. Finally, comparing the 2011 Egyptian with the 1979 Iranian cycles of contention, the chapter by Rasler builds on the *dynamics of contention* research program as developed by McAdam, Tarrow, and Tilly (2001) and demonstrates how similar mechanisms operated in both cases yet combined differently in driving forward processes of mobilization, coalition formation, and scale shift, and how the combination of these processes suggests a great deal of the outcomes of both cycles.

As with contributions to the first section of the book, contributors to the section on processes and trajectories of cycles of contention were attentive to how the particularities of MENA cases help inform theories of social movements and contentious politics. This attentiveness has yielded several meaningful adjustments and refinements to the theory, namely, how issues of both regional *relational* and *cultural* structures inform our understanding of processes of diffusion (i.e., the spread of a contentious performance, issue, or interpretive frame from one site to another) and externalization (i.e., the vertical projection of domestic claims onto international institutions or foreign actors).[9]

The Structure and Agency of Diffusion and Internationalization

One outstanding aspect of the Arab revolts was their quick travel across borders. Beginning in Tunisia and traveling through Egypt into other parts of the Arab world, the spread of contention was reminiscent of the 1989 demonstrations in East Europe that led to the fall of the Berlin Wall and the "Iron Curtain." The comparison of European and Arab cases of diffusion of mass discontent reveals similar dynamics of the transfer from one site to another of innovative challenges to authoritarian leaders in terms of issues, claims, or repertoires of action, which subsequently held sway across the region.

Much of the diffusion of protest across borders, though not necessarily of the same pattern, participants, and dynamics, can be explained in the context of *regionalism*—a notion connoting certain character traits ascribed to a group of geographically contiguous or proximate states, sharing distinct history, religion, and culture and maintaining relatively intensive interactions among them compared to relations with nonregional actors. Hence, in addition to the mediated and nonmediated agency-based drivers (Givan, Roberts, and Soule 2010), what facilitated the quick diffusion of demonstrations in all three waves further related to relational and cultural structural dimensions, namely the shared regional social and political features and characteristics among states in each region, rendering them a "regional society."

In explaining the dynamics and processes of diffusion of ideas and social and political upheavals across borders, resembling the "domino syndrome" (Mustafa and Hammada 2012, 28–32), theories of contentious politics may benefit from employing the international relations (IR) concept of regions or regionalism. Without underestimating the role of agency, which could be implied once the "domino syndrome" is treated narrowly, it is plausible to suggest that structural features of a given system render one agent more or less salient in projecting the prospects for and possibilities of contention and, therefore, becoming a role-model to emulate, based on either material or nonmaterial characteristics. Although it originally emerged as a medium-level analysis of IR, between the state and the global system (Binder 1958), the regional concept in fact reiterates the intertwinement of domestic and regional political and social factors in shaping regional players' conduct in the international arena. Beyond structural characteristics (national territory, interstate relations, and institutions), comparative regional studies in the early 1970s emphasized the common cultural, social, and historical bonds underpinning a shared sense of regional identity, which tends to increase in response to intrusive actions by nonregional players (Cantori and Spiegel 1970, 4; Falk and Mendlowvitz 1973; Thompson 1973; Feld and Boyd 1980). In the post–Cold War years, scholarship on regionalism further stressed the *socially constructed* nature and shared "regional awareness" of groups of players emanating from common historical experiences and identities (Hurrell 1995, 38–41, 53; Barnett 1995; Press-Bar-Nathan 2005, 283).

Regional state systems thus involve, in addition to the state, also social, economic, and security matters, all of which render national borders permeable and susceptible to cross-national dynamics along the continuum of conflict to interdependence. Regarding MENA, one of the world's defined regional systems, the group of Arab states represents a distinct supranational subregion unified by its Arab-Islamic culture and history (Matar and Hilal 1986; Tripp 1995; Sela 1998; Buzan and Wæver 2004). The diffusion of contention across this region, albeit with state-specific dynamics due to particular state capabilities and regime responses, was further instigated by social and political similarities such as authoritarian regimes, repressed freedoms, corrupt administrations, underdevelopment, and demographic structures (e.g., high percentage of youth) as well as a sense of dependence on non-Arab international actors (Mustafa and Hammada 2012, 31–32). Whether the Arab revolts were domestically based or represented "one revolution of multiple voices," thus representing the "new [type of] Arabism" (Mustafa and Hammada 2012, 34), or instigated the rise of a "new regionalism" (Fawcett 2013, 201–2) is still to be seen. There is, however, little doubt that the swift success of the Tunisian revolt in toppling an established autocrat, and even more so of Egypt's—in view of its pivotal role in the region—coupled by the impact of satellite TV networks and social media, was essential in the diffusion process.

Extrapolating from the national level of cycles of contention and reconnecting with the idea of "early riser" or "initiator" movements in processes of diffusion (McAdam 1995), the idea of regionalism is useful in a twofold manner. First, it provides us with important clues regarding which movement or episode of contention is likely to play the role of initiator (or spin-off—to use McAdam's term) in processes of diffusion and how it becomes a constitutive factor in the operation of both demonstration effects and transnational networks. Second, it points to a meaningful theoretical link between diffusion and structure of political opportunities; a potentially pivotal state may project to other regional states or signal or set in motion identifiable and similar claims, issues, and repertoires in other sites, which essentially means that this state's temporal location in the regional wave may indeed become part of the regional structure of political opportunities (Brockett 1991).

Diffusion, of course, is not the only process or trajectory of cycles of contention that may have cross-border, transnational features. Faced with brute repression, activists often look outside their state and seek to attract international attention in the hope that outside actors and institutions will intervene on their behalf vis-à-vis the local authorities. While attempts of local activists to broaden the scope of the conflict and to externalize their claims are a recurring feature that has been demonstrated convincingly by scholars of social movements and contentious politics in various structures of government and regime types, here too the particularities of the MENA region generated important refinement to models of externalization and international intervention.

Great Power politics and intervention in the Middle East, perhaps more than any other region, is a historical phenomenon manifested from the late eighteenth century to the present (Halliday 2005; Fawcett 2013). Elaborating on the geopolitical calculations behind this phenomenon is beyond the scope and length of this chapter. It would suffice to mention the well-researched and extensively studied structure of power relations between MENA regimes and Western or Eastern powers, characterized as a very tight system of alliance, typically one of asymmetrical mutual dependence. The implications of such structure of power relations are vast, covering various issues and domains, including not only regional/international politics but also domestic politics. Indeed, as shown by Goldstone, a given regime's international contexts of opportunities and constraints is one important factor to be taken into consideration in trying to make sense of the enormous diversity in terms of openings and trajectories of the Arab revolts.

And while the likelihood of international intervention is treated in Goldstone's analysis as one of several "independent variables," Alimi and

Mayer's chapter treats it as a phenomenon to be explained in light of similar and earnest attempts by activists in various Arab countries to mobilize international intervention, with striking differences not only in actual intervention but also in its type. To make sense of the striking differences among the cases of Egypt, Libya, and Syria, the authors make the case for the importance of moving beyond a sole focus on normativist and realist calculations on the part of outside, international actors and institutions and on the advocacy networks of activists operating beyond borders—a phenomenon well developed and conceptualized in Keck and Sikkink's "boomerang model" (1998). A fuller understanding of differences across those three cases is gained by examining the political opportunity structure each regime is nested in and presents dissidents—or relative power as captured by each state's degree of exclusivity (or dependency) and autonomy (or value) vis-à-vis other supranational institutions and authorities. The domestic contention and international intervention linkage discussed in the chapters by Goldstone and Alimi and Mayer further highlight the generation-long debate about the Western-based theory and practice of international humanitarian intervention fostered and exercised in the post–Cold War years.[10] The military interventions by NATO against Qadhafi's regime in Libya and by regional and international powers in Syria and Yemen effectively deepened ethnoreligious cleavages and further undermined already weak state organizations, with long-term disruptive effects on the process of transition in these countries. A reevaluation of international intervention in domestic crises, from public diplomacy to direct military intervention, be it under the banner of democratic ideals or humanitarian concerns, is indeed much needed.

The problematic of international intervention is attested by the intervention in Egypt of the United States and other Western powers and support for a quick transition to participatory democracy with full incorporation of the Muslim Brotherhood into the process, assuming that the latter's political worldview was compatible with the democratic rules of the game. Regardless of the questionable validity of this assumption, the quick transition from authoritarianism to democracy had its open-ended dynamics, implying that the process of transition opens a host of old and new issues and hence remains highly contentious. Practically, and in light of the leaderless and weakly organized non-Islamist groups, the Muslim Brotherhood took advantage of the quick transition to democracy, capitalizing on their vast resources and strong organizational infrastructure.[11]

Contentious Transition

Is it possible to define the starting and ending points of transition in a way that marks it clearly from processes of contention and regime change? Is it a sheer fall of the incumbent regime or the process toward a change of government and/ or reforms? And, is it accurate and analytically beneficial to treat it as a linear process? These questions relate directly to the tendency among scholars of social movements, regimes, and transitions to engage in a kind of a "parallel play."

All cycles of popular contention have some outcomes, which can be affected by authorities' responses to the claims made and which can be unpacked according to their biographical, cultural, and political aspects. Yet, not only is the notion of outcomes ambiguous (i.e., drawing a clear and conclusive link between popular contention and political change in its broad sense, whether such goals were originally intended or unintended by movements) but also some outcomes may take years to be ascertained and assessed (Giugni 2008; Bosi and Uba 2009). As is usually the case, assertions about success or failure are contentious, as they are made by the parties and actors involved; when made by analysts, these assertions are often based on normative judgments (e.g., strides toward democracy). These issues become more complex in cycles of popular contention that are mass-based; involve multiple, often opposing noninstitutional actors; and include claims and issues that are broad, at times systemwide. In these types of cycles of popular contention it is likely that outcomes may take on transitional features that, more often than not, given their societal and systemic consequences and implications are highly contentious and therefore become the bone of ongoing contention.

Consider, for example, the case of the Tunisian transition process—so far the most promising case of all Arab uprisings despite its continued fragility. The Tunisian case of transition is instructive not only because it is one of the more socially coherent and historically developed states in the region but also because an inclusive approach of coalitions and consensus building was consciously adopted by the rival political parties, including an Islamist one. Tunisia successfully enacted a new constitution and established new democratic institutions, with relatively little violence, amid the emergence of a dynamic public sphere. Tunisia became the only Arab country so far where an Islamist party, al-Nahda, assumed power following democratic elections in the spring of 2011 and then gave it up in response to popular demand, paving the road to new parliamentary elections in October 2014, in which the secular party Nida' Tunis won the most votes. Furthermore, the Islamist party accepted the results and participated in a peaceful transfer of power after the presidential race that December (Marzouki 2015).

Notwithstanding this progressive, albeit arduous transition, in the 6th year after toppling Ben 'Ali's authoritarian regime, Tunisia's process of transition is yet to be solidified, with no guarantee for consequent political stability and reinstated domestic security, without which international investments in its economy or resumed tourism would not take off. This lengthy process of transition is of the essence, because the primary reason behind the uprising against the regime was economic. Indeed, by late 2013, the Tunisian currency hit an all-time low, food prices soared, and unemployment reached 16 percent—34 percent among university graduates. The continued deterioration of the economic conditions resulted in a growing public impatience with the lingering betterment of their socioeconomic situation and significant loss of faith in the government expressed by massive demonstrations and fall of the coalition government (Transitions at Crossroads 2013). The economic difficulties were further aggravated by the growing scope of terrorist attacks against the regime, staged from neighboring Libya as well as from within, by Jihadists of both al-Qaeda in the Islamic Maghreb and the Islamic State (11 attacks between December 2014 and July 2015), culminating in the killing of 38 tourists at a seaside resort in June 2015 (Marzouki 2015; Zellin 2015).

Attentive to this and other aspects of the highly contentious nature of transition politics and moving beyond the tendency of scholars of transition to treat social movements more or less as epiphenomenal to a process driven by elite realignment, defection, and contestation, contributions to this section of the volume have built on recent developments in the study of contentious politics to provide a more process-sensitive and nuanced treatment of transition. By focusing on how popular contention shapes and is shaped by transition, chapters in this section have demonstrated both the theoretical and comparative payoffs of paying close analytical attention to the various phases and types of transition (i.e., shift from an established regime—political or economic or a combination of both—designation of a new one, and its operation) and to the role played by both regime incumbents and challengers—internally based and externally based—in driving, impeding, or reverting it altogether.

Such an approach and mode of investigation has paved the way for the identification of revealing similarities between MENA and non-MENA cases. Boudreau's chapter demonstrates the critical role of brokerage in mediating the salience of pre/existing tensions and divergent interests and orientations, both between and within the contending parties, and how this facilitates not only the shift from the contentious stage to political transition but also the shift from one transition phase to another. This line of explanation not only enables Boudreau to identify and make sense of the differences between the cases of Indonesia and the Philippines but also, as Boudreau goes on to show, has applicability and validity that go beyond case/region specificity. Although each case informs which actor can play the role of broker, the focus on brokerage suggests a great deal about the striking difference between the Egyptian experience of transition and that of Tunisia, much like the Southeast Asian cases. Whereas in Egypt (similar to Indonesia) newly empowered brokers were able to build only ephemeral links between different constituencies, and one movement actor in particular (i.e., the Muslim Brotherhood) had no match in terms of size and institutional heft, we saw something quite different in Tunisia and its Southeast Asian counterpart, the Philippines. In both cases, activist collectives were diverse and individually small, with some, most notably the Tunisian General Labor Union and the Tunisian National Order of Lawyers, capitalizing on their preexisting network and playing a critical role in brokering the vast majority of activists and groups into a post-transition arrangement.

Finally, the chapters by Sznajder and Talshir share a focus, first, on dynamics and features of popular contention *in* processes of transition; both chapters demonstrate how popular contention emerged and consolidated in the context of regime-imposed economic transition that deepened structural issues of socioeconomic gaps and their related grievances. Second, both chapters examine tensions and inconsistencies between *economic* and *political* transitions and how they bear on the primary object of claims and discontent (i.e., political authorities or corporations and other carriers of neoliberal policies [Soule 2010; McAdam and Tarrow 2011]). Whether or not we are dealing with an inexorable link between the two realms (and the salience of such a link) and the extent to which it shapes the claims, goals, and issues raised by popular contenders or is shaped by them, is not merely a matter of regime features and characteristics but just as well a matter of emergent features of the contentious politics of transition. Indeed, in contrast to liberal democracies, authoritarian regimes tend to monopolize and centralize the economy or control it through a system of business patronage and cronyism. This, as Sznajder shows about the impact of education's privatization, was the case in the fairly new and limited democracy of Chile as well as in Jordan; in both cases at least initially political authorities were seen as the prime object of claims—a fact that differed from the Israeli experience, where business corporations and moguls were targeted, as shown by Talshir. Yet, as also demonstrated in both chapters, the contentious nature of transition produced outcomes that went beyond regime features and case-specific political configurations of power. The combined influence of internal and external factors—some preexisting, others contingent and newly developing—gave rise to meaningful similarities between the authoritarian MENA and democratic non-MENA countries analyzed in both chapters in terms of the internal dynamics and features of the opposition groups and organizations as well as the goals, issues, and claims made on powerholders.

Similarities aside, there is at least one central aspect in Boudrau's chapter that helps inform the theory of social movements in contentious transition, namely, the role of the military in the process of transition, a recurring feature in the MENA countries.

The Military—Beyond Issues of Social Control

Despite their varied responses, the Arab militaries played a key role in shaping not only the trajectories of the revolts and the fate of the incumbent regimes but also, and no less importantly, the particular path of the transitional process. In Syria the military acted to ensure the survival of the regime despite growing loss of national territory to the rebel groups, underlining its ethnically based nature, while in Libya and Yemen it disintegrated in accordance with tribal, ethnic, or geographic allegiances. In both Egypt and Tunisia the military was central in shaping the trajectory of the popular cycle of contention and its immediate outcomes; in both countries, the military's decision to abandon its traditional role as protector of the regime was highly consequential. The fact that the Egyptian military eventually acted against the Muslim Brotherhood's elected president—despite previous understandings and the support of the military's international benefactors for the transition—offers one of many illustrations in support of this point. The Arab revolts provide ample evidence that speak to the need to think about the military in developing societies in general and the Arab world in particular not only as a symbol of national sovereignty and a body responsible for safeguarding the security and integrity of the state but also in fact as a full-fledged actor that may have vested political and economic interests and indirect connection to issues of power and influence (Cook 2007).

Scholars of social movements and contentious politics have paid only scant attention to the military; when they do, they have tended to treat it as part of the issue of law-and-order, as was the case with the mobilization of the US-based Patriot movement during the 1980s, precipitated, among other things, by the administration's policy of assigning the military to internal, domestic policing tasks (Wright 2007). Other scholars focus on military defection as part of explaining the success or failure of nonviolent revolts against authoritarians, listing numerous factors that are likely to shape security forces defection or loyalty to the regime (Chenoweth and Stephan 2011; Nepstad 2013; Ketchley 2014). Even here, however, there is little attempt to engage in a more process-sensitive approach to transition, one that is able to capture its various modalities, complexities, and inherently contentious features.

Even when the military is not going through a "policing" process, a situation in which the military has neither interest nor involvement in politics and the economy whatsoever, or in which the political–military relations follow the republican model of civilian control over the military in its strictest sense, is rare (Levy 2012). On top of those cases where popular contention centers on issues in which the military, and the security establishment more generally, is inherently involved and directly affected (i.e., popular contention over foreign and security issue domains), the highly precarious, uncertain, and open-ended features of transition make it exceptionally likely for the military to become actively involved.

Instances where the military completely takes over a state are admittedly rare outside the postcolonial states, yet nevertheless possible—a possibility that cannot be fully understood based on sole reliance on interest/value-based or structural types of explanations. Moreover, there are instances, as some of the recent Arab revolts revealed, where the military can play the role of broker. Indeed, the Arab revolts not only provide various examples of the roles military organizations played in response to contention and transition processes but also illustrate how these roles are informed by the military's social composition, relationships with the regime, and capability as potential brokers. Hence, contrary to the socially embedded Egyptian military (and Turkish, for that matter), such capabilities were nonexistent in other cases due to the military's marginal status (Libya) or to its tribally or ethnically based status (Yemen and Syria, respectively).

Thinking about the military as a broker allows for a more processual and continuous analysis of pretransition and post-transition stages and helps make sense of specific pathways processes of transition may end up taking. Recalling Boudreau's analysis, that the military played a key role in Indonesia and Egypt corroborates the literature's argument that regime change is often shaped by strong organizations from within the system rather than by the revolting movements. In Tunisia, where the military adopted a nonintervention policy— practically supporting the constitutional authority established following the flight of Ben ʿAli—and its Southeast Asian counterpart, the Philippines, however, we saw something quite different.

Brokerage, a recurring relational mechanism, may operate in two opposing ways. The first is *exclusionary*, which is about the connection of factions and groups on each side of an "us–them" boundary without establishing new connections across that boundary (i.e., in-group brokerage) (McAdam, Tarrow, and Tilly 2001, 26). The second mode of operation is *inclusionary*, which is about the production of a new connection between previously unconnected or weakly connected sides (i.e., out-group brokerage) (Tilly 2003a, 21). Although structural conditions and other factors—some preexisting, others newly developing, and some exogenous, others endogenous—certainly inform the initial brokerage role the military may take, it is how these conditions and factors gain or lose salience and consequentiality in the context of the specific interactive and relational patterns and practices brokerage generates that suggests a great deal about the pathways transition processes take. To illustrate the point, let us contrast briefly the Egyptian and Tunisian transition processes and the partisan stance the military took in the former case compared to the nonpartisan role the military took in the latter case.

Since the 1952 "Free Officers" coup, the status the military has assumed as the pillar of Egypt's social revolution had been demonstrated not only in deciding the fate of the incumbent regime but also in shaping the political process of transition. In the wake of mounting tension between the military establishment and the autocrat ruler, especially in view of the latter's attempts to bequeath power to his son Gamal, perceived as a threat to the military's autonomy and status, the military institution effectively reassumed the role of the state's caretaker, from toppling Mubarak (February 11, 2011) to the first democratic presidential elections of June 2012. This development coincided with the military's functioning as an exclusionary "in-group" broker, seeking to determine Egypt's transition of power, surprisingly by coalescing with the Muslim Brotherhood—practically recognizing their primary political influence—and marginalizing the unorganized secular groups, which were seen at the time as too revolutionary, hence threatening. Whether the military preferred the Muslim Brotherhood as its political partner due to a Machiavellian calculation aiming at exposing the latter's true totalitarian nature, or sought to follow the familiar pattern of coalition of military regimes with Islamist mass movements as their political base (e.g., Pakistan 1979–1987 and Sudan 1989–2000), is hard to determine. What matters most, and worth noting, is that throughout the process of transition, and even during President Mursi's year in office, both parties remained primarily guided by and committed to their political and economic interests rather than a commitment to ensure the consolidation of a free civilian system of power, and without any serious attempt to develop frameworks of cross-sector dialogue and negotiations that could have had alleviated past (and contemporary) sources of animosity and mistrust (e.g., the secular-religious boundary and the newly developing security threat of Islamist militants in the Sinai Peninsula). From this perspective, there is little wonder why the military took caution and went to such a considerable great length to frame the ultimatum of July 2013 as protecting and realizing the people's will.

Contrary to the Egyptian case, Tunisia's military, though being the most trusted institution, remained relatively small, with no real experience in battle throughout the state's history and never showed inclinations to be involved in politics. Part of the explanation to the relatively less contentious and violent experience of the Tunisian process of transition is found in the inclusionary "out-group" brokerage of the military. Compared to Egypt, the Tunisian military essentially adopted the General Tunisian Labor Union (UGTT) as de facto broker—enabling it to act behind-the-scenes and in a nonpartisan way to encourage and facilitate contacts and dialogues among the various sociopolitical forces. These forthcoming conditions and a military-led integrationist tenor unquestionably contributed to the success of the UGTT in forming consensus with the other actors and parties, agreeing on a new constitution, and setting a timetable for parliamentary and presidential elections amidst continued restlessness and political instability.

A Final Note

The recent wave of Arab revolts has unquestionably engendered two somewhat contradicting scholarly trends. The first one regards a process of reassessment and revision of previous conception of the Arab world as exceptional, one would even say "outside history," and as sharing highly similar features that set it apart from other regions. The enormous diversity among the more than a dozen cases of popular contention has certainly strengthened a trend according to which there is more receptivity and willingness to acknowledge and theorize on those differences and put them in comparative perspective. Yet, as argued in the introductory chapter of this volume, this trend still constitutes a minority and is also limited in its tendency to search for commonalities between MENA and non-MENA states in the impetus to rebel or in outcomes—usually the unfortunate rise to power of antidemocratic Islamist movements.

The second trend regards an idealistic view of the MENA region. The similar street scenes, slogans, and claims made by protesters in Arab and non-Arab countries led Arab scholars to make sweeping optimistic conclusions presenting the revolts as a historical turning point and the beginning of a new era—"end of post-colonialism," "second Arab awakening" (*nahda*), and "new Arabism" (Dawisha 2013; Muasher 2014). According to this vision, the authoritarian state will give way to a new political model of pluralism and democracy through negotiation and adaptation especially concerning the proper role of religion in government.

The editors and contributors of this volume have adopted a more balanced, in-between position, one that argues that similarities between Arab and non-Arab states go well beyond the impetus to rebel, and that spirited generalization regarding a fourth wave of democratization are too premature and offer little if any analytical value given the highly contentious and open-ended feature of any transition process. Recognizing that certain features score higher in Arab countries in particular and authoritarian regimes more generally, we have nonetheless demonstrated how a focus on the dynamics of popular contention, regimes, and transitions as well as their heightened interrelatedness during cycles of contention generates cross-state/regimes similarities. But our appreciation of the unique properties and traits of a given case has also led us to identify and propose several meaningful adjustments to existing theories and models of social movements and contentious politics, as this chapter has fleshed out and discussed.

We cannot close without a final note on the role of Islamist movements. The Arab revolts highlighted what was common knowledge for decades, namely that these movements were the most significant ideological, social, and political force in the Arab countries. The participation of Islamists in transitional processes following regime fall largely revealed their revivalist and militant facets. Notwithstanding Tunisia's exception, in the absence of a strong government and military institution, Islamist militancy became the hallmark of the transitional phase, a powerful legitimizing force behind sectarian and tribal intrastate conflicts as demonstrated in the cases of Libya, Syria, Yemen, and Iraq. Without falling into the trap of "exceptionalism" and essentialism—such as, whether or not Islamism and democracy are compatible—the manifestations of jihadism and intrastate violent conflicts in many of the MENA countries since the Arab revolts present two questions about transition processes in this region. First, keeping in mind that Islam, just like democracy and liberalism, is a system of worldviews, ideas, values, and norms that shapes and is shaped by real life events and developments, rather than being a hermetically isolated textual system, the question thus becomes: can Islamic revivalists, self-perceived emissaries of a single divine and morally superior mission, moderate and adjust to coexistence and equality of all men and women regardless of different religious and nonreligious value systems? Second, is political transition from authoritarianism to genuine participatory political system possible without a radical social transformation of the narrowly based divisions along tribal, ethnic, religious, and regional allegiances into state- and nation-based ones? The answer is found in the intricate, complex, and emergent features of contentious politics.

Acknowledgments

I am deeply indebted to Eitan Alimi for his true partnership and invaluable contribution to this chapter. I am also grateful to the Fritz Thyssen Stiftung whose generous funding of "The Public Political Thought of the Arab Spring" helped in putting this chapter together.

Notes

1. On the debate concerning the functions of urban informal networks, see Denoeux (1993, 13–26).
2. For an example of debating the "personalization of the state" (*shakhsanat al-Dawla*), see Baheyya (pseudonym of an Egyptian female citizen), "A Family Affair," April 26, 2005, http://baheyya.blogspot.com/2005_04_01_archive.html (accessed November 30, 2013).

3. The EU was especially active in its closer "neighbourhood" of south- and east-Mediterranean countries advancing human rights and democracy advocacy groups in addition to sustainable economic development (Aggestam 2008, 1).

4. According to Noueihed and Warren (2012), the highest scope of social media users was in Tunisia and Egypt: 30 and 25 percent of Internet; 17.6 and 5.5 percent of Facebook, respectively. In Libya, Yemen, and other republican states, the scopes of users were far lower.

5. I thank Wael Abu Uqsa for pointing this out to me.

6. For a vivid description of this reality, especially among young graduates, see Amin (2013).

7. Reminiscent of Hafiz al-Assad's 1982 total war in quelling the Muslim Brotherhood's rebellion in the city of Hama at the cost of 10,000–25,000 civilians dead and destruction of part of the city (Friedman 1989, 76–105).

8. Such calls were primarily expressed by the slogans "The people demands the removal of the regime" (*al-sha'b yurid 'isqat al-nizam*) or simply "go out" (*'irhal*).

9. These definitions are borrowed, respectively, from McAdam, Tarrow, and Tilly (2001), and Tarrow (2005).

10. On this debate, see Hoffman (2001). For a review of critical approaches of international intervention see especially Herbst (2001), Lutvak (2001), Talentino (2002), and Fleiz (2005).

11. Tibi (2013, 145–46—quoting Shahin 2012, 58), maintains that the Muslim Brotherhood joined the Tahrir Square demonstrations in a coalition with non-Islamist groups agreeing not to raise their religious slogans and gave assurance neither to field a candidate of their own to the presidency nor to run for more than 35 percent of the parliament seats, which they later squarely violated.

References

Abdalla, Nadine. 2012. "Social Protests in Egypt before and after the 25 January Revolution: Perspectives on the Evolution of their Forms and Features." *The Awakening of the Civil Society in the Mediterranean*. Retrieved from http://www.iemed.org/observatori-en/arees-danalisi/arxius-adjunts/anuari/med.2012/abdalla_en.pdf.

Abdel Hamid, Wael. 2011. "Egypt's Parliamentary Elections—The Roots of a Democracy in Denial." The Center for Voting and Democracy, January 18, 2011.

Abdelrahman, Maha. 2009. "'With the Islamists?—Sometimes. With the State?—Never!' Cooperation between the Left and Islamists in Egypt." *British Journal of Middle Eastern Studies* 36 (1): 37–54.

Abinales, Patricio. 1996. *The Revolution Falters: The Left in Philippine Politics after 1986*. Ithaca, NY: Southeast Asia Program Publications, Cornell University.

Abraham, Margaret, and Gregory M. Maney. 2012. "Transforming Place and Belonging through Action Research, Community Practice, and Public Policy: Comparing Responses to NIMBYism." *Current Sociology* 60 (2): 178–201.

Abraham, Margaret. 1995. "Ethnicity, Gender, and Marital Violence: South Asian Women's Organizations in the United States." *Gender and Society* 9 (4): 450–68.

Aburaiya, Issam. 2004. "The 1996 Split of the Islamic Movement in Israel: Between the Holy Text and Israeli–Palestinian Context." *International Journal of Politics, Culture and Society* 17 (3): 439–55.

Adams, Gerry. 1986. *The Politics of Irish Freedom*. Dingle, Ireland: Brandon Books.

Aday, Sean, Henry Farrell, Marc Lynch, John Sides, and Deen Freelon. 2012. "New Media and Conflict after the Arab Spring." Washington, D.C. United States Institute of Peace 2012. Retrieved from http://www.usip.org/files/resources/PW80.pdf.

Adserà, Alicia, and Carles, Boix. 2007. "Constitutions and Democratic Breakdowns." In *Controlling Governments: Voters, Institutions, and Accountability*, edited by José María Maravall, 247–302. Cambridge: Cambridge University Press.

Afrobarometer Data, Botswana, Ghana, Lesotho, Malawi, Mali, Namibia, Nigeria, South Africa, Tanzania, Uganda, Zambia, Zimbabwe, Cape Verde, Kenya, Mozambique, and Senegal, Round 2, 2002–2003, and Round 3, 2005–2006. Available at http://www.afrobarometer.org.

Akenson, Donald H. 1973. *The United States and Ireland*. Cambridge, MA: Harvard University Press.

Alberoni, Francesco. 1984. *Movement and Institution*. New York: Columbia University Press.

Al-Chaidar, Herdi Saharasad, and M. Fadjroel Rachman. 2000. *Gerakan mahasiswa, rezim tirani & ideologi reformasi*. Jakarta, Indonesia: Madani Press.

Aldaba, Fernando. 2002. "Philippine NGOs and Multistakeholder Partnerships: Three Case Studies." *Voluntas: International Journal of Voluntary and Nonprofit Organizations* 13 (2): 179–92.

Alexander, Christopher. 2000. "Opportunities, Organizations, and Ideas: Islamists and Workers in Tunisia and Algeria." *International Journal of Middle East Studies* 32 (4): 465–90.

Alexander, Christopher. 2010. *Tunisia: Stability and Reform in the Modern Maghreb*. London: Routledge.

Alexander, Jeffrey C. 2011. *Performative Revolution in Egypt: An Essay in Cultural Power*. London: Bloomsbury Academic.

Alfian. 1989. *Muhammadiyah: The Political Behavior of a Muslim Modernist Organization under Dutch Colonialism*. Yogyakarta, Indonesia: Gadjah Mada University Press.

Alimi, Eitan Y. 2007. *Israeli Politics and the First Palestinian Intifada: Political Opportunities, Framing Processes, and Contentious Politics*. London: Routledge.

Alimi, Eitan Y. 2009. "Mobilizing under the Gun: Theorizing Political Opportunity Structure in a Highly Repressive Setting." *Mobilization* 14 (2): 219–37.

Alimi, Eitan Y., Chares Demetriou, and Lorenzo Bosi. 2015. *The Dynamics of Radicalization: A Relational and Comparative Perspective*. New York: Oxford University Press.

Alimi, Eitan Y., and Sivan Hirsch-Hoefler. 2012. "Structure of Political Opportunities and Threats, and Movement-Countermovement Interaction in Segmented Composite Regimes." *Comparative Politics* 44 (3): 331–49.

Almeida, Paul D. 2002. "Los Movimientos Populares contra las Políticas de Austeridad Económica en América Latina entre 1996 y 2001." *Realidad: Revista de Ciencias Sociales y Humanidades* 86 (Marzo–Abril): 177–89.

Almeida, Paul D. 2003. "Opportunity Organizations and Threat-Induced Contention: Protest Waves in Authoritarian Settings." *American Journal of Sociology* 109 (2): 345–400.

Almeida, Paul D. 2008. *Waves of Protest: Popular Struggle in El Salvador, 1925–2005*. Minneapolis: University of Minnesota Press.

Al-Momani, Mohammad. 2011. "The Arab 'Youth Quake': Implications on Democratization and Stability." *Middle East Law and Governance* 3 (1–2): 159–70.

Amar, P. 2011. "Why Mubarak Is Out." *Jadaliyya Magazine* (jadaliyya.com online). February 1, 2011. Retrieved May 17, 2014, from http://www.jadaliyya.com/pages/index/516/why-mubarak-is-out.

Amin, Galal. 2003. *'Asr al-Jamahir al-Ghafira* [Age of the Huge Masses]. Cairo: Dar al-Shuruq (Arabic).

Amin, Galal. 2013. *Whatever Happened to the Egyptian Revolution?* Cairo and New York: American University in Cairo Press.

Anderson, Benedict, and Ruth McVey. 1971. *A Preliminary Analysis of the October 1, 1965, Coup in Indonesia.* Ithaca, NY: Modern Indonesia Project, Cornell University.

Anderson, Christopher J. 2007. "Structures and Voter Behavior." In *Oxford Handbook of Political Behavior*, edited by Russell J. Dalton and Hans-Dieter Klingemann, 589–609. Oxford: Oxford University Press.

Anderson, Lisa. 1987. "The State in the Middle East and North Africa." *Comparative Politics* 20 (1): 1–18.

Anderson, Lisa. 2006. "Searching Where the Light Shines: Studying Democratization in the Middle East." *Annual Review of Political Science* 9: 189–214.

Anderson, Lisa. 2012. "Demystifying the Arab Spring: Parsing the Differences between Tunisia, Egypt, and Libya." *Foreign Affairs* 90 (3): 2–7.

Antiov, Hans, Derick W. Brinkerhoff, and Elke Rapp. 2010. "Civil Society Capacity Building for Democratic Reform: Experience and Lessons from Indonesia." *Voluntas: International Journal of Voluntary and Nonprofit Organizations* 21 (3): 417–39.

Antonius, George. 1938. *The Arab Awakening: The Story of the Arab National Movement.* London: H. Hamilton.

Arce, Moises. 2008. "The Repoliticization of Collective Action after Neoliberalism in Peru." *Latin American Politics and Society* 50 (3): 37–62.

Ardıç, Nurullah. 2012. "Understanding the 'Arab Spring': Justice, Dignity, Religion and International Politics." *Afro Eurasian Studies* 1 (1): 8–52.

Armstrong, Elizabeth A., and Mary Bernstein. 2008. "Culture, Power, and Institutions: A Multi-Institutional Politics Approach to Social Movements." *Sociological Theory* 26 (1): 74–99.

Arthur, Paul. 1974. *The People's Democracy, 1968–1973.* Belfast, Northern Ireland: Blackstaff Press.

Aspinall, Edward. 2005. *Opposing Suharto: Compromise, Resistance, and Regime Change in Indonesia.* Stanford, CA: Stanford University Press.

Atria, Fernando. 2012. *La mala educación.* Santiago, Chile: Catalonia.

Atria, Fernando, Guillermo Larrain, José Miguel Benavente, Javier Couso, and Alfredo Joignant. 2013. *El otro modelo: Del orden neoliberal al régimen de lo público.* Santiago, Chile: Debate.

Ayeb, Habib. 2011. "Social and Political Geography of the Tunisian Revolution: The Alfa Grass Revolution." *Review of African Political Economy* 38 (129): 467–79.

Ayubi, Nazih. 1995. *Over-Stating the Arab State: Politics and Society in the Middle East.* London and New York: I.B. Tauris.

Bach, Daniel C. 2012. "Patrimonialism and Neopatrimonialism: Comparative Receptions and Transcriptions." In *Neopatrimonialism in Africa and Beyond,* edited by Daniel C. Bach and Mamoudou Gazibo, 25–45. New York: Routledge.

Bakary, Tessy D. 1997. "Political Polarization over Governance in Cote d'Ivoire." In *Governance as Conflict Management,* edited by I. William Zartman, 49–94. Washington DC: Brookings Institution Press.

Barany, Zoltan. 2011. "The Role of the Military." *Journal of Democracy* 22 (4): 28–39.

Barker, Rodney. 1990. *Political Legitimacy and the State.* Oxford: Clarendon Press.

Barnes, Samuel H., Barbara G. Farah, and Felix Heunks. 1979. "Personal Dissatisfaction." In *Political Action: Mass Participation in Five Western Democracies,* edited by Samuel H. Barnes and Max Kaase, 381–407. Beverly Hills, CA: Sage.

Barnes, Samuel H., and Max Kaase, eds. 1979. *Political Action: Mass Participation in Five Western Democracies.* Beverly Hills, CA: Sage.

Barth, Fredrik. 1969. *Ethnic Groups and Boundaries: The Social Organization of Cultural Difference.* Boston, MA: Little, Brown and Company.

Bayat, Asef. 1998. "Revolution without Movement, Movement without Revolution: Comparing Islamic Activism in Iran and Egypt." *Society for Comparative Studies in Society and History* 40 (1): 136–69.

Bayat, Asef. 2002. "Activism and Social Development in the Middle East." *International Journal of Middle East Studies* 34 (1): 1–28.

Bayat, Asef. 2005. "Islamism and Social Movement Theory." *Third World Quarterly* 26 (6): 891–908.

Bayat, Asef. 2007. *Making Islam Democratic—Social Movements and the Post-Islamist Turn.* Stanford, CA: Stanford University Press.

Bayat, Asef. 2010. *Life as Politics—How Ordinary People Change the Middle East.* Amsterdam, CA: Amsterdam University Press.

Bayat, Asef. 2010. *Life as Politics: How Ordinary People Change the Middle East.* Stanford, CA: Stanford University Press.

Bayat, Asef. 2012. "Politics in the City-Inside-Out." *City and Society* 24 (2): 110–28.

Beblawi, Hazem. 1987. "The Rentier State in the Arab World." *Arab Studies Quarterly* 9 (4): 383–98

Beetham, David. 2005. "Freedom as the Foundation." In *Assessing the Quality of Democracy,* edited by Larry Diamond and Leonardo Morlino, 32–46. Baltimore, MD: Johns Hopkins University Press.

Beinin, Joel. 2011. "A Workers' Social Movement on the Margin of the Global Neo-Liberal Order, Egypt 2004–2009." In *Social Movements, Mobilization and Contestation in the Middle East and North Africa,* edited by Joel Beinin and Frederic Vairel, 181–201. Stanford, CA: Stanford University Press.

Beinin, Joel. 2011. "Egypt's Workers Rise Up." *The Nation*, March 7/14, 8–9.

Beinin, Joel. 2012. "The Working Class and the Popular Movement in Egypt." In *The Journey to Tahrir: Revolution, Protest, and Social Change in Egypt*, edited by Jeannie Sowers and Chris Toensing, 92–106. London:: Verso Books.

Beinin, Joel, and Frédéric Vairel, eds. 2011. *Social Movements, Mobilization, and Contestation in the Middle East and North Africa*. Stanford, CA: Stanford University Press.

Beinin, Joel, and Frédéric Vairel, eds. 2013. *Social Movements, Mobilization, and Contestation in the Middle East and North Africa*. 2nd edition. Stanford, CA: Stanford University Press.

Beissinger, Mark R. 1998. "Event Analysis in Transitional Societies: Protest Mobilization in the Former Soviet Union." In *Acts of Dissent: New Developments in the Study of Protest*, edited by Dieter Rucht, Ruud Koopmans, and Friedhelm Neidhardt, 284–316. Berlin: Sigma Press.

Beissinger, Mark R. 2002. *Nationalist Mobilization and the Collapse of the Soviet State*. Cambridge: Cambridge University Press.

Beissinger, Mark R. 2011. "Mechanisms of Maidan: The Structure of Contingency in the Making of the Orange Revolution." *Mobilization* 16 (1): 25–43.

Beissinger, Mark R. 2013. "The Semblance of Democratic Revolution: Coalitions in Ukraine's Orange Revolution." *American Political Science Review* 107 (3): 574–92.

Beissinger, Mark R., Amaney Jamal, and Kevin Mazur. 2012. "Who Participates in Democratic Revolutions? A Comparison of the Tunisian and Egyptian Revolutions." Paper presented at the American Political Science Association meeting, August 29–September 2, New Orleans, Louisiana.

Beissinger, Mark R., and Gwendolyn Sasse. 2012. "An End to Societal Patience? The Economic Crisis and Political Protest in Eastern Europe." Oxford: University of Oxford College. Nuffield Working Papers Series in Politics.

Bellei, Cristián, Cristian Cabalín, and Víctor Orellana. 2014. "The 2011 Student Movement against Neoliberal Educational Policies." *Studies in Higher Education* 39 (3): 426–40.

Bellin, Eva R. 2002. *Stalled Democracy: Capital, Labor and the Paradox of State-Sponsored Development*. Ithaca, NY: Cornell University Press.

Bellin, Eva R. 2004. "The Robustness of Authoritarianism in the Middle East: Exceptionalism in Comparative Perspective." *Comparative Politics* 36 (2): 139–57.

Bellin, Eva R. 2012. "The Robustness of Authoritarianism Reconsidered: Lessons of the Arab Spring." *Comparative Politics* 44 (2): 127–49.

Bennani-Chraïbi, Mounia, and Olivier Fillieule, eds. 2003a. *Résistances et protestations dans les sociétés musulmanes*. Paris: Presses de Sciences Po.

Bennani-Chraïbi, Mounia, and Olivier Fillieule. 2003b. "Appel D'air(e)." In *Résistances et protestations dans les sociétés musulmanes*, edited by Mounia Bennani-Chraïbi and Olivier Fillieule, 17–42. Paris: Presses de Sciences Po.

Berins Collier, Ruth, and James Mahoney. 1999. "Adding Collective Action to Collective Outcomes: Labor and Recent Democratization in South America and Southern Europe." In *Transitions to Democracy*, edited by Lisa Anderson, 97–119. New York: Columbia University Press.

Bermeo, Nancy. 2003. *Ordinary People in Extraordinary Times: The Citizenry and the Breakdown of Democracy.* Princeton, NJ: Princeton University Press.

Bhardawaj, Maya. 2012. "Development of Conflict in Arab Spring Libya and Syria: From Revolution to Civil War." *Washington University International Review* 1: 76–96.

Bhuiyan, Serajul I. 2011. "Social Media and Its Effectiveness in the Political Reform Movement in Egypt." *Middle East Media Educator: Research Online* 1 (1): Article 3.

Bicchi, Federica. 2009. "Democracy Assistance in the Mediterranean: An Overview." *Mediterranean Politics* 14 (1): 61–78.

Bishara, Dina. 2012. "The Power of Workers in Egypt's 2011 Uprising." In *Arab Spring in Revolt: Revolution and Beyond*, edited by Babgat Korany and Rabab El-Mahdi, 83–104. Cairo: American University in Cairo Press.

Bishara, Marwan. 2012. *The Invisible Arab: The Promise and Perils of the Arab Revolutions.* New York: Nation Books.

Bob, Clifford. 2005. *The Marketing of Rebellion: Insurgents, Media, and International Activism.* Cambridge: Cambridge University Press.

Bobbio, Norberto. 1996. *Left and Right: The Significance of a Political Distinction.* Chicago: University of Chicago.

Bockman, Johanna, and Gil Eyal. 2002. "Eastern Europe as a Laboratory for Economic Knowledge: The Transnational Roots of Neoliberalism." *American Journal of Sociology* 108 (1): 310–52.

Booth, John A., and Mitchell A. Seligson, eds. 1978. *Political Participation in Latin America. Vol. 1: Citizen and State.* New York: Holmes and Meier.

Bosi, Lorenzo, and Katrin Uba. 2009. "Introduction: The Outcomes of Social Movements." *Mobilization* 14 (4): 409–15.

Boubakri, Amor, and Susanne Lindhal. 2009. *The European Union and Challenges to Democracy Building in the Arab World.* Stockholm, Sweden: International Institute for Democracy and Electoral Assistance.

Boudreau, Vincent. 1996. "Northern Theory, Southern Protest: Opportunity Structure Analysis in Cross-National Perspective." *Mobilization* 1 (2): 175–89.

Boudreau, Vincent. 2001. *Grass Roots and Cadre: In the Protest Movement.* Manila, Philippines: Ateneo de Manila University Press.

Boudreau, Vincent. 2004. *Resisting Dictatorship: Repression and Protest in Southeast Asia.* New York: Cambridge University Press.

Boudreau, Vincent. 2009. "Elections, Repression and Authoritarian Survival in Post-Transition Indonesia and the Philippines." *Pacific Review* 22 (2): 233–53.

Bradley, John R. 2012. *After the Arab Spring: How Islamists Hijacked the Middle East Revolts.* New York: Palgrave.

Brady, Henry E., Sidney Verba, and Kay L. Schlozman. 1995. "Beyond SES: A Resource Model of Political Participation." *American Political Science Review* 89 (2): 271–94.

Bratton, Michael. 2009. "Democratic Attitudes and Political Participation: An Exploratory Comparison across World Regions." Paper presented at the Congress of the International Political Science Association, Santiago de Chile.

Bratton, Michael, E. Gyimah-Boadi, and Robert B. Mattes. 2005. "Afrobarometer Round 3: The Quality of Democracy and Governance in 18 African Countries, 2005–2006." Retrieved February 8, 2011, from http://www.afrobarometer.org.

Bratton, Michael, and Eldred Masunungure. 2006. "Popular Reactions to State Repression: Operation Murambatsvina in Zimbabwe." AfroBarometer Working Paper, 59. Retrieved from http://pdf.usaid.gov/pdf_docs/Pnadg661.pdf.

Bratton, Michael, and Nicholas van de Walle. 1992. "Protest and Political Reform in Africa." *Comparative Politics* 24 (4): 419–42.

Brockett, Charles D. 1991. "The Structure of Political Opportunities and Peasant Mobilization in Central America." *Comparative Politics* 23 (3): 253–74.

Brockett, Charles D. 2005. *Political Movements and Violence in Central America*. Cambridge: Cambridge University Press.

Brooks, Courtney, and Milos Teodorovic. 2011. "Exporting Nonviolent Revolution, from Eastern Europe to the Middle East." *Radio Free Europe/Radio Liberty*, February 21.

Brown, Archie. 1996. *The Gorbachev Factor*. Oxford: Oxford University Press.

Brown, James F. 1991. *Surge to Freedom: The End of Communist Rule in Eastern Europe*. Durham, NC: Duke University Press.

Brownlee, Jason. 2002. "The Decline of Pluralism in Mubarak's Egypt." *Journal of Democracy* 13 (4): 6–14.

Brownlee, Jason, Tarek Masoud, and Andrew Reynolds. 2013. "Why the Modest Harvest?" *Journal of Democracy* 24 (4): 29–44.

Brumberg, Daniel. 2014. "Theories of Transition." In *The Arab Uprisings Explained: New Contentious Politics in the Middle East*, edited by Marc Lynch, 29–53. New York: Columbia University Press.

Brym, Robert, Melissa Godbout, Andreas Hoffbauer, Gabe Menard, and Tony Huiquan Zhang. 2014. "Social Media in the 2011 Egyptian Uprising." *British Journal of Sociology* 65 (2): 266–92.

Buechler, Steven M. 2004. "The Strange Career of Strain and Breakdown Theories of Collection Action." In *Blackwell Companion to Social Movements*, edited by David A. Snow, Sarah A. Soule, and Hans-Peter Kriesi, 47–66. Oxford: Blackwell.

Bunce, Valerie. 1981. *Do New Leaders Make a Difference? Executive Succession and Public Policy under Capitalism and Socialism*. Princeton, NJ: Princeton University Press.

Bunce, Valerie. 1999. *Subversive Institutions: The Design and the Destruction of Socialism and the State*. New York: Cambridge University Press.

Bunce, Valerie. 2012. "The MENA Uprisings in Comparative Perspective: The Transition from One Uprising to Many." Paper presented at the Conference on

"The Revolutions of 2011: One Year On" at the University of Texas at Austin, February 16–19.

Bunce, Valerie. 2014. "Rebellious Citizens and Resilient Authoritarians." In *The New Middle East: Protest and Revolution in the Arab World*, edited by Fawaz Gerges, 446–68. Cambridge: Cambridge University Press.

Bunce, Valerie, and Sharon L. Wolchik. 2011. *Defeating Authoritarian Leaders in Postcommunist Countries*. New York: Cambridge University Press.

Bunce, Valerie, and Sharon L. Wolchik. 2013. "Bringing Down Dictators: Waves of Democratic Change in Communist and Postcommunist Europe and Eurasia." In *Why Communism Didn't Collapse: Regime Resilience in China, Vietnam, Laos and Cuba*, edited by Martin Dimitrov, 123–48. Cambridge: Cambridge University Press.

Buzan, Barry, and Ole Wæver. 2004. *Regions and Powers: The Structure of International Security*. Cambridge: Cambridge University Press.

Cabalin, Cristian. 2012. "Neoliberal Education and Student Movements in Chile: Inequalities and Malaise." *Policy Futures in Education* 10 (2): 219–28.

Cambridge Union Society. 2012. "This House Believes the Arab Spring Is a Threat to Global Stability." *Huffington Post*. Retrieved from http://www.huffington-post.co.uk/the-cambridge-union-society/arab-spring-threat-global-security-this-house-believes_b_1259904.html.

Carapico, Sheila, Lisa Wedeen, and Anna Wuerth. 2002. "The Death and Life of Jarallah Omar." *Middle East Report Online*. Retrieved from http://www.merip.org/mero/mero123102.

Carey, Sabine C. 2009. *Protest, Repression and Political Regimes—An Empirical Analysis of Latin America and Sub-Saharan Africa*. New York: Routledge.

Castells, Manuel. 2012. *Networks of Outrage and Hope. Social Movements in the Internet Age*. Cambridge: Polity.

Chalmers, Douglas A., Carlos A. Vilas, Katherinne Hite, Scotte B. Martin, Kerianne Piester, and Monique Segarra, eds. 1997. *The New Politics of Inequality in Latin America: Rethinking Participation and Representation*. New York: Oxford University Press.

Chambers, Simon. 2002. "A Critical Theory of Civil Society." In *Alternative Conceptions of Civil Society*, edited by Simon Chambers and Will Kymlicka, 90–110. Princeton, NJ: Princeton University Press.

Chandra, Siddarth, and Douglas Kammen. 2002. "Generating Reforms and Reforming Generations: Military Politics in Indonesia's Democratic Transition and Consolidation." *World Politics* 55 (1): 96–136.

Chatham House Meeting Summary. 2012. *Syria: Prospects for Intervention*. Middle East and North Africa Programme, International Law Programme, and International Security Research Department. London, UK.

Chaudhry, Kiren Aziz. 1994. "Economic Liberalization and the Lineages of the Rentier State." *Comparative Politics* 27 (1): 1–25.

Chenoweth, Erica, and Maria J. Stephan. 2011. *Why Civil Resistance Works: The Strategic Logic of Non-Violent Conflict*. New York: Columbia University Press.

Choi, Jungug. 2001. "Philippine Democracies Old and New: Elections, Term Limits, and Party Systems." *Asian Survey* 41 (3): 488–501.

Cinalli, Manlio, and Marco G. Giugni. 2011. "Institutional Opportunities, Discursive Opportunities and the Political Participation of Migrants in European Cities." In *Social Capital, Political Participation and Migration in Europe: Making Multicultural Democracy Work?*, edited by L. Morales and M. G. Giugni, 43–62. New York: Palgrave Macmillan.

Citrin, Jack. 1974. "Comment: The Political Relevance of Trust in Government." *American Political Science Review* 68 (3): 973.

Clark, Janine. 2004a. "Islamist Women in Yemen: Informal Nodes of Activism." In *Islamic Activism: A Social Movement Theory Approach*, edited by Quintan Wiktorowicz, 164–84. Bloomington: Indiana University Press.

Clark, Janine. 2004b. "Social Movement Theory and Patron-Clientelism: Islamic Social Institutions and the Middle Classes in Egypt, Jordan, and Yemen." *Comparative Political Studies* 37 (8): 941–68.

Clark, Janine. 2006. "The Conditions of Islamist Moderation: Unpacking Cross-Ideological Cooperation in Jordan." *International Journal of Middle East Studies* 38 (4): 539–60.

Clark, Janine, and Bassel F. Salloukh. 2013. "Elite Strategies, Civil Society, and Sectarian Identities in Postwar Lebanon." *International Journal of Middle East Studies* 45 (4): 731–49.

Clarke, Killian. 2014. "Unexpected Brokers of Mobilization: Contingency and Networks in the 2011 Egyptian Uprising." *Comparative Politics* 42 (4): 38.

Cole, Juan. 2011. "Egypt's New Left versus the Military Junta." *Social Research* 79 (2): 487–510.

Cole, Juan. 2014. "Putinism in Cairo: The Rise of the Russian Model." Retrieved from http://www.juancole.com/2014/02/putinism-cairo-russian.html.

Coleman, Katharina P. 2007. *International Organisations and Peace Enforcement: The Politics of International Legitimacy*. Cambridge: Cambridge University Press.

Committee for Economic and Social Change. 2012. "Towards Forming a More Israeli Society." Retrieved from http://hidavrut.gov.il 10/5/2013.

Cook, Steven A. 2007. *Ruling but Not Governing: The Military and Political Development in Egypt, Algeria and Turkey*. Baltimore, MD: Johns Hopkins University Press.

Cook, Steven A. 2011. *The Struggle for Egypt: From Nasser to Tahrir Square*. Oxford: Oxford University Press.

"Conflicto estudiantil en (Chile)." Retrieved from http://www.taringa.net/posts/info/15155705/Conflicto-estudiantil-en-Chile.html.

Cordesman, Anthony. 2011. "Rethinking the Arab 'Spring'." Center for Strategic and International Studies, November 8. Retrieved from http://csis.org/files/publication/111102_MENA_Stability_Security.pdf.

Costello, Matthew, J. Craig Jenkins, and Hassan Ali. 2015. "Bread, Justice, or Opportunity? The Determinants of the Arab Awakening Protests." *World Development* 67, 90–100.

Craig, Ann L., and Joe Foweraker, eds. 1990. *Popular Movements and Political Change in Mexico*. Boulder, CO: Lynne Rienner.

Craig, Stephen C., and Michael A. Maggiotto. 1981. "Political Discontent and Political Action." *Journal of Politics* 43 (2): 514–22.

Cunningham, David. 2003. "State Versus Social Movement: FBI Counterintelligence against the New Left." In *States, Parties, and Social Movements*, edited by Jack A. Goldstone, 45–77. Cambridge: Cambridge University Press.

Dabashi, Hamid. 2012. *The Arab Spring: The End of Postcolonialism*. London: Zed Books.

Dagg, Christopher. 2007. "The 2004 Elections in Indonesia: Political Reform and Democratisation." *Asia Pacific Viewpoint* 48 (1): 47–59.

Dahl, Robert A. 1970. *After the Revolution? Authority in a Good Society*. New Haven, CT: Yale University Press.

Dahl, Robert A. 1971. *Polyarchy: Participation and Opposition*. New Haven, CT: Yale University Press.

Dalacoura, Katerina. 2012. "The 2011 Uprisings in the Arab Middle East: Political Change and Geopolitical Implications." *International Affairs* 88 (1): 63–79.

Dalton, Russell J. 1988. *Citizen Politics in Western Democracies: Public Opinion and Political Parties in the United States, Great Britain, West Germany, and France*. Chatham, NJ: Chatham House.

Dalton, Russell J. 2008. *Citizen Politics: Public Opinion and Political Parties in Advanced Industrial Democracies*. Chatham, NJ: Chatham House.

Dalton, Russell J., Alix Van Sickle, and Steven Weldon. 2010. "The Individual-Institutional Nexus of Protest Behaviour." *British Journal of Political Science* 40 (1): 51–73.

Davenport, Christian. 2005. "Repression and mobilization: Insights from Political Science and Sociology." In *Repression and Mobilization*, edited by C. Davenport, H. Johnston, and C. Mueller, vii–xli. Minneapolis: University of Minnesota Press.

Davenport, Christian, Hank Johnston, and Carol Mueller, eds. 2005. *Repression and Mobilization*. Minneapolis: University of Minnesota Press.

David, Assaf. 2010. "The Revolt of Jordan's Military Veterans." *Foreign Policy*, June 16, 2010. http://www.unz.org/Pub/ForeignPolicyWeb-2010jun-00213.

Dawisha, Adeed I. 2013. *The Second Arab Awakening: Revolution, Democracy, and the Islamic Challenge from Tunis to Damascus*. New York: Norton.

De Nardo, James. 1985. *Power in Numbers: The Political Strategy of Protest and Rebellion*. Princeton, NJ: Princeton University Press.

De Vasconcelos, Álvaro, ed. 2011. "The Arab Democratic Wave: How the EU Can Seize the Movement." Paris: European Union Institute for Security Studies Report no. 9.

Della Porta, Donatella. 1995. *Political Violence and the State*. New York: Cambridge University Press.

Della Porta, Donatella. 1996. "Social Movements and the State: Thoughts on the Policing of Protest." In *Comparative Perspectives on Social Movements*, edited by D. McAdam, J. McCarthy, and M. Zald, 62–92. Cambridge: Cambridge University Press.

Della Porta, Donatella, ed. 2009. *Another Europe: Conceptions and Practices of Democracy in the European Social Forums*. London: Routledge.

Della Porta, Donatella. 2012. "Eventful Protest, Global Conflicts: Social Movements in the Reproduction of Protest." In *Contention in Context: Political Opportunities and the Emergence of Protest*, edited by Jeff Goodwin and James M. Jasper, 256–75. Stanford, CA: Stanford University Press.

Della Porta, Donatella. 2014. *Mobilizing for Democracy: Comparing 1989 and 2011*. Oxford: Oxford University Press.

Della Porta, Donatella, and Mario Diani. 2006. *Social Movements: An Introduction*. Malden, MA: Blackwell.

Della Porta, Donatella, Hanspeter Kriesi, and Dieter Rucht, eds. 1999. *Social Movements in A Globalizing World*. London: Macmillan.

Desposato, Scott, and Barbara Norrander. 2009. "The Gender Gap in Latin America: Contextual and Individual Influences on Gender and Political Participation." *British Journal of Political Science* 39 (1): 141–62.

Diamond, Larry. 2002. "Thinking about Hybrid Regimes." *Journal of Democracy* 13 (2): 21–35.

Diamond, Larry, and Leonardo Morlino, eds. 2005. *Assessing the Quality of Democracy*. Baltimore, MD: Johns Hopkins University Press.

Diani, Mario. 1992. "The Concept of Social Movements." *Sociological Review* 40 (1): 1–25.

Diani, Mario. 2009. "The Structural Bases of Protest Events: Multiple Memberships and Networks in the February 15th 2003 Anti-War Demonstrations." *Acta Sociologica* 52 (1): 63–83.

Diani, Mario. 2012. "Modes of Coordination of Collective Action: What Actors in Policy Making?" In *Networks in Social Policy Problems*, edited by Marco Scotti and Balazs Vedres, 101–23. Cambridge: Cambridge University Press.

Diani, Mario. 2013. "Organizational Fields and Social Movement Dynamics." In *The Future of Social Movement Research: Dynamics, Mechanisms, and Processes*, edited by Jacquelien van Stekelenburg, Conny Roggeband, and Bert Klandermans, 145–68. Minneapolis: University of Minnesota Press.

Diani, Mario. 2015. *The Cement of Civil Society: Studying Networks in Localities*. Cambridge: Cambridge University Press.

Diani, Mario, and Maria Kousis. 2014. "The Duality of Claims and Events: The Greek Campaign against the Troika's Memoranda and Austerity 2010–2012." *Mobilization* 19 (4): 387–404.

Diani, Mario, and Doug McAdam. 2003. *Social Movements and Networks: Relational Approaches to Collective Action*. Oxford: Oxford University Press.

Dix, Robert H. 1983. "The Varieties of Revolution." *Comparative Politics* 15 (3): 281–94.

Domber, Gregory F. 2008. "Supporting the Revolution: America, Democracy, and the End of the Cold War in Poland, 1981–1989." Ph.D. dissertation, Department of History, George Washington University, Washington DC.

Donker, Teije Hidde. 2013. "Re-Emerging Islamism in Tunisia: Repositioning Religion in Politics and Society." *Mediterranean Politics* 18 (2): 207–24.

Dooley, Brian. 1998. *Black and Green: Civil Rights Struggles in Northern Ireland and Black America*. London: Pluto.

Dorsey, James M. 2012. "Pitched Battles: The Role of Ultra Soccer Fans in the Arab Spring." *Mobilization* 17 (4): 411–18.

Duboc, Marie. 2011. "Egyptian Leftist Intellectuals' Activism from the Margins: Overcoming the Mobilization/demobilization Dichotomy." In *Social Movements, Mobilization and Contestation in the Middle East and North Africa*, edited by Joel Beinin and Frederic Vairel, 61–80. Stanford, CA: Stanford University Press.

Eaton, Kent. 2003. "Restoration or Transformation? 'Trapos' versus NGOs in the Democratization of the Philippines." *Journal of Asian Studies* 62 (2): 469–96.

Economist. 2008. "The Economist Intelligence Unit's Index of Democracy 2008." Retrieved June 18, 2011, from http://graphics.eiu.com/PDF/Democracy%20 Index%202008.pdf.

Editors. 2000. "Changes in Civil-Military Relations since the Fall of Suharto." *Indonesia* 70: 125–38.

Eggert, Nina, and Katia Pilati. 2014. "Networks and Political Engagement of Migrant Organisations in Five European Cities." *European Journal of Political Research* 53 (4): 858–75.

Einwohner, Rachel L. 2009. "The Need to Know: Cultured Ignorance and Jewish Resistance in the Ghettos of Warsaw, Vilna, and Łódź." *Sociological Quarterly* 50 (3): 407–30.

Eisenstadt, S. N. 1978. *Revolution and the Transformation of Societies: A Comparative Study of Civilizations*. New York: Free Press.

Eldridge, Philip. 1989. *NGOs in Indonesia: Popular Movement or Arm of Government?* Clayton, Victoria, Australia: Centre of Southeast Asian Studies, Monash University.

El-Gobashy, Mona. 2012. "The Praxis of the Egyptian Revolution." In *The Journey to Tahrir: Revolution, Protest, and Social Change in Egypt*, edited by Jeannie Sowers and Chris Toensing, 21–40. London: Verso Books.

Eljahmi, Mohamed. 2006. "Libya and the US: Qadhafi Unrepentant." *Middle East Quarterly* 13 (1): 11–20.

El-Mahdi, Rabab. 2009. "Enough: Egypt's Quest for Democracy." *Comparative Political Studies* 42 (8): 1011–39.

El Sharnoubi, Osman. 2013. "Revolutionary History Relived: The Mahalla Strike of 6 April 2008." *AhramOnline*, 6 April. Retrieved from http://english.ahram.org.eg/NewsContent/1/64/68543/Egypt/Politics-/Revolution-take--The-April--Mahalla-strike-.aspx.

Escobar, Arturo, and Sonia E. Alvarez, eds. 1992. *The Making of Social Movements in Latin America: Identity, Strategy, and Democracy*. Boulder, CO: Westview Press.

Esterkin, Johnathan. 2012. "Why She Needs Politics Now" [in Hebrew]. *Zman Tel Aviv*, November 20, 2012. Retrieved from http://www.nrg.co.il/online/54/ART2/415/838.html.

Evangelista, Matthew. 1999. *Unarmed Forces: Transnational Movements to End the Arms Race*. Ithaca, NY: Cornell University Press.

Ezbawy, Yusery Ahmed. 2012. "The Role of the Youth's New Protest Movements in the January 25th Revolution." *IDS Bulletin* 43 (1): 26–36.

Faris, David. 2009. "The End of the Beginning: The Failure of the April 6th Movement and the Future of Electronic Activism in Egypt." *Arab Media and Society* 9. Retrieved from http://www.arabmediasociety.com/?article=723.

Faris, David M. 2013. *Dissent and Revolution in the Digital Age: Social Media, Blogging and Activism in Egypt*. London: I. B. Tauris.

Fawaz, Mona. 2014. "The Politics of Property in Planning: Hezbollah's Reconstruction of Haret Hreik (Beirut, Lebanon) as Case Study." *International Journal of Urban and Regional Research* 38 (3): 922–34.

Fawcett, Louise. 2013. *International Relations of the Middle East*. 3rd ed. Oxford: Oxford University Press.

Fearon, James, and David Laitin. 2003. "Ethnicity, Insurgency, and Civil War." *American Political Science Review* 97 (1): 75–90.

Fearon, James, and David Laitin. 2004. "Neotrusteeship and the Problem of Weak States." *International Security* 28 (4): 5–43.

Feng, Yi. 1997. "Democracy, Political Stability and Economic Growth." *British Journal of Political Science* 27 (3): 391–418.

Ferree, Myra Marx. 2003. "Resonance and Radicalism: Feminist Framing in the Abortion Debates of the United States and Germany." *American Journal of Sociology* 109 (2): 304–44.

Filali-Ansary, Abdou. 2012. "The Languages of the Arab Revolutions." *Journal of Democracy* 23 (2): 5–18.

Filiu, Jean Pierre. 2011. *The Arab Revolution: Ten Lessons from the Democratic Uprising*. Oxford: Oxford University Press.

Fillieule, Olivier, and Mounia Bennani-Chraïbi. 2003. "Exit, Voice, Loyalty et bien d'autres choses encore." In *Résistances et protestations dans les sociétés musulmanes*, edited by Mounia Bennani-Chraïbi and Olivier Fillieule, 43–126. Paris: Presses de Sciences Po.

Findlay, Trevor. 2002. *The Use of Force in UN Peace Operations*. Stockholm, Sweden, and Oxford: SIPRI and Oxford University Press.

Finkel, Evgeny, and Yitzhak M. Brudny. 2012. "No More Colour! Authoritarian Regimes and Colour Revolutions in Eurasia." *Democratization* 19 (1): 1–14.

Fishman, Robert M. 1990. "Rethinking State and Regime: Southern Europe's Transition to Democracy." *World Politics* 42 (3): 422–40.

Flanigan, Shawn Teresa. 2008. "Nonprofit Service Provision by Insurgent Organizations: The Cases of Hizballah and the Tamil Tigers." *Studies in Conflict and Terrorism* 31 (6): 499–519.

Fleitz, Fredrick. 2002. *Peacekeeping Fiascoes of the 1990s.* London: Praeger.

Fligstein, Neil, and Doug McAdam. 2012. *A Theory of Fields.* New York: Oxford University Press.

Flynn, M. K. 2000. *Ideology, Mobilization and the Nation: The Rise of Irish, Basque and Carlist Nationalist Movements in the Nineteenth and Early Twentieth Centuries.* Basingstoke, Hampshire, England: Palgrave Macmillan.

Foran, John. 1997. "The Comparative-Historical Sociology of Third World Social Revolutions: Why a Few Succeed, Why Most Fail." In *Theorizing Revolutions,* edited by John Foran, 227–67. London: Routledge.

Foran, John. 2005. *Taking Power.* Cambridge: Cambridge University Press.

Forbrig, Joerg, and Pavol Demes, eds. 2007. *Reclaiming Democracy: Civil Society and Electoral Change in Central and Eastern Europe.* Washington, DC: German Marshall Fund.

Forum for Social Justice. 2011. "Document of Demands." Retrieved July 7, 2013, from http://drishot.org.il/?page_id=271.

Freedom House. 2006. "Freedom in the World 2006 Country Subscores." Retrieved June 18, 2011, from http://www.freedomhouse.org/template.cfm?page = 278&year = 2006.

Freedom House. 2012. "Freedom in the World." Retrieved April 2012, from http://www.freedomhouse.org.

Friedman, Thomas L. 1989. *From Beirut to Jerusalem.* New York: Farrar Straus Giroux.

Frisch, Hillel. 2013a. "The Egyptian Army and Egypt's 'Spring'." *Journal of Strategic Studies* 36 (2): 180–204.

Frisch, Hillel. 2013b. "The Role of Armies in the Arab Uprisings: An Introduction." *Journal of Strategic Studies* 36 (2): 177–79.

Fukuyama, Francis. 1995. "Reflections on the End of History, Five Years Later." *History and Theory* 34 (2): 27–43.

Fuster, Morell M. 2012. "Composition of 15M Mobilization in Spain: Free Culture Movement a Layer of 15M Ecosystem Movement." *Social Movement Studies* 11 (3–4): 386–92.

Gamson, William A. 1990. *The Strategy of Social Protest.* 2nd ed. Belmont, CA: Wadsworth.

Gamson, William A., and David S. Meyer. 1996. "Framing Political Opportunity." In *Comparative Perspectives on Social Movements,* edited by Doug McAdam, John D. McCarthy, and Mayer N. Zald, 275–90. Cambridge: Cambridge University Press.

Garretón, Manuel A. 1989. "Popular Mobilization and the Military Regime in Chile: The Complexities of the Invisible Transition." In *Power and Popular Protest: Latin American Social Movements*, edited by Susan Eckstein, 259–77. Berkeley: University of California Press.

Garretón, Manuel A. 2012. *Neoliberalismo corregido y progresismo limitado: Los gobiernos de la Concertación ne Chile 1990–2010*. Santiago, Chile: Arcis.

Gause, F. Gregory, III. 2011. "Why Middle East Studies Missed the Arab Spring: The Myth of Authoritarian Stability." *Foreign Affairs* 90 (4): 81–90.

Geddes, B., J. Wright, and E. Frantz. 2014. "Autocratic Breakdown and Regime Transitions: A New Data Set." *Perspectives on Politics* 12 (2): 313–31.

Geddes, Barbara. 1999. "What Do We Know about Democratization after Twenty Years?" *Annual Review of Political Science* 2: 115–44.

Gelman, A., and J. Hill. 2006. *Data Analysis Using Regression and Multi-level/ Hierarchical Models*. Cambridge: Cambridge University Press.

Gelvin, James L. 2012. *The Arab Uprisings: What Everyone Needs to Know*. Oxford: Oxford University Press.

Gholz, Eugene, Daryl Press, and Harvey Sapolsky. 1997. "Come Home, America: The Strategy of Restraint in the Face of Temptation." *International Security* 21 (4): 5–48.

Ghonim, Wael. 2012. *Revolution 2.0: The Power of the People Is Greater Than the People in Power: A Memoir*. New York: Houghton Mifflin Harcourt.

Giliberti, Luca. 2014. "Bandas latinas en España? Grupos juveniles de origen inmigrante, estigmas y síntomas." *Revista Española de Investigaciones Sociológicas* 148: 61–78.

Gitelman, Zvi. 1974. *The Diffusion of Innovation from Eastern Europe to the Soviet Union*. Beverly Hills, CA: Sage.

Giugni, Marco. 2008. "Political, Biographical, and Cultural Consequences of Social Movements." *Sociology Compass* 2 (5): 1582–600.

Givan, Rebecca K., Kenneth M. Roberts, and Soule, Sarah A. 2010. "Introduction: The Dimensions of Diffusion." In *The Diffusion of Social Movements: Actors, Mechanisms, and Political Effects*, edited by Rebecca K. Givan, Kenneth M. Roberts, and Sarah A. Soule, 1–18. New York: Cambridge University Press.

Glenn, John K., III. 2001. *Framing Democracy: Civil Society and Civic Movements in Eastern Europe*. Stanford, CA: Stanford University Press.

Goldstone, Jack A. 1980. "Theories of Revolution: The Third Generation." *World Politics* 32 (3): 425–53.

Goldstone, Jack A. 1991. *Revolution and Rebellion in the Early Modern World*. Berkeley: University of California Press.

Goldstone, Jack A. 1998. "Social Movements or Revolutions? On the Evolution and Outcomes of Collective Action." In *From Contention to Democracy*, edited by Marco Guigni, Doug McAdam, and Charles Tilly, 125–45. Lanham, MD: Rowman and Littlefield.

Goldstone, Jack A. 2001. "Towards a Fourth Generation of Revolutionary Theory." *Annual Review of Political Science* 4: 139–87.

Goldstone, Jack A. 2003. "Revolutions in Modern Dictatorships." In *Revolutions: Theoretical, Comparative, and Historical Studies*, 3rd ed., 69–75. Independence, KY: Cengage Learning.

Goldstone, Jack A., ed. 2003. *States, Parties, and Social Movements*. Cambridge: Cambridge University Press.

Goldstone, Jack A. 2004. "More Social Movements or Fewer? Beyond Political Opportunity Structures to Relational Fields." *Theory and Society* 33 (3/4): 333–65.

Goldstone, Jack A. 2011. "Understanding the Revolutions of 2011: Weakness and Resilience in Middle Eastern Autocracies." *Foreign Affairs* 90 (3): 8–16.

Goldstone, Jack A. 2014. "Regimes, Resources, and Regional Intervention: Understanding the Openings and Trajectories for Contention in the Middle East and North Africa." Working Manuscript. Fairfax, VA: George Mason University.

Goldstone, Jack A., Robert H. Bates, David L. Epstein, Ted Robert Gurr, Michael B. Lustik, Monty G. Marshall, Jay Ulfelder, and Mark Woodward. 2010. "A Global Model for Forecasting Political Instability." *American Journal of Political Science* 54 (1): 190–208.

Goldstone, Jack A., and C. Tilly. 2001. "Threat (and Opportunity): Popular Action and State Repression in the Dynamics of Contentious Action." In *Silence and Voice in the Study of Contentious Politics*, edited by Ronald R. Aminzade, Jack A. Goldstone, Doug McAdam, Elizabeth J. Perry, William H. Sewell, Jr., Sidney Tarrow, and Charles Tilly, 179–94. Cambridge: Cambridge University Press.

Goodwin Jeff. 1994. "Old Regimes and Revolutions in the Second and Third Worlds: A Comparative Perspective." *Social Science History* 18 (4): 575–604.

Goodwin, Jeff. 1997. "State-Centered Approaches to Social Revolutions: Strengths and Limitations of a Theoretical Tradition." In *Theorizing Revolutions*, edited by John Foran, 11–37. New York and London: Routledge.

Goodwin, Jeff. 2001. *No Other Way Out: States and Revolutionary Movements, 1945–1991*. Cambridge: Cambridge University Press.

Goodwin, Jeff, and James Jasper. 1999. "Caught in a Winding, Snarling Vine: The Structuralist Bias of Political Process Theory." *Sociological Forum* 14 (1): 27–54.

Goodwin, Jeff, and Theda Skocpol. 1989. "Explaining Revolutions in the Contemporary Third World." *Politics and Society* 17 (4): 489–509.

Grand, Stephen R. 2011. "Starting in Egypt: The Fourth Wave of Democratization?" Washington, DC: Brookings Institution. Retrieved from http://www.brookings.edu/opinions/2011/0210_egypt_democracy_grand.aspx.

Gunning, Jeroen, and Ilan Zvi Baron. 2013. *Why Occupy a Square? People, Protests and Movements in the Egyptian Revolution*. London: Hurst.

Gurr, Ted R. 1968. "A Causal Model of Civil Strife: A Comparative Analysis Using New Indices." *American Political Science Review* 62 (4): 1104–24.

Gurr, Ted R. 1970. *Why Men Rebel*. Princeton, NJ: Princeton University Press.

Habermas, Jurgen. 1975. *Legitimation Crisis*. Boston, MA: Beacon Press.

Haddad, Bassam. 2012. "Syria, the Arab Uprisings, and the Political Economy of Authoritarian Resilience." *Interface* 4 (1): 113–30.

Hadiz, Vedi R. 2008. "Understanding Social Trajectories: Structure and Actor in the Democratization Debate." *Pacific Affairs* 81 (4): 527–36.

Hafez, Mohammed M. 2003. *Why Muslims Rebel: Repression and Resistance in the Islamic World.* Boulder, CO: Lynne Rienner.

Haggard, Stephan, and Kaufman, Robert R. 1995. *The Political Economy of Democratic Transitions.* Princeton, NJ: Princeton University Press.

Hagopian, Frances, and Scott P. Mainwaring, eds. 2005. *The Third Wave of Democratization in Latin America: Advances and Setbacks.* New York: Cambridge University Press.

Hale, Henry E. 2013. "Regime Change Cascades: What We Have Learned from the 1848 Revolutions to the 2011 Arab Uprisings." *Annual Review of Political Science* 16: 331–53.

Hamayotsu, Kikue. 2011. "Beyond Faith and Identity: Mobilizing Islamic Youth in a Democratic Indonesia." *Pacific Review* 24 (2): 225–47.

Hamid, Shadi. 2014. *Temptations of Power: Islamists and Illiberal Democracy in a New Middle East.* New York: Oxford University Press.

Hariman Robert. 1995. *Political Style: The Artistry of Power.* Chicago, IL: University of Chicago Press.

Harnischfeger, Johannes. 2003. "The Bakassi Boys: Fighting Crime in Nigeria." *Journal of Modern African Studies* 41 (1): 23–49.

Hassenpour, Navid. 2014. "Media Disruption and Revolutionary Unrest: Evidence from Mubarak's Quasi-Experiment." *Political Communication* 31 (1): 1–24.

Heaney, Michael, and Fabio Rojas. 2008. "Coalition Dissolution, Mobilization, and Network Dynamics in the U.S. Antiwar Movement." *Research in Social Movements, Conflicts and Change* 28: 39–82.

Hegghammer, Thomas 2010. *Jihad in Saudi Arabia.* New York: Cambridge University Press.

Herbst, Jeffrey. 2004. "Let Them Fail: State Failure in Theory and Practice: Implications for Policy." In *When States Fail: Causes and Consequences*, edited by Robert Rotberg, 302–18. Princeton, NJ: Princeton University Press.

Hess, David, and Brian Martin. 2006. "Repression, Backfire, and the Theory of Transformative Events." *Mobilization* 11 (1): 249–67.

Heydemann, Steven, and Reinoud Leenders, eds. 2013. *Middle East Authoritarianism.* Stanford, CA: Stanford University Press.

Heydemann, Steven. 2007. "Social Pacts and Persistence of Authoritarianism in the Middle East." In *Debating Arab Authoritarianism: Dynamics of Durability in Non-Democratic Regimes*, edited by Oliver Schlumberger, 31–38. Stanford, CA: Stanford University Press.

Hirschman, Albert. 1970. *Exit, Voice and Loyalty: Responses to Decline in Firms, Organizations and States.* Cambridge, MA: Harvard University Press.

Hoffman, Stanley. 2001. "The Debate about Intervention." In *Turbulent Peace*, edited by Chester Crocker, Fen O. Hampson, and Pamela Aall, 273–84. Washington, DC: United States Institute of Peace.

Holden, William. 2009. "Ashes from the Phoenix: State Terrorism and the Party-List Groups in the Philippines." *Contemporary Politics* 15 (4): 377–93.

Holmes, Amy Austin. 2012. "There Are Weeks When Decades Happen: Structure and Strategy in the Egyptian Revolution." *Mobilization* 17 (4): 391–410.

Horovitz, Dan, and Moshe Lissak. 1989. *Trouble in Utopia: The Overburdened Polity of Israel*. Albany, NY: State University of New York Press.

Howard, Lise Morje. 2012. "The Ethnocracy Trap." *Journal of Democracy* 23 (4): 155–69.

Howard, Philip N., Aiden Duffy, Deen Freelon, Muzammil Hussain, Will Mari, and Marwa Mazaid. 2011. "Opening Closed Regimes: What Was the Role of Social Media during the Arab Spring?" SSRN Scholarly Papers ID 2595096. Rochester, NY: Social Science Research Network. Available at http://papers.ssrn.com/abstract=2595096.

Howard, Philip N., and Muzammil M. Hussain. 2011. "The Role of Digital Media." *Journal of Democracy* 22 (3): 35–48.

Howard, Philip N., and Muzammil M. Hussain. 2013. *Democracy's Fourth Wave: Digital Media and the Arab Spring*. Oxford: Oxford University Press.

Human Rights Watch. 2012. *World Report—Events of 2011*. New York: Seven Stories Press. Retrieved from https://www.hrw.org/sites/default/files/reports/wr2012.pdf.

Hunter, Helen-Louise. 2007. *Sukarno and the Indonesian Coup: The Untold Story*. Westport, CT: Praeger Security International.

Hunter, Wendy. 1998. "Negotiating Civil-Military Relations in Post-Authoritarian Argentina and Chile." *International Studies Quarterly* 42 (2): 295.

Huntington, Samuel. 1991. *The Third Wave of Democratization in the Late Twentieth Century*. Norman: University of Oklahoma.

Hurrell, Andrew. 1995. "Regionalism in Theoretical Perspective." In *Regionalism in World Politics*, edited by Louise Fawcett and Andrew Hurrell, 37–73. Oxford: Oxford University Press.

Ibrahim, Saad Eddin. 2010. "Maghza al-Iktisah Ghair al-Masbuq lil-Hizb al-Watani" [The Significance of the Unprecedented Sweeping of the National Party]. *al-Misri al-Yawm*, December 11, 2010. Retrieved from http://www.almasryalyoum.com/node/268327 (Arabic).

Idle, Nadia, and Alex Nunns, eds. 2011. *Tweets from Tahrir: Egypt's Revolution as It Unfolded, in the Words of the People Who Made It*. New York: OR Books.

Ikelegbe, Augustine. 2001. "Civil Society, Oil and Conflict in the Niger Delta Region of Nigeria: Ramifications of Civil Society for a Regional Resource Struggle." *Journal of Modern African Studies* 39 (3): 437–69.

"Index Mundi". 2012. "Yemen Economy Profile 2012." Retrieved from http://www.indexmundi.com/yemen/economy_profile.html.

Inglehart, Ronald. 1979. "Political Action: The Impact of Values, Cognitive Level and Social Background." In *Political Action: Mass Participation in Five Western Democracies*, edited by Samuel H. Barnes and Max Kaase, 343–80. Beverly Hills, CA: Sage.

Inglehart, Ronald. 1990. *Culture Shift in Advanced Industrial Society*. Princeton, NJ: Princeton University Press.

International Crisis Group. 2011. *Popular Protest in North Africa and the Middle East (I): Egypt Victorious?* Crisis Group Middle East/North Africa Report No.101, February 24, 2011. Retrieved May 17, 2014, from http://www.crisisgroup.org/en/publication-type/reports.aspx?year=2011&page=8.

International Crisis Group. 2011. "Popular Protests in North Africa and the Middle East (IV): Tunisia's Way." *Middle East/North Africa Report 106*. Retrieved from http://www.merip.org/mero/mero123102.

International Institute for Strategic Studies. 2012. "Russia's Syrian Stance: Principled Self-Interest." *Strategic Comments* 18 (7): 1–3.

International Labour Office (ILO). 2009. "Truth, Reconciliation and Justice in Zimbabwe." International Labour Office. Retrieved from http://www.ilo.org/wcmsp5/groups/public/---ed_norm/---relconf/documents/meetingdocument/wcms_123293.pdf.

International Labour Office (ILO) and ITUC. 2012. "Nigeria—The State of Trade Unionism and Industrial Relations Practice in Export Processing Zones." International Labour Organization. Retrieved from http://www.ituc-csi.org/IMG/pdf/epz_nigeria.pdf.

Ishani, Maryam. 2011. "The Hopeful Network." *Foreign Policy*. February 7. Retrieved from http://www.foreignpolicy.com/articles/2011/02/07/the_hopeful_network.

Itani, Faysal. 2013. "Stability through Change: Toward a New Political Economy in Jordan." *Atlantic Council*, December 2013: 1–6. Retrieved from http://www.atlanticcouncil.org/publications/issue_briefs/stability_through_change_toward_a_new_political_economy_in_jordan.pdf.

Jamal, Amaney A. 2006. *Barriers to Democracy: The Other Side of Social Capital in Palestine and the Arab World*. Princeton, NJ: Princeton University Press.

Jasper, James M. 2004. "A Strategic Approach to Collective Action: Looking for Agency in Social Movement Choices." *Mobilization* 9 (1): 1–16.

Jasper, James M., and Jane D. Poulsen. 1995. "Recruiting Strangers and Friends: Moral Shocks and Social Networks in Animal Rights and Anti-Nuclear Protests." *Social Problems* 42 (4): 493–512.

Jenkins, Philip. 2006. *Decade of Nightmares: The End of the Sixties and the Making of Eighties America*. New York: Oxford University Press.

Jensen, Jon 2011. "Behind Egypt's Revolution: Youth and the Internet." *Global Post Special Report on the Arab Awakening*. February 13, 2011. Retrieved May 17, 2014, at http://www.globalpost.com/dispatch/egypt/110213/social-media-youth-egypt-revolution.

Johnston, Hank. 2014. *What is a Social Movement?* Cambridge, UK: Polity Press.

Johnston, Hank, and Paul Almeida, eds. 2006 *Latin American Social Movements: Globalization, Democratization, and Transnational Networks.* Lanham, MD: Rowman & Littlefield.

Johnston, T. 2011. *What's Old Is New Again: Social Media, Protests and the Enduring Role of Civil Society.* Unpublished paper. Retrieved May 17, 2014, from http://site-maker.umich.edu/comparative.speaker.series/files/cpw.2011.10.7.johnston.pdf.

Jones, Gregg. 1989. *Red Revolution: Inside the Philippine Guerrilla Movement.* Boulder, CO: Westview Press.

Joppke, Christian. 1995. *East German Dissidents and the Revolution of 1989: Social Movement in a Leninist Regime.* New York: New York University Press.

Kaase, Max, and Kenneth Newton. 1995. *Beliefs in Government.* Oxford: Oxford University Press.

Kadivar, Mohammad Ali. 2013. "Perception Profiles, and Alliances in the Iranian Reform Movement, 1997–2005," *American Sociological Review* 78 (6): 1063–86.

Kamete, Amin Y. 2009. "'For Enhanced Civic Participation in Local Governance': Calling Tyranny to Account in Harare." *Environment and Urbanization* 21 (1): 59–75.

Kamete, Amin Y. 2010. "Defending Illicit Livelihoods: Youth Resistance in Harare's Contested Spaces." *International Journal of Urban and Regional Research* 34 (1): 55–75.

Kandil, Hazem. 2011. "Interview: Revolt In Egypt." *New Left Review* 68 (March–April): 17–55.

Kandil, Hazem. 2012. *Soldiers, Spies and Statesmen: Egypt's Road to Revolt.* New York: Verso.

Kaplan, Robert. 2011. "One Small Revolution." *New York Times*, January 23, p. 11.

Kashiam, Mustafa Abdalla A. 2012. "The Italian Role in the Libyan Spring Revolution: Is It a Shift from Soft to Hard Power?" *Contemporary Arab Affairs* 5 (4): 556–57.

Kaufmann, Daniel, Aart Kraay, and Massimo Mastruzzi. 2009. "Governance Matters VIII: Aggregate and Individual Governance Indicators for 1996–2008." World Bank Policy Research Paper No. 4978, Washington D.C.: World Bank.

Keck, Margaret E., and Kathryn Sikkink. 1998. *Activists beyond Borders: Advocacy Networks in International Politics.* Ithaca, NY: Cornell University Press.

Kelidar, Abbas. 1993. "States without Foundations: The Political Evolution of State and Society in the Arab East." *Journal of Contemporary History* 28 (2): 315–39.

Kenig, Ofer, and Anna Kneplmann. 2013. "De'ikhat ha-Miflagot ha-Gdolot: Israel be-Mabat Hashva'ati" [The Decline of the Big Parties: Israel in a Comparative Perspective]. In Tikkun Shitat ha-Mimshal be-Israel [Reforming Israel's Political System], edited by Gideon Rahat, Shlomit Barnea, Chen Friedberg, and Ofer Kenig, 145–183. Jerusalem: Israel Democracy Institute and 'Am 'Oved (Hebrew).

Kennedy, Ryan. 2010. "The Contradiction of Modernization: A Conditional Model of Endogenous Democratization." *Journal of Politics* 72 (3): 785–98.

Kenney, P. 2002. *Carnival of Revolution: Central Europe, 1989.* Princeton, NJ: Princeton University Press.

Keohane, Robert O., and Joseph S. Nye, eds. 1973. *Transnational Relations and World Politics*. Cambridge, MA: Harvard University Press.

Kerton, Sarah. 2012. "Tahrir, Here? The Influence of the Arab Uprisings on the Emergence of Occupy." *Social Movement Studies* 11 (3–4): 302–8.

Ketchley, Neil, 2014, "The army and the people are one hand!" Fraternization and the 25th January Egyptian Revolution. *Comparative Studies in Society and History* 56 (1): 155-86.

Khamis, Sahar, and Katherine Vaugh. 2011. "Cyberactivism in the Egyptian Revolution: How Civic Engagement and Citizen Journalism Tilted the Balance." *Arab Media and Society* 14 (Summer). Retrieved April 25, 2014, from http://www.arabmediasociety.com/?article=769.

Khawaja, M. 1993. "Repression and Popular Collective Action: Evidence from the West Bank." *Sociological Forum* 18 (1): 47–71.

King, Stephen J. 2009. *The New Authoritarianism in the Middle East and North Africa*. Bloomington: Indiana University Press.

Kitschelt, Herbert. 1986. "Political Opportunity Structures and Political Protest: Anti-Nuclear Movements in Four Democracies." *British Journal of Political Science* 16 (1): 57–85.

Knights, Michael. 2013. "The Military Role in Yemen's Protests: Civil-Military Relations in the Tribal Republic." *Journal of Strategic Studies* 36 (2): 261–88.

Koesel, Karrie, and Valerie Bunce. 2013. "Diffusion-Proofing: Chinese and Russian Responses to the Color Revolutions and the Arab Uprisings." *Perspectives on Politics* 11 (3): 753–68.

Koopmans, Ruud. 2004. "Protest in Time and Space: The Evolution of Waves of Contention." In *The Blackwell Companion to Social Movements*, edited by David A. Snow, Sarah A. Soule, and Hanspeter Kriesi, 19–46. Malden, MA: Blackwell.

Koopmans, Ruud, and Paul Statham. 1999. "Ethnic and Civic Conceptions of Nationhood and the Differential Success of the Extreme Right in Germany and Italy." In *How Social Movements Matter*, edited by Marco Giugni, Doug McAdam, and Charles Tilly, 225-51. Minneapolis: University of Minnesota Press.

Kousis, Maria. 2012. "Greek Protests against Austerity Measures: A Relational Approach." Paper for Session LOC03: Political Systems Crisis of Legitimacy, 22nd World Congress of the International Political Science Association, "Reshaping Power, Shifting Boundaries," July 8-12, Madrid, Spain.

Kriesi, Hanspeter. 2004. "Political Context and Opportunity." In *The Blackwell Companion to Social Movements*, edited by David Snow, Sarah Soule, and Hanspeter Kriesi, 67–90. Malden, MA: Blackwell.

Kriesi, Hanspeter. 2011. "The Political Consequences of the Financial and Economic Crisis in Europe: Electoral Punishment and Popular Protest." *Swiss Political Science Review* 18 (4): 518–522.

Kriesi, Hanspeter, Edgar Grande, Martin Dolezal, Marc Helbling, Dominic Hoeglinger, Swen Hutter, and Bruno Wuest. 2012. *Political Conflict in Western Europe*. Cambridge: Cambridge University Press.

Kriesi, Hanspeter, Rudd Koopmans, Jan W. Duyvendak, and Marco Giugni. 1995. *New Social Movements in Western Europe: A Comparative Analysis*. Minneapolis: University of Minnesota Press.

Kriesi, Hanspeter, and Anders Westholm. 2007. "Small-Scale Democracy: The Determinants of Action." In *Citizenship and Involvement in European Democracies: A Comparative Analysis*, edited by Jan W. Van Deth, José R. Montero, and Anders Westholm, 255–79. London and New York: Routledge.

Kurtoglu Eskisar, Gul M., and Sherrill Stroschein. 2009. "Moderating Effects of Patronage in the Middle East and Eastern Europe." SSRN Scholarly Paper ID 1449061. Rochester, NY: Social Science Research Network. Retrieved from http://papers.ssrn.com/abstract=1449061.

Kurzman, Charles. 1994. "A Dynamic View of Resources: Evidence from the Iranian Revolution." *Research in Social Movements, Conflicts, and Change* 17: 53–84.

Kurzman, Charles. 1996. "Structural Opportunity and Perceived Opportunity in Social-Movement Theory: The Iranian Revolution." *American Sociological Review* 61 (1): 153–70.

Kurzman, Charles. 2003. "Une Déploration Pour Moustafa. Les Bases Quotidiennes de L'activisme Politique." In *Résistances et protestations dans les sociétés musulmanes*, edited by Mounia Bennani-Chraïbi and Olivier Fillieule, 177–96. Paris: Presses de Sciences Po.

Kurzman, Charles. 2004a. *The Unthinkable Revolution in Iran*. Cambridge, MA: Harvard University Press.

Kurzman, Charles. 2004b. "Conclusion: Social Movement Theory and Islamic Studies." In *Islamic Activism: A Social Movement Theory Approach*, edited by Quintan Wikrorowicz, 289–303. Bloomington: Indiana University Press.

Kurzman, Charles. 2012. "The Arab Spring Uncoiled," *Mobilization* 17 (4): 377–90.

Lagi, Marco, Karla Z. Bertrand, and Yaneer Bar-Yam. 2011. "The Food Crises and Political Instability in North Africa and the Middle East." Working paper. Cambridge, MA: New England Complex Systems Institute.

Lapavitsas, Costas, Annina Kaltenbrunner, Duncan Lindo, J. Michell, Juan Pablo Painceira, Eugenia Pires, Jeff Powell, Alexis Stenfors, and Nuno Teles. 2010. "Eurozone Crisis: Beggar Thyself and Thy Neighbour." *Journal of Balkan and Near Eastern Studies* 12 (4): 321–72.

Latinobarometro Corporation. 2009. "Latinobarometro Serie de Tiempo 1995–2009." Version 2005-07-21. Available at http://hdl.handle.net/1902.29/10528.

Layton, Azza Salama. 2000. *International Politics and Civil Rights Policies in the United States, 1941–1960*. Cambridge: Cambridge University Press.

Leef, Dafni. 2011. Speech, July 23, 2011. Retrieved from http://www.youtube.com/watch?v=HNzmKcAqakg.

Leenders, Reinoud. 2012. "Collective Action and Mobilization in Dar'a: An Anatomy of the Onset of Syria's Popular Uprising." *Mobilization* 17 (4): 419–34.

Levitsky, Steven, and Lucan A. Way. 2010. *Competitive Authoritarianism: The Origins and Evolution of Hybrid Regimes in the Post–Cold War Era.* Cambridge: Cambridge University Press.

Levy, Yagil. 2012. *Israel's Death Hierarchy: Casualty Aversion in a Militarized Democracy.* New York: New York University Press.

Lichbach, Mark I., and Ted R. Gurr. 1981. "The Conflict Process: A Formal Model." *Journal of Conflict Resolution* 25 (1): 3–29.

Linz, Juan J. 2000. *Totalitarian and Authoritarian Regimes.* Boulder and London: Lynne Reinner.

Linz, Juan J., and Alfred Stepan. 1996. *Problems of Democratic Transition and Consolidation.* Baltimore, MD: Johns Hopkins University Press.

Lipset, Symor, and Stein Rokkan. 1967. *Party Systems and Voters Alignments.* New York: Free Press.

Lipsky, Michael. 1968. "Protest as a Political Resource." *American Political Science Review* 62 (4): 1144–58.

Lotan, Gilad, Erhardt Graeff, Mike Ananny, Devin Gaffney, Ian Pearce, and Danah Boyd. 2011. "The Revolutions Were Tweeted: Information Flows during the 2011 Tunisian and Egyptian Revolutions." *International Journal of Communication* 5: 1375–405.

Luders, Joseph E. 2010. *The Civil Rights Movement and the Logic of Social Change.* Cambridge: Cambridge University Press.

Luttwak, Edward. 2001. "The Curse of Inconclusive Intervention." In *Turbulent Peace*, edited by Chester Crocker, Fen O. Hampson, and Pamela Aall, 229–48. Washington, DC: United States Institute of Peace.

Lynch, Marc. 2011. "After Egypt: The Limits and Promise of On-Line Challenges in the Authoritarian Arab States." *Perspectives on Politics* 9 (2): 301–18.

Lynch, Marc. 2012. *The Arab Uprising.* New York: Public Affairs.

Lynch, Marc. 2014a. "Introduction." In *The Arab Uprisings Explained: New Contentious Politics in the Middle East*, edited by Marc Lynch, 1–28. New York: Columbia University Press.

Lynch, Mark, ed. 2014. *The Arab Uprisings Explained: New Contentious Politics in the Middle East.* New York: Columbia University Press.

MacFarlane, Neil S., and Thomas Weiss. 2000. "Political Interest and Humanitarian Action." *Security Studies* 10 (1): 112–42.

Magadia, Jose J. 2003. *State Society Dynamics: Policymaking in a Restored Democracy.* Quezon City, Philippines: Ateneo de Manila University Press.

Magen, Zvi. 2012. "Russia ba-Mizrah ha-Tikhon - Mediniyut be-Mivhan" [Russia and the Middle East: Policy Challenged]. Memorandum, No. 118, Tel Aviv University: The Institute for National Security Studies (Hebrew).

Mainwaring, Scott, and Anibal Perez-Linan. 2005. "Why Regions of the World Are Important: Regional Specificities and Region-Wide Diffusion of

Democracy." Kellogg Institute, University of Notre Dame, Working Paper 322, October.

Mainwaring, Scott, and Anibal Perez-Linan. 2014. *Democracies and Dictatorships in Latin America: Emergence, Survival and Fall.* Cambridge: Cambridge University Press.

Majol, Alberto. 2012. *El derrumbe del modelo: La crisis de la economía de mercado en el Chile Contemporáneo.* Santiago, Chile: LOM.

Majol, Alberto. 2013. *No al lucro: De la crisis del modelo a la nueva era política.* Santiago, Chile: Debate.

Maney, Gregory M. 2000. "Transnational Mobilization and Civil Rights in Northern Ireland." *Social Problems* 47 (2): 153–79.

Maney, Gregory M. 2007. "From Civil War to Civil Rights and Back Again: The Interrelation of Rebellion and Protest in Northern Ireland, 1955–1972." *Research in Social Movements, Conflicts and Change* 27: 3–35.

Maney, Gregory M. 2012. "Agreeing for Different Reasons: Ideology, Strategic Differences, and Coalition Dynamics in the Northern Ireland Civil Rights Movement." In *Strategies for Social Change,* edited by Gregory Maney, Rachel Kutz-Flamenbaum, Deana Rohlinger, and Jeff Goodwin, 170–96. Minneapolis: University of Minnesota Press.

Maney, Gregory M., and Margaret Abraham. 2008/2009. "Whose Backyard? Boundary Making in NIMBY Opposition to Immigrant Services." *Social Justice* 35 (4): 66–82.

Mann, Michael. 1984. "The Autonomous Power of the State: Its Origins, Mechanisms and Results." *European Journal of Sociology* 25 (2): 185–213.

Mann, Michael. 1986. *The Sources of Social Power. Vol. I: From the Beginning to 1760 AD; Vol. II: The Rise of Classes and Nation-States, 1760–1914.* Cambridge: Cambridge University Press.

Maoz, Zeev. 2011. *Networks of Nations: The Evolution, Structure, and Impact of International Networks, 1816–2001.* Cambridge: Cambridge University Press.

Marsh, Alan, and Max Kaase. 1979. "Measuring Political Action." In *Political Action: Mass Participation in Five Western Democracies,* edited by Samuel H. Barnes and Max Kaase, 57–97. Beverly Hills, CA: Sage.

Martin, Megan. 2012. "The Arab Spring: Youth, Freedom, and the Tools of Technology." *Al Arabiya,* April 6. Available at: http://english.alarabiya.net/views/2012/04/06/205837.html.

Marx, Anthony. 2005. *Faith in Nation: Exclusionary Origins of Nationalism.* Oxford: Oxford University Press.

Marzouki, Nadia. 2015. "Tunisia's Rotten Compromise." *Middle East Research and Information Project.* July 10, 2015. Retrieved from http://www.merip.org/mero/mero071015.

Matar, Jamil, and ʿAli al-Din Hilal. 1986. *Al-Nizam al-Iqlimi al-ʿArabi: Dirasa fi al-ʿAlaqat al-Siyasiyya al-ʿArabiyya* [The Arab Regional Order: A Study of the Political Arab Relations]. Beirut: Markaz Dirasat al-Wahda al-ʿArabiyya (Arabic).

McAdam, Doug. 1982. *Political Process and the Development of Black Insurgence, 1930–1970*. Chicago, IL: University of Chicago Press.

McAdam, Doug. 1993. "The Cross National Diffusion of Movement Ideas." *Annals of the American Academy of Political and Social Sciences* 528, Citizens, Protest, and Democracy: 56–74.

McAdam, Doug. 1996. "Conceptual Origins, Current Problems, Future Directions." In *Comparative Perspectives on Social Movements: Political Opportunities, Mobilizing Structures and Cultural Framings*, edited by Doug McAdam, John D. McCarthy, and Mayer N. Zald, 23–40. Cambridge: Cambridge University Press.

McAdam, Doug. 1999. *Political Process and the Development of Black Insurgency, 1930–1970*. 2nd ed. Chicago, IL: University of Chicago Press.

McAdam, Doug, John D. McCarthy, and Mayer N. Zald, eds. 1996. *Comparative Perspectives on Social Movements: Political Opportunities, Mobilizing Structures and Cultural Framings*. Cambridge: Cambridge University Press.

McAdam, Doug, and Sidney Tarrow. 2010. "Ballots and Barricades: On the Reciprocal Relationship between Elections and Social Movements." *Perspectives on Politics* 8 (2): 529–42.

McAdam, Doug, and Sidney Tarrow. 2011. "Introduction: Dynamics of Contention Ten Years On." *Mobilization* 16 (1): 1–10.

McAdam, Doug, Sidney Tarrow, and Charles Tilly. 1997. "Towards an Integrated Perspective on Social Movements and Revolution." In *Ideals, Interests, and Institutions: Advancing Theory in Comparative Politics*, edited by Marc I. Lichbach and A. Zuckerman, 142–73. Cambridge: Cambridge University Press.

McAdam, Doug, Sidney Tarrow, and Charles Tilly. 2001. *Dynamics of Contention*. Cambridge: Cambridge University Press.

McCammon, Holly J., Courtney Sanders Muse, Harmony D. Newman, and Teresa M. Terrell. 2007. "Movement Framing and Discursive Opportunity Structures: The Political Successes of the U.S. Women's Jury Movements." *American Sociological Review* 72 (5): 725–49.

McCarthy, John D. 1997. "The Globalization of Social Movement Theory." In *Transnational Social Movements and Global Politics: Solidarity beyond the State*, edited by Jackie Smith, Charles Chatfield, and Ron Pagnucco, 243–59. Syracuse, NY: Syracuse University Press.

McClurg, Scott D. 2003. "Social Networks and Political Participation: The Role of Social Interaction in Explaining Political Participation." *Political Research Quarterly* 56 (4): 449–64.

McKinney, Seamus. 1998. "Journey Took 30 Years." *Irish News*, Souvenir Supplement. October 5, 1998, 12.

McRae, Dave. 2001. *The 1998 Indonesian Student Movement*. Clayton, Victoria, Australia: Centre of Southeast Asian Studies, Monash Asia Institute, Monash University.

Meijer, Roel. 2005. "Taking the Islamist Movement Seriously: Social Movement Theory and the Islamist Movement." *International Review of Social History* 50 (2): 279–91.

Meller, Patricio. 2011. *Universitarios, ¡el problema no es el lucro, es el Mercado!* 3rd ed. Santiago, Chile: Uqbar Editores.

Melucci, Alberto. 1989. *Nomads of the Present: Social Movements and Individual Needs in Contemporary Society.* London: Hutchinson Radius.

Menaldo, Victor. 2012. "The Middle East and North Africa's Resilient Monarchs." *Journal of Politics* 74 (3): 707–22.

Menoret, Pascal. 2011. "Leaving Islamic Activism Behind: Ambiguous Disengagement in Saudi Arabia." In *Social Movements, Mobilization, and Contestation in the Middle East and North Africa,* edited by J. Beinin and F. Vairel, 43–60. Stanford, CA: Stanford University Press.

Merkel, Wolfgang. 2012. "Embedded and Defective Democracies: Where Does Israel Stand?" In Herman Tamar (Ed.), *By the People, for the People, without the People? The Emergence of (Anti)Political Sentiment in Western Democracies and in Israel,* 185–225. Jerusalem: Israel Democracy Institute. http://en.idi.org.il/media/1430593/EB1ByThePeople.pdf.

Merkel, Wolfgang. 2013. "Democracy and European Integration: A 'Trade-off'?" Neue Gesellschaft/Frankfurter Hefte, *International Quarterly Edition—Journal of Social Democracy* 2: S2–S7.

Meyer, David S. 1993. "Institutionalizing Dissent: The United States Political Opportunity Structure and the End of the Nuclear Freeze Movement." *Sociological Forum* 8 (2): 157–79.

Meyer, David S. 2003. "Political Opportunity and Nested Institutions." *Social Movement Studies* 2 (1): 17–35.

Miall, Hugh, Oliver Ramsbotham, and Tom Woodhouse. 1999. *Contemporary Conflict Resolution: The Prevention, Management and Transformation of Deadly Conflicts.* Cambridge, UK: Polity Press.

Migdal, Joel S. 1988. *Strong Societies and Weak States: State-Society Relations and State Capabilities in the Third World.* Princeton, NJ: Princeton University Press.

Migdal, Joel S. 2001. *State in Society: Studying how States and Societies Transform and Constitute One Another.* New York: Cambridge University Press.

Migdal, Joel S., Atul Kohli, and Vivienne Shue, eds. 1994. *State Power and Social Forces: Domination and Transformation in the Third World.* Cambridge: Cambridge University Press.

Milani, Abbas. 2011. *The Shah.* New York: Palgrave Macmillan.

Miller, Benjamin. 2006. "Balance of Power or the State-to-Nation Balance: Explaining Middle East War-Propensity." *Security Studies* 15 (4): 658–705.

Miller, Laurel, Jeffrey Martini, and F. Stephen Larrabee. 2012. *Democratization in the Arab World: Prospects and Lessons from Around the Globe.* Washington DC: Rand Corporation.

Miller, Warren E. 1980. "Disinterest, Disaffection, and Participation in Presidential Politics." *Political Behavior* 2 (1): 7–32.

Mishal, Shaul, and Avraham Sela. 2006. *The Palestinian Hamas: Vision, Violence, and Coexistence.* New York: Columbia University Press.

Moaddel, Mansoor. 2002. "The Study of Islamic Culture and Politics: An Overview and Assessment." *Annual Review of Sociology* 28: 359–86.

Moaddel, Mansoor. 2005. *Islamic Modernism, Nationalism, and Fundamentalism: Episodes and Discourse.* Chicago, IL: University of Chicago Press.

Moaddel, Mansoor. 2013. "The Birthplace of the Arab Spring: Values and Perceptions of Tunisians and a Comparative Assessment of Egyptian, Iraqi, Lebanese, Pakistani, Saudi, Tunisian, and Turkish Publics." National Consortium for the Study of Terrorism and Response to Terrorism (START), College Park, University of Maryland.

Mohammed, Arshad, and Jason Lange. 2012. "U.S. Sends Warning to Saleh Backers in Yemen." *Reuters* online, US edition. May 16. Retrieved from http://www.reuters.com/article/2012/05/16/us-usa-yemen-assets-idUSBRE84F1GS20120516.

Moloney, Ed, and Andy Pollak. 1986. *Paisley.* Dublin: Poolbeg Press.

Moodie, Dubar T. 2002. "Mobilization on the South African Gold Mines." In *Social Movements. Identity, Culture, and the State,* edited by David S. Meyer, Nancy Whittier, and Melinda Robnett, 46–65. Oxford: Oxford University Press.

Moreira Alves, Maria H. 1989. "Interclass Alliances in the Opposition to the Military in Brazil: Consequences for the Transition Period." In *Power and Popular Protest: Latin American Social Movements,* edited by Susan Eckstein, 278–98. Berkeley: University of California Press.

Morlino, Leonardo. 1998. *Democracy between Consolidation and Crisis: Parties, Groups, and Citizens in Southern Europe.* Oxford: Oxford University Press.

Morlino, Leonardo. 2011. *Changes for Democracy: Actors, Structures, Processes.* Oxford: Oxford University Press.

Moskos, Charles C. 1990. "Peace Soldiers: United Nations Military Forces." In *Making War Making Peace: The Social Foundations of Violent Conflict,* edited by Francesca M. Cancian and James William Gibson, 398–407. Belmont, CA: Wadsworth.

Muasher, Marwan. 2014. *The Second Arab Awakening and the Battle for Pluralism.* New Haven, CT: Yale University Press.

Mueller, Carol. 1999. "Claim 'radicalization'? The 1989 protest cycle in the GDR." *Social Problems* 46 (4): 528–47.

Muller, Edward N., and Thomas O. Jukam. 1977. "On the Meaning of Political Support." *American Political Science Review* 71 (4): 1561–95.

Mustafa, Nadia, and Amal Hammada, eds. 2012. "Al-Thawra al-Misriyya wa-Dirasat al-'Ulum al-Siyasiyya: A'mal al-Mu'tamar al-Sanawi al-Awwal li-Shabab A'dha' Hay'at al-Tadris" [The Egyptian Revolution and the Study of Political Sciences: Proceedings of the First Annual Conference of the Young Faculty Members]. June 14–15, 2011. Cairo: Cairo University (Arabic).

National Committee on American Foreign Policy. 2012. "The United States and a Changing Middle East." *American Foreign Policy Interests* 34 (5): 255–62.

Navarro, Marysa. 1989. "The Personal Is Political: Las Madres de Plaza de Mayo." In *Power and Popular Protest: Latin American Social Movements,* edited by Susan Eckstein, 241–58. Berkeley: University of California Press.

Ndlovu-Gatsheni, Sabelo. 2012. "The Death of the Subject with a Capital 'S' and the Perils of Belonging: A Study of the Construction of Ethnocracy in Zimbabwe." *Journal of Critical Arts* 26 (4): 525–46.

Nepstad, Sharon E. 2011a. "Nonviolent Resistance in the Arab Spring: The Critical Role of Military-Opposition Alliances." *Swiss Political Science Review* 17 (4): 485–91.

Nepstad, Sharon E. 2011b. *Nonviolent Revolutions: Civil Resistance in the Late 20th Century.* New York: Oxford University Press.

Nepstad, Sharon E. 2013. "Mutiny and Nonviolence in the Arab Spring: Exploring Military Defections and Loyalty in Egypt, Bahrain, and Syria." *Journal of Peace Research* 50 (3): 337–49.

Nettle, J. P. 1968. "The State as a Conceptual Variable." *World Politics* 20 (4): 559–92.

Njotorahardjo, Niko. 2003. *Transformasi Indonesia: pemikiran dan proses perubahan yang dikaitkan dengan kesatuan tubuh Kristus.* Jakarta, Indonesia: Metanoia.

Noland, Marcus, and Howard Pack. 2007. *The Arab Economies in a Changing World.* Washington, DC: Peterson Institute for International Economics.

Noonan, Rita K. 1995. "Women against the State: Political Opportunities and Collective Action Frames in Chile's Transition to Democracy." *Sociological Forum* 10 (1): 81–111.

Norris, Pippa, Stefaan Walgrave, and Peter Van Aelst. 2005. "Who Demonstrates? Antistate Rebels, Conventional Participants, or Everyone?" *Comparative Politics* 37 (2): 189–205.

Norris, Pippa. 2002. *Democratic Phoenix: Reinventing Political Activism.* New York: Cambridge University Press.

Northern Ireland Civil Rights Association (NICRA). 1978. *We Shall Overcome: The History of the Struggle for Civil Rights in Northern Ireland, 1968–1978.* Belfast: Author.

Norton, Augustus, ed. 1995. *Civil Society in the Middle East.* Boston, MA: Brill.

Noueihed, Lin, and Alex Warren. 2012. *The Battle for the Arab Spring: Revolution, Counter-Revolution and the Making of a New Era.* New Haven, CT: Yale University Press.

O'Donnell, Guillermo, Philippe Schmitter and Laurence Whitehead. 1986. *Transitions from Authoritarian Rule: Tentative Conclusions about Uncertain Democracies.* Baltimore, MD: Johns Hopkins University Press.

Obach, Brian. 2010. "Political Opportunity and Social Movement Coalitions: The Role of Policy Segmentation and Nonprofit Tax Law." In *Strategic Alliances: Coalition Building and Social Movements*, edited by Nella Van Dyke and Holly J. McCammon, 197–218. Minneapolis: University of Minnesota Press.

Obi, Cyril I. 2009. "Structuring Transnational Spaces of Identity, Rights and Power in the Niger Delta of Nigeria." *Globalizations* 6 (4): 467–81.

ÓDochartaigh, Niall, and Lorenzo Bosi. 2010. "Territoriality and Mobilization: The Civil Rights Movement in Northern Ireland." *Mobilization* 15 (4): 405–24.

Olavarría, Margot. 2003. "Protected Neoliberalism: Perverse Institutionalization and the Crisis of Representation in Post-Dictatorship Chile." *Latin American Perspectives* 30 (6): 10–38.

Olukotun, Ayo 2002. "Traditional Protest Media and Anti-Military Struggle in Nigeria 1988–1999." *African Affairs* 101 (403): 193–211.

Olzak Susan. 1983. "Contemporary Ethnic Mobilization," *Annual Review of Sociology* 9: 355–74.

Ondetti, Gabriel. 2006. "Repression, Opportunity, and Protest: Explaining the Takeoff of Brazil's Landless Movement." *Latin American Politics and Society* 48 (2): 61–94.

Ottaway, Marina, and Julia Choucair-Vizoso, eds. 2008. *Beyond the Façade: Political Reform in the Arab World*. Washington, DC: Carnegie Endowment for International Peace.

Owen, Roger. 2012. *The Rise and Fall of Presidents for Life*. Cambridge, MA: Harvard University Press.

Ozler, S. Ligu. 2009. "Out of the Plaza and into the Office: Social Movement Leaders in the PRD." *Mexican Studies/Estudios Mexicanos* 25 (1): 125–54.

Pace, Michelle. 2012. "Egypt." In *The European Union and the Arab Spring: Promoting Democracy and Human Rights in the Middle East*, edited by Joel Peters, 49–64. Lanham, MD: Lexington Books.

Parry, Geraint, George Moyser, and Neil Day. 1992. *Political Participation and Democracy in Britain*. Cambridge: Cambridge University Press.

Parsa, Misagh. 1989. *The Social Origins of the Iranian Revolution*. New Brunswick, NJ: Rutgers University Press.

Patel, David. 2012. "Preference Falsification, Diffusion, and the Centrality of Squares in the Arab Revolutions." Prepared for the August 30–September 2 APSA Convention, New Orleans.

Patel, David, and Valerie Bunce. 2012. "Turning Points and the Cross-National Diffusion of Popular Protest." *Comparative Democratization* 10 (1): 10–13.

Patel, David, Valerie Bunce, and Sharon Wolchik. 2014. "Diffusion and Demonstration." In *The Arab Uprisings Explained: New Contentious Politics in the Middle East*, edited by Mark Lynch, 57–74. New York: Columbia University Press.

Peisakhin, Leonid. 2013. "Why Are People Protesting in Ukraine? Providing Historical Context." Retrieved March 12, 2014, from http://www.washington-post.com/blogs/monkey-cage/wp/2013/12/19/why-are-people-protesting-in-ukraine-providing-historical-context/.

Peleg, Ilan. 2004. "Jewish-Palestinian Relations in Israel: From Hegemony to Equality?" *International Journal of Politics, Culture and Society* 17 (3): 415–37.

People's Democracy. 1969. "Why PD?" Linen Hall Library Political Collection, Belfast, Northern Ireland.

Perkins, Kenneth. 2004. *A History of Modern Tunisia*. Cambridge: Cambridge University Press.

Perry, Elizabeth J. 2002. *Challenging the Mandate of Heaven: Social Protest and State Power in China*. New York: M. E. Sharpe.

Petonito, Gina. 2000. "Racial Discourse and Enemy Construction." In *Social Conflicts and Collective Identities*, edited by Patrick G. Coy and Lynne M. Woehrle, 19–40. New York: Rowman & Littlefield.

Pharr, Susan, and Robert Putnam, eds. 2000. *Disaffected Democracies: What's Troubling the Trilateral Countries?* Princeton, NJ: Princeton University Press.

Pilati, Katia. 2011. "Political Context, Organizations and Protest Activities in African Countries." *Mobilization* 16 (3): 351–68.

Pilati, Katia. 2016. *Migrants' Political Participation in Exclusionary Contexts. From Subcultures to Radicalization*. Basingstoke, Hampshire: Palgrave-Macmillan.

Piven, Frances F., and Richard Cloward. 1993. *Regulating the Poor: The Functions of Public Welfare*. New York: Pantheon Books.

Polletta, Francesca. 2002. *Freedom Is an Endless Meeting*. Chicago, IL: University of Chicago Press.

Pop-Eleches, Grigore, and Graeme Robertson. 2015. "Information, Elections and Political Change." *Comparative Politics* 47 (4): 459–95.

Posusney, Marsha Pripstein. 1997. *Labor and the State in Egypt: Workers, Unions and Economic Restructuring, 1952 to 1996*. New York: Columbia University Press.

Posusney, Marsha Pripstein, and Michele Penner Angrist. 2005. *Authoritarianism in the Middle East: Regimes and Resistance*. Boulder, CO: Lynne Rienner.

Powell, Bingham G. Jr. 2005. "The Chain of Responsiveness." In *Assessing the Quality of Democracy*, edited by Larry Diamond and Leonardo Morlino, 62–76. Baltimore, MD: Johns Hopkins University Press.

Przeworski, Adam. 2008. "Constraints and Choices: Electoral Participation in Historical Perspective." *Comparative Political Studies* 42 (1): 4–30.

Przeworski, Adam, and Francis Limongi. 1997. "Modernization: Theories and Facts." *World Politics* 49 (2): 155–83.

Queirolo Palmas, Luca., ed. 2009. *Dentro le gang. Giovani, migranti e nuovi spazi pubblici*. Verona, Italy: Ombre Corte.

Quimpo, Nathan. 2005. "The Left, Elections, and the Political Party System in the Philippines." *Critical Asian Studies* 37 (1): 3–28.

Rafizadeh, Majid. 2012. "The Four Axes of the East: Russia, China, Syria, and Iran." *International Affairs Review* (July 8). Retrieved from http://www.iar-gwu.org/node/424.

Rahat, Gideon, and Mario Sznajder. 1998. "Electoral Engineering in Chile: The Electoral System and Limited Democracy." *Electoral Studies* 17 (4): 429–42.

Rasbash, Jon, and Browne, Michael W. 2008. "Non-Hierarchical Multilevel Models." In *Handbook of Multilevel Analysis*, edited by Jan De Leeuw and Erik Meijer, 301–34. Berlin: Springer.

Rasler, Karen. 1996. "Concessions, Repression and Political Protest." *American Sociological Review* 61 (1): 132–52.

Reid, Ben. 2001. "The Philippine Democratic Uprising and the Contradictions of Neoliberalism: EDSA II." *Third World Quarterly* 22 (5): 777–93.

Richards, Alan, and John Waterbury. 2008. *A Political Economy of the Middle East.* Boulder, CO: Westview.

Rieff, David. 2000. "Moral Principles, Strategic Interests, and Military Force." *World Policy Journal* 17 (2): 39–47.

Risse, Thomas, and Kathryn Sikkink. 1999. "The Socialization of International Human Rights Norms into Domestic Practices." In *The Power of Human Rights: International Norms and Domestic Change*, edited by Thomas Risse, Stephen C. Ropp, and Kathryn Sikkink, 1–38. Cambridge: Cambridge University Press.

Ritter, Daniel. 2015. *The Iron Cage of Liberalism: International Politics and Unarmed Revolutions in the Middle East and North Africa.* New York: Oxford University Press.

Rivera, Temario. C. 2002. "Transition Pathways and Democratic Consolidation in Post-Marcos Philippines." *Contemporary Southeast Asia* 24 (3): 466–83.

Roberts, Adam. 2004. "United Nations and Humanitarian Intervention." In *Humanitarian Intervention and International Relations*, edited by Jennifer M. Welsh, 71–97. Oxford: Oxford University Press.

Roberts, Kenneth M. 2014. *Changing Course: Party Systems in Latin America's Neoliberal Era.* New York and Cambridge: Cambridge University Press.

Robertson, Graeme B. 2011. *The Politics of Protest in Hybrid Regimes: Managing Dissent in Post-Communist Russia.* Cambridge: Cambridge University Press.

Robinson, Glenn E. 2004. "Hamas as Social Movement." In *Islamic Activism. A Social Movement Theory Approach*, edited by Quintan Wiktorowicz, 112–39. Bloomington: Indiana University Press.

Robinson, Glenn E. 2005. "Organizational Imperative and the Limits to Alliance: The PFLP-Hamas Relationship since 1991" Presented at the Cooperation Across Ideological Divides in the Middle East, Rockefeller Foundation, Bellagio.

Rodan, Gary, and Caroline Hughes. 2012. "Ideological Coalitions and the International Promotion of Social Accountability: The Philippines and Cambodia Compared." *International Studies Quarterly* 56 (2): 367–80.

Roniger, Luis, and Mario. Sznajder. 1999. *The Legacy of Human Rights Violations in the Southern Cone, Argentina, Chile and Uruguay.* Oxford: Oxford University Press.

Rosenberg, Tina. 2011. "Revolution U: What Egyptians Learned from the Students Who Overthrew Milosevic." *Foreign Policy*, February 16, 1–6. Retrieved from www.foreignpolicy.com/articles/2011/02/16/revolution_u.html.

Rosenhak, Zeev, and Michael Shalev. 2013. "The Political Economy of Israel's 'Social Justice' Protests: A Class and Generational Analysis." *Contemporary Social Science*. Retrieved from http://dx.doi.org/10.1080/21582041.2013.851405.

Ross, Michael. 2012. *Oil Curse.* Princeton, NJ: Princeton University Press.

Rothman, Franklin Daniel, and Pamela E. Oliver. 1999. "From Local to Global: The Anti-Dam Movement in Southern Brazil, 1979–1992." *Mobilization* 4: 41–57.

Rouhana, Nadim. 1998. "Israel and its Arab Citizens: Predicaments in the Relationship between Ethnic States and Ethnonational Minorities." *Third World Quarterly* 19 (2): 277–96.

Rucht, Dieter. 1996. "The Impact of National Contexts on Social Movement Structures: A Cross-Movement and Cross-National Comparison." In *Comparative Perspectives on Social Movements*, edited by Doug McAdam, John D. McCarthy, and Mayer Zald, 185–204. Cambridge: Cambridge University Press.

Rueschemeyer, Dietricht. 2005. "Addressing Inequality." In *Assessing the Quality of Democracy*, edited by L. Diamond and L. Morlino, 47–61. Baltimore, MD: Johns Hopkins University Press.

Rutherford, Bruce K. 2008. *Egypt after Mubarak: Liberalism, Islam and Democracy in the Arab World*. Princeton, NJ: Princeton University Press.

Ryan, Curtis R. 2002. *Jordan in Transition: From Hussein to Abdullah*. Boulder, CO: Lynn Reinner.

Sale, Kirkpatrick. 1973. *SDS*. New York: Vintage Books.

Salinas, Daniel, and Pablo Fraser. 2012. "Educational Opportunity and Contentious Politics: The 2011 Chilean Students Movement." *Berkeley Review of Education* 3 (1): 17–47.

Salloukh, Bassel F. 2006. "The Limits of Electoral Engineering in Divided Societies: Elections in Postwar Lebanon." *Canadian Journal of Political Science/Revue Canadienne de Science Politique* 39 (3): 635–55.

Salman, Ton. 2007. "Bolivia and the Paradoxes of Democratic Consolidation." *Latin American Perspectives* 34 (6): 111–30.

Sartori, Giovanni. 1987. *The Theory of Democracy Revisited*. Chatham, NJ: Chatham House.

Savun, Burcu, and Daniel Tirone. 2011. "Foreign Aid, Democratization, and Civil Conflict: How Does Democracy Aid Affect Civil Conflict?" *American Journal of Political Science* 55 (2): 233–46.

Sazegara, Mohsen, and Maria J. Stephan. 2009. "Iran's Islamic Revolution and Nonviolent Struggle." In *Civilian Jihad: Nonviolent Struggle, Democratization and Governance in the Middle East*, edited by Maria J. Stephan, 185–204. New York: Palgrave Macmillan.

Schattschneider, Erik E. 1960. *The Semi-Sovereign People*. New York: Holt, Rinehart and Winston.

Schechter, Asher. 2012. *Chronika shel Meha'a* [Chronicles of Protest]. Tel Aviv: Ha-Kibbutz ha-Me'uhad (Hebrew).

Schneider, Cathy L. 1995. *Shantytown Protest in Pinochet's Chile*. Philadelphia, PA: Temple University Press.

Schneider, Cathy L. 2005. "Police Power and Race Riots in Paris." *Politics and Society* 36 (1): 133–59.

Schock, Kurt. 2005. *Unarmed Insurrections: People Power Movements in Nondemocracies.* Minneapolis: University of Minnesota Press.

Schofer, Evan, and Marion Fourcade-Gourinchas. 2001. "The Structural Contexts of Civic Engagement: Voluntary Association Membership in Comparative Perspective." *American Sociological Review* 66 (6): 806–28.

Schulte Nordholt, H., and Ireen Hoogenboom. 2006. *Indonesian Transitions.* Yogyakarta, Indonesia: Pustaka Pelajar.

Schumaker, Paul D. 1975. "Policy Responsiveness to Protest-Group Demands." *Journal of Politics* 37 (2): 488–521.

Schwartz, Stephanie. 2011. "Youth and the 'Arab Spring.'" Washington, DC: United States Institute of Peace. http://www.usip.org/publications/youth-and-the-arab-spring.

Schwarz, Rolf. 2008. "The Political Economy of State-Formation in the Arab Middle East: Rentier States, Economic Reform, and Democratization." *Review of International Political Economy* 15 (4): 599–621.

Schwedler, Jillian, and Janine Clark. 2006. "Islamist-Leftist Cooperation in the Arab World." *IMIS Review* 18: 10–11.

Scott, James 1985. *Weapons of the Weak: Everyday Forms of Peasant Resistance.* New Haven, CT: Yale University Press.

Seddon, David. 1990. "The Politics of Adjustment: Egypt and the IMF, 1987–1990." *Review of African Political Economy* 17 (47): 95–104.

Sela, Avraham. 1998. *The Decline of the Arab-Israeli Conflict: Middle East Politics and the Quest for Regional Order.* Albany, NY: State University of New York Press.

Seligson, Mitchell A., and John A. Booth, eds. 1979. *Political Participation in Latin America. Vol. 2: Politics and the Poor.* New York: Holmes and Meier.

Shalev, Michael. 2013. "Class-Based Analysis of the Israeli Social Protest." Paper presented in the social protest conference, Eshkol Center, Hebrew University of Jerusalem June 2013; work in progress.

Shallam, Hesham. 2011. "Striking Back at Egyptian Workers." *Middle East Research and Information Report*, MER259. Retrieved May 17, 2014, from http://www.merip.org/mer/mer259/striking-back-egyptian-workers.

Sharabi, Hisham. 1992. *Neopatriarchy: A Theory of Distorted Change in Arab Society.* Oxford: Oxford University Press.

Shatz, Adam. 2010. "Mubarak's Last Breath." *London Review of Books* 32 (10): 6–10.

Shepard, Benjamin H. 2012. "Labor and Occupy Wall Street: Common Causes and Uneasy Alliances." *WorkingUSA: The Journal of Labor and Society* 15 (1): 121–34.

Shmuli, Itzik. 2011a. Speech, September 3, 2011. Retrieved from http://goo.gl/2hcqc (Hebrew).

Shmuli, Itzik. 2011b. Speech, August 13, 2011. Retrieved from http://goo.gl/S9WPa (Hebrew).

Shmuli, Itzik. 2011c. Speech, August 6, 2011. Retrieved from http://www.youtube.com/watch?v=NW8wtqeJIJk (Hebrew).

Shugart, Matthew Sobart. 1989. "Patterns of Revolution." *Theory and Society* 18 (2): 249–71.

Sikkink, Katheryn. 2005. "Patterns on Dynamic Multilevel Governance and the Insider-Outsider Coalition." In *Transnational Protest and Global Activism*, edited by Donatella della Porta and Sidney Tarrow, 151–73. Lanham, MD: Rowman & Littlefield.

Singerman, Diane. 2003. "Réseaux, cadres culturels et structures des opportunités politiques: Le mouvement islamiste en Égypte." In *Résistances et protestations dans les sociétés musulmanes*, edited by Mounia Bennani-Chraïbi and Olivier Fillieule, 219–42. Paris: Presses de Sciences Po.

Singerman, Diane. 2004. "The Networked World of Islamic Social Movements." In *Islamic Activism. A Social Movement Theory Approach*, edited by Quintan Wiktorowicz, 143–63. Bloomington: Indiana University Press.

Skaaning, Svend-Erik. 2006. "Political Regimes and Their Changes: A Conceptual Framework." Stanford, CA: Center on Democracy, Development, and the Rule of Law, Stanford University (Working Paper no. 55).

Skocpol, Theda. 1979. *States and Social Revolutions: A Comparative Analysis of France, Russia, and China*. Cambridge: Cambridge University Press.

Skocpol, Theda. 1994. *Social Revolutions in the Modern World*. Cambridge: Cambridge University Press.

Slater, Dan. 2004. "Indonesia's Accountability Trap: Party Cartels and Presidential Power after Democratic Transition." *Indonesia* 78: 61–92.

Slater, Dan. 2009. "Revolutions, Crackdowns, and Quiescence: Communal Elites and Democratic Mobilization in Southeast Asia." *American Journal of Sociology* 115 (1): 203–54.

Slater, Dan. 2010. *Ordering Power: Contentious Politics and Authoritarian Leviathans in Southeast Asia*. Cambridge: Cambridge University Press.

Slim, Hugo. 1997. *Doing the Right Thing: Relief Agencies, Moral Dilemmas and Moral Responsibility in Political Emergencies and War*. Uppsala, Sweden: Oxford Brookes University.

Smith, Jackie. 2011. "Globalizations Forum on Middle East Protests: Commentary." *Globalizations* 8 (5): 655–59.

Smith, Jackie, and Bob Glidden. 2012. "Occupy Pittsburgh and the Challenges of Participatory Democracy." *Social Movement Studies* 11 (3–4): 288–94.

Smooha, Sammy. 1990. "Minority Status in an Ethnic Democracy: The Status of the Arab Minority in Israel." *Ethnic and Racial Studies* 13 (3): 389–413.

Snow, David A., and Robert Benford. 1992. "Master Frames and Cycles of Protest." In *Frontiers in Social Movement Theory*, edited by Aldon D. Morris and Carol McClurg Mueller, 133–55. New Haven, CT: Yale University Press.

Snow, David A., Sarah A. Soule, and Hanspeter Kriesi. 2004. "Mapping the Terrain." In *The Blackwell Companion to Social Movements*, edited by David A. Snow, Sarah A. Soule, and Hanspeter Kriesi, 3–16. Malden, MA: Blackwell.

Snyder, Robert. 1998. "Paths Out of Sultanistic Regimes: Combining Structural and Voluntarist Perspectives." In *Sultanistic Regimes*, edited by Houchang E. Chehabi and Juan J. Linz, 49–81. Baltimore, MD: Johns Hopkins University Press.

Solt, Frederick. 2008. "Economic Inequality and Democratic Political Engagement." *American Journal of Political Science* 52 (1): 48–60.

Soule, Sarah, A. 2010. *Contentious Politics and Corporate Social Responsibility*. New York : Cambridge University Press.

Sowers, Jeannie, and Chris Toensing, eds. 2012. *The Journey to Tahrir: Revolution, Protest, and Social Change in Egypt*. London: Verso Books.

Soyer, Michaela. 2014. "'We Knew Our Time Had Come': The Dynamics of Threat and Microsocial Ties in Three Polish Ghettos under Nazi Oppression." *Mobilization* 19 (1): 47–66.

Spalding, Rose J. 2007. "Civil Society Engagement in Trade Negotiations: CAFTA Opposition in El Salvador." *Latin American Politics and Society* 49 (2): 85–114.

Stiglitz, Joseph. 2011. "The Globalization of Protest." *Project Syndicate*, November 4.

Stiglitz, Joseph. 2012. *The Price of Inequality*. New York: Norton & Company.

Stokes, Gale. 1993. *The Walls Came Tumbling Down: The Collapse of Communism in Eastern Europe*. Oxford: Oxford University Press.

Strang, David, and Sarah A. Soule. 1998. "Diffusion in Organizations and Social Movements: From Hybrid Corn to Poison Pills." *Annual Review of Sociology* 24: 265–90.

Swed, Ori, and Alexander Weinreb. 2015. "Military Westernization and State Repression in Post-Cold War Era." *Social Science Research* 53: 270–87.

Swidler, Ann. 1986. "Culture in Action: Symbols and Strategies." *American Sociological Review* 51 (2): 273–86.

Sznajder, Mario, and Luis Roniger. 2009. *The Politics of Exile in Latin America*. Cambridge: Cambridge University Press.

Talentino, Andrea. 2005. *Military Intervention after the Cold War*. Athens, OH: Ohio University Press.

Talshir, Gayil. 2014. "Ha-Meha'a ha-Hevratit be-Re'i Mashber ha-Demokratia ha-Isra-elit: Bein Kalkala, Politika, ve-Zehut" [Social Protest in View of the Crisis for Israeli Democracy: Between Economy, Politics and Identity]. *Politika* 23: 5–45 (Hebrew).

Talshir, Gayil. 2015. "Ha-Israelim ha-Hadashim: Mi-Meha'ah Hevratit le-Behirot Miflagtiyot" [The New Israelis: From Social Protest to Party Elections]. In *Elections in Israel 2013*, edited by Michal Shamir, 37–69. Jerusalem: Israel Democratic Institute (Hebrew).

Tan, Paige. 2002. "Anti-Party Reaction in Indonesia: Causes and Implications." *Contemporary Southeast Asia* 24 (3): 484–508.

Tarrow, Sidney. 1983. "Struggling to Reform: Social Protest and Policy Response during Cycles of Protest." Western Societies Paper, No. 15. Ithaca, NY: Center for International Studies, Cornell University.

Tarrow, Sidney. 1994. *Power in Movement. Social Movements and Contentious Politics*. New York: Cambridge University Press.

Tarrow, Sidney. 1995a. "Mass Mobilization and Elite Exchange: Democratization Episodes in Italy and Spain." *Democratization* 2 (3): 221–45.

Tarrow, Sidney. 1995b. "Mass Mobilization and Regime Change: Pacts, Reform, and Popular Struggle in Italy (1918–1922) and Spain (1975–1978)." In *The Politics of Democratic Consolidation: Southern Europe in Comparative Perspective*, edited by Richard Gunther, Nikiforos P. Diamandouros, and Hans-Jürgen Puhle, 204–30. Baltimore, MD: Johns Hopkins University Press.

Tarrow, Sidney. 1996. "States and Opportunities: The Political Structuring of Social Movements." In *Comparative Perspectives on Social Movements*, edited by Doug McAdam, John D. McCarthy, and Mayer N. Zald, 41–61. Cambridge Studies in Comparative Movements. Cambridge: Cambridge University Press.

Tarrow, Sidney. 1998. *Power in Movement: Social Movements and Contentious Politics*. 2nd ed. Cambridge: Cambridge University Press.

Tarrow, Sidney. 2001a. "Contentious Politics in a Composite Polity." In *Contentious Europeans*, edited by D. Imig and S. Tarrow, 233–51. Lanham MD: Rowman and Littlefield.

Tarrow, Sidney. 2001b. "Transnational Politics: Contention and Institutions in International Politics." *Annual Review of Political Science* 4: 1–20.

Tarrow, Sidney. 2005. *The New Transnational Activism*. Cambridge: Cambridge University Press.

Tarrow, Sidney. 2011. *Power in Movement: Social Movements and Contentious Politics*. 3rd ed. Cambridge: Cambridge University Press.

Tarrow, Sidney. 2015. *Wars, States, and Contention: A Comparative Historical Study*. Ithaca, NY: Cornell University Press.

Taylor, Marcus. 2002. "Success for Whom? An Historical-Materialist Critique of Neoliberalism in Chile." *Historical Materialism* 10 (2): 45–75.

Taylor, Verta, and Nancy Whittier. 1992. "Collective Identity in Social Movement Communities: Lesbian Feminist Mobilization." In *Frontiers in Social Movement Theory*, edited by Aldon D. Morris and Carol McClurg Mueller, 104–29. New Haven, CT: Yale University Press.

Tejerina, Benjamín. 2001. "Protest Cycle, Political Violence and Social Movements in the Basque Country Nations and Nationalism." *Nations and Nationalism* 7 (1): 39–57.

Teti, Andrea, and Gennaro Gervasio. 2011. "The Unbearable Lightness of Authoritarianism: Lessons from the Arab Uprisings." *Mediterranean Politics* 16 (2): 321–27.

The Australian. 2011. "Extremist Threat to the Arab Spring." October 11, 2011. Retrieved from http://www.theaustralian.com.au/news/opinion/extremist-threat-to-arab-spring/story-e6frg71x-1226163359427.

Thomas, Daniel. 2001. *The Helsinki Effect: International Norms, Human Rights and the Demise of Communism*. Princeton, NJ: Princeton University Press.

Thompson, Mark. 1995. *The Anti-Marcos Struggle: Personalistic Rule and Democratic Transition in the Philippines*. New Haven, CT: Yale University Press.

Thompson, Mark. 1996. "Off the Endangered List: Philippine Democratization in Comparative Perspective." *Comparative Politics* 28 (2): 179–205.

Tibi, Bassam. 2013. *The Shari'a State: Arab Spring and Democratization*. London: Routledge.

Tilly, Charles. 1978. *From Mobilization to Revolution*. Reading, MA: Addison-Wesley.

Tilly, Charles. 1984. "Social Movements and National Politics." In *State-Making and Social Movements*, edited by Charles Bright and Susan Harding, 297–317. Ann Arbor, MI: University of Michigan Press.

Tilly, Charles. 1993. *European Revolutions 1492–1992*. Oxford: Blackwell.

Tilly, Charles. 2002. *Stories, Identities and Political Change*. Lanham, MD: Rowman & Littlefield.

Tilly, Charles. 2003a. *The Politics of Collective Violence*. Cambridge: Cambridge University Press.

Tilly, Charles. 2003b. "When Do (and Don't) Social Movement Promote Democratization?" In *Social Movements and Democracy*, edited by Ibarra Pedro, 21–46. New York: Palgrave.

Tilly, Charles. 2004a. *Social Movements, 1768–2004*. Boulder, CO: Paradigm Press.

Tilly, Charles. 2004b. *Contention and Democracy in Europe, 1650–2000*. Cambridge: Cambridge University Press.

Tilly, Charles. 2006. *Regimes and Repertoires*. Chicago, IL: University of Chicago Press.

Tilly, Charles, and Sidney Tarrow. 2007. *Contentious Politics*. Boulder, CO: Paradigm Press.

Tilly, Charles, and Sidney Tarrow. 2006. *Contentious Politics*. Lanham, MD: Paragon Press.

Tilly, Charles, and Sidney Tarrow. 2007. *Contentious Politics*. Boulder, CO: Paradigm Press.

Toledano, Ehud R. 2011. "Middle East Historians and the Arab Spring: Early-Days Assessment." *Sharqiyya* (Fall): 4–11.

Toro, Sergio Y. 2007. "La inscripción electoral de los jóvenes en Chile: Factores de incidencia y aproximaciones al debate." In *Modernización del Régimen Electoral Chileno*, edited by A. Fontaine, 101–122. Santiago, Chile: PNUD.

"Transition at Crossroads: Tunisia Three Years after the Revolution." 2013. Hearing before the Subcommittee on the Middle East and North Africa of the Committee on Foreign Affairs, United State Congress, House of Representatives, December 4, 2013.

Trejo, Guillermo. 2012. *Popular Movements in Autocracies: Religion, Repression, and Indigenous Collective Action in Mexico*. Cambridge: Cambridge University Press.

Tripp, Charles. 1995. "Regional Organizations in the Arab Middle East." In *Regionalism in World Politics: Regional Organization and International Order*, edited by Andrew Hurrell and Louise Fawcett, 283–308. New York: Oxford University Press.

Tripp, Charles. 1998. "Egypt 1945–52: The Uses of Disorder." In *Demise of the British Empire in the Middle East: Britain's Response to Nationalist Movements, 1943–1955*, edited by Cohen Michael J. and Martin Kolinsky, 112–41. London: Frank Cass.

Tripp, Charles. 2014. "The Politics of Resistance and the Arab Uprisings." In *The New Middle East: Protest and Revolution in the Arab World*, edited by Gerges Fawaz, 135–54. New York: Cambridge University Press.

Tugal, Cihan. 2009. "Transforming Everyday Life: Islamism and Social Movement Theory." *Theory and Society* 38 (5): 423–58.

Tuma, Elias H. 1980. "The Rich and the Poor in the Middle East." *Middle East Journal* 34 (4): 413–37.

Turam, Berna. 2006. *Between Islam and the State*. Stanford, CA: Stanford University Press.

Ufen, Andreas. 2012. "Party Systems, Critical Junctures, and Cleavages in Southeast Asia." *Asian Survey* 52 (3): 441–64.

Urzúa, Sergio. 2012. "La Rentabilidad de la Educación Superior en Chile. ¿Educación Superior Para Todos?" Documento de Trabajo No.386 CEP, Santiago de Chile, 20 Marzo 2012.

Vairel, Frédéric. 2011. "Protesting in Authoritarian Situations: Egypt and Morocco in Comparative Perspective." In *Social Movements, Mobilization, and Contestation in the Middle East and North Africa*, edited by J. Beinin and F. Vairel, 27–42. Stanford, CA: Stanford University Press.

Van de Donk, Wim, Brian D. Loader, Paul G. Nixon, and Dieter Rucht. 2004. *CyberProtest*. London: Routledge.

Van Den Bosch, Jeroen. 2013. "Political Regime Theory: Identifying and Defining Three Archetypes." *Copernicus Journal of Political Studies* 2 (4): 78–96.

Van Dyke, Nella, and Holly McCammon, eds. 2010. *Strategic Alliances: New Studies of Social Movement Coalitions*. Minneapolis: University of Minnesota Press.

Vardys, Stanley. 1983. "Polish Echoes in the Baltics." *Problems of Communism* 32: 21–34.

Varon, Jeremy. 2004. *Bringing the War Home*. Berkeley : University of California Press.

Verba, Sidney, Kay L. Schlozman, and Henry E. Brady. 1995. *Voice and Equality: Civic Voluntarism in American Politics*. Cambridge, MA: Harvard University Press.

Vogt, Achim. 2011. "Jordan's Eternal Promise of Reform." *Internationale Politik und Gesellschaft* 4: 61–76.

Ward, Stephen R. 2009. *Immortal: A Military History of Iran and Its Armed Forces*. Washington, DC: Georgetown University Press.

Waterbury, John. 1983. *The Egypt of Nasser and Sadat: The Political Economy of Two Regimes*. Princeton, NJ: Princeton University Press.

Weber, Max. 1922 (1978). *Economy and Society*. Translated and edited by Guenther Roth and Claus Wittich. Berkeley: University of California Press.

Wehnert, Barbara. 2005. "Diffusion and Development of Democracy, 1800–1999." *American Sociological Review* 70 (1): 53–81.

Weiss, Thomas G. 2012. *Humanitarian Intervention*. Cambridge, UK: Polity Press.

Western, Bruce. 1998. "Causal Heterogeneity in Comparative Research: A Bayesian Hierarchical Modeling Approach." *American Journal of Political Science* 42 (4): 1233–59.

Weyland, Kurt. 2010. "The Diffusion of Regime Contention in European Democratization, 1840–1940." *Comparative Political Studies* 43 (8/9): 1148–76.

Weyland, Kurt. 2014. *Making Waves: Democratic Contention in Europe and Latin America since the Revolution of 1848*. New York: Cambridge University Press.

Whitehead, Laurence. 2002. *Democratization: Theory and Practice*. Oxford: Oxford University Press.

Wickham, Carrie R. 2002. *Mobilizing Islam: Religion, Activism and Political Change in Egypt*. New York: Columbia University Press.

Wickham, Carrie R. 2013. *The Muslim Brotherhood: Evolution of an Islamist Movement*. Princeton, NJ: Princeton University Press.

Wickham-Crowley, Timothy. 1992. *Guerrillas and Revolution in Latin America*. Princeton, NJ: Princeton University Press.

Wiktorowicz, Quintan. 2000. "The Salafi Movement in Jordan." *International Journal of Middle East Studies* 32 (2): 219–40.

Wiktorowicz, Quintan. 2004. "Introduction: Islamic Activism and Social Movement Theory." In *Islamic Activism. A Social Movement Theory Approach*, edited by Quintan Wiktorowicz, 1–33. Bloomington, Indianapolis: Indiana University Press.

Wiktorowicz, Quintan, ed. 2004. *Islamic Activism: A Social Movement Theory Approach*. Bloomington: Indiana University Press.

Wilkes, Rima. 2004. "First Nation Politics: Deprivation, Resources, and Participation in Collective Action." *Sociological Inquiry* 74 (4): 570–89.

Wilson, Harold. 1976. *The Governance of Britain*. London: Weidenfeld and Nicolson.

Wolfsfeld, Gadi, Elad Segev, and Tamir Sheafer. 2013. "Social Media and the Arab Spring: Politics Comes First." *International Journal of Press/Politics* 18 (2): 115–37.

World Bank. 2011. *World Development Indicators*. Accessed March 2011 from http://data.worldbank.org/data-catalog

Wright, Stuart A. 2007. *Patriots, Politics, and the Oklahoma City Bombing*. Cambridge: Cambridge University Press.

Yakobson, Alexander, and Amnon Rubinstein. 2008. *Israel and the Family of Nations: The Jewish Nation-State and Human Rights*. London: Routledge.

Yashar, Deborah J. 2005. *Contesting Citizenship in Latin America: The Rise of Indigenous Movements and the Postliberal Challenge*. Cambridge: Cambridge University Press.

Yayasan Lembaga Bantuan Hukum Indonesia. 1998. *Pokok-pokok pikiran YLBHI tentang reformasi politik perburuhan nasional*. Jakarta, Indonesia: Author.

Yiftachel, Oren. 2006. *Ethnocracy: Land and Identity Politics in Israel/Palestine*. Philadelphia: University of Pennsylvania Press.

Yom, Sean L., and F. Gregory Gause III. 2012. "Resilient Royals: How Arab Monarchies Hang On." *Journal of Democracy* 23 (4): 74–88.

Yona, Yossi, and Spivak Avia, eds. 2012. *Efshar Gam Aheret [To Do Things Different]*. Tel Aviv: Ha-Kibbutz ha-Me'uhad (Hebrew).

Zavadskaya, Margarita. 2013. "Protests under Non-Democratic Regimes: 'Contingent Democrats' versus 'Real Democrats.' Progress Report." St. Petersburg, Russia, Laboratory for Comparative Social Research, Higher School of Economics: 29.

Zelin, Aaron Y. 2015. "Tunisia's Fragile Democratic Transition." Washington Institute for Near East Policy. July 14, 2015. Retrieved from http://www.washingtoninstitute.org/policy-analysis/view/tunisias-fragile-democratic-transition.

Zemni, Sami, Brecht De Smet, and Koenraad Bogaert. 2013. "Luxemburg on Tahrir Square: Reading the Arab Revolutions with Rosa Luxemburg's The Mass Strike." *Antipode* 45 (4): 888–907.

Zirakzadeh, Cyrus E. 2008. "Crossing Frontiers: Theoretical Innovations in the Study of Social Movements." *International Political Science Review* 29 (5): 525–41.

Zolberg, Aristide. 1972. "Moments of Madness." *Politics and Society* 2 (2): 183–207.

Zukerman, Ethan R. 2011. "The First Twitter Revolution?" *ForeignPolicy.com*. January 14.

Index

'Abdallah II, King, 247. *See also* Jordan

Adams, Gerry, 152. *See also* Northern Ireland

advocacy networks. *See* networks

agency, 158, 162, 163, 164, 284, 288, 295–298

Alawites, 107, 293. *See also* Syria

Algeria, 3, 98, 109, 110, 127, 159, 277, 278, 280, 284

Allende, Salvador, 221, 229, 231, 239, 252n16. *See also* Chile

alliances, 48, 100, 123, 165, 166, 206, 217; international, 217, 240, 289, 298; political, 163, 172, 218, 222, 224; social, 217, 240, 289; with social movements, 30, 31, 33, 35–37

al-Nahda (Islamic Party), 291, 299

al-Qaeda, in the Arabian Peninsula, 107; in the Islamic Maghreb, 300

Amin, Galal, 279

Aquino, Corazon, 212. *See also* Philippines

Arab League (League of Arab States), 165, 168, 173. *See also* supranational institutions

Arab revolts, 3, 4, 17, 18, 19, 22, 43, 68, 99, 115, 116, 126–128, 129, 131, 132, 133n1; 135, 154, 157, 258; comparative historical perspective of, 16–17, 276–307; differences among Arab States, 290–291; mass character and, 255; network social movement, 42; political reform, 102; popular accounts of, 110; popular and analytic focus on, 97; popular nature of, 289; reforms, 262; role of youth, 98; similarities with non-Arab cases, 285, 294, 305; as social movements, 7, 10, 27, 30–31, 33, 39, 44, 286, 288

"Arab Spring." *See* Arab revolts

Arabism, 290, 296, 305

Argentina, 79, 239, 264(figure), 265(figure); authoritarian regime, 94

Assad, Bashar al-, 31, 108, 171. *See also* Syria

Assad, Hafiz al-, 171, 293, 307n7. *See also* Syria

authoritarian regimes. *See* regimes

authoritarianism, 4, 28–32, 173–176, 280, 298; communist version of, 122; elite-backed constitutional, 207; repressive context, 18, 39, 46, 47, 48, 49, 50, 51, 52, 56, 66, 67, 69, 72, 88, 286; rulers, 19, 115, 116, 117, 118, 119, 124, 127, 138, 129, 131, 132, 158, 280, 289, 294; states, 284; transition to democracy, 298, 306. *See also* nondemocracies

renovation, 47, 50; repertoire of
actions, 47, 49; repression and
mobilizing structures, 48–50;
repressive contexts, 46, 47, 49, 56, 66,
67, 70; resource allocation, 33, 35; scale
shift, 295; social movement, 44, 111;
transnationalization, 66, 67, 69, 294;
Zimbabwe, 50, 55, 61
media coverage, 137, 143
MENA (Middle East & North Africa),
2–3, 4–5, 7, 9, 10, 14, 16–17, 18, 20, 22,
24n8, 27, 28–32, 37, 38, 41, 43, 44, 47,
67, 93, 95, 100, 105, 108, 111, 126, 127,
128, 129, 131, 157, 158, 159, 276, 277, 281,
282, 286, 287, 295, 296, 297, 300, 301,
305, 306
Middle East: authoritarianism, 28–32,
98–100; coalitional modes, 35–37,
36(table); communitarian or
subcultural modes, 38–40;
comparative historical perspective of
Arab revolts, 276–307; comparisons
with other case studies, 220–226;
democracy, 275; democratization
of societies, 4; elites, 28–32; ethnic
democracies, 135; exceptionalism,
4, 277, 306; modes of coordination,
32–33, 40–43; monarchies, 100–102;
multiple cleavages, 28–32;
organizational modes, 37–38;
personalist regimes, 102–109; popular
contention, 157; regime collapse,
109 (figure); regimes, 257; social
movement theory, 27–28, 33–35;
uprisings, 126–128, 135. *See also*
Egypt; Iraq; Israel; Jordan; Lebanon;
MENA; Syria; Tunisia; Yemen
military, 1, 18, 20, 118, 199n13, 276m,
289m, 302; Algeria, 110; Argentina,
9; authoritarian regimes and, 94–95,
156; Bahrain, 293; British in Northern
Ireland, 151–152; Chile, 94, 227, 228,

229, 230, 231, 232, 233, 234, 235, 239,
240, 243, 244, 245, 246; civil control,
302; comparison between Egypt and
Tunisia, 303–304; contention, 303;
corporatist regime, 127; coups, 1, 9,
23n1, 44, 215, 216; cycle of
contention, 17, 292; DA'ISH, 108;
defection, 108, 180, 183, 191–192, 211,
302; dictatorship, 21, 141; differences
between Egypt and Tunisia, 106;
divisions within, 94; Egypt, 3, 31, 44,
106, 109, 170, 171(figure), 182, 191, 215,
223, 224, 259, 291, 292, 293, 302, 303,
304; elites, 101, 103, 163; Indonesia,
197, 208, 213, 214–215, 219, 221, 303;
intervention, 3, 44, 101, 141, 157,
158, 159m, 160(table), 173, 298; Iran,
172, 183, 193, 195, 196, 197; Israel, 12;
Jordan, 247, 248, 291; Latin American
countries, 93; level of trust in, 93;
Libya, 98, 106, 159, 168, 168(figure),
292, 293; marginalized, 105; military-
industrial complex, 13; NATO,
107, 159, 298; Nigeria, 52; nonviolent protests, 141; occupation, 153;
paralysis, 183, 196–197; Philippines,
210, 211, 212, 221; political role of, 7;
post-transition, 223; regimes, 99, 100,
102, 103, 110, 165, 167, 304; repression,
170, 231; role as a political player, 22,
48, 302; role in developing societies,
302; role in the Arab world, 302; role
in translation, 292, 301, 302; role of
brokers, 303; Saudi Arabia, 101, 108;
Slovenia, 119; Somali, 165; Soviet
Union, 127; Syria, 98, 107, 108; 172,
173(figure), 302; transfer of arms, 166,
169; transition, 303; Tunisia, 94, 106,
127, 128, 291, 302, 303, 306; Ukraine,
175; United Nations, 159, 172; United
States aid, 104; Yemen, 94, 293;
Zimbabwe, 54

organizational structure, 18, 46–72, 286, 288, 289; in Nigeria, 52–55, 57–62; in Sub-Saharan Africa, 62–66; in Zimbabwe, 52–55, 57–62. *See also* organizations

organizations, 13, 14, 15, 16, 20, 32, 33, 35, 37, 39, 40, 46, 47, 48–49, 50–52, 54, 53, 61, 66, 70, 71, 94, 96, 116, 184, 211, 281, 283, 294; activist, 209, 216; advocacy, 167, 207, 281; business, 53, 56, 61, 62, 63–65(table); Chilean, 237, 238; civil society, 204, 268, 274; development, 56, 61, 61(figure), 62, 63–65(table), 66; Egyptian, 67, 68, 223, 303; human rights, 198; Indonesian, 209, 210, 213, 214, 216, 303; international governmental organization, 153; intervention by, 178n1; Iranian, 193, 195; Islamist, 30, 32, 34, 35, 37, 38, 39, 41, 43, 44, 67, 213, 214; labor, 109; labor unions, 207; left-wing, 41, 212, 249; local, 50; MENA, 67, 301; migrant, 69, 70; military, 303; Moroccan, 69; movement, 204, 205, 207, 211, 216, 220, 221, 222, 224, 225; Muslim Brotherhood, 223, 224, 249; Nigerian, 52, 53, 57–67; nongovernmental (NGOs), 49, 51, 118, 124, 158, 193, 207, 229, 272, 281; Northern Ireland, 142; Philippines, 207–208, 209, 210, 216, 219, 220; political, 42, 49, 142, 195, 291; popular contention, 5; popular security, 182; professional, 54, 109; protest, 28, 68, 207; religious, 37, 49, 56, 61(figure), 62, 63–65(table), 66; Shiite, 41; social, 287, 291; social movements, 21, 33, 39, 62, 207; state, 289, 290, 292, 298; student, 207, 237; trade unions, 51, 53, 54, 56, 59–60(table), 61(figure), 62, 63–65(table), 67, 191, 193, 288; Tunisian, 41, 43, 222; voluntary, 271;

working-class, 38; Zimbabwean, 52, 54, 57–67. *See also* organizational structure

Owen, Roger, 279

Paisley, Ian, 145, 150, 151. *See also* Northern Ireland

Pakistan, 163, 177(chart), 304

Palestinians, 174, 248, 249, 253n23, 257, 291, 292; Al-Aqsa intifada, 35; Gaza Strip, 12, 109, 215, 257; Intifada, 7, 35, 110, 134, 153, 174; Islamic Jihad, 34; occupied territories, 12, 35, 260; Palestine Liberation Organization (PLO), 12; Palestinian Authority (PA), 109; Popular Front for the Liberation of Palestine (PFLP), 34; territories, 98; West Bank, 12, 253n23

path dependency, 181, 206. *See also* scientific explanation

Penguins Revolution, 232, 250n5. *See also* Chile

Philippines, 103, 104, 123, 124, 125, 166, 180, 224, 225, 301, 302; antidictatorship movements, 207–210; compared to Indonesia, 21, 205, 207–221, 300; Maoist insurgency, 212

Piñera, Sebastián, 237, 238, 240, 241(figure), 242, 244, 245. *See also* Chile

Pinochet, Augusto, 123, 125, 230, 231, 235, 246, 250n2. *See also* Chile

PISA (Programme for International Student Assessment) (Chile), 235

pivotal case, 191–192

police: brutality, 176, 184, 185–186, 187, 189; Chile, 230, 236, 237, 238, 245; corruption, 187; detention, 238; Egypt, 42, 98, 184, 186, 187, 188, 189–190, 190, 198n5; Iran, 193, 196; Israel, 266; Jackson State University, Mississippi, 11; military, 170; Nigeria, 52;